Disengaging from Terrorism

This book presents an in-depth case study of 13 individuals who moved away from terrorist activity in Turkey. Setting their life stories in the context of political violence in support of Kurdish independence and a leftist revolution, and the response of the Turkish state, the book examines how the individuals were motivated to become involved in terrorism, how they participated, why they became disillusioned, and above all how they coped with the difficult process of disengagement. The book then draws out general lessons on how individuals can be encouraged to move away from terrorism, and especially on how states can construct repentance mechanisms, and protection mechanisms, to assist with this. The book is a particularly rich, valuable source on why people move away from terrorism as most books in the field concentrate on why people become terrorists, and on "terrorist profiling."

Kamil Yılmaz is Chief Superintendent in the Turkish National Police. He completed his doctorate at Columbia University, USA.

Routledge Transnational Crime and Corruption Series

Published in association with the Terrorism, Transnational Crime and Corruption Center, School of Public Policy, George Mason University, USA

1 **Russian Business Power**
 The role of Russian business in foreign and security relations
 Edited by Andreas Wenger, Jeronim Perovic and Robert W. Orttung

2 **Organized Crime and Corruption in Georgia**
 Edited by Louise Shelley, Erik Scott and Anthony Latta

3 **Russia's Battle with Crime, Corruption and Terrorism**
 Edited by Robert W. Orttung and Anthony Latta

4 **Human Trafficking and Human Security**
 Edited by Anna Jonsson

5 **Irregular Migration from the Former Soviet Union to the United States**
 Saltanat Liebert

6 **Human Security, Transnational Crime and Human Trafficking**
 Asian and Western perspectives
 Edited by Shiro Okubo and Louise Shelley

7 **Labour Migration, Human Trafficking and Multinational Corporations**
 The commodification of illicit flows
 Edited by Ato Quayson and Antonela Arhin

8 **Environmental Crime and Corruption in Russia**
 Federal and regional perspectives
 Edited by Sally Stoecker and Ramziya Shakirova

9 **Disengaging from Terrorism**
 Lessons from the Turkish Penitents
 Kamil Yılmaz

Disengaging from Terrorism
Lessons from the Turkish Penitents

Kamil Yılmaz

LONDON AND NEW YORK

First published 2014
by Routledge

2 Park Square, Milton Park, Abingdon, Oxon OX14 4RN

711 Third Avenue, New York, NY 10017, USA

Routledge is an imprint of the Taylor & Francis Group, an informa business

First issued in paperback 2017

Copyright © 2014 Kamil Yılmaz

The right of Kamil Yılmaz to be identified as author of this work has been asserted by him in accordance with the Copyright, Designs and Patent Act 1988.

All rights reserved. No part of this book may be reprinted or reproduced or utilised in any form or by any electronic, mechanical, or other means, now known or hereafter invented, including photocopying and recording, or in any information storage or retrieval system, without permission in writing from the publishers.

Notice:
Product or corporate names may be trademarks or registered trademarks, and are used only for identification and explanation without intent to infringe.

British Library Cataloguing in Publication Data
A catalogue record for this book is available from the British Library

Library of Congress Cataloging in Publication Data
Kamil Yılmaz.
Disengaging from terrorism : lessons from the Turkish penitents / Kamil Yılmaz.
    pages cm. – (Routledge transnational crime and corruption ; 9)
    Includes bibliographical references and index.
    1. Terrorism – Turkey. 2. Kurds – Civil rights – Turkey. 3. Terrorism – Turkey – Prevention. 4. Terrorists – Turkey. 5. Turkey – Politics and government – 1980–6. Partiya Karkerên Kurdistanê. I. Title.
HV6433.T92Y55 2014
363.32509561–dc23   2013040866

ISBN: 978-0-415-71904-9 (hbk)
ISBN: 978-1-138-07918-2 (pbk)

Typeset in Times New Roman
by HWA Text and Data Management, London

Contents

List of illustrations vi
About the author vii
Foreword viii
Preface x

1 Introduction 1

2 Historical and social contexts 12

3 Separation stage: Turkish Penitents' paths to political violence 50

4 Transition stage I : life in the PKK and revolutionary groups 98

5 Transition stage II: causes of disillusionment and exit from the groups 119

6 Transition stage III: difficulties and resources for disengagement 166

7 Reincorporation: politics of repentance and life after violence 200

8 Conclusion 227

Bibliography 241
Index 250

Illustrations

Figures

3.1	Rite of passage (ROP) model for political violence	94
3.2	Turkish Penitents' processes towards political violence	96
4.1	Cell structures (networks) in revolutionary groups	118
6.1	Processes of individual disengagement from (imagined) communities of violent practices	197
6.2	Legitimate peripheral participation (LPP) in communities of practice	198

Tables

2.1	Introductory information about the Turkish Penitents	44
3.1	Separation stage – Turkish Penitents' paths to political violence	95
6.1	Information about the Turkish Penitents' entry and exit	195
6.2	Factors contributing to the Turkish Penitents' disengagement from political violence	196
7.1	Statistical data about the repentance laws in Turkey	209

About the author

Kamil Yılmaz has a PhD in applied (political) anthropology from Columbia University (2012) and has worked for the Turkish Ministry of Interior since 1998. He is currently based at the International Center for Terrorism and Transnational Crime (UTSAM) in Ankara where he works as a researcher and a lecturer. Before his PhD, he obtained a Master's degree in Criminal Justice from John Jay College of Criminal Justice in New York and three Master's degrees from Columbia University in the fields of international affairs, political anthropology, and applied anthropology, respectively. His research interests include political violence, radicalization and deradicalization processes related to terrorism, identity politics, elite formation and circulation, as well as international security and international relations. His publications include *Politics of Repentance in Turkey* (2012), *The Emergence and Rise of Conservative Elite in Turkey* (2009), *Iran as a Nuclear Power: A Precarious Dilemma for Turkey* (2009), *The Rise of Radical Islam in Post-Soviet Space: Fiction or Reality?* (2007), *US Preemption on Iran? An Estimative Analysis in Light of the Neo-Realist Theory* (2006).

Foreword

Many books have been produced on the subject of terrorism since 9/11. But very few have discussed disengagement from terrorism. This rarely researched topic is very important. If the phenomenon of terrorism is to be contained in the coming decades, it is important that individuals leave terrorist groups and have the ability to reengage with society.

There are several societies that have faced this challenge on a significant scale. Colombia, with its many decades history of terrorist groups, has established peace with some demobilized groups and has allowed members of terrorist groups to reengage with society. In fact, one of Colombia's most popular politicians was once a member of a highly active terrorist group. Ireland has also had many individuals disengage from involvement with the IRA. Saudi Arabia runs significant reeducation programs to try and get individuals once part of terrorist groups to leave behind their past behavior. Apart from the IRA case, little has been written in the academic literature about the process of disengagement from terrorism and reintegration into society.

The book by Kamil Yılmaz on *Disengaging from Terrorism* is unique in that it draws on interviews with terrorists who have severed their ties from two different types of terrorist movements in Turkey – leftist and PKK. Using the tools of an anthropologist, Dr. Yılmaz has drawn on over one hundred hours of interviews to explain the motivations to join these organizations, the life within the organizations and the reasons that the members of these terrorist groups chose to disengage.

Turkey provides fertile ground for this analysis as it has many diverse terrorist groups operating simultaneously in the country that have been responsible for tens of thousands of fatalities in recent decades. One of the great strengths of this pioneering book is that it does not focus on former participants of one terrorist group but compares and contrasts the experiences of individuals who have participated in very different types of terrorist groups and come from very different backgrounds within Turkey.

Even though Turkey has had success in getting terrorists to disengage from terrorism, Dr. Yılmaz book does not whitewash the difficulties in leaving behind the terrorist life and reentering one's family and the society. As he shows, some families of terrorists are supportive of the terrorist organizations they joined and their disengagement is not welcomed by their family. This makes their return to society even more fraught with difficulty.

The realities of life within the terrorist organization and of life after disengagement are captured by Dr. Yılmaz in the text of his probing interviews. His success as an interviewer brings his subjects to life. He presents their travails both as terrorists, the problems they observed in the terrorist groups that precipitated their exit, and their current daily realities post-disengagement.

The interviews are placed in the context of anthropological and social science research making this a contribution not only to terrorism studies but to a broader academic literature.

This book lets you enter into terrorist communities that are rarely revealed to the external world. It will help you understand the motivations of terrorists and what facilitates disenchantment with terrorist groups.

Louise I. Shelley

Preface

Terrorism has been one of the most intractable issues that humanity has faced in recent decades. Global and local efforts in responding to the scourge of terrorism have provided us with valuable insights as to why individuals resort to violent means to achieve political ends (radicalization); what kinds of people resort and are susceptible to terrorism (profiling); and what measures have been taken by governments, private enterprises, and international institutions to tackle this menace (counter-terrorism). Such efforts, nevertheless, revealed very little in terms of understanding why and how people disengage from terrorism (deradicalization) and what happens to individuals when they leave terrorism behind (reincorporation).

I was intrigued by the dearth of studies on disengagement from terrorism because, while many people join terrorist groups, a considerable number exit them globally every year. Working as a chief superintendent at the Turkish National Police, I have personally been privy to the fact that thousands of individuals left various terrorist groups in Turkey since the inception of terrorist acts in the 1970s. Despite the existence of disengagement from terrorism, our knowledge of the processes that lead people to leave terrorism remains limited. Furthermore, as a person who has tried to understand various issues on terrorism both professionally and academically, I have always been curious to know the lived-experiences of actual terrorists or of those who have been members of a terrorist organization. I believe that knowing the personal experiences of ex-terrorists is important and worthy of scientific inquiry within itself. But I also think that there is much to be learned from such experiences in terms of understanding why a person joins a terrorist organization in the first place. For example, we may go to great lengths to decipher the mental and emotional landscapes of individuals like the Christmas Day bomber Umar Abdulmuttallab, Oklahoma bomber Timothy McVeigh, Norwegian terrorist Anders Breivik or the Tsarnaev brothers who came to be known as the "Boston bombers." It will not be erroneous, however, to argue that anyone who ventures an opinion to fathom individual pathways to terrorism will concede the fact that ex-terrorists are better positioned to understand the aforementioned individuals, simply because they can relate to them better than outsiders. In addition, because of their innate credibility, former terrorists can better communicate counter narratives to at-risk populations and make significant contributions to prevention activities. For all these reasons, I thought that a well-researched and clearly analyzed book on disengagement would be a notable addition to the existing literature on terrorism and political violence.

To write this book, I personally collected *oral histories* of thirteen "formers" whom I call "the Turkish Penitents." My lengthy interviews with them generated about 120 hours of video-recorded data and provided me with a unique opportunity to get under their skins. Six of my informants had engaged in political violence in various Marxist-Leninist groups in Turkey; while seven of them had left the PKK (Partiya Karkerên Kurdistan – Kurdistan Workers' Party), a Kurdish separatist group that established itself within Turkey and various "mountains" in the northern parts of Iraq and has been committing terrorist acts since 1984.

The word "mountain" has a symbolic significance both for Kurds and Turks and its meaning transcends the regular lexicon; yet, we do not know much about the "mountain." Likewise, Marxist-Leninist groups have largely operated within urban environments from their "cells," but what happens within those cells remains unknown to most of us. Since most of the causes of disillusionment of the Turkish Penitents are related to their lives within the aforementioned enigmatic structures, i.e., "the mountain" and "urban cells," a specific emphasis in this book has been made to decipher what really happens in those structures.

Because of a paucity of guiding research on the topic and in order to allocate more space to the "voices" of the Turkish Penitents, this book will not include a separate theory section. Relevant theories are chapter specific and will be used when convenient throughout the text. More importantly, my method will be my main conceptual tool as I propose a "theoretically informed methodology," i.e., life histories organized by using rites of passage (ROP) as a model that is supported by Bourdieu's (1993) *Practice Theory* and Lave and Wenger's (1991) concepts of *situated learning* in *communities of practice* through *legitimate peripheral participation*, in an effort to make sense of various processes, stages, and transition points in the life continuum of the Turkish Penitents. This model will be undergirded by an inter-disciplinary approach, incorporating theories and methods from political and psychological anthropology, criminology, and political psychology.

So, why did I define my informants as "penitents"? I use "penitent" as a descriptive term by placing a special emphasis on the *cognitive* and *behavioral* aspects of the disengagement processes. That is, during the interviews I asked specific questions to understand whether my informants were repentant or detached, or a combination of both. Although details of these nuances will be explained later, to put it briefly, the common denominator for all of these nomenclatures is "non-violence" and a complete rupture with former terrorist groups. Thus, I use the term "penitent" simply for practical reasons to include all of my informants.

Shortly put, Turkish Penitents are individuals who joined a violent group *voluntarily or involuntarily* (e.g., through forced recruitment, in the case of the PKK), who practiced political violence or stayed in such groups albeit not participating in violence for a certain period of time, and who either left the group *voluntarily*, its ideology and violence (repentants) or left the armed struggle while retaining the group's ideological aspirations (detacheds). My informants are unique in the sense that despite extreme difficulties, they managed to make a decision and implement it. They were not simply resilient people, but individuals who transcended serious difficulties and their own liminal situation. Thus, I was interested in understanding my subjects' *gradual progression* toward increased involvement in terrorist activities and whether there is a *gradual retrogression* from the terrorist groups. To this end, it was important to understand the continuities and changing elements in their character and motivations, as well as the effects of the changing social situation throughout their lives. That is why, the life-history method appeared to be perfect and chosen as the main method for this book.

Within this frame of mind, a semi-structured, in-depth life-history interview was employed in this study, asking Turkish Penitents to reconstruct their own lives. All interviews were conducted in Turkish, my mother tongue, though some of my informants spoke both Turkish and Kurdish. The interviews usually took upward of four hours or more (the longest being about 16 hours), and were split up over a number of days. The total length of the interviews was about 120 hours, which I recorded with a video-recorder, transcribed them verbatim myself and content-analyzed.

Since this book is exploratory in nature and purpose, I believe that little was to be gained by imposing the criterion of representativeness on the sample I interviewed. Moreover, given its sensitive and in-depth nature, it was hard to find volunteers for this research. Most of my informants would be chosen among people who are living in "disguise" in society as they are *betwixt and between* the wrath of their former groups on the one hand and the potential harassment by their former communities for being labeled as "traitors" on the other. I was privileged, however, to have access to 13 such individuals who received rewards from the state for their expiatory confessions and repentance in the form of reduced or no sentences.

The recruitment of my informants was based on snowballing. I found my first two informants (one from the PKK and one from a revolutionary group) through my private contacts, and thenceforth asked each informant to nominate other individuals from their networks for my next interview. The groups from which my informants came emerged arbitrarily even though I had intended initially to talk with equal number of individuals from the PKK and other revolutionary groups. To specify, my technique led to *seven* informants from the PKK and *six* from the revolutionary groups. To protect their confidentiality, I do not specify which revolutionary group these six informants came from. For the other seven informants, I attach their group to their names because the PKK is the only separatist group in Turkey anyway. In an effort to provide an easier reading, I will use my informants' pseudonyms in hyphenated form by attaching the letter "P" to my informants from the PKK and "R" to those from revolutionary groups (example: "Zilan-P" means she is from the PKK; "Hakan-R" signifies that he was a member of a revolutionary group).

More importantly, after interviewing this nearly equal number of informants from two types of groups (i.e., separatist *versus* revolutionary-leftist) at the end of the fieldwork and reading my transcriptions over and over again, I decided to make a comparison between the Turkish Penitents who left the PKK and revolutionary groups, for such a comparison appeared to have a potential to yield some meaningful results with regard to Turkish Penitents' entry into and exit from terrorist groups. Lastly, and to my surprise, most of my informants were eager to talk, proven by the fact that almost all of them agreed to be recorded, in addition to their open statements about their desire to tell their stories.

As a penultimate note, I am indebted to many people who contributed to the writing of this book in different ways. First and foremost, I am heartily thankful to Professor Charles Harrington, my professor at Teachers College-Columbia University, for his sincerity, wholehearted support and invaluable insights from the initial to the final stages of my research. His guidance and expert knowledge on psychological anthropology were especially indispensible for the finalization of this study. Second, I thank Professor Louise Shelley for her encouragement to turn my study into a book and her kind support during the write-up.

As a person who joined the PhD program from outside the field of anthropology, I am especially pleased to thank Professor Comitas, Professor Varenne, and Professor Bond from whom I learned a great deal about the discipline. It was during my formal and informal interactions with ProfessorComitas that I became acquainted with the nuts and bolts and the joy of the fieldwork. It is also a great honor for me to have known Professor Bond whose intellect and in-depth theoretical knowledge of political anthropology provided me with enormous inspiration for the writing of this book.

My special appreciation and gratitude goes to my informants who opened themselves up to me with great sincerity as much as enthusiasm. This book would surely not be possible without their help and willingness to tell their stories. I would also like to thank three of my friends in the Turkish government, whose names I cannot provide, for introducing me to some of my informants. I am also pleased to thank my friends Mustafa Bal, Sinan Celiksu, Isa Karasioglu, Mehmet Afacan, Oguzhan Demir, Niyazi Ekici, Murat Ozkan, Alper Sozer, Murat Gunestas, Selcuk Atak, Ertugrul Zorlu, Yusuf Yuksel, Ahmet Celik, Muvaffak Citak, Spiro Ardavanis, Angelica Fulga, Amina Tawasil, Lisa Le Fevre and many others for their unsparing emotional support and advice during my research and being there for me all the time. Also, I am most grateful to my immediate family, my parents, brother, and sisters for their love, patience and constant support that has kept me going in life.

To conclude, the analyses I make in this book should not be generalized; for I can only talk about my informants based on the data I generated during my fieldwork. However, many of the terrorist organizations from which my informants came still maintain their salience not only for public life, but also for the current political discourse in the country. Therefore, it is possible to make meaningful extrapolations from my discussions that may be applicable for understanding the notions of entry into and exit from terrorist groups within Turkey in general and other places as well. Even so, although my data is limited to the life histories of 13 individuals who practiced political violence in Turkey, the information it generates can be still useful to understand not only the environmental factors that may lead one towards political violence, but also the behaviors of those who are currently positioned somewhere in the paths that my informants took before they became members of a terrorist organization.

As this book is based on interviews with individuals who formerly participated in political violence in Turkey where the current political debate is around the active terrorists' *reinstatement into society*, I hope that both the content and timing of this book may render it particularly noteworthy for the small body of cross-cultural literature on individual disengagement from political violence and terrorism.

1 Introduction

The stories of Zilan and Hakan

As she tells her story, Zilan was 13 when she found herself in the Kurdistan Workers' Party (better known by its patronymic, the PKK) camps located in the mountains of the southeastern parts of Turkey and Northern Iraq, respectively. Zilan's life was shaped by a series of "turning points." As the eldest of five girls within a poor Kurdish family living in the Kurdish dominated Şırnak province, she was forced by her father to drop out of school after the sixth grade in order to help her ailing mother at home. Both of her parents were illiterate. Zilan had a big culture shock when they moved to Istanbul for economic reasons. While she was coming to terms with with this disruption, her aunt who was living in Izmir province persuaded Zilan's family to move to Izmir, arguing that although providing many opportunities to the newcomers, the process of adaptation to Istanbul was disheartening and that it would be easier for them to make a living in Izmir, a smaller city but offering almost equal possibilities of survival and success nonetheless. However, what her aunt had in mind was that she wanted Zilan to marry her 25-year-old son who was a member of the PKK. By doing so, she had wished to keep her son out of *politics*. Feeling that she was being "instrumentalized" and saying, "I hadn't even lived my maidenhood and hadn't even seen my menarche," Zilan rejected outright marrying her cousin who was "like a brother" to her. However, her father said, "You accept this or else I will kill you." She had no choice but to acquiesce; she felt "very little and powerless."

Rather reluctantly, she got married (a religious ceremony conducted by an *Imam*) to her cousin who was involved in political violence with the PKK in urban Turkey. Not so long after their marriage, he was asked to go to "the mountain"[1] to receive more sophisticated training. He convinced Zilan to go with him by saying that "we will stay there for a few days and come back." Trusting him, being convinced by their "promised" return, and thinking that it would be an interesting experience for a young girl, she agreed to go to the mountain. She was not sure if she had any other choice anyway. The journey, nonetheless, was far from being an interesting adventure, as it marked for her the beginning of 17 years of "wasted time" and "debilitating idleness" in the mountains, broken only by occasional internecine encounters with the Turkish military.

Zilan's disengagement process started from the outset, even before joining the PKK. Despite joining the group involuntarily, various factors such as daily practice of violence and being in a state of "point of no return" allowed her to grow accustomed to the environment for a short period of time. However, albeit thinking that violence against Turkish soldiers could be justified in a state of war, witnessing a plethora of "inhumane, unjust, and deplorable" acts dictated by the PKK leaders against her own friends (PKK guerillas) and other Kurds (peshmerges in Northern Iraq) confirmed her desire to run away from the group very early on. But only after 17 years, several months before my interview with her in February 2010, did she be able to escape from the PKK and turn herself in to the Turkish authorities with her second husband whom she met on the mountain. Since then, she has been living in a small town in Turkey's southeast with her husband and four children, but as she put it, life after violence is "extremely difficult" and "she doesn't know what the future has in store for them." The only resource they have in securing their lives in society is "invisibility."

Hakan, a 55 year old "professional revolutionary," says he was a member of a leftist-revolutionary terrorist organization for over 25 years. In contrast to Zilan, he grew up in a relatively affluent (middle-class) and traditional family (ideologically Republican, ethnically Turkish) in Turkey's financial capital Istanbul, and both of his parents were educated. His mother finished primary school, whereas his father graduated from high school and worked in several factories to provide him and his two younger brothers "the best lives possible" in the country at the time. Believing that his father's efforts as a "worker" were not given the credit he deserved, i.e., "exploited" by the Turkish bourgeoisie and the elite class, he was already into the "leftist ideology" even before beginning high school. The humanistic rhetoric of the leftist groups in high school, coupled with the camaraderie of charismatic schoolmates, seemed quite appealing for him to join the activities of such groups. Unlike Zilan, Hakan entered the leftist group voluntarily and even had a formal initiation ceremony into the group. Furthermore, his continued practice within the group, his occasional arrests by the police, and the disparaging ways his father was treated when he came to collect him from the police stations, contributed only to his transition from a leftist utopian to a radical, violent, and professional revolutionary.

Hakan practiced political violence in various parts of Turkey, but mainly in Istanbul for more than 25 years. He had many different responsibilities within the group, the most important being his position in the group's "military committee." For him, the state was solely responsible for the "heartbreaking" conditions of the "people of Anatolia," and to eliminate this exploitative and oppressive state and to bring about a revolution, any action could be justified no matter how brutal that action would be. Hakan describes himself as a "professional revolutionary" which means that he was busy day and night, both physically and mentally, with activities and thought practices in order to bring about *the* revolution. He made a lot of sacrifices, for example, despite living in the same city with his mother, he did not see her for more than 18 years lest the police would find him. But over the years, numerous factors contributed to his *process of disillusionment,* to be examined in the ensuing chapters in more detail. Just to give an example, which emanated from him being sidelined by the group leaders albeit his "lifetime sacrifices," his accumulated anger against his own group was so strong that when he finally gave in after going through several "epiphanies" and "introspections" on the thirteenth day of a two-week detention at the terrorism division of the Istanbul Police Department, and expressed his desire to divulge the location of his group's one and only weapons' cache in the country, even his interrogators were taken aback. They thought that he was simply joking, because his group was a relatively small but an influential one, known by its brutal attacks against state officials, state institutions, and private enterprises, and the disclosure of its single arsenal would impair the group significantly at the time. In retrospect, so it did.[2]

Hakan believed that "when the heart is convinced, the mind would follow." As he emphasized, the first *seed of doubt* had come to him long before he was captured by the police in 1999. But he struggled for a long time to actualize his physical disengagement from the group, which was quite arduous. In other words, his seemingly instantaneous conversion to non-violence was just the final stage in a long, painful but also irreversible dissociation from armed struggle. Thinking retrospectively, however, Hakan does not think that he did something wrong; squinting his watering eyes, he recounts that "he was made" by the state and he did not have any alternatives to violence. For him, there was a blurred line between the victim and the perpetrator; his one-time torturers were none but the "mirror image" of what one calls a "terrorist." Although going through a relatively easier process of reincorporation into society due to inherited financial resources, he describes his current state of mind as "less than jubilant" as he is still struggling with some psychological issues, which I shall explore in Chapter 7.

Statement of the problem

This book explores ethnographically and in depth the processes of individual disengagement from political violence in Turkey by reconstructing the lives of 13 individuals including Zilan and Hakan whom I call "Turkish Penitents" from the PKK, a separatist group, and various Marxist-Leninist revolutionary groups that practice political violence in Turkey and elsewhere (e.g., Europe, Iran, Iraq, and the Russian Federation). Today, these individuals are trying simultaneously to make sense of the history of political violence in their country and of their role in that history, "to undo past wrongs and mend spoiled identities, and to resume interrupted lives" (Scheper-Hughes 2007).

The research for this book is exploratory since there are only few guides for it. In an effort to understand why certain individuals become terrorists, the bulk of research has hitherto focused on the causes of political violence and terrorism. Accordingly, most research has emphasized the importance of understanding the nature of *paths to* political violence, while little attention has been paid to individual *paths from* political violence and terrorism. The specific purpose of this book, then, is to contribute to the existing small body of literature on disengagement from terrorist groups (e.g., Bandura 1998; Barrett and Bokhari

2008; Dugan and Huang 2008; Ashour 2009; Bjorgo and Horgan 2009; Reinares 2011) by reconstructing the processes of disengagement of 13 detached or repentant individuals who are ethnically Turkish and Kurdish. Following Bjorgo and Horgan (2009), a distinction has been made between "behavioral" and "cognitive" aspects of disengagement. That is, there are some individuals who distance themselves from the extremist group and its violent means, but retain their extremist views on society and their ideology; while there are others who feel remorse and repent, and consequently help state authorities in their fight against terrorist organizations. My informants fall into both categories, but mostly into the latter one. Hence, it was of interest to ask whether they followed this path in exchange for security by police against the wrath of the groups they left or they sincerely felt remorse and repented, which will be explored under the discussion of the "politics of repentance" in Chapter 7.

A second aim is to compare and contrast the experiences of those who left politically-motivated *leftist-revolutionary groups* and those abandoned a politically and ethnically motivated *separatist* organization, the PKK. The reason why they are comparable has to do with these groups' ideology, history, membership types, internal dynamics, etc., which appears to have important ramifications on individual experiences of disengagement (Chapters 5 and 6). Moreover, even though the main focus of this book is on individual disengagement from political violence, in order to obtain a more "comprehensive" understanding, it explores also the preceding and aftermath phases of Turkish Penitents' disengagement, i.e., "how they took part in violent actions in the first place" and "how they left the groups and who they have become after leaving political violence."

In order to achieve the above-mentioned tasks, I collected *oral histories* of Turkish Penitents through video-recorded lengthy interviews, which provided me with a sizable amount of information about their lives *before, during*, and *after* their participation in political violence. This method also allowed me to take into account the internal (psychological) as well as the external (social, economic, and political) factors affecting the above-mentioned stages. Put differently, with life histories, I attempted to generate data about the socio-political and cultural contexts within which the Turkish Penitents are embedded.

Significance of the research

If one looks at the number of studies conducted around the notions of paths *to* and *from* political violence, it will be easy to see that there is a disproportionate number in favor of the former. Even in the media and reports written by political pundits, much of the attention has been given to violence and its perpetrators, while little attention has been dedicated to non-violence and individuals who converted from violence to non-violence. Moreover, among the few studies that focus on disengagement from terrorism, most studies looked at the issues of "collective disengagement," i.e., groups' transition from violent struggle to politics, while only a handful of studies focused on the notion of individual disengagement, some of which are compiled by Bjorgo and Horgan (2009) in their book *Leaving Terrorism Behind*. Many authors emphasized the need for studies on this relatively unexplored phenomenon, most notably Horgan (2005) and Bjorgo and Horgan (2009). In addition, even though there are a few studies on the "exit" from political violence, most of these studies used secondary data, largely due to the difficulty of accessing first-hand, private accounts of individuals who have participated in political violence. Horgan also attracts attention to the importance of such research by urging researchers to do "fieldwork" and by saying that "if one is to study terrorism and terrorists effectively ... one *must* meet with and speak to individuals who are, or who have been directly involved with a terrorist organization" and adds that "unfortunately the research from this approach is extremely limited" (2005:33). White (1999) lists the number of researchers who have done this:

> J. Bowyer Bell's (e.g., 1979, 1993), Frank Burton's (1978), and Jeffrey Sluka's (1989) work on Irish Republicans, and Steve Bruce's (1992), and Sarah Nelson's (1984) work on Protestant Paramilitaries. Donatella della Porta's (1992;1995) work on violence in Italy ... Each of these authors interviewed former active violent activists.

Absent from this list, Horgan adds, "are Jamieson for her work with Italian Red Brigade 'leaders' and 'followers,' and Taylor for research on Loyalist terrorist organizations in Northern Ireland, Islamic fundamentalist groups in the Middle East, and Italian terrorist movements" (2005:33). Apart from these, Vincent's (1988) study on political violence in County Fermanagh, Northern Ireland, Kassimeris' (2011) study of individual exit in Greece, and Reinares' (2011) empirical study of "disengagement and deradicalization" of ETA members in Spain, should also be added to the foregoing list.

Wishing to be a worthy addition to the studies based on private data, this book takes up the call by the foregoing authors and chooses a methodology that is based on one-year of fieldwork in Turkey (January 2010–December 2010), generating about 120 hours of video-recorded individual accounts of the Turkish Penitents as well as the necessary archival data. By using such data, I also aim to contribute to the efforts of those scholars (Feldman 1991; Mahmood 1996; Nordstrom 1997; Sluka 2000) who promote the idea that the essence of ethnographic writing is the voice given to the subjects of their studies – the subjugated, the tortured, the violated, the dislocated, the émigré, the feminine "other" and those who are identified as terrorists by modern governments.

Historically, attempts and the discussions of explaining terrorism and politically violent behavior have taken place in a highly contested terrain. In recent years, however, there seems to be more consensus over the use of multi-dimensional approaches in terrorism research as opposed to the more frequently used psychological approach (e.g., Post 2003; Horgan 2005; Victoroff 2005; and Khan and Azam 2008). These authors believe that the search for merely psycho-pathological origins is fruitless because terrorists are psychologically heterogeneous. Thus, another significance of this book lies in the fact that in understanding the making of paths *to* and *from* political violence of individuals who transcend the difficulties and their own situation, it focuses on a creative interaction of both social and psychological factors to define human *agency* (Harrington and Boardman 1997). Doubtless, the Turkish Penitents constructed new outcomes for themselves in the face of odds against them. Thus, it is also valid to ask "how did the Turkish Penitents make their decisions despite the threats from their respective groups on the one hand and anxiety (and fear) over the level of acceptance by the society upon return?" Answers to this question will be explored in Chapters 5, 6 and 7.

Furthermore, there are no a priori qualities or characteristic traits of a person that would help us understand who is likely to become a terrorist or stop being one. Literature on terrorism and political violence shows that individuals who practice political violence or terrorism have diverse backgrounds, coming from all races, all religions, different age groups, from both sexes, and so on and so forth. Yet, as Colvin writes, "a strong tendency [still] exists in the political science and terrorism literature to reduce the perpetration of violence to ultimate types and causes and to classify perpetrators in relation to these causes (religious zealot, Marxist guerilla, tribal warrior, criminal gang member)" (2007:465). As White suggests, we should not ask "what type of person would do this," or even "what are the indigenous labels applied to perpetrators of this type," but "what kinds of cultural and political dynamics had to come into play to make this type of person necessary or thinkable?" (1992:21–46). Thus, the focus of this book is not on understanding "who" the terrorists are, but instead focusing on "what" they do. To specify, rather than focusing solely on *terrorist profiling*, i.e., "the similarities between terrorist behavior and the predominant traits of those who might be characterized as one or more of a number of personality types" (Horgan 2005:134), it focuses on understanding the factors, roles, functions, and processes, as well as the interplay between these and *individual psychologies* and *styles of coping* that influence the Turkish Penitents' paths to and from political violence. I simply attempt to come up with a taxonomy of processes and potential factors by which I ask "what factors, what processes, what motivations, what group dynamics, what turning points," etc., merge with individual personality orientations, strategies, and perhaps serendipities that would help us understand the aforementioned paths.

In describing the psychologies of Turkish Penitents, I use various variables, e.g., "inner *versus* other directedness, internal *versus* external locus of control, reward *versus* punishment orientedness, and their "styles of coping" (Vaillant's model), all borrowed from Harrington and Boardman (1997). In so doing, I simply aim to describe what type of individuals the Turkish Penitents are, rather than assuming that they are in some way "abnormal" or seeking some predictors of future behavior.

To conclude this section, before doing the fieldwork, I had proposed using a "theoretically informed methodology" i.e., the *rites of passage* (Van Gennep 1960) and various forms of *practice theory* for designing my interviews. These approaches were useful both conceptually and methodologically as they provided me with an opportunity to ask the most relevant questions and organize the interviews in a systematic way. In the same fashion, for the write-up of this book, the resulting interviews were divided into three main sections after the fieldwork in order to make better sense of the lives of the Turkish Penitents. I am proposing a new *process-based* conceptual approach for political violence; hence its explanation is in order.

Conceptual framework: rite of passage (ROP) model for political violence

Bourdieu's practice theory reconciles the distinction between structure and the social agent and breaks with the prominent objective-subjective dichotomy of the social sciences. The notions of *habitus* and *field* that Bourdieu developed are proposed to achieve the foregoing tasks together as he believed that habitus and field exist only in relation to each other. According to him, "although a field is constituted by the various social agents participating in it (and thus their habitus), a habitus, in effect, represents the transposition of objective structures of the field into the subjective structures of action and thought of the agent" (Bourdieu 1990:x). Since my subjects practiced political violence, oral histories provided me with an understanding of this dialectical relationship between the subjective and objective structures of the Turkish Penitents in order to identify the causes of their disengagement. The question remained, however, "how to make a high volume of data more intelligible?" Therefore, I had to organize the data in some way which would allow me to follow a systematic approach when asking questions during the interviews, and to position myself such that I could be able to see my subjects' lives as a whole, while also being able to focus on micro details of their life continuum. Arnold Van Gennep's concept of the *rites of passage* proved to be useful in that it allowed me to delve into the aforementioned (dialectical) relationship in different phases of the lives of Turkish Penitents.

Van Gennep's most important contribution to social sciences is thought to be his analysis of ceremonies accompanying a person's "life crises" which he called *rites de passage*. He suggested that when the activities associated with such ceremonies are analyzed in terms of their content and order, it was possible to distinguish three major phases: separation (*separation*), transition (*marge*), and incorporation (*agrégation*). Considered as a whole, he is said to have labeled these the *schéma* of *rites de passage* (Kimball 1960:vii). Van Gennep cautions us, however, that these three categories are not developed to the same extent by all peoples or in every set of ceremonies, e.g., "rites of separation are prominent in funeral ceremonies, rites of incorporation at marriages" (1960:viii). Van Gennep was not concerned with particular rites in any case; his main interest lay in the similarities of all rites that entail:

- The essential significance of the rites and their relative positions within ceremonial wholes, that is, their *order*.
- The existence of transitional periods which sometimes acquire a certain *autonomy*.

- The relationship between actual spatial passage and the change in social position, expressed in such ritualization of movements from one status to another as an "opening of the doors" (1960:x).

This third feature interests me most, for, like Van Gennep, I am also convinced that there is no evidence that a secularized global world has lessened the need for ritualized expression of an individual's transition from one status to another. Every day, we pass from one position to another, one state of mind to another, and so on and so forth. Since my informants have gone through a transition from one status to another and one state of mind to another, following Van Gennep's tri-partite formulation, I will focus on and explore Turkish Penitents' lives in three stages:

1. *Separation stage – paths to political violence*: This stage symbolizes Turkish Penitents' participation in ordinary social life and their separation from it, until (and including) their joining terrorist groups.
2. *Transition stage – life in terrorist groups and paths from political violence*: This stage covers Turkish Penitents' lives in groups, i.e., the stage of practicing political violence, ending in (and including) their processes of disengagement.
3. *Incorporation stage – politics of repentance and life after violence:* This final stage is about the role of repentance laws in Turkish Penitents' disengagement (i.e., politics of repentance), their present status in society and states of mind after practicing political violence for a certain period.

* * *

A similar effort to my ROP model was proposed earlier by the applied psychologist John Horgan. In his *The Psychology of Terrorism*, Horgan outlines an approach that he calls the *process model of terrorism*. He views terrorism as a process having discrete phases to "becoming" a terrorist," "being" a terrorist, and "disengaging" from terrorism (2005:69). Horgan aims at understanding "what factors" influence and limit involvement and engagement in the field of terrorism as they were used successfully in understanding the same issues pertaining to juvenile delinquency, involvement in gangs, and other criminal activity (2005:70). In developing this approach, Horgan was inspired by Clarke and Cornis, the founders of the Rational Choice Theory (RCT) of criminal behavior. They argue, "offenders, like the rest of us, seek to benefit themselves by making decisions that are to some degree "rational" or shaped by supportive qualities" (2005:70). Horgan is perhaps the first researcher who translated their RCT into terrorism.

While Rational Choice Theory was applicable to some of my informants, at least some of them did not enter into political violence through calculation. For instance, several of them from the PKK became members through "forced recruitment," which was a popular recruitment method of the group in the 1990s. Several others entered by chance in addition to those whose gradual progression towards political violence took place on a voluntary basis. These issues will be discussed later. It suffices here, however, to say that using a *process* model is still important. Like Horgan, in my ROP model, I place a greater emphasis on decisional processes in terms of understanding the entering, staying, and exiting phases of political violence. A process model is especially helpful in deciphering the disengagement processes of the Turkish Penitents, because decisional processes occur before the actions associated with these processes (Horgan 2005:131). Even though decisions are made by improvisation, which was the case for some of my informants, the timing of that improvisation is usually determined by a triggering factor, or a "turning point" (Sampson and Laub 1993), which is preceded by a complex process of rumination and calculation in the face of changing social situations, with regard to leaving the groups in particular.

Besides these commonalities between our foregoing two approaches, my ROP model adds several complementary features to Horgan's process model of terrorism. First, the ROP model I propose is based on a richer private data; that is my own in-depth interviews with 13 Turkish Penitents. Second, from my reading of his book, it appeared to me that in Horgan's tri-partite approach of "becoming a terrorist," "being a terrorist," and "disengaging," even though each stage has been thought out as a part of a whole (process), they are supported by different data collected in different places by different researchers including some of his own. These seem to have created hindrances in addressing the importance of a holistic view; i.e., connections and transitions between these stages were not clearly addressed. In my study, I had proposed to use the ROP model before going into the field, which means that I was particularly vigilant *inter alia* about the connections and transitions between the three different stages that I explained ealier: *separation, transition,* and *incorporation*. All explanations about the processes that impinge upon the individual in all three stages, as well as the connections between them and transitions from one to the next, will be supported with the same dataset which may have more potential to offer a more coherent analysis. I now turn to my research questions and the elaboration of how the three stages in the ROP model will be presented in this book.

Guiding questions and objectives

The guiding research questions are: What motivational (individual/internal) and structural (environmental/external) factors did influence the Turkish Penitents in their processes of disengagement from terrorist organizations? How did they disengage, and what are their current positions in society and their states of mind? This involves the following specific objectives and questions:

- To reconstruct individual experiences pertinent to Turkish Penitents' decision-making processes in leaving the organization.
- To explore the differences and similarities between Turkish Penitents who left a leftist-revolutionary group and those who exited from a separatist organization, the PKK. In this quest, my specific aim is to explore the impact

of *internal* and *external* factors on denouncing violence and adopting an anti-violence position.
- What were the obstacles and inhibiting factors for leaving the group? How did they overcome such factors?
- What can we learn from their experiences that may contribute to the facilitation of disengagement processes for others who are still involved in political violence?

As mentioned before, I aimed to achieve these tasks by collecting life histories that focus not only on the processes of Turkish Penitents' participation in violence and disengagement but also its *wake* and *aftermath*. Below, I will summarize the function of the three stages, which are also the main chapters of this book.

In the third chapter, I will explore various issues in the "Separation Stage" (*Paths to political violence*) that include Turkish Penitents' incremental journey towards political violence. Specifically, I will explore (a) important events, people, and turning points during my informants' childhood and education years; (b) their political socialization and personality orientations; (c) the effects of these and the combination of ideas/narratives/symbols/leaders in their gradual radicalization; and (d) their entry into political violence. Turning points in the life-course will be explored particularly to understand the transitions between these phases.

The examination of the "Transition Stage" (*Lives in terrorist groups and causes of disengagement*) will be divided into several chapters. Chapter 4 is dedicated to my informants' lives and behaviors in their respective groups, i.e., their first impressions, educational activities, practices, and duties in groups. In Chapter 5, I will explore their feelings about the issues examined in the previous chapter. To specify, the following issues will be investigated and analyzed: (a) Turkish Penitents' perceptions of, and relations with, other members and the leaders; (b) their first "*seeds of doubt*" and causes of disillusionment (greater focus will be given to this section); and (c) difficulties and fears when disengaging. In the last chapter of the "Transition stage," i.e., Chapter 6, I will explain how my informants managed to overcome the difficulties associated with leaving terrorist groups. In other words, opportunities and resources related to disengagement, as well as the turning points and serendipities, will be discovered.

These three chapters, i.e., the stage of *practicing* political violence, will bear a great deal of weight as they allowed me to obtain information about not only the subjective structures (psychology of Turkish Penitents, their personality patterns, feelings, thoughts, actions, etc.) but also the objective/external structures (e.g., the Turkish state, the notion of "deep state," the economic and social conditions, the groups and attraction of their ideologies, etc.) from the perspective of people who have first-hand information about these structures. It also allowed me to delve into the interplay between these two structures, i.e., how Turkish Penitents' perceptions of the objective structures affected their disengagement. To be more specific, in light of Lave and Wenger's (1991) concepts of *situated learning* in *communities of practice* through *legitimate peripheral participation*, I will explore "how it is that one's transposition of the objective structures of the field into his subjective structure of action and thought leads him/her to enter into political violence and a similar process then causes his/her disengagement. Where does the change occur, in the objective or subjective structures, or in both?

In Chapter 7, the "Incorporation Stage" (*Politics of repentance and life after violence*), I will try to explain (a) the politics of repentance in Turkey from a Maussian perspective. To do this, I will conceptualize Turkish Penitents' confessions and collaboration and the state's promise of rewards as "gift-exchange"; (b) Turkish Penitents' current status in society and states of mind, which include their current difficulties and fears, as well as their personal resources and social support. The final chapter of the book, Chapter 8, will include the concluding remarks, as well as policy implications and suggestions for future research regarding the notion of individual disengagement from political violence and terrorism.

Notes

1 Within the terrorism discourse in Turkey, both for Turks and Kurds, the word "mountain" signifies "the PKK camps" in the mountainous areas within Turkey and beyond, mostly in Northern Iraq.
2 In Chapter 7, using a Maussian perspective I will discuss the value of such "information" as a commodity in a type of gift exchange between the state and members of terrorist organizations including the Turkish Penitents.

2 Historical and social contexts

Introduction

This purpose of this chapter is to provide the historical and social contexts within which the Turkish Penitents are embedded. Although the main focus of this book is placed on their individual disengagement from political violence, a better understanding of the phenomenon requires a consideration of what Marett (2007 [1912]) calls the "social present," which refers to a time span of at least three generations in the study of societies and individuals. In other words, considering that the present problems related to political violence in Turkey are deeply rooted in the nature and the historical evolution of the country's political and social structures, it is necessary to describe those structures from an historical perspective.

The violence exerted by the Kurdish-separatist group PKK and various leftist-revolutionary groups in contemporary Turkey is indeed linked to a variety of ethnic, economic, and socio-cultural problems that date back to the time of the Ottoman Empire and especially to the incipient stages of the Turkish Republic. To specify, the country has always been a multiethnic and multicultural society and the problem of how to incorporate different ethnic, economic and religious groups into the system, both politically and economically, has always maintained its salience in the country's politics throughout history. Many reforms were carried out in this light in order to ameliorate the conditions and preempt potential violent reactions (rebellions) by these groups by aiming to guarantee them better security for their lives, honor, property, and more importantly, equal rights of citizenship (e.g., the Imperial Decree of 1839, known as *Tanzimat Fermanı*). In addition, the stratified nature of society during the Ottoman and Republican (post-1923) periods has complicated the incorporation of such groups into society further, those from the peripheries in particular. With the process of modernization, and in the context of the establishment of a new nation-state, the problems of the "differential incorporation" (Smith 1998) of the foregoing groups intensified and manifested themselves in the discourses and practices related to the familial and politico-jural domains (Fortes 1970), or in, what is commonly called as, the public and private spheres.

In what follows, I will describe Turkey's social and political structures diachronically with a particular emphasis on the relationship between the state and its citizens, a relationship that seems to have created conditions conducive to political violence. To achieve this task, I will use a center-periphery analysis approach which will take into account the role of stratification and differential incorporation in conflictual relationships between the state and society, most conspicuously in the public domain. Following Heper, I use "center" to define "those groups which try to uphold the state's autonomy and supremacy in the polity; [while] "periphery" refers to those who try to escape from the regulation of the state" (1980:20) and desire to place themselves in the center. I will then explain the emergence and evolution of the groups I studied, revolutionary groups and the PKK, respectively.

Society and politics in Turkey

Turkey is a country of approximately 78 million people that straddles the European and Asian continents (Thrace and Anatolia respectively) and is surrounded by water on three sides. It is bordered by ten countries: Iraq and Syria to the south; Greece, Romania, and Bulgaria to the west; Iran, Armenia, and Georgia to the east; and Ukraine and Russia to the north. The majority of its population is Sunni Muslim (98 percent),[1] while the remaining population includes mostly Christians and Jews. Despite the controversial estimates on its ethnic composition, according to most estimates, 70–75 percent is Turkish, 18 percent Kurdish and other minorities make up the 7–12 percent of its population (CIA Factbook 2008). The Republic is a parliamentary democracy, founded in 1923 after World War I as one of the successor states of the Ottoman Empire.

During the era of the Ottoman Empire, all social and political affairs were under the monopoly of the state. In contrast to the nature of conflicts that took place in the West as a result of various polarizations such as Church/state; feudality/bourgeoisie/industrial proletariat; local groups/national groups, conflicts in the Ottoman Empire took place along the axis of state/community (*devlet/cemaat*) (Mardin *et al.* 1990:20). Most Western accounts focused on the notion that the Sultan governed the Empire through a "slaved" bureaucracy, a system generally referred to as "Eastern despotism," where there were no intermediary institutions between the Sultan's authority and his subjects (*teb'a*). Whereas the vassals' (*kuls*) lives and property were under the control of the Sultan, ordinary citizens' (*teb'a*) lives were more secure, due to the protection provided by religious law (*şeriat*) and intellectuals (*ulema*) (1990:21). In this respect, it is possible to say that the supporters of the view of "Eastern despotism" overlooked the private property domain of ordinary citizens guaranteed for them by the *şeriat*.

One of the most distinguishing aspects of the Ottoman political system was the centrality of the state. During the reign of Sultan Bayezid I (1389–1403) and thereafter, Ottomans were quite successful in using all the tools and the structures of a centralized government: "periodic surveys of population and land, a central treasury, a bureaucracy which sought the capital to regulate affairs of state throughout provinces, and a system of control through the Sultan's own slaves" (Inalcik 1976:28; Szyliowicz 1977:105; Heper 1980:83). Likewise, the state's supremacy increased by the fact that Islam was never an autonomous force or power *vis-à-vis* the state, given that "the members of the religious institution were appointed and could be dismissed by the sultan" (Shaw 1976:135). Additionally, one of the key aspects of the centralized system was that the children of religious minorities were taken from their families, educated in special schools (*enderuns*) and placed into the ruling elite by integrating them with the administrative class.

The "Leviathan" style of government systems, which emerged in the West in the middle of the seventeenth century and the system of nation-states created later influenced the creation of Ottoman institutions in a significant way (Mardin 1990:31). However, although various confrontations between central and peripheral forces in the West (e.g., between the state and the Church, state builders and locals, the owners of the means of production and those who lacked them) led to some reconciliation between these forces and resulted in the integration of the periphery into the center, these confrontations and integrations did not take place in the Ottoman Empire until the nineteenth century (1990:32). What is more, the main confrontation was unidimensional that manifested itself in the form of conflict, because the centralized system was inappropriate for general public, particularly those who pursued a nomadic life on the periphery. The relationship between the state and the nomads of Anatolia, who were indeed the nuclei of the Empire, was a special one. Not only did the state have issues with these nomads but there was also a real conflict between them and the city-dwellers and the Ottoman elite, which resulted in the conviction of the latter that civilization was indeed a struggle between urban dwellers and nomads. This perception was also molded into the idea that nomadism (an aspect of the periphery) is nothing but a life-style that deserves condescension (1990:33). According to Ozankaya, residual effects of such clashes between the nomads and the settled population were observed even in the late 1960s especially in the eastern parts of Turkey (1971:136).

Another constitutive element of the center-periphery discord was the center's suspicions about local notables and religious orders. When the periphery was seen as a fertile ground for those who claimed right on the throne (*taht*), it became the focus of rebellions throughout the Ottoman history. As a result of these rebellions, the center gave semi-autonomous status to the peripheral elites and thus conflict was prevented for a long time (Mardin 1990:33). However, when the Empire started to suffer social disorganization in its period of decline, the center-periphery divide again became one of the biggest problems. The Sultan and his officials were diametrically opposed to the Anatolian people (1990:34). Since Anatolia was the major constitutive element of the modern Turkey, it is important to understand this opposition in terms of understanding the contemporary problems and conflicts in the country. A major grievance of the masses at the time had to do with state officials (*kuls*) who were non-Muslims. Ordinary citizens were frustrated as they thought that the system was excluding freely born Muslims while providing more opportunities for non-Muslims (1990:40).

A further problem of the centralized system was related to economics. State officials were richer than the tradesmen; the state enjoyed an economic monopoly that favored state officials whose treatment of the periphery was less than oppressive. In addition, the Sultan enjoyed a monopoly on all agricultural land except for the city centers (1990:35–6), which proved in a way that the Ottoman land regime, too, displayed patrimonial characteristics (Heper 1980:83). In brief, until the nineteenth century, the major problem in the Ottoman Empire was the subjugating policies of the state in the fields of the economy, politics, and culture. The periphery could benefit from only one of the center's educational institutions, that is, religious education. This subjugation led in turn to the creation of counter-cultures and a coalition between the villagers and the local elite who saw the center as their enemy (Mardin 1990:38). Although the center tried to prevent the formation of this coalition by various strategies, such as the granting of benefits in return for service to the Sultan (the "fief system"– *timar*), it did not bestow any political-territorial rights (Heper 1980:83); thus it could not succeed in preventing numerous rebellions.

A popular conviction among historians about the Ottoman centuries is that, from the second half of the sixteenth century to the nineteenth century, there was a progressive development from a centralized system to a quasi-feudal polity, a conviction that was based on the idea of "the gradual weakening of the center and the growing 'autonomy' that the periphery acquired during this period" (Heper 1980:81). Heper argues, however, that the wealth of the local notables came largely from their exploitation of the weaknesses of the center in the localities and thus, "they were never and/or interested in translating their economic power into central political power" (1980:96). Similarly, with regard to the same period, Karpat claims that despite the establishment of the modern capitalist order and a rational bureaucratic system, the old social order needed to be eliminated elsewhere, whereas "in the Ottoman empire the old political system was preserved despite social changes" (1972:257). The state maintained its sovereignty, its multi-national character, and resisted Turkish nationalism almost until the end of the World War I (1972:257).

On the other hand, it has been also suggested that during the process of modernization in the nineteenth century, the political system underwent several important innovations and reforms that affected particularly the center given that "progress was made towards a constitutional government in the Ottoman polity" (Heper 1980:81). There was a move from hereditary-based (or Sultan-based) bureaucracy to a "rational bureaucracy" (Weber 1968). Bureaucrats took control of the notion of patrimonial constitutionalism from the Sultan and reduced his influence in politics. At the same time, they were able to secure their livelihoods and property (Mardin 1990:26–7). In the *Tanzimat* (Regulations) period (1839–1876), the aim of reforms was "to establish a uniform and centralized administration linked directly with each citizen and working with its own rational principles of justice, applied equally to all" (Heper 1980:92). Despite these sanguine intentions, the lack of institutions and legal framework did not provide suitable ground for the implementation of "equality" that these *fermans* had aimed for (Karpat 1972:259). In effect, the equality of all citizens, promulgated both in the *Tanzimat Fermanı* in 1839 and the *Islahat Fermanı* in 1856, was considered by the center "to be a practical means to mobilize the masses behind the state and against the local notables" (1972:258).[2]

16 *Historical and social contexts*

Consequently, the alienation of the periphery from the center increased, which compelled the center to search for other means to incorporate the periphery to the system, e.g., giving the people of the periphery a feeling that they were same as those of the center. For this, the word "Ottoman" was used as a unifying force which was only relatively successful, because the terms "Kurdish," "Albanian," Lezgi," "Arab," etc., still remained as quite salient concepts for understanding social reality (Mardin 1990:42). Before Mustafa Kemal Atatürk, the founder of the Turkish Republic, the Young Turks tried to do the same by promoting a new concept of the *Vatan* (fatherland) in order to create a new form of identity "to supersede religious, ethnic, and local divisions" (Karpat 1972:264). Furthermore, "the recognition of the Ottoman citizenship for all inhabitants regardless of religion, the abolition of the *millets*,[3] and the introduction of general military service (which had been in practice limited to Turks) prepared the ground for the successful dissemination of the new political culture" (1972:264). However, they also failed to succeed because their laicist approach *inter alia* did not resonate with the religious periphery (Mardin 1990:42). The periphery's turn to religion was in fact its response to the failure of the center to incorporate them into the system and to the center's conviction that the periphery was the center of backwardness (1990:45). More importantly, the state's fear between 1920 and 1923 of disintegration along the ethnic lines and the fear of backwardness (*irtica*) continued until the 1950s, which has also remained hitherto the main problem of Kemalist politics in Turkey (1990:42).

The notion of stratification in the Ottoman and Republican periods

Many Western and Turkish researchers have claimed over the years that there was no hereditary aristocracy in the Ottoman social system, while arguing about the existence of a patrilineal upper class in Republican Turkey (Mardin 1990:67). According to Inalcik (1970), there were two main strata in the Ottoman Empire: (1) the ruler and his administrators (*kuls*) and (2) the ruled (*reaya*). To be more specific, the first class was the "*askeri*" class that comprised religious personnel and administrators, i.e., palace and military personnel, state officials and intellectuals (*ulema*). The second class (*reaya*) included all Muslim and non-Muslim individuals (*teb'a*) who paid taxes but did not participate in government affairs. In a nutshell, the delegation of the Sultan's authority was a political condition, which was responsible for stratification in the Empire (Göcek 1993:513). Moreover, another condition for stratification was religion and in the Ottoman context, "the identification of Ottoman religious communities as minority groups preceded their identification as ethnic groups" (1993:514).

A crucial feature of the Ottoman stratification was that *reaya* could not benefit from the privileges that the *askeri* class had. However, a constant feature and common orientation of the center was the protection of *reaya*, or "the flock," in particular the peasants, so that the state would obtain revenues in a consistent manner (Karpat 1977:90). As mentioned earlier, within the *askeri* class, *kuls* were chosen among non-Muslims. In fact, all state officials were non-Muslims except for the *ulema* (religious intellectuals), and this system was designed as such to prevent the creation of dynasties. At the same time, the *kul* system was not unchecked, because *kuls* had no security against the Sultan (Mardin 1990:73). To reemphasize here, in the Ottoman socio-political system, a person's status in society was determined by the Sultan's decision (1990:75); for instance, "through the granting or withdrawing of imperial certificates (*berats*), the Sultan could decide whether a person belonged to a tax-free or a tax-paying group" (Mardin 1967:272).

According to Mardin, this dichotomous model of stratification in the Empire could only be considered as an "ideal type," as he argues that understanding the objective dimensions of stratification in the Empire required a consideration of not only the official classes but also unofficial ones, which are indeed multifarious (1990:75). Besides Inalcik's dual model of Ottoman stratification, for example, the famous seventeenth-century itinerant Evliya Çelebi's depiction of Ottoman city systems should also be taken into account. During his visit to Istanbul, Evliya Çelebi (1640[1971]) observed five different classes in the city, which included the managerial class (*askeri*), gardeners, beggars, boatmen, and tradesmen. Mardin suggests, however, that the Empire tried incessantly to suppress any possibility that did not fit to the dichotomous model, while adding that "this contention is one of the major characteristics of the Ottoman social history" (1990:76). Lastly, the administrative (*askeri*) class was not homogenous; it was fragmented and prone to violence while, despite their differences, the hostility of the *reaya* classes (artisans and villagers) towards the *askeri* class made it look like a unified bloc (1990:77).

What was significant in the Empire was that class consciousness permeated all politics because "knowing one's own position" was the basic rule that was common to all in society (1990:83). This rule manifested itself as such; for instance, individuals from a certain profession had to carry an identifier on them that signified their profession, members of certain *millet* had to wear clothes with their cultural identifiers, or members of the lower class were not allowed to were clothes that belonged to the elites (1990:83). Such rules and regulations limiting "regular or exuberant consumption" have existed ubiquitously in the world, be it the West, China, or the Ottoman Empire. The crucial point here is that such rules and regulations meant that "economic power, or wealth, is not the single determinant of the right of consumption" (Barber 1957:191). It is also possible to argue that the same rule applies to modern Turkey.

In any event, regardless of the model taken for analysis, whoever examines Ottoman political development will find, in the words of Heper, that "there is an unmistakable continuity from the classical Ottoman period to the centuries of decline and into the nineteenth century" (1980:98). One of the crucial characteristics of Ottoman political culture was an "ever-present tension" (1980:98), which attests to the common theme that the administrative class was hated by the lower classes (*reaya*). Economic inequalities stemming from the privileged position of the administrative class, coupled with their condescending approach to other classes, were among the major causes of rebellions throughout Ottoman history. Most of the city rebellions were orchestrated by tradesmen, janissaries, and discontented people of the palace (Mardin 1990:78). In short, the relationships between the different strata of this system played an important role in terms of political violence throughout Ottoman history.

Studying the notion of stratification in modern capitalist societies, Giddens (1973) suggests that three fundamental social elements – property, education, or professional skills, and manual labor – lead to a tri-partite model of class structuring. These three elements produce three nuclei of power in the economic domain, i.e., three different classes: (i) an upper class, who own productive property and thereby control the means of production; (ii) a middle class comprised of individuals who do not own property but nevertheless create a position of power for themselves in the social hierarchy by virtue of the special education or skills they possess that they can use as currency in the market; and finally, (iii) a lower or working class who occupy the last rung of such a socio-economic ladder, and who can only offer manual labor in exchange for subsistence wages. With respect to the social structuring in modern Turkey, despite the existence of these three categories of classes, it is plausible to argue that the abovementioned patterns of Ottoman stratification have remained intact, as many researchers have found that the country's peculiar political structure, i.e., "patrimonial, bureaucratic sovereignty" and the "center-periphery" divide have continued and reproduced the Ottoman pattern of two ideal social classes, i.e., the ruler and the ruled (Frey 1975; Heper 1976; Mardin 1980; Aydin 2006: 499).

The late nineteenth century, the establishment of the Republic and the problems of differential incorporation (1923–present)

In the latter part of the nineteenth century, there was already a move from Ottoman nationalism to Turkish nationalism due to various turning points in the political system concerning three major organized forces: the throne, the intelligentsia, and the military (Karpat 1972:270). As Karpat asserts, these developments were in fact "the prelude to the establishment of the Republic and the formal abolition of the monarchy and the Caliphate in 1922–4" (1972:270). During this period, numerous innovations[4] were made to the political system, the motivating ideology of which was the adoption of Western models in lieu of the previous Islamic models and institutions. It is important to note that, as these structural changes were made due to internal forces, i.e., they were not imposed upon the country by colonizing agents, the experience of the country's modernization has been generally called as a "voluntary modernization" (Göle 2002).

The latter part of the nineteenth century was important in terms of understanding the political modernization of the Ottoman Empire and the rise of Turkish nationalism. As Akçura (1976 [1904]) points out in his classic Üç Tarz-ı Siyaset ("Three Ways of Politics"), Pan-Islamism and Ottomanism had already failed and "nationalism" was the rational choice for modernization. As Karpat suggests, "nationalism consequently appeared not only as a political solution to the survival of the state and of Turks as a cultural-political group, but also as a channel for the introduction of science and progress for the new political unit: the nation" (1972:280). Accordingly, the intelligentsia of the time started to search for ways to promote a national Turkish history and culture. To this end, they organized a secret association known as the Young Turks in 1889, whose aim was "to protest against [Sultan] Abdulhamid's suppression of freedoms and ask for the reinstatement of the constitution of 1876," which marked the birth of Turkish nationalism (1972:280).

When the Young Turks escaped abroad and organized a network of political organizations (Ittihad ve Terakki, "Unity and Progress"), they expressed themselves as Turks, and from that time onwards, "to be a Turk meant not only having an ethnic identity, but also a political one" (1972:280). Their first rebellion against Sultan Abdulhamid, orchestrated by Besneli Niyazi on July, 1908, took place in Monaster. Sultan Abdulhamid failed to suppress the uprising and he was compelled to sign the Declaration of the Second Constitutional Period in 1908 (*II. Meşrutiyet*). The second constitutional government was established on 23 July 1908, which was the beginning of a new phase in the political development of Turkey. In this period (1908–1918), many new social groups – such as civil and military officers, civil bureaucrats, and professionals – first began to emerge among the political elites (Arslan 2005:133). The Young Turk era was also significant in the sense that during this period "secularism" became the main feature of Turkish nationalism, which in turn encouraged the Arab intelligentsia to abandon their loyalties to the Ottoman state and fight for the creation of their own national states (Karpat 1972:281). The culmination point in the transformation of the Ottoman state in the latter part of the nineteenth century was the establishment of the Republic of Turkey in 1923 by Mustafa Kemal, an Ottoman officer who is popularly known as "Atatürk" (the Father of the Turks).

Not so long after Turkey's defeat in World War I, the victorious Allies started to dismember Turkey. The Sultan, Mehmet VI, living in Istanbul "felt helpless and was forced to accept and abide by the terms of armistice" (Rahman 1984:158). This decision, as the famous Pakistani Muslim poet Muhammad Iqbal puts it, was one of *Aql*, "the way of reason," because the Sultan accepted the Allies' humiliating terms after a rational calculation. However, the way Mustafa Kemal chose was one of *Ishq*, "creative love." Instead of succumbing to extreme difficulties, he decided to confront and overcome them, and "with the aid of sympathetic and like-minded forces, turned Turkey from a helpless, defeated nation into an independent and sovereign power" (1984:158). In much of the Islamic world, Mustafa Kemal was seen as a revitalizing figure, a trailblazer for Muslims so to speak, that they might take back their long-awaited self-hood through a recultivation of *Ishq*. This euphoria did not last long, however, given that on 3 March 1924, Mustafa Kemal abolished the Caliphate which was interpreted as the nationalist isolation of Turkey from the rest of the Muslim world. In his "wholesale" program of Westernization, Islam ceased to be the basis of the state, secularism was adopted in its place, and accordingly religious education was prohibited in the state education (1984:158).

The innovations Atatürk had in mind were not limited to the religious sphere. The main impetus behind his actions was a Western-style "modernization," which is generally defined as "a societal process that involves the whole of the society including its economy, belief system, culture and politics" (Arslan 2005:131). As such, he did not falter in penetrating each of the fields mentioned above. Establishing the Republic on 29 October 1923, he abolished the Sultanate and the Caliphate, respectively. The religious law of şeriat was replaced by a modern civil code adopted from the Swiss civil code, and a penal code was devised based on the Italian penal code. The new system was based on Roman law (1925–1926). Legal reforms were followed by a number of cultural reforms, the most important being the reform of the alphabet. The Arabic script was replaced by the Roman one in 1928. After that, the status of women in society was ameliorated as they acquired the right to vote and to be elected to parliament before their counterparts in many European countries. The reforms also affected political and social life: the first political party of the Republic, the Republican People's Party, was established, the wearing of the *hijab* (veil) outside religious buildings was forbidden and the Western calendar and time standards were adopted. In addition, a national railway network was built, a national educational system was established, and the expansion of a secular higher education began. Last but not least, in an effort to provide a framework for language reform, a "sun theory of languages" was designed by the Turkish Language society. This main argument of this theory was that Turkish was a major language that had spread from Central Asia to other parts of the world. According to this theory, new textbooks were prepared by the Ministry of Education for use in primary and secondary schools. Words of non-Turkic origin (Arabic, Persian) were excised from dictionaries. The crucial point with the language reform was the intention of the elites to reduce the possibility of foreign connections to other cultural reference groups (e.g., Kurds) in favor of a more autonomous culture (Arslan 2005:134; Turan 1984:177–84).

Theoretically, Atatürk's approach to social transformation is an *induced* rather than an *organic* model of change. The key to the organic model is that change comes from the bourgeoisie, continues with the establishment of a centralized state with a elite bureaucracy, and ends with a constitutional government in which royal bureaucracy develops into a public bureaucracy. Most states in Western Europe had achieved this type of change during the second part of the nineteenth century (Organski 1965; La Palombara 1969). According to the induced change model, the initial impetus for change does not come from the bourgeoisie.

> Induced development evinces, in order of time, (1) an outside stimulus, usually in the form of overwhelming power; (2) the emergence of a leader (or leaders) who seek to elevate their nation to a position of like power; (3) the creation of a new bureaucracy and a change in the political structure; (4) economic change, planned and in part executed by the central government, and (5) the emergence of a middle class followed by a variety of further expressions of collective economic interest.
>
> (Heper 1976:485–6)

It appears that there is a consensus in the analyses of the Turkish polity that the developments until the transition to a multiparty system in the 1940s may be based on the first four steps of the induced change model (1976:486). Military threats that the Ottoman Empire faced led to a move from the earlier patrimonial bureaucracy to a modernizing bureaucracy. Atatürk's emergence as a leader coincides with this period. In addition, despite the fact that this recently emerged bureaucratic ruling tradition was challenged toward the end of the century, it remained an Ottoman legacy to Republican Turkey, and the period of single-party rule (1923–1950) further strengthened that tradition (Karpat 1972; Heper 1976:486; Lewis 2002).

Another characteristic of the Turkish polity during the republican period has to do with the nature of its stratified society bequeathed by the Ottoman polity. As Van Nieuwenhuijze noted, "in the Ottoman-Turkish polity one certainly comes across (1) factual ascendancy of one sector of society over another, simultaneously in terms of economic and political power and in terms of (mutual) cultural rating, (2) a worldview containing a hierarchical element – characteristics of a stratified society" (1965:9). Van Nieuwenhuijze's depiction of the Ottoman-Turkish polity is much akin to Smith's (1998) concepts of "pluralism" and "differential incorporation." Historically, the key areas of controversy regarding the notion of socio-political structure have ranged from "the role of consensus and/or dominance in the maintenance of social order to the assignment of causality in social transformations" (Leon and Leons 1977:560). Smith emphasized the inherent disunity in highly segmented social systems and the need for explicit and implicit coercion to maintain such systems as a political unit (1977:560). According to him, in societies characterized by pluralism, one of the components must be dominant over the others in order to prevent social disintegration. In addition, societies that manifest the characteristics of pluralism are further split into pluralistic societies and plural societies.

> Pluralistic societies occur when the dominant section constitutes a majority of the total population. When the dominant section constitutes a minority, the result is the plural society, a type in which the structural implications of cultural pluralism have their most extreme expression, and the dependence on regulation by force is greatest.
>
> (1977: 561)

The reason for dependence of force, as explained by Smith, stems from the idea that such plural societies are "characterized by internal intersectional conflict that may be expressed or latent, and they depend for their maintenance on 'the monopoly of power by one cultural section'" (1977:562). Since plural societies are held together by political coercion, how do these societies transform themselves, or simply put, "how does the system change in such societies?" Smith's answer to that is simple: "the plural society is subject to revolutionary rather than evolutionary change" (1977:565). Put differently, for Smith, if change is to come in plural societies it will be violent and revolutionary in nature (1977:566). This necessity of change by violence, on the other hand, is linked to Smith's political typologies which he termed "political incorporation" that has three alternatives: *universalistic*, *consociation*, and *differential* incorporation. In universalistic incorporation, distinct sections are incorporated based on "consent and equity" (Britain and Holland); in consociation, distinctions are based on "equivalent or complementary rights and status" (Lebanon and tribal Terik-Tiriki); and in differential incorporation, different groups are incorporated based on "unequal basis." Where this "differential incorporation" prevails, "one corporate group or corporate section of a society enjoys superior rights and privileges, while others suffer corresponding disabilities" and this one "distinct section dominates the others, normally for its own advantage, and by various means which may include naked force where this seems necessary" (Smith 1974:180–98; Leon and Leons 1977).

Within the frameworks envisaged by Smith, I place Turkey within the category of plural societies for the following reasons: (1) during the Republican period (from 1923 to the late 1980s in particular), a minority group (the bureaucratic-military elite) was dominant in social and political affairs of the country;[5] (2) the main goal of this elite was to transform Turkish society top-down, which can be seen as a supply-led imposition of *their* ideals on society instead of allowing a demand-driven social change; (3) although there was the initial intention of establishing and maintaining a *de jure* "universalistic incorporation" of different ethnic, religious, and economic groups into the system, the *de facto* "differential incorporation" of these groups has permeated the Turkish polity during this period, although the ethnic groups are not distinguished based on physical criteria (race), but instead on cultural criteria (Smith 1960:774–5); (4) the "perceived" subjugation (e.g., of Kurds, Alevis, minorities, and religiously conservative people) by the state has created a contention within society, leading eventually to a belief among the supporters of the PKK (claiming Kurdish rights) and numerous revolutionary groups that the system must change, and that change can only come about by revolutionary violence.

The problems emanating from the differential incorporation of different groups into Turkish society have manifested themselves mostly within the public domain, although there were times when the dominant group penetrated even into the private domains of groups and individuals. What is crucial here is that an "authoritarian modernism," as implicated above, underpins the public domain in Turkey. The major problem with this is that, "while the Turkish public sphere adheres to some of the basic universal principles of the Western public sphere, these principles are selectively highlighted, coupled, and translated into social practices that are creatively altered as well" (Göle 2002:177). If we examine the ways in which Islam, being a minority, Kurdishness or Alewism is problematized in the public sphere, in the words of Göle, "we become aware of the unspoken, implicit borders and the stigmatizing, exclusionary power structure of the secular public sphere" (2002:178). This secular public sphere covers various spaces that range *inter alia* from "Parliament and educational institutions to the street and public transportation" (2002:177). To explain further, this modern/secular public sphere incorporates "regular," "Sunni Muslims" who are ethnically "Turkish," while confining *pious Muslim practices* to the private domain and *excorporating* those Sunni Muslims who display signs of piety in public. It also excludes from the system religious minorities (meaning "Christians and Jews," according to the Treaty of Lausanne), ethnic minorities (especially the "Kurds"), and Alevis.

Göle asserts that the public sphere is not a pre-established arena and that it is constantly constituted and negotiated through performance (2002:183). In light of this assertion, it will not be erroneous to say that in recent years the Turkish public sphere has gone through various transformations for the improvement of excluded groups. However, since this book takes into account the role of the aforementioned exclusionary structures on the Turkish Penitents' entry into and exit from political violence, and given that most of them joined their respective groups before these transformations, it is necessary to describe the problem areas historically by focusing on various time-periods and turning points in Republican history and with a particular emphasis on their relation to the emergence and significance of the terrorist groups that this book has set out to explore. The remainder of this chapter will then be split into three sections: (1) from the establishment of the Republic in 1923 to the 1960 military coup and the execution of the Prime Minister Adnan Menderes in 1961; (2) from 1960 to the military coup of 1980; and (3) from the 1980 coup to the present.

The Turkish polity between 1923–1960

The crucial aspect of this period was about the absolute leadership of Atatürk (1923–1938) and secularists' attempts at gaining hegemony, which was marked by drastic examples of exclusion that manifested themselves in multifarious ways and almost ubiquitously in society (Mardin 1967–1990; Turan 1984; Yavuz 2001; Kongar 2002; Arjmand 2008). I have already mentioned the type and nature of some social and political reforms. I will now talk about several specific incidents and the center's praxes that are significant for Turkish political development particularly in relation to the ruler/ruled relationship and the construction of Kurdish nationalism and other reactionary sentiments. Being fueled by the fear of disintegration, these praxes were portrayed to be necessary in consolidating the fledgling nation-state. In reality, however, a consideration of their latent functions (Smith 1998:28; Mamdani 2009) shows that such practices were but "excesses of secularism" as "the fetish of modernity" (Göle 2002:184), which left indelible marks in the popular imagination, some of which have reflected upon society in the form of political violence.

Sheikh Said Rebellion (Sunni Kurdish) – 1925

This rebellion, led by Sheikh Said in the country's southeast, was the first crucial incident that took place after the establishment of the Turkish Republic in 1923. It was a reaction against the abolition of the Caliphate in 1924. I will return to this later, but in order to make its significance more intelligible, it is necessary to provide a brief background. Historically, the Kurdish tribes were organized under emirates (principalities) that had "de facto independence" from the center until the sixteenth century (Gavan 1958). This independence came largely because of the Ottoman Empire's encouragement of the hostility between the Sunni-Kurdish emirates and Shiite Iranian Empire, which resulted in Kurdistan's inclusion in the Ottoman Empire (Yeğen 2006:217). The logic behind the political organization of the Ottoman Empire was the articulation of the confederation of Kurdish tribes as "sub-systems" within the broader system of the Empire, while ensuring that the autonomous status of the former remained intact. It is thus sensible to conclude, as Yeğen does, that "the political, economic, administrative and cultural aspects of the relationship between the Ottoman state and the Kurds were almost entirely defined by the dialectic between the sub-systems (i.e., autonomous Kurdish emirates) and the general system (i.e., the Ottoman Empire)" (2006:218). Under this framework, the autonomous status of the Kurdish tribes was recognized by the Ottoman state until the mid-1800s, and such autonomy seemed to have constituted and defined the politico-social space where "Kurdishness" was constituted (2006:217).

The problems that the Ottoman Empire faced at the beginning of the nineteenth century, however, brought about several changes in terms of the autonomy of the Kurdish emirates. A major consequence of these problems was the erosion of the aforementioned devolved aspects of the Ottoman Empire, which resulted eventually in the destruction of the periphery, and thus of the Kurdish emirates (2006:218). The abolition of the emirates was intended as the destruction of the dominant political-administrative organization in "Kurdistan," as a bond had been created, which connected the Kurdish tribes under a tribal confederation (2006:219). The abolition of the emirates eventually led to confrontations between individual tribes. Consequently, the failure of the center to prevent tribal conflicts and restoring order in "Kurdistan" resulted in the emergence of new actors in Kurdish politics: *the sheikhs* (Olson 1989:xvi). The sheikhs had the power and legitimacy to restore order among the conflicting tribes; they functioned as mediators between the center and the periphery. From the beginning of the 1800s, most Kurdish rebellions were led by the sheikhs, the most important of which were the "revolt of the Sheikh Ubeydullah in the 1870s" and the "Sheikh Said rebellion in 1925" (Yeğen 2006:219). As well as their mediating role between central government and the peripheral tribes, the sheikhs also functioned also as mediators between the Islamic faith and Kurdish nationalism. As Tucker suggests, "for Kurds nationalism and religion became intertwined from the beginning" (1989:xvii). And summarizing the Sheikh Said rebellion, Tucker said:

> The Sheikh Said rebellion showed ... the possibility of a symbiotic relationship between nationalism and religion ... Said's rebellion had shown that nationalism in its seemingly modern western sense (shared language, cultural forms, history, contiguous territory etc.) and religion, in this case Sunni Islam, were by no means incompatible, at least at the level of political policy and struggle.
>
> (1989:xix)

In addition, in "Kurdistan," as Olson asserts, "the nationalist ideas found their way into the *tarikats* (religious sects) and *tekiyyes* (dervish lodges) where the sheikhs became their ardent supporters" (1989:16). Proceeding from the foregoing, in his analysis of the construction of Kurdish identity, Yeğen argues that "*sheikhs, tarikats* and *tekiyyes* had all been the constitutive components of the social space wherein Kurdishness was constituted" (2006:20). This point is quite interesting, as I will explain later, that when the PKK was established in 1978, it adopted initially a Marxist-Leninist ideology and almost ignored the fact that most of its recruits came from religious families. In any event, besides the fact that the Sheikh Said rebellion was an attempt to show the compatibility of Islam and nationalism, what really triggered it was the abolition of the Caliphate in 1924. The Caliphate, as one of the two power sources of the Ottoman Empire (the other being the Sultanate), was "an institution which guaranteed that the bond between the Ottoman political center and the Muslim elements of the "periphery" was to be a loose one, so as to tolerate the ethnic plurality of the 'periphery'" (2006:221). The abolition of the Caliphate therefore meant the elimination of this loose bond that was replaced by the oppressive treatment by the center of the (ethnic, cultural, economic, administrative, and political) elements of the periphery. From this perspective, it was the second "strike" (after the removal of the emirates) against the periphery, i.e., "the social space wherein Kurdishness was constituted" (2006:221).

To conclude, according to Olson, the Sheikh Said rebellion took several forms including tribal, religious, and national ones (1989:153–5). Despite the fact that Turkish authorities captured Sheikh Said and hanged him in 1925 in Diyarbakır, "his rebellion, the first ethno-religious uprising, made the Turkish Republic very suspicious of any form of Kurdish activities" (Yavuz 2001:7–8). Put differently, "the articulation of ethnic-based politics with tribal politics increased the pressure on the Kurdish tribes" (Yeğen 2006:222). As a result, as Van Bruinessen suggests, a project of detribalization was adopted in Turkey and in his view, "everything that recalled a separate Kurdish identity was to be abolished: language, clothing, names and of course the tribes themselves" (1978:10). Republican history in fact proves the denial of the existence of Kurds by the Turkish authorities who for a long time insisted that Kurds were actually Turks and that the Kurdish language was a corrupted version of Turkish. In addition, Kurdish history was not mentioned in the textbooks, "the country's Kurdish region was dotted with the slogan reminding inhabitants that 'happy is he who calls himself a Turk'" (Marcus 2007:10), the names of the Kurdish villages were altered and substituted by Turkish ones, "the word Kurdistan was expunged from books and the language was essentially banned" (2007:18). All in all, the upshot of the radical nation-building practices of the Kemalist ideology led to the construction of the Kurdish identity as "reactionary," "tribal," and an outcome of "regional backwardness" (Yavuz 2001:2), which hitherto dominated the public and state discourses concerning the Kurdish as well as the PKK problem. Instead, as Yavuz suggests, a better conceptualization would be to view these issues "as an outcome of the tension between the forces of homogenization and the struggle to maintain cultural and local autonomy" (2001:3).[6]

Dersim rebellion (Alevi Kurdish)–1938

Assimilation policies of the center led to another rebellion (in addition to the Koçgiri rebellion of 1920 and the Sheikh Said rebellion in 1925) in and around the mountainous areas of Dersim inhabited mostly by Alevi Kurds, known as Zazas,[7] in 1937–1938. According to Van Bruinessen, Alevis are a heterodox religious minority who later (in the 1990s) began to manifest themselves as another ethnic group (1996:2). Yet, in the Turkish legal context, Alevis are not recognized as a different religious or ethnic group; they are (approximately 7 million) subsumed under the Muslim population that is said to constitute the 98 percent of Turkish society. Although various factions of Alevis accept that Alevism is part of Islam, others claim that it is more like a tradition, folklore, or a way of life. In general, there are several strands of Alevism in Turkey which include "sympathizers of Iranian Shiism," "mystical Islamic Alevism," "Marxist-atheist Alevis," "Kemalist traditionals," and "Republican Alevism."

The significance of Dersim[8] rebellion is to do with the renewed alienation between the center and the periphery (i.e., Kurdish Alevis, whereas the Sheikh Said rebellion was of Sunni-Kurdish origin). Dersim was a part of a region that was marked for evacuation by the central government in Ankara. The crux of the issue was that Dersim residents refused to pay taxes and recognize any authority other than their own and Ankara concentrated on solving this problem (White 2011:7). A report made on behalf of the Interior Minister to the parliament in as early as 1926 read: "Dersim is an abscess on the Turkish Republic and it must be removed, for the sake of the country's well-being" (Beşikçi 1990:29). After ten years, it was apparent in Atatürk's speech that the aforementioned approach worsened as he said, "We have to remove this abscess at its roots. To deal with this problem, we will give greater powers to the government" (Hasretyan 1995:262).

Consequently, in order to tame this recalcitrant region, a new law called the "Tunceli Law" (official name, "*Munzur Vilayeti Teşkilat ve İdaresi Hakkında Kanun*") was introduced to the parliament, which contained extreme measures to bring the Dersim residents under the jurisdiction of the Turkish Republic (Beşikçi 1990:11–12). These extreme measures[9] prompted the Dersim revolt led by some local leaders, most notably by Seyit Riza. The revolt did not succeed; the leaders including Seyit Riza were executed and, according to official army records, 13,806 people were killed and 11,683 people were relocated between 1936–1939 (Şen 2011). Although most of the previous governments generally chose to justify these killings by the concept of "counter insurgency," 73 years later, Prime Minister Tayyip Erdogan disclosed considerable classified information about the Dersim massacre and openly apologized to the public in a televised speech in November 2011 by saying, "If it is necessary to apologize on behalf of the state and if there is such literature, I apologize" (2011:1).

The Democrat Party's ascendance to power and 1960 military coup

The second half of the 1940s is another historical period for Turkey as it marks the transition from a single-party to multiparty state or alternatively, from a totalitarian system to democracy. Although many parties were established during this period, only the Democrat Party (DP), founded by Adnan Menderes and three others who were former members of the Republican People's Party (CHP), became successful. The ascendance of the DP to power represents the fifth stage in the aforementioned "induced change model," for, as Heper writes, "the étatist policies of the 1930s created a bourgeoisie which could challenge the 'center' in the 'ruralizing election' of 1950" (1976:486). Until the introduction of a multiparty system, the entrepreneurial groups were subordinate to the ruling bureaucratic order and functioned as an economic auxiliary to it (Karpat 1966:173). As Karpat argues, however, "the growth in their size, power, and function within the national economy made them potential candidates for political power" (1966:174). Eventually, they achieved power under the Democrat Party in 1950 when the public voted against the centralized statist tradition that was intent on transforming society top-down (Keyder 1990:102). After its victory in the 1950 elections (the DP received 53.35 percent of the popular vote and 83.57 percent of the seats in the Grand National Assembly), the DP also won the next two elections and stayed in power through majority party governments (Arslan 2005:135; Sayarı and Bilgin 2011:741).

The DP's approach of "growth from below" fundamentally changed the country's social organization and the power relations in it. It marked a significant diminution in the power of the bureaucrats who ruled the country since the nineteenth century and replaced them with "a new economic elite drawn from landed and business groups and their associates" (Karpat 1966:178). In the latter part of the decade, however, the party's influence started to dwindle, as Turkey's bourgeoning democracy suffered from "increasing strains amidst growing polarization and conflict between the government and the opposition" (Sayarı and Bilgin 2011:741). As a result of the escalation of the tension, a group of middle-ranking officers ousted the DP from office,[10] replaced it with a military government on 27 May 1960, and arrested Prime Minister Menderes and two of his cabinet members who were eventually hanged in 1961.

The causes of the 1960 military coup and three others that followed it have long been the foci of political debates and public discourses in Turkey. According to Özbudun, for instance, what brought the DP down were the deviation from democracy, increasing cronyism in the DP, and the departure from Kemalist principles (in Kırçak 1993). On the other hand, Keyder argues that the 27 May coup could be seen as an attempt by the bureaucratic-statist elite to regain the power they had lost a decade earlier (1990:117). This elite was regarded as a social set composed of "military-civilian intellectuals," on which I will elaborate below.

A popular alternative conception meanwhile points to the fact that, far from protecting the country's democracy, the military coup in 1960 and others that followed it in 1971, 1980 and 1997 (called "post-modern coup") not only truncated the development of the country's democracy but also destroyed its economy, social life and the aspirations of its citizens. In addition, social groups (mostly religiously conservative people) that respected the legacy of the Democrat Party and its leader Adnan Menderes viewed the post-coup constitution of 1961 as an instrument that prevented the manifestation of the "public will" through the creation of institutions such as the "Constitutional Court," the "National Security Council," which allowed the military to meddle in politics, and the "Turkish Council of State" (Danıştay). The common conviction of individuals who subscribed to the latter conceptualization is that conditions for the abovementioned coups were fabricated by secret forces, which has come to be known as "the deep-state" in Turkey. Using Perlmutter's (1969) concept of "praetorian state" and Smith's concept of "institutionalized repression" (1998:102–3), I will delve into the notion of the deep state and its significance in the last section of this chapter, which will be preceded by a discussion of the emergence of various leftist-revolutionary groups and the PKK.

The rise of the Turkish Left and the emergence of revolutionary groups and the PKK (1961–1980)

A modern secular left-wing movement in Turkey emerged as a force with the aim of establishing a new social and political system which depended, "first and above all on the elimination of the traditional concepts of authority and social organization" (Karpat 1966:169). Leftist conceptualization of government systems is based on a materialist concept of power and an economic explanation of social organization, which is diametrically opposed to the traditionalist moral explanations of government and authority (1966:169). In light of this, the elimination of traditionalism was natural, which began towards the end of the Ottoman Empire and gathered momentum in Republican Turkey. According to Karpat, "the reforms in government prepared the ground not only for modernization of the country in the general sense, but also for the development of leftist movements" (1966:169). In particular, the relatively democratic environment created by the 27 May coup (1960) and the constitution of 1961[11] was the period when the masses and young people became politicized, the working class developed noticeably both in quantity and quality and the platform of the Turkish left started to gain momentum in Turkish politics. According to Aydınoğlu,

> the military coup staged by a group of politically backward officers who did not have any clear program but the aim of toppling the Democrat Party, laid in fact the foundations of a new political superstructure and culture. [Hence] it paved the way for the lower classes to turn to political action and created its instruments.
>
> (1992:28, my translation)

At the same time, national liberation movements and social mobilizations taking place around the world also influenced greatly Turkish youth and intellectuals. It is in this context that the TİP, "Türkiye İşçi Partisi" (Turkey's Labor Party) was born and gained popularity among the youth, mostly because of the lack of alternative options at the time.[12] Two political movements emerged from the TİP at this time although they opposed each other in terms of ideology and methods as to how to bring about *the* revolution: the MDD, "Milli Demokratik Devrim" Hareketi (National Democratic Revolutionary Movement) and the SD, "Sosyalist Devrim" Hareketi (Socialist Revolutionary Movement). Since these movements greatly influenced Turkey's illegal revolutionary groups, it is necessary to understand their major arguments.

The most important aspect of the MDD was Mihri Belli[13] and other founders' belief in the "gradual revolution," which was envisaged by the Soviet Bolsheviks. The crucial point here has to do with their conception of Turkey's "peculiar" conditions. To clarify, they argued that since Turkey was a pseudo-feudal country that lacked a proletariat, what they needed first was a democratic revolution which would be brought about by the social set of "military-civilian intellectuals." At the very least, this revolution would be anti-imperialist in nature; it would achieve the idea of "independent Turkey" and solve other "democracy" problems. In fact, Marxist ideology found a suitable ground to flourish in Turkey at that time, because a particular social set (military-civilian intellectuals) in the country that had indeed proved their success in an anti-imperialist revolution 40 years ago. For the MDD members, this social set was the "Kemalists" who had established the Republic in 1923. It is therefore possible to suggest that the MDD was a movement that created a type of Marxism out of the combination of Kemalism and Stalinism in the 1960s. The key ideological concepts that defined the MDD were "anti-imperialism" and, instead of the power of classes, their "trust" in national powers and some sections of the military and bourgeoisie.

The SD (Socialist Revolutionary) movement, on the other hand, wanted to proceed "by the book" and bring about a revolution along Marxist lines, i.e., instead of seeking to build alliances like the MDD with villagers and the petit-bourgeoisie, they believed in the idea that the revolution would be possible only by the proletariat. Despite their conviction of changing the regime through revolution, they were aware that the new regime after the revolution would be built through an evolutionary reform-making process. To this end, the SD ideologues believed that the working class had to do the following:

> the land reform, nationalization of foreign trade, banking sector and insurance companies; rapid industrialization through the state; and the elimination of factors that cause national humiliation such as the NATO, bilateral agreements, etc. In addition, private sector would depend on the "development plan" and be protected.
> (Aybar 1968:663–6)

As implied above, despite their differences, the MDD and the SD shared similar values and goals, i.e., they were both anti-imperial and democratic in nature and defining the state's role, which Karpat called "the new statism" (1966:184), was imperative for both movements.

An important point about these two movements has to do with their relationship to the Fikir Kulüpleri, "FKs" (Idea Clubs), established in the Political Science Department of Ankara University in 1956. These clubs were then transformed into Fikir Kulüpleri Federasyonu, "FKF" (Federation of Idea Clubs) in 1965. By the end of the decade, the MDD movement increased its influence the FKF and the association's name was changed to Dev-Genç, "Turkiye Devrimci Gençlik Federasyonu" (Turkey's Revolutionary Youth Federation). The establishment of the Dev-Genç is crucial in that it trained the most elite that pursued revolutionary armed struggle in 1970 and the ensuing years. It supported, and more often organized, all activities for the rights of workers and villagers. Among these activities, workers' marches held on 15–16 June 1970 were the most significant ones in terms of the role of Dev-Genç in their planning and implementation. However, the effects of the 15–16 June actions on the Dev-Genç was also crucial in the sense that most of the Dev-Genç militants participated in these events within the THKP-C, "Türkiye Halk Kurtuluş Partisi Cephesi" (Revolutionary People's Liberation Party/Front) and became more radicalized because of witnessing the radicalization of the worker's movement to which they were thenceforth distant, if not indifferent.

The THKP-C, along with the THKO, "Türkiye Halk Kurtuluş Ordusu" (People's Liberation Army of Turkey), is the most important group in understanding future revolutionary groups founded in the late 1970s because they all claimed to be the descendants of one of these two groups. Some of these groups include the DHKP-C (Revolutionary People's Salvation Party-Front), the MLKP (Marxist-Leninist Communist Party) or the TKP/ML-TIKKO (Turkey's Communist Party/ Marxist-Leninist), of which provided topics for this research.

The THKP-C was established in 1970 by Mahir Çayan and his friends, who rejected the idea of taking control of the TİP (Turkey's Labor Party) and transforming it to a war party of the proletariat. The main reason for this rejection was that it would delay the process of revolution that they wanted to start as soon as possible. They wanted to shape the structure of the organization of proletariat and other laborers *vertically* without further delay. Although the discussion about starting the revolution from the village or city centers remained ambiguous at the beginning, Çayan and his friends eventually thought that village conditions were not suitable and, being electrified by the dynamism of the proletariat during 15-June events, turned towards the urban environment for the revolution. Even though the 15–16 June events marked the defeat of the proletariat, they demonstrated to the THKP-C that the masses were ready for mobilization, provided that it was impossible to have them join the revolutionary struggle through trade-union structures or activities. What was needed instead was to show the masses the weakness of the state, which could be done through a war strategy which Çayan called "Politicized Military War Strategy" (Koç 2008:3). Most of his ideas were contained in his "Uninterrupted Revolution I-II-III." For him, Turkey was an oligarchic state but since the income level was relatively better in comparison with earlier decades, a balance seemed to exist between the state and the people. This balance, on the other hand, was an "artificial" one which could be eliminated through an armed revolutionary struggle.

Most of his actions were directed towards imperialist institutions and figures such as robbery of Istanbul Trade Bank and the kidnapping of the Israeli Consul General Ephrahim Elrom. He was imprisoned many times, but he escaped in 1971 and decided to cooperate with the THKO of Deniz Gezmiş and his friends who were sentenced to life in prison. In January 1972, Çayan and his friends kidnapped three British technicians working at a radar station in Turkey's Fatsa province, brought them to Kızıldere village in Niksar, and declared that they would be released as a *quid pro quo* for the release of Deniz Gezmiş and his friends. Çayan and nine of his friends, however, were surrounded by the army in that village and were killed on 30 March 1972 in a gun-battle.

The THKO emerged in the latter part of 1968 under the political and ideological leadership of Hüseyin İnan, although its popular leader was Deniz Gezmiş. Like the THKP-C, all members of the THKO were affiliated with the Turkish Labor Party (TİP), but they were not content with its relaxed position with respect to the revolution. What is more, in the face of increasing dynamism and radicalization among the youth, the TİP was seen as an obstacle rather than an enabling force for the revolution. Despite the TİP's laid-back attitude, many workers' strikes, student boycotts and anti-imperialist actions[14] took place in the latter part of 1960s. Defending the idea of revolution through violence, not being bound by laws and reaction against revisionism and all bourgeois groups may be listed as the most distinguishing features of the THKO. In contrast to the THKP-C that was focused on cities, the THKO's main interest lay in the countryside and it turned to the urban environment only after seeing the dynamism and successful actions in the cities. Despite its relative success, however, its focus on the revolution through a small group of armed individuals led to its decline in 1970 and it was eventually defeated when its leader cadre was eliminated. After the amnesty of 1974, the remaining cadre of the THKO restructured the group and started the group's process of self-criticism. This process resulted in the discussions of revisionism, which marked the THKO's transition from being a petit bourgeois to a Marxist group. Finally, the group changed its name to TDKP- İÖ "Türkiye Devrimci Komünist Partisi-İnşa Örgütü" (The Revolutionary Communist Party of Turkey-Build up Organization) in 1978 (Yalçıner 1988:2178–9).

As a penultimate note, the most crucial developments with regard to the period (1960–1980) took place in the latter part of the 1970s when the country saw mass mobilization and a high level of political polarization; namely, rightists and leftists. Leftists comprised aforementioned Marxist-Leninist groups that struggled to bring about a communist revolution through violence, while the rightists were composed of various nationalist and religiously conservative sections who tried to prevent a communist "take-over" of the country. The strongest faction among the rightists was the followers of the MHP "Milliyetçi Hareket Partisi" (Nationalist Action Party) who are commonly known as the "Ülkücüs" (singular Ülkücü). The multiplicity of explanations regarding the causes of the foregoing polarization notwithstanding, bloodletting clashes between rightists and leftists that took place between 1975 and 1980 were generally cited as the most important causes of the 12 September military coup.

Finally, another important aspect of the period here is to do with Kurdish identity and Kurdish movements. According to Yavuz, this period (particularly the 1960s and 1970s) marks the "secularization" of the Kurdish identity as a result of its interaction with socialist ideology, during which Alevi Kurds played an important role (2001:9). The relative liberalization that came with the 1961 constitution enabled Kurdish intellectuals to express Kurdish concerns and grievances in socialist terms to promote the self-determination of Kurds (2001:9). An important development in this regard was the establishment of the DDKO "Devrimci Doğu Kültür Ocakları" (The Revolutionary Cultural Society of the East) in 1969, "the first organizational attempt to raise the consciousness of the Kurdish population by stressing the uneven economic development within the regions of the country" (2001:10). In other words, the DDKO blended Kurdish nationalism and Marxism to mobilize youth "in the name of social justice and identity" (2001:10). Abdullah Öcalan took part in DDKO activities and created contacts with other students when he was in Istanbul in 1970 (Birand 1992:83). After the 1971 military coup, the DDKO was outlawed and its ex-members later tried to revive the DDKO under the DDKD, "Doğu Devrimci Kültür Dernekleri" (Revolutionary Democratic Cultural Associations), but they could not succeed in creating a unified Kurdish organization largely due to the existence of rival ideologies and personalities (Yavuz 2001:10; Marcus 2007).

The PKK was born in 1978 in Fis Village of Diyarbakır province under the leadership of Abdullah Öcalan, who is also known by the diminutive "Apo." As the eldest of seven children, Öcalan grew up in an environment dominated by disappointment and violence: "Ever since I was conscious, in my family there was always fighting ... there was an overwhelming unhappiness," he once said (Marcus 2007:16). His aggressive behavior was shaped during childhood when he learned of the importance of revenge and the uses of violence by his parents. As Marcus writes,

> When Öcalan was beaten badly by other boys and he ran crying home to his mother, she threw him out of the house, warning him not to return until he had exacted revenge. He quickly developed a reputation of being a wild, bold child: "even though it was forced on me the first time, my tendency for action [toward taking revenge] had started. I began to be attacker; I cracked the heads of many children," he recalled [internal references deleted].
>
> (2007:16)

Although founding the PKK in 1978, Öcalan explained in many interviews that the idea of establishing a Kurdish movement came to his mind at the beginning of 1970s during his encounters with leftist revolutionaries in prison. Marcus argues that being imprisoned for attending peaceful demonstrations convinced him that Turkey's undemocratic environment allowed little room for peaceful pursuit of political goals and that an armed revolution was the only answer (2007:25). Another consequence of his time in prison was that his awareness of the Kurdish problem had started to merge with a basic Kurdish nationalism which led him to start thinking of forming his own group. He described this time as his transition to becoming a professional revolutionary (2007:25). The main problem for Öcalan was about Turkey's "colonization" of the Kurdish region, which was coupled with "imperialism" and "capitalism." In addition, he was extremely critical of the traditional structure of the Kurdish society, an aversion that he extended later to the Turkish state (Yavuz 2001:12). The solution for him, then, was an "armed struggle" and "socialism," through which he would destroy the traditional Kurdish societal structure and create a socialist pan-Kurdish state (Marcus 2007:38; Yavuz 2001:12). To this end, Öcalan tried to recruit supporters who had high political consciousness, which is why he focused his attention on the provinces where the youth population was highest. He describes the importance of the youth as follows:

> Our activities were directed towards young intellectuals, because they had a unique character. First of all, as a social category, youth are more open to revolutionary ideas and have proclivity to internalize them. Second, because they are young intellectuals, they are more open to science and they have more contact with science and revolutionary ideas. Third, youth have dynamic, vibrant and intrepid characteristics. From this perspective as well, it was natural and obligatory to work with them...
> (EGM 2000:126, my translation)

On the other hand, Öcalan had numerous rivals who also claimed to defend Kurdish rights but rejected the use of violence such as Kemal Burkay who founded Turkey's Kurdistan Socialist Party and the Kurdish movement of Özgürlük Yolu (The Path of Freedom). Öcalan did not hesitate to attack his rivals brutally, and through such attacks, he and his small group became known as "Apocular" (followers of Apo), a formidable group that instilled significant fear in the region at the time. According to Marcus, even though Öcalan's attacks were not always justified, they resonated among "twenty-something Kurds who were eager for an independent state ... and frustrated by the history of failed uprisings and forced assimilation" (2007:35). Albeit his group's increasing popularity among Kurds, Marcus argues that the combination of pressure in the first part of 1980 from rival groups and the state authorities led Öcalan to secretly flee across border into Syria in July 1980, shortly before the upcoming military coup on 12 September 1980. However, despite such an interpretation of Öcalan's move to Syria, there are other arguments about it in that the timing of his escape from Turkey *inter alia* led many people, including most of my informants from the PKK and revolutionary groups, to think that Öcalan and his entourage were in reality taken to Syria by the instruments of the deep state to protect him from the wrath of the upcoming military coup. This is an important point with regard to the relationship between the PKK and the deep state, to which I will turn in the concluding section of this chapter.

The 12 September military coup, the rise of the PKK and its evolution (1980–present)

The real causes of the 12 September coup have been debated for more than three decades in Turkey. Generally, however, economic problems, political instability created by polarization in society between rightists and leftists (especially between 1975 and 1980), increased violence among these groups and the inability of the civil governments to quell that violence have been cited as the obvious causes of the 12 September coup. Although violence did not stop suddenly and completely, as commonly argued by various people, the most conspicuous result of the coup was the significant decrease in terms of political violence on the streets given that the average number of people killed monthly between 12 September 1980 and 11 September 1981 was 24, whereas 234 individuals were killed every month in the same period during the preceding year (Turkish General Staff 1983:199). The most important factor contributing to this decrease was that the scope of the Martial Law instituted in the provinces was expanded from 22 provinces to include the whole country. It remained in place until 1987, during which time the Martial Law Commanders were given extreme powers for countering terrorism which they had demanded before the military coup. In this regard, a crucial change was made in terms of the detention of political criminals which was increased to 30 days and 90 days, respectively. Another important change was that Martial Law Commanders were given the authority to sack public officials "whose works were seen as harmful for the public order" (Demirel 2001:60). What was more significant, in fact, was the enactment of the "Law on the Constitutional Order" on 28 October 1980 as it clearly demonstrated the army's desire to be the "constituent power" of the country. According to this law, the National Security Council (NSC) was given enhanced authority and control in the fields of executive, legislative, and judicial powers (Mumcu 1987).

Furthermore, in terms of its duration in power and the harshness of policies implemented for countering political violence, the 12 September intervention was different from those of 1960 and 1971. In 1960, the Committee of National Unity had directed its pressure against the avant-garde of the Democrat Party, while mostly leftist movements were targeted in 1971. However, in 1980, not only did the military try to suppress violently the leftist groups that were believed to be the major cause of terrorism, but it also turned towards extreme-nationalist rightist groups and individuals (Demirel 2001:62–3). According to one estimate, from 1980 to the 1984 democratic election, a total of 43 individuals, nine of whom rightist and 34 leftist, were executed for political crimes; 650 thousand people were detained; 171 people died in custody due to torture and misconduct. and 43 people were reported to have died as a result of "suicide" while in custody (Birand *et al.* 1999:231–2). It is important, though ironic, to note that public support for the military intervention in 1980 was quite high, which in turn increased the military's distrust of civilians and democratic regimes and fed into the military's ideology of being the "regime protectors."

Broadly speaking, after the 12 September coup, the state identified Kurdish nationalism, the left, and radical Islam as its enemy, and banned all forms of cultural expression (Yavuz 2001:10). After the coup, the organizational power of Kurdish networks was destroyed and many Kurdish activists fled to Europe, where they formed "the core of transnational Kurdish activism" (2001:10). More importantly, several traumatic examples can be mentioned as having left indelible wounds in the collective memories of Kurdish people in Turkey, which have more direct ramifications on PKK violence. The most frequently invoked example among them has been the infamous narratives of torture in Diyarbakır prison in the aftermath of the 1980 military coup. What really happened in that prison was depicted by Marcus through her quotation from Mehdi Zana (an influential Kurdish politician), as follows:

> Every night the sound of men screaming under torture was heard ... prisoners were sodomized with batons, dunked into vats filled with excrement, left in rat-infested cells, terrorized by a dog, given water mixed with detergent to drink, and forced to lie in the snow in their underwear ... In order not to undergo ... torture, the prisoners submitted ... So they were forced to shout, "I am proud to be Turkish" or "A Turk is worth the whole universe".
> (2007:67)

It is in this context that the PKK started to rise in 1984 as a force which captured the minds of the Kurdish people and raised their political consciousness. As Yavuz writes, it also played an important role "in establishing a web of networks in and outside Turkey to recruit militants, undermining the religio-tribal structure of the region by presenting new opportunities for the middle class and urbanized Kurdish youth, and unexpectedly popularizing and consolidating Turkish nationalism in Turkey" (2001:11). In this regard, one of the most important latent functions of the PKK campaign was the deepening of Turkish nationalism, for the PKK encouraged its supporters to criticize "not the 'political authority' in Ankara, but rather Turkish nationalism as a construct, in order to legitimize their own separatist nationalism" (2001:11). This new conception of being critical of Turkish nationalism instead of state power marks a turning point in terms of the separation between Kurdish nationalism and the leftist movement of Turkey (2011:11).

From the time he fled to Syria in 1980 until 1984, Öcalan and his leader cadre gave the PKK militants theoretical, political, and weapons training in Lebanon's Bekaa Valley that was controlled by Syria. The same year, the PKK established its armed faction HRK, "Kürdistan Kurtuluş Birliği" (Union of Kurdistan's Salvation), by illegally infiltrating the country, and staged its first attacks on Turkey in the towns of Eruh and Şemdinli on 15 August 1984[15] and declared its war against the Republic of Turkey. Two years later, the PKK established the ARGK "Kürdistan Halk Kurtuluş Ordusu" (Kurdistan People's Salvation Army) on 30 October 1986 (Ballı 1991:206; Demirel 1996:25–6). After this date, the group increased its armed propaganda and dominated the region especially in the latter part of the 1980s and the first part of 1990s. Being caught unprepared, the Turkish government faltered for a moment but eventually decided to deal with the problem via issuing a "state of emergency" in the region in 1987 that lasted until 2002. In this respect, it is possible to argue that the PKK attacks backfired in that they led to the "securitization" of normal life in heavily Kurdish populated areas (Yavuz 2001:13). In addition, it has been suggested that more than 40,000 people, most of whom were Kurds, were killed by 1999 by the PKK or the state security forces. The PKK gained the largest mass support between 1989 and 1994 that led to an increase in its attacks, but after that period there was a significant decline in terms of its attacks and support base, largely due to the decisive work of Turkish security forces. In an effort to revitalize itself and its supporters, the PKK decided to launch suicide attacks in 1996 (Alkan 2006; Karademir 2000). Later it tried to move to the Black Sea region by forming alliances with other leftist-revolutionary groups by signing a "Unity Protocol" in December 1996 (Kılıç and Güner 1996). These efforts were fruitless, nevertheless, leading to internal strife within the PKK and providing Turkish security forces with an opportunity to launch targeted operations. In one of those operations, Şemdin Sakık, one of the most influential group leaders, was captured in northern Iraq and brought to Turkey (Çiloğlu 1998:42). However, the most significant turning points for the PKK and the state's struggle against it took place in 1999, when the PKK leader Öcalan was captured and put into prison on İmralı Island near Istanbul. The significance of this event is twofold: First, when captured by the Turkish security forces, Öcalan stated that his mother was Turkish and he was ready to help the state, which shocked not only the PKK militants and the group's Kurdish supporters but also the general public in the country. Second, the group declared a ceasefire which continued until 2004, a period when "peace doves were flying" in the country.[16]

Having borne the brunt of the state violence before and after the September 12 coup, revolutionary-leftist groups had directed their activities towards the state, but as most of my informants from the revolutionary groups mentioned, leftist groups could not respond to the coup by regaining their energy and reorganizing themselves. For this, they were never forgiven by the masses until the beginning of 1990s, the years when they reached their apex in terms of exerting violence and gaining support of the masses. In generating this mass support, revolutionary groups continued to capitalize on socio-economic inequalities in the country and torture by law enforcement officials. However, as the country's economy started to show a steady improvement and the concept of democratic policing became popular in society, the aforementioned inequalities and torture were largely eliminated. These developments helped contribute to the end of the Turkish Left and rendered the leftist-revolutionary groups almost irrelevant especially after the year 2000.

At this point, it is necessary to note that the Gezi Park incidents, which unfolded in May 2013 and continued for several months, might have changed the foregoing argument about the Turkish leftist-revolutionary groups. To explain briefly, the AKP government removed a number of trees in Istanbul's Taksim Gezi Park for a massive urban development project. A group of people with environmentalist concerns organized a sit-in to protest against this project; but the government's initial response to these protests was too harsh, as expressed by Prime Minister

Erdoğan himself. The rather brutal eviction of the sit-in outraged many people and within several hours thousands of individuals went to the Taksim Square to support the protesters. In the following days, protests over Gezi Park created an opportunity for those who wanted to address their grievances over the AKP's recent policies. At the core of the issues were freedom of press, freedom of expression, and freedom of assembly. The most important issues, however, had to do with the Prime Minister's growingly authoritarian behavior and rhetoric, as well as his party's encroachment on Turkey's secularism. Another important issue with regard to the Gezi Park events was the police's response to the protests, which was perceived by many as less than humane and undemocratic. It is possible therefore to argue that many people, youngsters in particular, might have been radicalized due to popular discontent with the government and excessive use of force by the police during the aforementioned protests. It is also possible that leftist-revolutionary groups might have taken advantage of this opportunity to increase their propaganda within society and to find more recruits.

On the other hand, since the end of its ceasefire in 2004, the PKK, and recently the KCK, "Koma Ciwaken Kurdistan" (Union of Communities in Kurdistan) remains the most salient problems in terms of political violence in Turkey. When it became public in 2007, the KCK announced that it was the "urban wing" of the PKK. But as a result of later investigations and indictments, prosecutors have argued that the KCK is an umbrella (terrorist) organization that encompasses the PKK, rather than being one of its subordinate factions. In fact, the origin of this organization can be found in Öcalan's article "Kurds in the 2000s" which he wrote in İmralı prison. In this article, Öcalan articulates the "democratic republic thesis" and talks about a "modeling" which matured over time into "democratic autonomy" (Söylemez 2011:1). In this autonomous system, Öcalan proposes that the people of Kurdistan have the right of self-determination; in other words, he makes the definition of a "semi-federative" political structure (2011:1). Despite these ideas, however, the KCK remained an elusive organization until 2007; but in an article published in 2008 in the *Aksiyon* magazine, the KCK was depicted as an organization which had established a de-facto Kurdistan state in some pilot-cities in Turkey's southeast region. Consequently, the KCK operations intensified in 2009 in which nearly 2,500 people (some of whom are elected municipal officials) have been taken into custody and 900 among them, as of March 2011, were arrested.

The public opinion about the KCK and operations against it is fragmented and volatile, but vacillates between two different viewpoints in general. According to one view, adopted largely by liberal intellectuals and people sympathetic to the Kurdish cause, the KCK should be seen as the politicization of the PKK and the operations against it are no more than the AKP government's attempt to restrict Kurdish political expression and action. Proponents of the other view argue instead that the KCK derives its power from "weapons" and it has no desire to detach itself from the PKK and violence. They also argue that rather than being a civilian sub-group of the PKK, the KCK is bent on establishing a "parallel state" structure in which the PKK is designated as its army. This state is believed to have its own legislative, executive, and judicial divisions,[17] and a type of social organization, in addition to a constitution that defines the design of its flag, citizenship, economy, political system, defense system, party and so forth (Söylemez 2011:2–4). Between 2009 and 2012, the KCK has been thought to be behind many violent acts attributed to the PKK as well as *serhildan* (awakening) and civil disobedience actions taking place in various locations, predominantly in the country's southeast. Furthermore, Uslu argues that the system propounded by the KCK is not unique, for it is nothing but a bad imitation of the "Mandela model," as he writes, "from the names of organizational structures and strategy to the division of the network, Öcalan and other PKK leaders borrowed the idea from South Africa and tried to apply it to Turkey without even thinking whether the model would work for Kurds" (2011:1).[18]

To conclude, the government of the Justice and Development Party (the AKP), which came to power in 2002, turned the previous governments' approach to terrorism on its head. Whereas its predecessors believed that terror must be eradicated before implementing democratic policies, the AKP saw democratization as a crucial antidote to terrorism. Accordingly, its policymakers strove to design policies that would distinguish fighting with "terrorists" and fighting with "terrorism" that would in turn establish a balance between democracy and security. More specifically, the AKP seems to have realized that long years of forced assimilation and policies of denial did not bring any result in eradicating the Kurdish identity and nationalism. Hence they have adopted new approaches by expanding the rights of Kurdish people, by increasing investment in the places they live, and by seeking new conciliatory avenues in order to prevent the PKK from capitalizing on problems that are rooted in longstanding policies of denial and subjugation by some of the former administrations. However, as the PKK/KCK has increased the level of violence and Turkish society saw more "martyr funerals," the AKP government has had difficulty in explaining their new approaches to the general public, especially to those with the nationalistic tendencies, which resulted in their resorting to the old traditional/ statist policies.[19] This, in turn, has translated itself into an increase in state use of violence, prompting more violence by the PKK/KCK, and thereby leading to the perpetuation of the cycle of violence (Turk-on-Kurd violence and Kurd-on-Turk violence) that has turned the country to a cauldron of instability for almost three decades in various ways.[20]

Instead of a conclusion: praetorian army and the concept of deep state in Turkey

The contentious relations between the center and the periphery have affected Turkish politics and society since the incipient years of the Republic up until the end of the past century in particular. This tension conducive to *conflict* was exacerbated by inherent conundrums with regard to the *formation of a nation-state* (Mamdani 2009) in a country that used to be a home for different ethnic and religious groups. Put differently, the policies of the secularization of Sunnis,

Sunniization of the Alevis, and Turkification of the Kurds continued to dominate and adversely affect politics throughout Republican history. Thus, in addition to the Ottoman polity, understanding the social and political structures of the Republican Turkey is a *sine qua non* for making sense of the Turkish Penitents' involvement and dissociation from political violence.

As I tried to explain above, one of the most significant aspects of the Republican polity was the repression of the forces of the periphery that was institutionalized, to a great extent, with the 27 May coup in 1960 and the constitution made by the junta in its aftermath. This institutionalized repression (Smith 1998:102–3) manifested itself as the "military tutelage" under the guise of *protecting the secular regime* and *preventing territorial disintegration* through which the ruling elite has maintained its stronghold on power and the country's social and political affairs. It is commonly believed that in order to ensure that the military tutelage has continued, the ruling elite did not hesitate, among other things, to create a culture of terror in the country by either founding terrorist groups[21] or supporting them. Since this aspect of the ruling elite has been construed as the "deep state," and because my informants often spoke about it during the interviews, a theoretical explanation of the deep state is necessary for a better understanding of issues related to political violence in contemporary Turkey.

Perlmutter's (1969) concepts of "praetorian state" and "praetorian army" are helpful in terms of making sense of the deep state in Turkey. According to Perlmutter,

> A modern praetorian state is one in which the military tends to intervene and *potentially* could dominate the political system. The political processes of this state *favor* the development of the military as the core group and the growth of its expectations as a ruling class; its political leadership (as distinguished from bureaucratic, administrative, and managerial leadership) is chiefly recruited from the military, or from groups sympathetic, or at least not antagonistic, to the military. Constitutional changes are affected and sustained by the military and the army frequently intervenes in the government. In a praetorian state, therefore, military plays a dominant role in political structures and institutions.[22]
>
> (1969:383, italics in the original)

Social conditions contributing to praetorianism are listed by Perlmutter as "low degree of social cohesion," "the existence of fratricidal classes," "social polarity and a non-consolidated middle class," and "the recruitment and mobilization of resources," whereas political conditions comprise "center-periphery discord," "low level of political institutionalism," "weak and ineffective political parties," and "frequent civilian intervention in the military" (385–91).

Furthermore, praetorian armies are divided into two types: an arbitrator-type and a ruler-type. The former "tends to be more professionally oriented (with a particular emphasis on expertise), has no independent political organization and little interest in manufacturing a political ideology" (1969:392). The ruler-type, in contrast, is distinguished by its independent political organization ("an instrument for maintaining order") and so often, "a fairly coherent and elaborate political ideology" (1969:392). That an arbitrator-type army puts a time limit to its rule before handing over the power to an "acceptable" civilian government does not mean that it desires to relinquish its political influence when it returns to the barracks. In practice, and in most cases, the arbitrator-type army acts "as guardian of civilian authority and political stability," which, according to Perlmutter, is exemplified by the Kemalist legacy in Turkey where "the army serves as the guardian of the constitution" (1969:392). An arbitrator-type army may also become a ruler army if the conditions for the transfer of power to civilians are not met, while it is equally possible for a ruler-type "to turn the reins of power to the civilian regime, if the conditions for the return of the civilian rule are fulfilled" (1969:393). But in general, an arbitrator-type army has a time limit to its rule, while the ruler-type does not confine itself to a time limit. In Perlmutter's words, "the ruler-type sacrifices professionalism for political expediency" (1969:393). Lastly, another aspect of praetorian states has to do with the "basic democracy" they create, which Perlmutter calls as "tutelary political structures." He suggests that these structures "are no guarantee for relieving the praetorian syndrome, although they are established in the hope that political stability and progress may be achieved (1969:403). In other words, some tutelary political structures created by military rule display weaknesses similar to those they replace; and "others are no more than a shadow of the military-dominated state" (1969:403).

Based on the foregoing formulations by Perlmutter, it is plausible to suggest that the Republican political system in Turkey has demonstrated all characteristics of praetorianism. This system also produced also an arbitrator-type army which influenced, and more often "controlled," *politics* by way of military tutelage since the foundation of the Republic, albeit the effects of this military tutelage was felt more deeply since the 27 May coup in 1960. The italicization of the term "politics" above was intentional as it resonates with Smith's (1960) distinction of "politics" from "administration" and "power" from "authority." In his "Government in Zazzau," he argues that political and administrative activities constitute the "analytically distinctive" and essential components of the structure and process of government (1960:15). In addition, the system of political action by which government is directed is a system of power relations that is prone to competition, compromise, coalition, and similar activities; whereas "the system of administrative action through which the business of the government is carried on is a system of authority and authorized relations, order, obligations, and rights" (1960:15). Thus, Smith writes, "power characterizes political action, authority characterizes administrative action" (1960:15). In other words, "just as political action is based and focused on the appropriation of power, so administrative action derives from, and remains preoccupied with, authority and its problems" (1960:18).

Furthermore, political groups and units, according to Smith, are characterized by their active interest in the determination of policy and in obtaining the power; hence the competition for power is "inherently segmentary in form and process"

(1960:17). Since there is a constant competition for power in society, it is misleading to speak about the concept of a "monopoly of power" over the policy-making processes (1960:17). Thus, Smith argues,

> any situation characterized by an apparently complete concentration of power over these policy-making processes really turns out to be one in which competition about policy formation is confined to the cadre or group which exercises governmental control behind a *mask* of unanimity.
> (1960:17, emphasis added)

To clarify, even though political action and process are defined by the relativity of power relations, "it is in the final analysis, competition for the supreme power which is diacritical, that is, for the capacity to make decisions on policy affecting the total population of the unit concerned" (1960:18).

In light of the abovementioned concepts envisaged by Smith (1960) and Perlmutter (1969), I define the deep state in Turkey, broadly, as the ruling *bureaucratic-military elite* which seems to have exercised *manifest* or *latent control* on the country's political system through *a military tutelage* created by an arbitrary-type army with the 27 May coup in 1960 and institutionalized, *inter alia*, with the following military coups (the 12 September coup in 1980, in particular) and *institutions* which were established and secured within the constitutions designed by the stagers of these coups. On the other hand, rather than seeing terrorist violence as a constitutive element of the deep state, it would perhaps be more accurate to look at it as a *function* of the deep state, which manifests itself as the deep state's efforts of latent control of the country's socio-political affairs, among other things, by way of creating conditions conducive to military interventions through founding violent groups or manipulating and instrumentalizing the existing ones. For instance, with regard to the relationship between terrorist groups and the deep forces in the military, Fatih, one of my informants from a revolutionary group, said the following:

> I used to go to the headquarters of the Turkish Gendarme Forces to meet the head of Special Forces (called A Team) who would give me the bombs in a bag and I would get out normally. Also, I came to know later that the same person provided the intelligence for the assassination of General Ismail Selen who was killed on 23 May 1991 in Ankara.

Such latent control is the essence of the Turkish deep state, which guaranteed to a great extent the maintenance of the military tutelage for almost half a century.

Moreover, even though being amorphous and elusive in form, ideological underpinnings of the deep state have been generally articulated in society as "Kemalism," that is, a "secularist," "ultra-nationalist" (and can be read as exclusionary and Pan-Turkic) and "anti-imperialist" ideology. Whenever democratic elections resulted in the rise of groups that did not conform to the Kemalist legacy and ideology, the ruling elite (i.e., deep state) demanded a military intervention; the military intervened, stayed in power for a while, and transferred the power to civilian governments after making sure that the influence of the ruling elite remained intact by way of legal and political institutions created by them while in power.

I will provide more specific information about the deep state in the upcoming chapters when it will be relevant to my theoretical explanations of Turkish Penitents' individual disengagement (in Chapters 5 and 6, in particular). I will say here that conditions that paved the way for the September 12 military coup in 1980 are generally cited as an example for understanding the workings of the deep state.[23] To specify, the events in the Maraş and Malatya provinces in 1978 and the Çorum events in 1980 were commonly understood to be fabricated by the deep state actors who aimed to create a chaotic environment by staging provocations that would potentially lead to bloody clashes between Alevis and Sunnis or the leftists and rightists.[24] In addition, the PKK leader Öcalan's transfer to Syria before the coup in the company of "Pilot Necati," an army officer and a MİT (Turkish Central Intellligence Agency) member (Tayyar 2011:20–35), unresolved murders of around 2,000 Kurds during the first part of the 1990s, the burning of the Madımak hotel in Sivas in 1993 (37 Alevi intellectuals were killed), the events in the Gazi neighborhood in 1995, countless murders thought to be committed by the notorious deep-state actor Mahmut Yıldırım (known as *yeşil* which means "green" in Turkish);[25] are believed to be some examples of deep-state operations.

In the last decade, according to Uslu for instance, the potential success of the Annan Plan in 2004 was strongly desired by the Turkish deep state that has been at loggerheads with the AKP government since its rise to power, given that such success would mean the unification of Cyprus, which would in turn create a pretext for military intervention in Turkey (2010:265–8). Moreover, the Şemdinli incident in 2005, the attack on the Council of State in 2007, the Republican meetings in the wake of Presidential elections of 2007, the 2003 army-plan known as "The plan for ending the AKP and the Gülen movement" which was unveiled in 2009 and the assassination of Armenian-Turkish journalist Hirant Dink in 2007 were also attributed to the deep state (2010:261–312). Lastly, the most vivid example of the deep-state operation has been cited as the "Reşadiye incident" on 7 December 2009 when seven soldiers were killed by the terrorists, because this incident occurred shortly before the AKP's announcement of the "Democratic Opening" which had aimed to expand the rights of Kurdish citizens and giving the PKK militants a "second chance" to return to society after laying down their arms.

The excerpts from my interview below with Hakan, one of my informants from a revolutionary group, briefly describes the deep state, its *modus operandi*, and the relationship between the deep state and terrorist groups:

> After the 1980 military coup, I became convinced that my group had such a relationship. I mean, it started to be controlled and managed by the deep state. After the Gazi neighborhood incidents in 1995, this relationship became crystallized in my mind. I should add that when you look at the incidents in Maraş and Malatya in 1978 and Çorum in 1980, neither revolutionaries nor fascists [he means the rightists] were guilty of these events. There was

a third force that created conditions for their headlong clashes. I mean what happened in Gazi is no different from what happened in Maraş.

Today people talk about Ergenekon or the deep state. But we knew these thirty years ago, although we used to call it "counter-guerilla." Why did we call that? Or, how did we know about it? Because we knew other examples from all around the world ...We knew these from Gladio and NATO operations, as well as from the discussions about them. In our country, everybody knew the existence of counter-guerilla that was nothing but the army's "Special Forces Command." How does it work? Simple ... a rumor is spread in neighborhoods. You can see what they did in the wake of the September 12 coup. I mean, if you want to create chaos in a place, you have to organize some actions in that place. For instance, if we look at what happened in Maraş, Sivas to Alevis, we can see this. History always repeated itself in this respect. During the Gazi events in 1995, the same game was played; the deep state actors attacked Alevis' coffee houses in police uniforms. So, naturally people became disturbed and reacted. Then all revolutionary groups started to strike on behalf of the people, which meant that chaos was created.

So, why do they do these? It is pretty straightforward. Instability, chaos, and insecurity: Who benefits from these? It is obvious; we have one savior in this country. People do not even turn to God, because we have our army! Because, it is always there for us [speaking sarcastically]. I mean, this is my opinion. I think the army has a role in many incidents in this country. Or else, you have to look for the counter-guerilla in the institutions that were created by the army. I mean, you have to search for it in the Special Forces Command.

... in prison, those guys from JİTEM [Gendarme Intelligence and Counter-terrorism] and we were put in different wards. They used to be taken from the Kirklareli prison sometimes; for instance, there was Ibrahim Babat ... If they investigate thoroughly, they will find that he was one of those who shot those victims of the *triangle*[26] in the head. When he came back, he used to tell us that he was in Sapanca. Why did he tell us this? Obvious; because next day, we read what happened in Sapanca in the newspapers. [Being in shock, I asked where were the people being taken from? he continued] ... From the prison. These guys are former PKK members who had turned into *itirafci* [repentants]. They were being taken, used and returned to prison by some people.

The deep state was unveiled for the first time in 1996 when a Mercedes car crashed into a truck in Susurluk, where a police chief, a mafia leader, and his girlfriend were killed while a tribal chief, who was also a parliamentarian, was injured. This incident came to be known as the "Susurluk Incident," about which the public became enthusiastic as the case increased hopes for the exposure of the face of deep state. However, the incumbent government at the time viewed the case as "trivial nonsense"[27] which manifested itself as the covering-up of the case after the publication of several dubious reports. At the very least, still, the case provided the public with a glimpse of the deep state, even though from behind an opaque window.

Table 2.1 Introductory information about the Turkish Penitents

Name	Group name	Age	Sex	Education	Number of siblings	Parental involvement in childhood	Parents' and his/her religious views	Parents' economic status	Parents' education and job
Zilan	PKK	32	F	Elementary	4 girls	Yes	Religious/Sunni	Not good	Mother: illiterate, housewife Father: elementary, construction worker
Selim	PKK	32	M	Elementary	8 (7 boys, 1 girl)	Yes	Religious/Sunni (He went to Quran courses during childhood)	Good	Both illiterate, both farmers
Nadir	PKK	36	M	Continuing Elementary (After exit at the age of 35)	5 (3 boys, 2 girls)	Yes	Religious/Sunni	Moderate	No education in the village, "Culture of ignorance"
Savaş	PKK	41	M	Elementary	5 (1 boy, 4 girls)	Yes	Religious/Sunni	Good But gets worse after migration to Cizre	Both illiterate, both farmers
Recep	PKK	34	M	Elementary	6 (5 boys, 1 girl)	Yes	Not religious, Alewite	Not good	Mother: elementary, housewife Father: high school, construction worker
Azad	PKK	34	M	University	3 (2 boys, 1 girl)	Mother died when he was 8 Father was away when he was 2–8	Not religious, Alewite	Pretty good. His personal finances were very good during his adolescence	Mother: elementary, housewife Father: elementary, worked abroad and remitted money home

Name	Group	Age	Sex	Education	Siblings	Parental	Religion	Economic	Parents
Gürkan	PKK	40	M	Elementary	2 (1 boy, 1 girl)	Yes	Religious	Not good	Mother: illiterate, housewife; Father: illiterate, village administrator
Hikmet	Rev.*	37	M	High school drop out	3 (2 boys, 1 girl)	Yes, but loss of parental control during high school	Not religious, Alewite	Good	Mother: elementary, housewife; Father: elementary, mine worker
Gökhan	Rev.	41	M	High school	4 (3 boys (stepbrothers), 1 girl)	With father, but often away from home as he worked as a truck driver. Met his mother at 17. (Absence of parental control)	Not religious, Sunni	Not good (He had to work when he was a child)	Mother: elementary, housewife; Father: high school, retired from army and truck driver
Ahmet	Rev.	50	M	High school (a prestigious one)	1 girl	Yes	Not religious, Sunni	Good	Mother: elementary, housewife; Father: high school, shopkeeper
Hakan	Rev.	55	M	High school drop out	2 boys	Yes (After joining the group, he did not see his mother for 18 years)	Not religious, Sunni	Affluent	Mother: elementary, housewife; Father: high school, factory worker
Soli	Rev.	42	M	Elementary	7 (3 boys, 4 girls)	Yes	Not religious, Sunni (but he became religious after exit)	Poor	Mother: illiterate, housewife; Father: elementary, construction worker
Fatih	Rev.	51	M	High school	2 (1 boy, 1 girl)	Yes	Not religious, Alewite	Good	Mother: elementary, housewife; Father: secondary: shopkeeper

*Revolutionary group

The second opportunity arose in 2007 with the launch of the case of Ergenekon and a chain of other connected cases that followed it. Ergenekon is a clandestine organization, which is "allegedly" nested within the state, media, universities, and business enterprises. Around 500 individuals were taken into custody and more than 300 of them were charged with plotting to create commotion in society by various actions, among other things by the assassination of significant individuals and bombing of symbolic places, with an ultimate goal of overthrowing the AKP government. The effects of the Ergenekon case on the public are manifold, but an overarching effect of it seems to be public's perception of the arrests of military personnel including army's top-brass as a normal occurrence, which was previously unthinkable.[28] This, and other improvements made in terms of the civilian–military relations,[29] have been generally welcomed in domestic and international circles as they whittled away military's influence on politics and have likely contributed to Turkey's democratization efforts.

Some people, on the other hand, are not as sanguine about the Ergenekon case as those who view it as a precursor of more democracy in the country. An important part of Turkish society and some in the international community think that the case is politically motivated and it lacks substantial evidence. In a nutshell, such people believe that the main purpose of the Ergenekon case is to sideline critics of the AKP government.[30]

All in all, despite the foregoing legitimate concerns, the majority of the Turkish public seems to support the cases on the basis that they have checked in a way the impunity and arrogant power (Fullbright 1966) of the Turkish deep state.

Notes

1 Alevis are also included in this number. According to the estimates of the Turkish Statistics Institute (TUIK), there are around seven million Alevis in Turkey, some of whom are ethnically Turkish, while others are Kurdish or Zaza. In addition, whether Alevism is a separate religion or a denomination has long been a topic for discussion in Turkish society.
2 Local notables resisted Tanzimat reforms because, as Davison perceptively observed, "they profited from disorganization and inefficiency in the central government to maintain their political and financial control." For details, see Davison (1963).
3 According to the *millet* system, all Muslim ethnic groups, including the Kurds, Laz, Pomaks, Arabs, Bosnians, Albanians, Turks, were grouped in one category called "nation of Islam," while non-Muslims were identified as minority within the Empire (Kirisci and Winrow 1997). Hence, in the Ottoman Empire, Muslim ethnic groups were bound together by Islam, and "ethnic identities among the Muslim population did not carry much significance beyond the cultural and the linguistic" (Kirisci 2004:276).
4 For details about these innovations, see for example, Karpat (1972)," The Transformation of the Ottoman State, 1789–1909, *International Journal of Middle East Studies*, Vol. 3. No. 3 (July), pp. 243–81.
5 The ideology of these bureaucratic-military elites has been "top-down secularism." For the effects of this top-down secularism on the emergence of a new elite, see Yılmaz (2009) "The Emergence and Rise of Conservative Elite in Turkey," *Insight Turkey*, Vol.11 No.2 pp. 113–36.

Historical and social contexts   47

6   The Sheikh Said rebellion was also significant in the sense that the Terakkiperver Cumhuriyet Firkasi (Progressive Republican Party), the opposition forces of the periphery, was closed down in 1925 because of its alleged connection with the Sheikh Said rebellion. Similarly, Serbest Cumhuriyet Firkasi (The Free Republican Party) was closed down in 1930; another aspect of the period analyzed above showing the strong desire of the center to curb the influence of the periphery in the country's political and social life.

7   Following Bruinessen, I use the term "Kurdish Alevis" as shorthand for "Alevis whose native language is Kurdish or the related Zaza language" and this does not mean that I consider Zaza people as Kurds given that the majority of Zazas do not identify themselves as Kurds.

8   Dersim was the old name of the present-day Tunceli province of Turkey; but historically it stretched from Gaziantep and Kahramanmaras in the south through Adiyaman and Malatya to Sivas in the north (Van Bruinessen 1996:4).

9   These extreme measures were explained in the Reform Program of 1937 (Islahat Programı). For details, see Dersimi (1988:299–303).

10   The officers behind the 27 May coup had established a committee outside the traditional army hierarchy which they called "Milli Birlik Komitesi" (The Committee of National Unity). In staging the coup, this committee was able to gain the support of youth, universities, and the press.

11   This sentence sounds paradoxical in that military coups and democracy are almost mutually exclusive concepts. Murat Belge explains this paradox by comparing it with the DP's "paradoxical" victory in 1950 by saying, "These two incidents displayed paradoxical and opposite results. The 1950 election was a democratic incident which brought up backward outcomes, whereas the 1960 coup d'état was apparently undemocratic but it provided, none the less, the liberal reforms of Turkish political life" (my translation). See Belge (2003) "Sol", in *Geçiş Sürecinde Türkiye*, Eds. Irvin C. Schick and Ertugrul A. Istanbul: Belge Yayinlari, p.166.

12   It is important to note here that the publication of the *Yön* (*Direction*) and its sequel *Devrim* (*Revolution*) played a significant role in terms of theoretical discussions of socialism that influenced not only the future leftist political and social movements, but also illegal revolutionary groups that emerged in the beginning of 1970s. The famous "Declaration of *Yön*," signed by a total of 1,042 intellectuals posited numerous demands covering three major goals, i.e., "Westernization," "development," and "enlightenment," and prioritized the role of the state for the achievement of these goals. For details, see, Kürkçü (1988), "Kapitalizm ile Komünizm Arasında Geleneksel Aydınlar: Yön Hareketi," *STMA*, C6. pp. 2006–7.

13   The "National Democratic Revolution" thesis was first suggested by Mihri Belli in an article which he penned with the pseudonym "E. Tufekci" and published in the hundred and seventy-fifth volume of the *Yön* Magazine on 5 August 5 1966.

14   The most influential actions were directed against the visit of the US Army's Sixth Fleet in Istanbul. A series of actions were organized by Deniz Gezmis and other revolutionary youngsters who were not happy with the US's stance *vis-à-vis* the issues in Cyprus and Vietnam, and its unrelenting support of Israel in the Arab-Israeli war.

15   After these attacks, 15 August became one of the PKK's red-letter days as the group attacked almost every year on that day to commemorate its launch of struggle in Turkey.

16   Öcalan was initially sentenced to death, but due to the legal changes based on Turkey's European Union Accession Process, his death sentence was commuted to aggravated life imprisonment (Yıldırım 2004:90).

17   Since 2009, the police found and reported many instances that show the KCK's de-facto domination in some cities in the southeastern Turkey. It has been reported that the KCK levied various taxes on the people of the region, tried individuals for their crimes at its so-called "people's courts" on the mountain and dominated social and political life in the region.

48 Historical and social contexts

18 For the similarities between the KCK and the ANC in terms of their structure and goals, see, Uslu (2011), "KCK mimics ANC," *Todays Zaman*, 11 December 2011, Istanbul. For a detailed account of the KCK's goals, structure, ideology and modus operandi, see for example, Soylemez (2011), "Terror in the flat savannah: KCK," *Aksiyon*, 3 October 2011, Istanbul.

19 This phenomenon was described by Turner as "liminality of redress" in his analyses of social dramas where he asserted, "Redress has its liminal nature ... its being between and betwixt furnishes a distanced replication and critique of the events leading up to and composing the crisis... [Thus] if redress fails, there is usually regression to crisis (1974:41).

20 The Turkish state initiated a dialogue with the PKK in February 2013, which is dubbed as "democratic resolution process." According to this, the PKK agreed to start a ceasefire and withdraw its members from Turkish territory. Although there has been a significant decrease regarding the number of attacks perpetrated by the PKK, the prospects of the resolution process remain unknown to many in Turkish society.

21 For example, Turkish Hezbollah is said to have been founded by the state (deep-state) as an antidote to the PKK, which, ironically, was also thought to be supported by the deep-state since its inception in 1978.

22 Similarly, Rapoport defines praetorianism as "a constitutional form of government without consent" (1960:14–15).

23 For an example of the military's construction of chaotic atmosphere to be used as a pretext for the September 12 coup, consider the testimony of Nahit Menteşe, the General Secretary of the Justice Party in 1980, in Gürsoy (2012), "The Military was Exploding the Bombs in Kizilay" (Kizilay'da Bombalari Asker Patlatiyordu), *Aksiyon*, 9–15 Ocak.

24 With regard to the maturity of conditions for the coup, General Kenan Evren, one of the leaders of the coup, stated the following in retrospect: "I was always thinking not to intervene unless it was obligatory and the situation was unendurable, and I was hoping that politicians would get a grasp of themselves and become sober minded" (Evren 1990, my translation). The former President Süleyman Demirel's statement below is quite telling for the same issue: "Instead of protecting the state by using your legal authority, you made the bloodshed of individuals who dynamited the foundation of the state a stepping stone for your future ... Through the blood and tears that was shed and lost lives; you tried to create legitimacy for your coup" (Demirel 1990, my translation).

25 For detailed information about these murders, see, Uslu (2010), "The Intimidation Map of the Deep-State: Kurds Yesterday and Cemaats Today," [in Turkish] pp. 103–47.

26 By *triangle*, he is referring to three cities, namely Izmit, Sapanca, and Hendek (only 200 km from Istanbul) where thousands of people, mostly Kurds, were thought to be killed by the deep state.

27 The phrase "trivial nonsense" was used by Necmettin Erbakan, then the Prime Minister, but many people believe that he was forced by the deep-state actors to utter such words. This, in turn, was interpreted by many as a manifestation of the power of the deep-state.

28 The most striking of such arrests culminated in the unprecedented arrest of General İlker Başbuğ, former Chief of General Staff, on 6 January 2012, with charges of "leading a terrorist organization" (i.e., the "alleged" Ergenekon Terror Organization) and "attempting to stage a coup to overthrow the government." Additionally, in a landmark move, the Turkish court accepted the indictment for the September 12 coup on January 10, 2012, which paved the way for the trial of the coup leaders (General Kenan Evren, the former President of Turkey, and General Tahsin Sahinkaya, then the commander of the Turkish Air Force), for whom the prosecutor asked for life imprisonment without parole. For details see, Today's Zaman (2012).

29 Most important reforms in terms of civilian-military relations were made between 2002 and 2007, the most important of which being the change in the structure and other issues related to the MGK (National Security Council). For details, see, Akay (2011), "Civilian-Military relations in Turkey: An evaluation of 2000–2011 period," HYD: Istanbul.
30 The thirteenth High Criminal Court handed down severe punishments for Ergenekon suspects on 5 August 2013, including a life sentence for former Chief of Staff İlker Başbuğ. For details see, Hurriyet Daily (2013). Also, for alternative views on the Ergenekon case, see Jenkins (2009) and Demiroz and Kapucu (2012).

3 Separation stage

Turkish Penitents' paths to political violence

> The human essence is no abstraction inherent in each single individual. In its reality it is the ensemble of the social relations.
>
> (Karl Marx 1888)

Conceptual framework: a psychological-anthropological approach

In this chapter, I will explore the processes of Turkish Penitents' incremental journeys towards political violence. To this end, I will adopt a process-based psychological-anthropological approach that focuses on individual and social factors, as well as the interactions between them. Given that individuals are born into a culture and they do not grow alone, I will pay particular attention to the surroundings of the individual, or say, "environmental" factors, while considering the importance of rational "human action" in its role of shaping the environment. As Dollard argues, this sensitive balance can be captured adeptly if we consider that, "first, the group exists before the individual; and second, a new organism envisioned as approaching this functioning collectivity" (1935:14). The most important group that exists before the individual and into which the child comes is not the group in general; "the child is not born into the church or the army; rather he is born into a very definite specification of the larger group, namely the family" (1935:21). Dollard adds that we should also consider that "the family into which the child comes has a cultural lineage" (1935:21). Considering that the family is one of the most important *agents* of political socialization along with others such as school, media, and religion; these last two points that Dollard makes have a particular significance for my study in terms of understanding the Turkish Penitents' political socialization. Political socialization is generally used to mean the processes by which children and adolescents acquire political ideas, attitudes, and behaviors (Jennings and Niemi 1974; Powell and Cowart 2003; Sapiro 2004). According to Harrington, political socialization is "a person's ability to survive in a political system which depends on his/her mastery of the tools and knowledge that will enable him to reap premiums which are in short supply in a society, such as material goods, power, status, or safety" (1976:131). He argues that as there are no societies in which all of the premiums like status, power, and material goods are in an unlimited supply, "there is always the problem of distribution: Who gets what and who does not?" (1976:131). In an effort to answer this question, Harrington suggests, "whether a man succeeds or fails in this quest for premiums, the *activities* are the products of their socialization" [emphasis added] (1976:131). While warning that socialization-centered approaches cannot account for all of politics, he encourages the students of socialization by saying that "although they cannot account for the occurrence of social structural variables such as caste or clan systems, they can help account for how such systems are maintained" (1976:131). This point is made explicit in another article by Harrington and Whiting who argue that it is their purpose to explain not only how the content of a social role is learned but also how a society induces its members to "willingly to accept" such role responsibilities (quoted in Harrington 1976:132). Finally, they ask an important question. Why do some members accept their lot, and some rebel against it?

Given that my informants were involved in political violence against the state, i.e., they "rebelled" against it, Harrington's formulation of political socialization has special significance in terms of understanding their processes of radicalization and entry into violence, i.e., the transition from being a marginal or frustrated individual, potentially as a result of various psychological, socio-political, or economic grievances, to one who sees violence as a justifiable *political action* to eliminate those grievances. To specify, it is a valid question to ask whether the Turkish Penitents' processes of political socialization had anything to do with their radicalization and entry into politically violent groups.

I had examined the socio-political conditions that are conducive to political violence in Turkey earlier in Chapter 2 diachronically. In what follows, I will try to account for the notion of radicalization and entry into the PKK and other revolutionary groups on a *macro level*, that is, the root causes of political violence and exploitation of these causes by various terrorist groups in Turkey will be discussed theoretically. I will then explore the same issues on a *micro level* by incorporating the voices of the Turkish Penitents excerpted from their personal stories. In doing so, I wish to demostrate the interplay between the objective structures of Turkey and my informants' subjective understandings of those structures and whether this interaction had any effect in decision-making processes of participation in political violence. This latter part is particularly crucial in that only by understanding the individuals' transposition of "external" factors into their "own world" can we overcome the inherent tautology in the theories that claim to account for political violence in general, a tautology emanating from the idea that such theories do not account for those, as Ferracuti suggested, who abstain from terrorism despite being "frustrated" by the same contextual factors (1982:139).

Frustration-aggression hypothesis, relative deprivation and the role of ideology

The frustration-aggression hypothesis (FAH), originally developed by Berkowitz (1965), describes the response to frustration, or blockage of attainment of one's personal or environmental goals, while frustration generally refers to the experience of being denied something to which one feels entitled. Friedland (1992) used this approach in order to explain what dictates the conditions leading minority groups to desire exerting social change, how and why such groups turn to violence and why such violence usually escalates. This model, as Horgan put it, "has been popular in one form or another with a multitude of commentators" (2005:49). One of the derivatives of FAH was envisaged by Gurr (1970) who argues that the frustration-aggression hypothesis was the most systematically developed and empirically supported psychological theory explaining human aggression. Building on that theory, he proposed a framework of a general theory of civil violence, which he called the "relative deprivation." His basic premise was,

> The necessary precondition for violent civil conflict is relative deprivation, defined as actors' perception of discrepancy between their *value expectations* and their environment's apparent value *capabilities*. Value expectations are the goods and conditions of life to which people believe they are justifiably entitled. The referents of value capabilities are to be found largely in the social and physical environment: they are the conditions that determine people's perceived chances of getting or keeping the values they legitimately expect to attain.
>
> (Magnarella 1998:203; original emphasis)

According to this approach,

> the primary causal sequence in political violence is first the development of discontent, second the politicization of that discontent, and finally its actualization in violent action against political objects and actors ... Discontent arising from the perception of relative deprivation is the basic, instigating condition for participants in collective violence.
>
> (1998:203)

Proceeding from Gurr's theory of relative deprivation, Magranella (1998) developed a theory of the "culture of contention," in an effort to understand political violence in Turkey in the aftermath of 1980 military coup. This era is particularly important, for it covers the formative years of the PKK and sheds light on the significance of most of the revolutionary groups in Turkey that include the DHKP-C and the MLKP. Magranella modified Gurr's causal sequence in civil violence and terrorism by suggesting that the *first* in the sequence is the existence of infrastructural and perceptual conditions leading to the development of discontent; *second*, the inability of the society to correct the infrastructural deficiencies (e.g., basic resource shortages in the face of rapid population growth); *third*, the acceptance of ideologies condemning those conditions creating discontent and advocating violent action to alter the conditions; *fourth*, violent action. The more extensive and intense the first two conditions, he argues, the more probable will be widespread (civil) political violence. In addition, education had a significant importance in this process given that many students graduated from the universities with an awareness of the inequalities in their societies, and saw no avenues open to them in the existing systems for rectifying them. Consequently, growing up in a long tradition of violence and *machismo* led them to join some urban guerilla groups whose aim was to exert pressure for internal political change (1998:204). Magranella also placed an emphasis on Turkish socio-cultural system (especially the tradition of "crimes of honor" and "blood feud") as having an important role in violence in the sense that in the countryside, for example, limited economic opportunities led to intense competition and their hopelessness *vis-à-vis* the state authorities, directing them to self-sufficient mechanisms to protect their families from enemies. Lastly, he argued that Turkish families raise their children to be warriors, with aggressive tendencies to be directed against any available outsider group. Furthermore, as examined earlier, the nature of Turkey's socio-political structure caused significant *trauma* especially among the subjugated/peripheral groups, largely due to the country's latent system of differential incorporation. Within social and psychological theory, the effects of such trauma were focused on by various authors as "unfinished mourning" wherein a group "that has experienced a defeat, tragedy, or humiliation has been prevented (or prevented itself) from properly mourning this loss" (Colvin 2007:460). Vamik Volkan, a world-renowned political psychologist, took this theory furthest in his notion of "chosen trauma" experienced by a group. According to this notion, the group, unable to "digest" or mourn this trauma properly, unconsciously passes down this humiliation and hatred to successive generations and this chosen trauma forms the basis of group identity and all imaginations of and relationships with the Other are mediated by this group dynamic of unfinished mourning (Volkan 1997). As I will show later, these concepts affected some segments of society and are exploited by all groups I studied, the PKK in particular, in order to maintain their recruitment inflow from youngsters. Specifically, in order to account for violence by various revolutionary groups, the following common denominators for most revolutionary groups in Turkey should be considered: (1) their stance against imperialism (e.g., anti-American, anti-NATO, etc.); (2) their conviction that the working class was being exploited by the capitalist elite class (i.e., inequalities); (3) their argument about state repression, to which they have thought to have been subjected to by state institutions such as the police and the military; and last but not least, (4) their agreement on the necessity of a revolution to bring about socialism and, in the long run, communism. As the subjects of this study put it, most of the grievances of the members of revolutionary groups in Turkey (i.e., their frustration and relative deprivation), and thus their justification for "revolutionary violence," can be subsumed under two issues, i.e., economic exploitation causing various types of inequalities and torture by state officials. The existence of infrastructural problems or the notion of differential incorporation is important but insufficient to fathom the existence of political violence, unless they are used as a basis for an ideology to justify violence. As one Greek *pentito* from the 17 November organization states, "Guns need hands but they also need ideas. If the ideas are not there, the guns won't work" (Kassimeris 2011:569). In fact, the groups I explore in this book have historically used ideologies in an effective way. While revolutionary groups have utilized variants of Marxist-Leninist ideology, the PKK used various ideologies including Marxist-Leninist ideology and ethnic nationalism. Ideology is usually defined as "a belief system centered around some social or collective ideal (e.g., based on the values of justice, fairness, or inalienable rights) (Kruglanski et al. 2009:5). According to Ricoeur, "an ideology is something in which men live and think; it operates behind our backs [and] we think from it rather than about it" (1981:227). Therefore, it is possible to say that ideologies can function as *powerful belief systems*, and can thereby be used in a multitude of ways by various entities and people which may include the states, international institutions, terrorist organizations, charismatic leaders, and so on. For example, the function of ideologies is demonstrated by Bond in his Northern Zambia study as follows:

> They [ideologies] are ideational constructions about the world that lead to a high degree of compliance or conformity to some normative order associated with relations of inequality in power, wealth and social position. They are intimately related to authority's claim to legitimacy, and at particular moments they may serve as the code of interpretation which secures integration by justifying the system of authority.
>
> (2000:79)

Bond adds that in Northern Zambia the construction of local narratives has been a crucial element in the processes not only of domination and subjugation but also resistance and collaboration between rulers and those they rule (2000:77). In the same way, I suggest that in an effort to contest authority's claim to legitimacy and reject compliance or conformity, ideologies can be constructed in the form of *narratives* by *leaders* of terrorist groups through exploitation and rebranding of *ideas* and *symbols* (Nawaz 2011). According to Nawaz, this strategy works in the following way:

> Recruits are at first presented with information or images designed to shock and produce an emotional response by experienced and charismatic recruiters. This is usually followed up with a framework that interprets the shock inducing stimuli, and then weaves a grand narrative, that incorporates local and international grievances in a way that relates them to the individual's personal circumstances and context. In this process, a potential recruit's identity is also recreated in a way that makes it highly exclusive and is subsequently portrayed as being under threat by perceived enemies. Finally, recruits are offered a pro-active plan of action in the form of an all-encompassing ideology that offers simplistic solutions to complex problems.
>
> (2011:2)

Within the context of Turkey, as I will try to demonstrate in the upcoming sections and chapters, it is possible to view political violence by the PKK and revolutionary groups as a product of such a kind of typology, in which ideas and symbols are turned into narratives by group leaders to recruit people for their causes through indoctrination and reconstruction of their identities. The question remains, however: "Although living under the same circumstances, and thus having the same frustrations and being subjected to the same ideologies, why do only a few people respond to those frustrations with aggression and resort to violence?" It is indeed a valid question, and in order to answer this question, studies must be conducted with those who do not get involved in violence. But since there are at least *some* people who resort to violence, it is also a valid attempt to understand whether their perception of such infrastructural problems played a role in their resorting to violence; and if it did, to what extent they invoked those problems in explaining their past violent behavior. It is necessary then to delve into the individual responses of the Turkish Penitents in order to understand the interplay between these structural problems and their individual motivations and logic for joining violent groups.

Individual motivations for violence: "significance quest" as an integrative approach

The notion of significance quest was suggested by Kruglanski *et al.* (2009) as an integrative framework that combines heterogeneous factors identified as "personal causes" of suicidal terrorism (e.g., trauma, humiliation, social exclusion) as well as the various "ideological reasons" assumed to justify it (e.g., liberation from foreign occupation, defense of one's own nation or religion), and that explains diverse instances of suicidal terrorism as attempts at *significance restoration, significance gain,* and *prevention of significance loss* (2). The authors argue that the diversity of motivations for suicidal terrorism necessitated an integrative framework, which would reduce this heterogeneity by classifying varied motives into several motivational categories. In developing the notion of significance quest, Kruglanski *et al.* employ the ideas of various psychological theorists who provided different ideas on motivational forces in human behavior. For example, the authors call Victor Frankl's argument of "self-transcendence is the essence of human existence" as *search for meaning*, and believe that it presents an obvious affinity to Abraham Maslow's influential theory of motivation that identifies self-esteem and *self-actualization concerns* as top-level human strivings (2007:8). Moreover, they suggest that the quest for meaning and significance stems from humans' awareness of their own mortality, which motivates people to do "well," and be "good" members of society. A "supreme goodness" in this sense is understood as the readiness to sacrifice oneself for the group when necessary because "putting the group first is highly valued and rewarded by the promise of immortality" (2007:9). On the other hand, although developing the notion of significance quest to understand suicidal terrorism, the authors suggest that the "motivations involved in suicidal and nonsuicidal types of terrorism may differ in *degree* rather than in *kind* ..." and added, "simply put, suicidal terrorism confers upon one greater prestige and represents a more auspicious opportunity for significance gain" (2007:12). The authors also link the notion of significance quest with relative deprivation and an early socialization process by saying,

> the notion of relative deprivation pertains to a *subjective* experience or a belief that one's group's just deserts have been unfairly denied ... It thus defines an opportunity for significance gain, inculcated early in the socialization process, or "bred in the bone."
>
> (2007:23)

The Turkish Penitents' paths to political violence: a theoretical exploration

Before delving into a general theoretical discussion of the Turkish Penitents' paths to political violence, I shall note several important issues at the outset. First, four of my 13 informants joined their groups (the PKK) involuntarily. Among them, Selim-P, Nadir-P, and Gürkan-P joined the group through forced recruitment, while Zilan-P entered her group because of her fiancé as mentioned in the introduction. Thus, I will not include their stories in this discussion simply because they did not have a process of radicalization that culminated in their entry into the PKK. Second, in exploring my informants' paths to political violence, and in an effort to introduce my informants in more detail, I will first narrate the stories of each of my informants by focusing on a number of phases in their separation stage. To specify, in my narration, I will take into account the importance of life within the "family" along with "schooling" for the personality development of my informants and their character formation, which impinge upon them throughout life. Thus, I will first delve into the lives of the Turkish Penitents in these two different settings, while giving particular attention to the following variables which I borrow from Harrington and Boardman (1997): (1) the types of families, e.g., disintegrated/dysfunctional or stable families; (2) loving, unloving, or tense homes; (3) whether or not my informants had high emotional conflicts with parents; (4) important people and events (turning points) during childhood and schooling. I will then explicate the processes of my informants' political socialization (which I conceive to cover the former two phases) and how those processes shaped their understanding of political issues and their stands towards the notion of terrorism in Turkey. In connection with this, I will trace the links between their political socialization and radicalization, i.e., the triggering events and turning points (e.g., particulars and irregularities such as luck and misfortune) that radicalized them and played a decisive role in their entry to their respective groups. Third, at the end of the narration of each case and by using the foregoing theories, I will discuss the ways in which the aforementioned processes as a whole functioned in catapulting Turkish Penitents, at least some of them, from extremism/radicalism to political violence and terrorism. Finally, the remarks I will make below should not be generalized; for I can only talk about my informants' paths to political violence based on the data I generated during my fieldwork. However, many of the terrorist organizations from which my informants came still maintain their salience not only for public life, but also for the current political discourse in the country. Therefore, it is possible to make meaningful extrapolations from my discussion that may be applicable for understanding the "notion of entry" into terrorist groups within Turkey in general and also elsewhere. Even so, although my data is limited to the life histories of 13 individuals who practiced political violence in Turkey, the information it generates can be still useful to understand not only the environmental factors that may lead one towards political violence, but also the behaviors of those who are currently positioned somewhere on the paths that my informants took before they became a member of a terrorist organization. All in all, incorporating the foregoing approaches to my study offers an opportunity to understand the motivations of the Turkish Penitents to join politically violent groups. To demonstrate, I will first explore the experiences and feelings of my informants from revolutionary groups in their separation stage, which will be followed by an examination of the same processes that my informants from the PKK have gone through.

Paths to political violence: cases of Turkish Penitents from "revolutionary groups"

Case 1: Hakan-R

I had mentioned briefly Hakan's life history in Chapter 1. Here, I will focus on the processes that made him a revolutionary. Hakan was a member of a leftist-revolutionary terrorist organization for over 25 years. He grew up in a happy and middle-class, "traditional" family (ideologically Republican, ethnically Turkish) in Turkey's financial capital Istanbul, and both of his parents were educated. His mother finished primary school, whereas his father graduated from high school and worked in various factories. He had very strong bonds with his father, while his relationship with his mother was relatively distant. What Hakan liked most in retrospect about his mother was her interest in reading, as he says "The most precious treasure I inherited from her is her infatuation with the books." This, in fact, had a crucial influence in Hakan's school life and afterwards when he started to engage in the writings of various leftist authors. When he was at the high school, the diversity of his knowledge was one of his most notable features which did not escape the attention of Kemal, a pupil older than Hakan and the president of a leftist student club at the school, who played a crucial role in Hakan joining his revolutionary group.

Family (better-off)

Hakan grew up in a political environment in which the sanctity of the Turkish state was always prioritized because his family and most of his extended family were stauch defenders of the Republican Party (the CHP) ideology. Hakan's father always voted for the CHP which does not sound sensible at first glance given that he was a "worker" and the CHP ideology was the ideology of the Turkey's bureaucratic-military elite. But for Hakan, it was fathomable because within the available political spectrum, the CHP was closest to bringing Turkey to his father's ideal level. "Despite being the party of elites, the CHP aspires to install social democracy in the country and, if it was achieved, that would be good for the workers too," he said. In addition, Hakan's political attitudes were largely shaped during his childhood and adolescent years by his observation of the lifestyle that his father provided for them as a laborer, as he said: "If I were the son of a rich capitalist person, the likelihood of me being a leftist may be one in one thousand. Since I was shaped by the lifestyle, I had to proceed from the notion of 'exploitation.' I had to do it, because I learned it from my father, who was a laborer at Sumerbank factory. I know how he lived, how he tried to educate and feed us ... and I know that he did extra work to achieve all of these." *[margin: Political socialization]*

> Naturally, I identify myself more with the left. Because my father was a laborer; because how much pocket money I will get depends on how much he makes. If he earns more, I will dress well and eat well accordingly. I won't have to work as a shoeblack as a child or I won't have to sell water in the bazaars in my childhood. We did all of these, didn't we? We did because we didn't have the money, because our fathers couldn't give that money to us. We saw this kind of world at such a young age; so, I shouldn't have been expected to become something else. *[margin: Political socialization]*

The most important era in Hakan's life seems to be his high school years for the following reasons. First, the political atmosphere in Turkey at the time was quite tumultuous because of student protests at universities. The schools were boycotted almost on a daily basis, and even though Hakan did not participate in the boycotts, he was watching the actors behind the boycotts quite closely. They were indeed the most successful and most charismatic students of the school, and Hakan gravitated slowly towards tem. Second, three of the most important figures (role models) of the Turkish left, i.e., Deniz Gezmis, Huseyin Inan and Yusuf Aslan, were hanged after the 1971 military coup. The images of these three people on the gallows left indelible marks on the memory of the supporters of what they strove for, i.e., the liberation of Turkey from the imperialist powers and and their institutions. Hakan considers this event to be one of *[margin: Turning point ... Turning point]* the most important "turning points" for him and for many of his generation.

Third, Hakan's father retired and he bought an old one-family house in the Maltepe district located on the outskirts of Istanbul. So, they had to move from a relatively affluent and apolitical neighborhood to this highly politicized suburb which was, coincidentally, the "breeding place" of most of Turkey's leftist movements. The official name of this place is Mustafa Kemal neighborhood, but leftist groups call it "May 1st neighborhood" for it was deemed to be a symbol of the solidarity between revolutionaries and migrant villagers which was controlled for a long time by "public committees." When he was in his senior year at high school, Hakan was touched especially by the events that took place in this neighborhood after the 1 May celebrations: "... I was a senior at the high school. There were 1 May celebrations, written into the history along with its dead. For example, Hasan Kizilkaya died in those celebrations. A lot of shantytown residents (*gecekonducu* in Turkish) died, it was a big demonstration of resistance. We had participated in a meeting with the *gecekonducus* where we spoke about how we could find the necessary material to build more houses. At that time, there were many youngsters coming from different schools; all organized students groups were trying to build houses for the *gecekonducus*. Everybody is united; we would tie up the watchman, tell him that we are taking the stuff for the people, and that we don't have any problem with him. We would take whatever was needed. Can you imagine, all of the shantytowns at the time were built like this, thanks to revolutonaries. Nobody is going to school. Everybody is going to the neighborhood. I mean you are doing something which is huge; you are in that kind of an atmosphere. Imagine, people came from Anatolia with their children; and you are building shelter for them. It is really worthwhile. It is incredible for a young person, for a human. They feel indebted to you, but you sit down with them, eat with them ... it's inexplicable. It's almost impossible not to be a revolutionary in such an atmosphere; it would be against human nature. I heard the name of X [his group's name] first time in there."

Apart from abovementioned feelings of fullfillment, Hakan mentioned two concrete examples of experiences that radicalized him. First, when he was in his sophomore year at high school, his after school activity was to deliver a journal in front of the factories promoting resistance and revolution. On one of those days, he and six of his friends were detained by the police and taken to the police station. He recounted this experience by saying, "As soon

Political socialization and identification with the left

Radicalization

as we stepped in the car, they started to beat us. We were several boys and several girls who were simply students at high school; we were children. But in those days, that was routine treatment by the police anyway. They were police officers what else they would do?"and added: "Anyway, they beat us until the X factory, and when we arrived at the police station, officers were waiting for us with planks in their hands; they beat us in there for 45 minutes. That was the first time I saw the naked face of the state. Anyway, they had informed our parents, so my father came to collect me and he even scolded me; and said "The police are right; I don't want you to to be involved in political stuff anymore." After my father took me home, I went to the party office as did the others. People in the office said "we are very sorry for what they did to you." Normally my father should have done this; he should have said to police, "How can you do this to a child?" Even if he thought that I did something wrong, he should have behaved like this before the police officers.The bottom line is, you leave your father and go to the office where everybody is united."

Turning point – state violence

Significance loss

Turning point – idealization of a peer

As it is clear from this anecdote, Hakan's first experience that led him to become radicalized worsened because of his father, given that he sided with the oppressive state when he was supposed to side with his child. The second experience which involved, again, the police and his father elicited opposite feelings for his father, albeit strenghtening his reasons for radicalization."... I told the police, directly to their faces when I was finally caught in 1999, that they were the ones who contaminated me. I am a child of an ordinary Turkish family; but they took me, humiliated me, brought my father to there [police station] and beat him. And they said [to his father] "What kind of undignified man are you?" You know, I tried hard to find those officers to kill them. One of those officers was working in Kadikoy, he said a lot of bad things to my father that made the the man cry [his father]... 'If you weren't undignified, if you weren't a rascal, this child wouldn't be like this,' he said... Then he handed me over to my father."

> ... I don't know, may be I could be something else, but I never forgot this incident. It impacted on all my revolutionary life, because I had never been reduced to such a level before. I am not saying this for me, it was Ok if they beat and released me. But what they did to my father; it was unacceptable. It was a huge trauma for me ... Moreover, in that police station, those officers proved what I have been told by the revolutionary groups about them. They proved how undignified the state was. I saw everything first hand, with my own eyes.

The worthy activities for the people in shantytowns, coupled with the foregoing incidents that radicalized him, Hakan felt himself closer to the causes of those revolutionary groups. He was a revolutionary in mind, but he was not connected to any group until then; he was in a state of browsing. One of the most influential figures who wanted Hakan to be an official member of their group was his friend Kemal. Kemal was the sort of student whom not only Hakan but most students at his school looked up to; thus, Hakan was very excited when he was asked to become an official member by Kemal. Saying that "the year 1974 was the year of my existence," Hakan recounts his feelings at the time as follows: "One day, Kemal, Fatih, and I were in an apartment in the 1 May neighborhood. Kemal had mentioned [about his joining to group] before ... He then said, 'Look comrade Hakan; we want to make you a member of the organization; what is your opinion?' Of course I was very happy, I was ready anyway. I mean ... can you imagine? I will become a party member. Even if I die, my name will always be on the party records. I will die as a party member; is there anything more important than this? Of course if I died before that, there would still be something, somewhere; but dying as a party member is the biggest honor for a revolutionary."

I asked him if he had been through a formal initiation rite, he continued: "In fact, yes. The dinner table was covered with a flag. It's a gecekondu, what would you expect? [he smiles]. Anyway, they gave me the text of the oath of loyalty to the revolution, and we read it together. All members read it out loud all together. I mean it wasn't something very special; but I read it from memory. There were words about 'loyalty' and stuff like that ... I forgot, but in general, you give assurances that you will remain loyal to your comrades, your people and you will not betray them. Then, all of them kissed me and congradulated me. There is no ID card, but you are now in the records nevertheless ..." Official entry to the group

Initiation rite

When Hakan's life is looked at through the foregoing theoretical lenses, it appears that his quest for significance played the most important part in his journey towards the revolutionary group he joined. All other actors and factors such as his personal observation of his father's condition in childhood and afterwards, the CHP dominated the socio-political context in which he grew up and his processes of political socialization and radicalization appear to be ancillary to his fundamental search for meaning and significance. It is plausible to suggest that those factors and processes seem to have functioned as a facilitator, providing him with reasons for justification to join a violent group and influencing his choice of group. In addition, his quest for significance was so powerful that his process towards political violence did not follow the sequential pattern I outlined earlier;

namely, political socialization in family and school, radicalization, and entry. To specify, Hakan's radicalization by being subjected to state violence, or his loss of significance, occurred after his voluntary entry into the group.[1] It can be said that his loss of significance played a contributing role in solidifying his interest in and loyalty to his group. On the other hand, the nature of revolutionary groups seems to have reinforce Hakan's quest for significance in that these groups, and especially their military committees, intrinsically contain a high potential for fatality, promising in turn the chances of "immortality." As some of my informants stated, if a person joins a terrorist group, it means that he is conscious of the high possibility of his mortality that is inherent in all actions he is supposed to undertake. Below the excerpt from my interview with Hakan not only exemplifies the foregoing argument but it also offers a general idea about motivational reasons to join a revolutionary group and the psychology of martyrdom:

> Yes, our approach to martyrdom is the same; but the place of arrival when you die is different. If you ask a Jihadist, he will say that he will go to the Heaven. He believes this, because that belief is given to him; when he is asked to blow himself, he blows himself up. He reaches to that level of mindset; I mean it's about sacrifice … It's the same in us [revolutionary groups]. When we are sent to an action, e.g., to an "expropriation" such as a bank robbery or burglary from an exchange office, we know that we will shoot and get shot at if requested. I know this, but it's not important. Because if I am dead, I know that I will be a revolutionary martyr. Can you imagine? I will be a martyr. It is not different from a jihadist's martyrdom; there is no difference. If I die, I will be elevated to Nirvana. It's something like this; I mean you will enter the literature. [In that case] what will I be? I will be like Einstein, which means that the whole world will not forget me.

When I asked Hakan what benefit he could get from such feeling if he does not believe the existence of hereafter, he continued:

> But this is not something like that. For instance, when an artist produces art, he rarely thinks that he will make money from it. Picasso did not paint to be rich; he wanted his name to be written in history; he knew this. I am making the history at the moment; I have this consciousness. For instance, when I am on my way to attack a police station, my real intention is not to kill the people in there; psychologically, I have the feeling that I am now a part of history, and that I will be written in the history of revolution. Just like Deniz Gezmis and his friends

Psychology of martyrdom

[symbolic figures for the Turkish left]. Can you imagine? I will be known by the whole world. If you don't have such a feeling, you are nothing. Everybody will die eventually. Look, in Karacaahmet [a cemetery in Istanbul], all of them dead; but when you talk about Menderes [a former respected Prime Minister who was executed by the military junta], do you think this name will be forgotten?

Lastly, considering his styles of coping, based on Vaillant's (1971) model of ego coping styles, my findings suggest that his most apparent coping styles were idealization (immature defense – level II) and altruism (mature coping styles – level IV). Altruism is defined as vicarious but gratifying service to others (Harrington and Boardman 1997), while idealization means unconsciously choosing to perceive another individual as having more positive qualities than he or she may actually have (Vaillant 1971). Both of these coping styles comply with Hakan's significance quest, at least for two reasons. First, Hakan's rapprochement with the leftist groups coincided with the execution of the abovementioned three charismatic figures of the Turkish left, and he explained their execution as "the most important turning point" in his life.

This [hanging of Deniz and his friends] was one of the most important turning points in my life. We were at school at that time and there was a boycott in the school. There were older brothers (senior students), and they were emptying the classrooms. I mean, everybody had to join the boycott; it means they had the control of the school. We were not revolutionary at that time, but of course we were aware of what was going on.

The second reason was indeed linked to this; because one of the "brothers" Hakan talked about was Kemal, who was the president of the leftist student club which Hakan would join later on. Apparently, he was deeply influenced by Kemal. In many occasions during our conversations, Hakan mentioned his charisma, his "terrifying knowledge" about everything, and his "flawless" grasp of political affairs in the country at the time.

Case 2: Ahmet-R

Ahmet joined a revolutionary group when he was very young, around the age of 13, and he assumed various leadership positions until he left the group after 28 years. He grew up in an affluent and loving family in Istanbul and lived with his family throughout his revolutionary life except for occasional absences for group-related activities. He was a very successful student proven by the fact that he was able to enroll at one of the most prestigious high schools in the country. In terms of his entry into the group, he placed the most crucial emphasis on the environment and socio-political

[Margin note: Family (affluent and loving)]

context within which he lived his adolescent years. In his childhood, the student riots of 1968 had ended, but their effects were still lingering when he was at secondary school. Ahmet explained this time by saying: "The student riots of 1968 had ended but they had been rekindled within a couple of years. After the 1970 military coup, Deniz Gezmis, Huseyin Inan, and Yusuf Aslan had been hanged; Ibrahim Kaypakkaya [the legendary figure of TKPML-TIKKO] had died. Socialist movements had been restarted by the people who remained at the universities or who were in and out of prisons during those years. Teachers who were very active in the 1968 riots were still teaching at secondary schools and high schools. These people knew about the theoretical side of the issue [socialism and communism]; they were not simply teaching the official curricula." Turning point

Moreover, Ahmet's house was near the Istanbul University, in whose vicinity there were many student hostels. One of these hostels was adjacent to his house, which was, coincidentally, the place where the foundations of Turkey's most influential leftist groups had been laid. He was witnessing every day numerous anti-imperialist protests taking place in the university quad, most of which were organized by the students resident in these hostels. On the other hand, Ahmet was a very good soccer player, and he was playing in an amateur team along with several of his friends from the neighborhood. In those years, there were very few soccer pitches in the city, but one of the best pitches was a field belonging to the aforementioned student hostel, the bastion of the revolutionary group, of which Ahmet would become a member later on. His friends and he dreamed about playing in that field for a long time. As it turned out, one of his teachers at his school, his physical education teacher was linked to this revolutionary group; thus he was a frequent visitor to the student hostel with their dream soccer pitch. One day he invited Ahmet and his friends to play with their team in the hostel. They went there, played soccer, but in fact the teacher had gotten his hooks into them. "We were curious what was happening inside the hostel. After the game, we sat down for a cup of tea and they gave us some books. Those books were important in shaping one's personality; you don't have to be a terrorist, they were important books, good for everyone. Anyway, we started to read these books and went to school. We started to act as a political group that was composed of about 25 people. In a few weeks, we joined them when they were writing leftist slogans on the walls. They were incredibly skillful in that; we couldn't even write it on paper with pen, but they were writing them on the walls perfectly. Of course this seemed quite appealing to us."

Political socialization

Incremental radicalization

In a few months, participating in numerous activities in which he was able to show his courage and intelligence, the group gave Ahmet responsibility for the secondary school section of his high school. This was not only an honor for him, but also provided him a sense of empowerment at such a young age. It is possible to say that his responsibility and activities within the group made a noticeable impact on his incremental radicalization. In addition, like Hakan, Ahmet's "idealization" of the members of his group played a very important role in his radicalization and entry processes. One of the most important events exemplifying this was his attendance at a funeral of a leftist university student who was killed by ultranationalist students at Istanbul University: "So, after the funeral, we returned to the hostel and started to evaluate what had happened after the funeral. Everybody was fired-up, telling each other: "Have you seen how brother Mehmet was throwing stones at the armored vehicle? He was right under the tracks, did you see? You remember the brother from Erzurum [a city in the east of Turkey], he was shooting at the police." Apart from these, these older brothers were analyzing the events theoretically; they were not more than 18–19 years old at the time, but they were formidably knowledgeable."

Idealization

Idealization of peers

As illustrated in his story, the socio-political context within which Ahmet was embedded was crucial to understand his journey towards the group. But these external factors alone appear to be insufficient to make a definitive causal link unless individual factors are taken into account. In this respect, Ahmet's paths to political violence demonstrate significant similarities to Hakan's. Considering Ahmet's whole life history, I can argue that significance quest and his coping styles (idealization and altruism), too, seem to be the main reasons behind his joining the group. Although growing up in a stable family, having good economic resources, and attending one of the best schools in the country, Ahmet seemed to be dissatisfied with the "ordinary" life style he was leading. When he started to become involved in the group, and indeed became an important part of his group through his increased participation in group activities, he started to feel a sense of empowerment and fulfillment, which boosted his self-esteem and sense of significance.

Case 3: Gökhan –R

Gökhan was born in early 1970s in Istanbul. His father met Gökhan's mother when serving as an army officer in an eastern province. Within a few months after the first meeting, they got married on the terms that Gökhan's father would take care of her three children from her first marriage. Gökhan and his sister the children of this second marriage. In a few years, they moved together to Istanbul because of his father's posting, and not so

Unstable family structure

long after, his parents separated because of severe differences between them. As a result, his mother stayed with her children in Istanbul while Gökhan's father took him and his sister to Manisa, a city in western Turkey, where his own parents lived. Gökhan spent his formative years in this city without his mother, while his father was practically absent for most of the time because of his new job as a truck driver. Gökhan recounts his childhood context with the following words: "As I grew up with no parents ... I mean I had a father, but I was longing for a mother-father dialogue. The type of relationship I was envious of was the relationship between my aunt and her husband; he was working in the air force, and their life together with my aunt was pretty decent. I envied them all the time, as well as their relations with their children, their interest in their schoolwork, success, etc. You may even call it jealousy, but the idea of "if only I had such a family" crossed my mind so often." *— Childhood*

For Gökhan, the best moments of his childhood were the times he spent with his grandparents. He expressed his feelings towards them by saying, "I was very happy with my grandparents' attention to me. I was experiencing something like a lack of love; I guess I grew up in such an environment." His unrivaled role model, however, was his grandfather who was also a former army officer. Another important memory from his childhood was his infatuation with guns and the stories of "heroism" because of having many family members that worked in the military. On the other hand, Gökhan did not like his father, because worse than his absence were his boring conversations when he was around. He was drinking a lot and pouring his own problems on him and his sister. Moreover, when he did not have money to buy alcohol, he was confiscating Gökhan's money, which he earned from selling shortcakes at the ages of six and seven. Because of having intense emotional conflicts at an early age, Gökhan developed a habit of self-reflection; he was constantly questioning his life and surroundings very early on, which stayed with him throughout his life. More importantly, his father's authoritarian behavior became unbearable as he started thinking, "If only my father was not in my life." *— Emotional conflict with the father*

Gökhan had similar problems with authoritarian behavior at school. "My biggest misfortune was to do with my teachers. As I was an obstreperous student, my teachers beat me frequently in order to tame me. And beating always agitated me; I mean as if being beaten was increasing my inclination towards doing the very thing that I was told not to do. I was assuming that a door would be opening to a different world if I did it. My oppositions developed like this. When someone wanted to exert authority on *— Emotional conflict at school (Reaction formation)* me, I started to develop alternative behaviors against it." To give an example, one day Gökhan was looking out of the window of the classroom when a female teacher was talking. She came to him, scolded, and pulled him by his earlobe. As a result of this humiliation before his classmates, he did not go to school for several weeks. After repeating such reactions several times, he was first excluded by the school administration, and finally expelled as a result of other similar incidents.

Gökhan's life was shaped by several important events. First, when he was about six years old, he was selling shortcakes to make pocket money. When he almost finished selling a full tray of cakes one day, three men approached him, asking if he had change for 20 Turkish liras. As he took the money out of his pocket to help them, they grabbed it and ran away. He explained the effect of this incident by saying, "I had cried a lot at that time. I was really enraged. I mean it is a heavy weight if the product of someone's elbow grease is taken away from him." Second, his father and grandfather passed away within the same month. Even though he hated his father, the loss of his father deeply affected him as he said: "When I got out of the hospital, I was on an emotional roller-coaster [indirect translation]. I didn't know what to do. I was shaken by my father's death. Yes, I was in constant competition and struggle with him and I thought it was a meretricious thing to oppose him. But I was really sorry for losing him; I remember crying on the lap of my friend's father. But after that, I did not cry." *[margin: Significance loss]*

Second, after these incidents, he and his sister had to go to his mother's in Istanbul. It would not be an easy encounter, since he had not seen her for 17 years. Until then, his mother was a perfect woman in his imagination, partly because of his need for love by his mother and the lack of it from the father. When they met, they were both excited; they hugged and cried. With the passage of several months, however, he realized that she was not the woman he imagined; she was indeed a "self-seeking" person who could do anything to get what she wanted. More important, she was very dominant in the house and exerted violence against her children. "This caused a real trepidation in me. I mean it is not something I would accept if physical violence were exerted on me. I ran away from home, for two weeks or so ..." He was 17 years old then. After two weeks, one of his stepbrothers persuaded him to return home, but her behavior became even worse when he came back. He could not believe that she was his mother, and frequently during the interview, Gökhan said that he "abhorred" her and even wanted to "kill" her numerous times. As these problems continued, eventually he went back to Manisa to *[margin: Turning point ... Emotional destruction]*

68 *Separation stage*

establish a new life for himself, which was not easy; he was wrestling with financial problems most of the time. These difficulties led to the start of his criminality, e.g., he committed several burglaries together with his friends.

The third, and the most significant turning point, was connected with this event; he was imprisoned for one of those burglaries where he became acquainted with the first person that held a leftist ideology. He was around 18 years old. He summarizes his first impressions and the effects of that person in him as follows: "I encountered the leftist rhetoric first time in prison. I was staying in Salihli prison. In that prison, there was a guy from the Resistance Movement whose name was Musa. He was talking about leftist narratives all the time. If I need to expand my target; the man's rising up against the state appeared to me as if there was a huge mountain before me and nothing could destroy him. I wanted to find somebody to hold to account what I have been through; but I didn't know exactly who did this to me. As I could not name it, it was as if I was looking for a target. To be more correct, I had been saying to myself that I should have a goal, a place in this world ... that I should be doing something good so that somebody realized and accepted my existence. I had such a perspective at that time." [Turning point – prison] [Significance quest]

After serving his time in prison, he wanted to start a new life in a different city; he decided to move to Izmir where he had some friends and relatives. In Izmir, he simply wanted to make a living; he had nothing in mind with regard to the leftist politics which he was introduced to while in prison. He started to work in a tea house; but coincidentally, this tea house was located in the same building as the offices of several leftist organizations. When delivering tea to these offices, he could not help but realize that there were many illegal posters on the walls. He told to himself: "How audacious these are people to hang this stuff on the walls." As a result of this realization, he started to lean towards these groups, without discriminating between them. He established good relations with people from the three different groups all of which promoted the leftist ideology but differed in some ways, e.g., the methods, which country to emulate (such as Cuba, Vietnam, and Russia), etc. One girl from one of these groups, her "wittiness" in particular, attracted him a lot. Hence he started to spend more time with that group, expanded his knowledge of politics through the debates that took place between group members, and eventually became a member. Over time, he gained the trust of these people through his dedication, courage, and astuteness in group's practices, which led his promotion as the leader of youth wing of this group. [Turning point] [Idealization]

Gökhan was touched to some extent by the leftist ideology, particularly by its much articulated humanistic narratives, its stance against the exploitation of workers, and its aspiration to emancipate not only the laborers but also women and humanity, and so on. One of the reasons why this ideology seemed appealing to him was the timing of his introduction to these views; as he put it: "What they say appears to be very logical. They are the things we encounter and witness as cycle of violence in our daily lives. I mean, they talk about things that surround us; or even if we don't experience personally, they are things that we see with our own eyes. More importantly, these [narratives] seem even more logical when a person is in limbo, searching for something which would give meaning to his life." *Significance restoration*

With the effects of his newly gained knowledge about the leftist ideology, Gökhan started to believe that the police and the military were in fact the protectors of the interests of the system, which led him to think that serving the system was wrong: "If one wants to be a hero, he needed to serve his people." To this end, he increased his involvement in the activities of his group, believing that that group was standing up against those institutions in order to protect the rights of people. Most of the activities he participated were minor illegal ones, but he did not pay attention if these activities were serious or not. The feelings that these activities elicited were more important than the size of the activities, i.e., psychological satisfaction emanating from the idea that "I am serving my people." Besides this, the "excitement" received from the implementation of these minor activities was a "bonus" for the group members. He said, for example, "Let's say you are carrying journals which are illegal. As if you need to carry highly valuable material, you need to hide it; you walk around 40 streets, looking whether or not the police are behind you. I cannot describe how attractive these things appear to you." After several years of practice, however, and mostly because of being subjected to torture many times, his proclivity towards violent methods increased, shifting his previously peaceful approach in a significant way. This time, he started to believe that "you can only be a hero if you rise up against something; that is, you have to stand up against the state for your people and the only tool at one's disposal for this is violence." Gökhan received the taste of violence abundantly as a result of his reassignment by his group to Istanbul, where he became involved in many crimes that could potentially result in physical injuries or fatalities for both sides, especially financial crimes for funding the group, e.g., robbing banks, jewelry shops, and exchange offices that held a huge sum of money any given time. *State violence-radicalization*

It was in Istanbul where he saw his cousin for the first time and fell in love with her. He expressed his love to her father, Gökhan's maternal uncle, who did not approve such an idea at the beginning. Over the months, however, his ideas started to change for several reasons. First, he himself was involved in crime, mainly committing burglaries from wealthy people's houses. Second, he came to know that Gökhan was a member of an illegal group, he was "good at" robbing places, and he was quite a "courageous" person; thus he saw some prospect of working together in his own criminal activities. Eventually, Gökhan got engaged to his cousin, but realizing not so long after that his uncle was an alcoholic and exerting physical violence against his wife and sometimes on his daughter. He warned his uncle not to harm them one more time, while asking his mother-in-law to inform him if such incidents occurred again. He noticed several times the bruises on the face of his mother-in-law that she denied by providing different excuses for them. However, one summer day, when they were eating melon in their house, a big fight started and all hell broke loose in the house as his uncle started beating his aunt in front of Gökhan. He tried to prevent his uncle verbally, but he went inside and came back with a switchblade and started to swing it at him. Gökhan took the kitchen knife, which was on the table and stabbed him in the shoulder, and asked him to give in. As he tried to strike back, several Gökhan stabbed him further; and the upshot was ... his uncle was dead.

Recounting murder in cold blood – splitting

Gökhan managed to live several months as a fugitive with his fiancé, but eventually he got caught during a police search for his terrorism related criminal record, while traveling to in eastern Turkey. During the police interrogation, he confessed both his membership of the illegal group and murdering his uncle. While benefiting from the repentance laws for his involvement in terrorism and for murder, he spent 17 years in prison. When I spoke with him, he had just been released.

Although being slightly different from the previous two cases, the notion of significance quest was also one of the most discernable aspects in Gökhan's paths to political violence in a revolutionary group. Considering the circumstances of the country at the time, Hakan-R and Ahmet-R had grown up in relatively affluent and stable families, and the life's prospects seemed quite positive for them. However, as mentioned earlier, it appears that they were not satisfied with their lives; they wanted to transcend themselves through idealization of legendary figures of the Turkish left and charismatic group members who struggled to emancipate the people of Anatolia from exploitation by the oppressive state. In this sense, they were the "initiators" of their quest for significance. In Gökhan's case, however, the quest for meaning and significance was not initiated by him, but was prompted by a significance loss inflicted by a dysfunctional family structure in his childhood and adolescent years. This argument is sensible but also insufficient to explain fully why Gökhan joined a revolutionary group. At this point, I am led to believe that Gökhan's meeting with Kemal, the first leftist-revolutionary he met in prison, followed by his "serendipitous" encounters with several revolutionary groups in Izmir when he was working at a tea house presented to him the revolutionary-leftist struggle as a potential avenue for significance restoration. Speckhard and Akhmedova (2005) argue that when individuals do not have strong role models or leaders on whom they can rely,

> the group can take on a sense of "fictive kin" and group loyalties can become as strong as blood ties ... [Moreover], when a person has lost his moral compass in this situation or feels alienated and uncertain of belonging anywhere, he can become very vulnerable to groups that offer strong messages that convey a positive identity and sense of belonging to something meaningful.
> (135)

As I tried to demonstrate above, Gökhan lacked strong role models until he joined his group; and he seemed to have lost his compass before finally meeting with the leftist groups.

Case 4: Fatih-R

A similar case to Gökhan's was the case of Fatih, who was a member of a revolutionary group for 20 years. The country's socio-political context and the environment in which Fatih lived were influential in his entry to political violence. In this sense, his case presented similarities to Hakan and Ahmet. Nevertheless, in terms of his childhood life, he is closer to Gökhan's case given that he also grew up in a dysfunctional family structure. The biggest problem was his father's authoritarian behavior, which threw him into the hands of revolutionary associations in the neighborhood. Let us read about how he describes his childhood context and entry into the group: "Everybody around me had leftist roots except for my father. He was a staunch supporter of the Democrat Party; but my neighborhood predominantly consisted migrants [from the Balkans]; which is why most of them had leftist ideologies. I mean the political structure of the neighborhood was like this; fathers would go to the CHP offices [Republican Party] whereas the children used to go to 'people's houses' [which were run by revolutionaries]. This was the environment in my childhood ... In addition, there were also university events at the time, between leftists and rightists. In the

[margin: Dysfunctional family structure]

[margin: Political socialization]

people's houses, we met a lot of leftist students, and what they were doing was quite interesting for my three friends and me. As a result, we increased our visits to these places, which caused my father to overreact. He said, 'if you want to preoccupy yourself with these, don't come home again.. I protested him and left home. I think this was a breaking point; had he not said those things, my life would perhaps have developed differently."The above-cited quote from Fatih describes his dissatisfaction with his life within the family as well as his search for an alternative that, among other things like socio-political context in his neighborhood and in the country, increased his rapport with his group. But the last straw, which radicalized him and strengthened his ties with his group, was his subjection to violence by the nationalists." [margin: Turning point] [margin: Radicalization]

"It was 1978; nationalists opened fire when we were sitting in a coffee house in the neighborhood; I was wounded. As a result of this, I became more fired-up and started to increase my involvement in these things [group activities] ... which sped up afterwards; and I was in organizational activities until 1981. Nevertheless, the key point is, the raid on the coffee house was the turning point that marked my entry into this business [group], both professionally and mentally. I mean after such an event, you think that you can be separated from home. You become mentally separated from everything but the organization. Making it your life style becomes very normal. In short, the first transformation happened at that time."

Although growing up in a relatively well-off traditional Turkish family, Fatih too was dissatisfied with his life within the family. More importantly, his father's authoritarian behavior was unbearable, which created in turn high emotional conflicts in him. He was already participating in some of the activities of revolutionary groups in his neighborhood, albeit not very consciously. However, as a result of a loss of significance emanating from his tense relations with his father, he ran away from home, started to stay in his group's apartments, and increased his involvement in their activities. Like Gökhan, revolutionary struggle manifested itself as a good opportunity for significance restoration for Fatih. Moreover, similar to Hakan's case, Fatih's radicalization took place after his entry into the group when they were attacked by the nationalists while they were in a coffeehouse. In addition, similar to the effects of Hakan's trauma created by the state violence, this incident appears to have solidified Fatih's identification with the leftist struggle, the main enemy of which at the time were the rightists (in his terms, "the fascists") and the state, which they thought to have supported them.

Case 5: Soli-R

Soli grew up in an extremely dysfunctional family. His father's "totalitarian" behavior was unbearable as he explained him as a "despot." When I asked him how the atmosphere was within the family during his childhood, he said, "There was no fight indeed, because my father used to talk and we all listened to. There was a complete dictatorship in the house." In addition, his father was always at loggerheads with his mother's family because they had not wanted this marriage from the beginning. As a result of long-term enmity between them, Soli's father prohibited his children to have any contacts not only with his wife's family, but also with many of the relatives on both sides. They were living in a kind of solitary confinement during his childhood. In terms of his relations with his mother, Soli said, "My mother was an illiterate person; she didn't have anything (education) to give us. She was busy with her own condition anyway; I hardly remember her face in its normal state." On the other hand, malnourishment was a big problem in his large family. He had eight siblings (four brothers and four sisters) that made it very difficult for his father even to feed them sufficiently, let alone meeting their social and educational needs. *(Dysfunctional family structure)*

Recounting his childhood years, Soli says: "I mean we were raised in the hands of God. We would feed ourselves (8 or 10 people) with one little bowl full of olives. I mean there was a lot of hunger at home. However, you cannot take outside what's going on inside home. After reading some psychological books, I now know that it would be better if my father had killed us. We have had many problems outside because of what we have been through in that home. Our relations with people were very problematic. One of my brothers still has difficulty in making friends. The home was unbearable; it was like a dungeon. I rescued myself from this dungeon only when I attended high school. There, a sense of rage and ability to hold my father to account for the problems that developed in me; because high school gave me a self-confidence that I lacked before. I mean, I thought that he could no longer harm me like in my childhood. Only at that time, I said to myself, 'Yes, I am a human. I also remember myself wanting to kill my father many times.'" *(Unloving home / School effect)*

"But when I was at high school, my father died. I was simply frozen, I was motionless. They said you father is dead, but I was still waiting for him to stand up. Death did not suit him, you know ... He was so cruel that I had never thought he would die one day. But despite that cruelty, I felt that I was in need of him." His father's death also created problems at home given that there *(Turning point)* was a constant struggle for power and domination within the house despite the fact that Soli was the eldest child in the family. As a result of these unending brawls, he left home and started to stay outside; sometimes at a friend's house, but most of the time he spent the nights sleeping on a bench in parks. It was then when he finally met with people from the mafia and eventually approached people from his future revolutionary group, thinking that maybe they would provide him with a place to stay. He simply needed a "shelter" and a "loving" environment, as he explained "I was not interested in what they were talking about; I didn't care about their ideology. I was more interested in the attention that I received from them." [By mafia, he is referring to organized criminal groups]

Over time, however, he became interested in their stories and narratives as he read various books on leftist ideology and participated in political debates. These readings and discussions functioned in a way that allowed him to identify the "liables" for his negative life experiences. "When I passed from reading novels to books on philosophy and politics, I started to understand that the source of my problems was, in fact, the state, the system, and capitalism. These altogether, are indeed the main cause not only of my problems but my father's and my family's too. I mean, I felt like I found an enemy. Finding that enemy and finding the thing to blame, I started to embrace the cause with four hands; and I started to finish very thick books within one breath. I became voracious in a way." [Significance restoration]

The most salient aspect of Soli's life history pertaining to his entry into a revolutionary group appears to be his dysfunctional family structure that created in him a significance loss very early on and prompted in turn a need for significance restoration. Whereas Fatih's encounter with and joining in a revolutionary group was facilitated by his socio-political context, Soli approached his group with hopes of finding a shelter and a loving environment. Also, while the leftist ideology resonated in Fatih from the beginning, Soli's interest in the leftist ideology did not occur until he realized that leftist narratives showed him who was behind his life-time suffering. From this perspective, in the cases of Soli-R and Gökhan-R, another phenomenon seems to be in the work vis-à-vis their feeling of significance loss, that is, their search for "moral agents" for their suffering (significance loss) stemming from the negative life experiences they had in childhood and adolescence. In their article on pain, mind perception, and morality, Gray and Wegner (2010) linked mind perception to morality and accounted for how people perceive the minds of a range of moral players – villains, victims, martyrs, self-harmers, despots, benefactors, etc. – in terms of the general distinction between moral agents and moral patients (8). The authors argued that, "as described by Aristotle, moral situations are divided into the two roles of moral agents and moral patients ... Moral agents are those who do good or bad, whereas moral patients are those who are the recipients of good or bad" (2009:8). They also argue that the dyadic structure of morality forces human mind to search for an agent in cases of, for instance, being beset by good or evil or of experiencing unjust suffering and underserved salvation. But if individuals cannot find anybody to blame or praise, they look to the supernatural for an agent, finding God (2009:8). In fact, anthropological evidence supports this issue, for various societies invoke supernatural agents, e.g., "witchcraft" for instances of death, injury, and even the theft of one's genitals (Lewis 1995; Boyer 2001; Gray and Wegner 2010:11). In light of these ideas, I argue that although morality has a dyadic structure since they require two people (as explained by the authors) (e.g., a theft requiring a thief and victim or a donation requiring a donor and a beneficiary), there is room for a third person or entity to play an intermediary role, when an individual is in search of a moral agent for his unjust suffering or undeserved salvation especially in the absence of religious beliefs. Considering the cases of Soli-R and Gökhan-R, the groups clearly played this intermediary role in showing them the moral agents of their suffering. As they expressed themselves, these moral agents were none but the police and the military that were the embodiments of the exploitative and oppressive state. Gray and Wegner also argued that, interestingly, harm leads us to God more strongly than help because "with help people may thank Him, but with harm people both curse and embrace Him" (2010:12). For people of no strong faith, however, as in the case of Gökhan-R and Soli-R, harm does not seem to lead to the embrace of the moral agent who is perceived to be the inflictor of that harm. In contrast, identifying the agents of harm as state institutions led to an increased animosity in them towards those agents. Lastly, the authors argue that

> harm violates people's implicit sense of justice, making them feel wronged, which then leads to the perception of a moral agent ... This feedback loop can then continue, as future harm can then be seen as intended from an agent, which makes people feel like even more of a victim, necessitating an even more powerful moral agent, and so on.
>
> (2010:130)

Just like the former arguments explain Gökhan's and Soli's entry into the group, this last point sheds light on their continuous involvement in political violence within their respective groups.[2]

Case 6: Hikmet-R

My last informant from the revolutionary groups was Hikmet, whose entry into the group was different from all others described above. Growing up in a middle-class family, he had a stable childhood and adolescence. His family was Alevi-Kurdish, but he learned about his Alevi identity quite late, around the age of 14, given that his parents tried everything to conceal their Alevi identity, largely due to the explicit and latent discrimination against them. As he tells his story, the main reason for his involvement in political violence was his brother's capture by the police for being a member of the same revolutionary group Hikmet would join later on. Until then, he was not very much interested in political issues despite having an Alevi-Kurdish working-class family and spending his childhood in an apartment complex for about 2000 "workers" and their families. He recounts the effects of his brother's capture as follows:

Entry into group

Importance of family ties

> His capture was a huge and special loss for me. As we were sharing the same bed with him during our childhood, I was deeply affected by it. At that time, I heard that he was tortured by the police while in custody. I learned these from the lawyers and from my mom. They said the soldiers beat him badly in prison. I mean, when you hear these things, when one of your family members is affected by these, even if you don't have an ideology, it undoubtedly creates anger in you. Whether it translates itself into violence is another issue, but the key point in my case is that that experience led to an accumulation of anger in me. And, it was the first time when I started to listen to the songs of leftist singers; I started to become a revolutionary; although just by outlook at the beginning. Also, it was the time when I started to learn about my Alevi identity which I had neglected until then.

Frustration–aggression

In the terrorism literature, family ties are presented to function at least in two ways in terms of recruitment. First, terrorist groups seek new recruits especially among youngsters who have loose or preferably problematic ties with their families. Dysfunctional, tense, or unloving homes are perfect places for them to reach out to those youngsters who are living in such homes and in the throes of finding a way out. As explained in the cases of Soli-R and Gökhan-R, for such individuals, terrorist groups and their humanistic rhetoric appear to be a perfect alternative to restore their significance which they lost within the family. Second, psychology of victimhood is another concept that terrorist groups often utilize in their recruitment processes. Victimhood can emerge as a result of personal or collective trauma. The latter usually manifests itself as the suffering of others such as, the suffering of an individual's family member, relative, or even a distant compatriot whom the individual identifies himself with. Hikmet's case exemplifies this second type and demonstrates vividly how important the psychology of victimhood and family ties are for an individual in joining a politically violent group. Additionally, during our conversations Hikmet often emphasized that even though he knew about his brother's involvement in the activities of an illegal group, he was not aware of the extent of his involvement and, in fact, he was almost indifferent to the political issues surrounded him. His brother's capture therefore had multiple effects on him. First, he was deeply wounded and frustrated by the torture his brother had to endure while in custody. Second, this incident provoked his interest in his Alevi identity and created in him a curiosity about the groups that claim to respect and protect that identity. Since many of his relatives including his brother was a member of a "certain" group (confidentiality issue), it was natural for him to join that group. The overall effect of this incident, in the words of Hikmet, was the following: "I had no choice but to replace my brother in his group. If he were a member of X group instead of Y, I would join that group. There is no doubt about it." Lastly, in addition to the influence of his brother and his Alevi identity, like Gökhan, his infatuation with guns and tales of "heroism" starting from childhood had significant impact on his entry into the group and his continued involvement within the "military committee" of that group.

Paths to political violence: cases of Turkish Penitents from "the PKK"

Case 1: Recep-P

Recep was born in the late 1970s in a little town in Şırnak province located in Turkey's southeast region. He has seven siblings; one elder brother, two younger brothers, and four younger sisters. Both of his parents were educated, his father having finished high school, while his mother finishing only primary school. With the effects of his larger family, however, his parents maintained a "feudal" family structure at home, which had an enormous impact on the interpersonal relationships both within and outside the family. Authority of elders, in particular, was never questioned. When he started primary school, Recep could not speak the Turkish language, which meant that he did not understand most of the lessons. For this reason, he was whacked by the teachers almost on a daily basis. Ironically though, most of the teachers who beat him were ethnically Kurdish individuals. He was not conscious of the effects of these beatings for a long time that haunted him much later as he put, "You realize over time where one slap on your face for not knowing the language can take you." [Family] [School]

Recep grew up during the heyday of the PKK, i.e., the late 1980s and the beginning of the 1990s. In those times, even those Kurdish families who did not support the group "had to pretend" to be at least sympathizers if they wanted to survive, given that the PKK had permeated all aspects of the people's life in the region. His family was not "patriotic" (yurtsever in Turkish), which meant that they neither supported the PKK nor sympathized with it. As Recep put it, it was in fact the "wrong policies of the Turkish state," that brought them closer to the PKK. In its efforts to tackle the PKK terrorism, the Turkish state had implemented via its military various policies at the time, one of which was the implementation of forcible village evacuations. [Political socialization]

78   Separation stage

If certain villages were thought to be providing logistical support to the PKK, inhabitants of those villages were asked to become village guards for the state or else evacuate them, while at times, some of those villages were burned down altogether. Recep recounts his experiences on this by saying: "My family had to support the PKK initially because of its potential oppression. But they became true patriots after the military came to our village to evacuate it. In our villages, elders are highly respected; people listen to what they say. Therefore, when they are beaten by an army sergeant, for instance, normally not wearing his uniform, there would be blood; it would instigate a blood feud. But it's not that sergeant who slaps our elderly on the face; it's the uniform. Then, automatically, the hatred is directed not to the person, but to the uniform; and since that uniform represents the state, it means that the target of reaction, in fact, is the state. On the other hand, the PKK comes and acts exactly in the opposite direction, which means that you don't even need to think; the side that you will take is automatically determined." Recep adds that he personally witnessed the beatings of his father and uncle many times, and that he could not look at them because of the blood and bruises on their body. "For the children who face such situations and who want to take revenge, the PKK was the only alternative," he continued.

Because of these problems in the village, Recep's family had to move to the city center; but even there problems continued, given that the state did not allow them to go back to the village, the most important source of his family's subsistence. In addition, Recep could not continue his education at the secondary school. One reason for this was his family's fear of Turkish Hezbollah that was kidnapping Kurdish children in the region. Turkish Hezbollah was "allegedly" founded and supported by the state against the PKK. Being in the middle of much shooting, be it the PKK, Hezbollah, or the oppressive state, Recep's family decided to migrate to Istanbul when he was 13 years old, just like thousands of other families for similar reasons. In Istanbul, they found an apartment in one of the shantytowns that was hosting people like Recep and his family, i.e., families who fled their homes because of oppression by PKK as well as the state. Moreover, having the same language and culture, the residents of these shantytowns shared a similar history of being subjected to physical and symbolic violence, as well as political persecution, which meant that future solidarity between them in big cities was already established before their arrival. Ironically, the policies of the state in large cities like Istanbul, Ankara, and Izmir, were significantly milder than its policies in the southeast regions.

[margin: Turning point]

[margin: The effect of migration]

Within such political realm, the PKK did not even try hard to promote its ideology and to get people involved in its activities and branches in the legal sphere.

Illustrating such political context, Recep says: "In those years, the PKK was more influential here [Istanbul] than in Diyarbakır or Şırnak. In that region, people were afraid of even whispering the names of 'Apo' [the PKK leader] or 'HADEP' [a now prohibited political party that was the extension of PKK in politics]. Entering the offices of HADEP was being perceived by the state as attacking a military post. In contrast, entering the HADEP offices here is nothing; you wrap the PKK flag around your body and go to the heart of the city. You are filled with cumulated rage, but you are more relaxed here. Nothing happens if you do those things; you don't get beaten up every time you do such things. This, in turn, leads to an increase of impudence in you; you want to strike back with so much more than you saw there [in the east] ... and you do indeed. In addition, people from HADEP come to your house and you go to their offices. There is no longer a distinction; you are all for one. They don't even try to cajole you or gain your trust, one contact is more than enough; but even if they don't initiate the contact, you go and find them. You go there, still with fear at the beginning; but you realize that there is no problem ... then you bring all of your progeny." [Change of socio-political context]

Despite relaxed conditions in Istanbul, however, Recep and his friends were knocked about occasionally by the police for selling illegal journals. Aside from being "exciting" and full of "adrenalin," such treatments by the police increased their political consciousness, providing them with a feeling of "Yes, I am the man of the cause now." [Radicalization]

Just like any other Istanbulite, Recep experienced some difficulties with adapting to the big city. His biggest problem, however, was his life within the family; because ten people had to share a small apartment and his family was economically in dire straits. He had to work at such a young age to support the family, but he felt that his efforts were not being valued by his father and elder brother. He even thought that he was being "used." In his feudal culture parents want to have a lot of children, on whom they dote during the childhood. But when the children reach a certain age, parents expect them to "lactate." Such a state of mind led him to spend more time outside with his peers. But there was not much to do without money in Istanbul. Eventually, they started to go to the HADEP office more often, and the treatment they received in there healed in a way the emotional injuries that were inflicted upon them elsewhere, particularly within the households. Recep expressed this feeling vividly by [Significance loss in family]

80 Separation stage

saying: "Think about it; you are a child and you see suppression at home by your father, brother, or mother. Your opinion has no value, because you are a child. So, can you persuade me to do something? However, you go there [to the party office], you are 13 years old, and you go as a person who became inured to being downgraded, humiliated ... 'sit down, do this, do that,' etc. But when you go to the HADEP, a man with a beard and moustache, a man who is as old as your father comes and says by tapping on your shoulder, "How are you *heval*? I mean he respects you, values you. If you ask him something, he gets it done for you; or when you want to speak, he gives you the right to speak. But you go back home with these feelings, as soon as you step in, you are whacked by your father or brother. So, what just happened? The party office has just become a center of gravity for you, nothing else ..."

> ...More importantly, after spending sometime in HADEP, you realize that everybody listens to you. When somebody of your age comes to your house from there, even your father listens to him. Why? Because he came on their behalf; then the only thing that crosses your mind is this: if I want to be respected too, I should do more with them.

Recep decided to do exactly what he said above; to do more because the routine activities such as delivering journals, newspapers and leaflets, or participating in meetings did not satisfy him at all. One day, he expressed his feelings to one of his friends and realized that he was also in a similar emotional landscape. When they went to the HADEP office next time, they realized that the pictures of some Kurdish youngsters who went to "the mountain" were hung on the walls. When people spoke of them in the office, they expressed enormous respect for them, because they were the "real warriors" of Kurdistan. In those years, for some Kurds, if one of their youngsters had gone to the mountain he would not only "deify" himself but also automatically "upgrade" the status of his/her family within the community (it's still the same). Eventually, Recep and his friend spoke with somebody in the party office and openly stated that they wanted to be "warriors." That man neither rejected nor accepted their request outright; he just said "Mountain conditions are not easy ... you are too young, you can't take this" and added "Take this book, go home and read; and we will talk about it later." The book he gave to Recep and his friend was a guerilla's diary entitled, *The Soil Smells of Homeland*. They, in fact, read the book all in one breath and ran back to him. He finally said, "OK,

Margin notes: Interest in PKK; *Heval* means comrade in Kurdish; Significance restoration; PKK recruitment strategy

come back tomorrow, I will send you with the next couriers." They did exactly what he said and after traveling three days with several stopovers, they arrived at the mountain. Recep was aged 16 at the time.

In talking to terrorists and their associates of Chechen and Palestinian origin, the deepest impression Speckhard and Akhmedova had was an overwhelming sense of personal trauma (2005:129). They argue that "personal trauma, feelings of alienation, and disenfranchisement, etc., may inspire a quest for meaning that in cases of severe intergroup conflict may be afforded by a terrorism-justifying ideology" and added that "trauma does not have to be personal to have a deep effect in the individual" (2005:136). In addition, the authors place emphasis on the notion of *victimization*, arguing that "as individuals begin to see themselves subjectively as victims, their cognitive frames begin to change and over time the moral basis of struggle through political violence becomes justified in their minds" (2005:139). Similarly, Peteet (1994) examines the effects of trauma as the attainment and enactment of manhood and masculinity among Palestinian male youths in relation to ritualized beatings in the occupied West Bank. She frames the beatings (and detention) as rites of passages and argues that they are crucial to understand the construction of an adult, gendered (male) self that has critical consequences for political consciousness and agency (1994:129). Both of these studies imply the importance of personal or collective exposure to violence in understanding individuals' political socialization, radicalization, and resort to political violence.

Proceeding from these approaches, it is plausible to argue that the ongoing conflict between the Turkish state and the PKK for almost three decades has had a potential effect on paving the way for the construction of political consciousness and resistant subjectivity among Kurdish youth through their processes of political socialization. As Speckhard and Akhmedova (2005) argued before, trauma does not need to be personal to have deep effects in the individual. I had formerly mentioned the impact of torture in Diyarbakır prison on general Kurdish population, even on those who do not sympathize with the PKK or vote for political parties commonly known as the extension of the PKK in politics. For understanding the effects of such traumatic events and the protracted cycle of violence in Turkey, consider the "shattered assumptions" approach envisaged by Janoff-Bulman (1992):

> According to the shattered assumptions approach, following traumatic events people often face major challenges to their basic assumptions about the world and about themselves. Two assumptions that are most influenced by severe events are the assumption of *personal invulnerability* and the *perception* of the world as *meaningful, predictable* and *benign*. Accordingly, psychological distress in response to traumatic events is associated with a perception of the world as malevolent and the *self* as *vulnerable to victimization*.
> (Emphasis added)

82 *Separation stage*

Among my informants from the PKK, Recep's case displays significant commonalities indicated in the three studies cited above. His personal exposure to political violence in his village during the forced village evacuation and his subjective feeling of the relative deprivation of the Kurdish people, coupled with his psychological distress caused by his intra-family relations, represented a significance loss which prompted an attempt at significance restoration. For instance, when I asked Recep what he felt about the village evacuation and the events afterwards, he said:

> We left our village and came to Diyarbakır. I witnessed a lot of beatings in the village. I remember, for instance, my uncles were not able to walk as a result of 15-day detention. You see this when you are a child; all of the children saw this. What can you do as a child? I can talk about my own experience; the only thing I thought in that psychology was 'We will take out revenge when we grow up.' I mean this is what happens in your soul, but you don't know how to do it [To take revenge]. At that time, the PKK seems to be the only alternative. I mean, even if you don't think about these, they put the weapon to your hand. This is it, you can't take it, because he is my grandfather, he is my father, or uncle. You look at them while they are lying on the ground with lots of bruises on their body.

It is clear from his story that Recep chose to restore his significance through a commitment to a culturally revered act (sacrificing one's self for a collective cause) identified as such in a prevalent ideological frame, i.e., the PKK ideology. The reason for such an embarkation on a collective cause emanates from the fact that significance restoration is usually beyond the power of individuals. We saw this also earlier in the cases of my informants from revolutionary groups such as Gökhan, Fatih, and Soli, when they saw the group as a means to significance restoration. This phenomenon is called by Kruglanski *et al.* (2009) a "collectivist shift":

> Personal traumas, and frustrations, represent a significance loss, motivating the quest for significance restoration. Often, however, it is *beyond the power of the individual* to restore her or his lost sense of personal significance. It is impossible to being back to life the loved ones lost to enemy violence. Nor is it easy to undo the deeds that brought one ostracism from one's community, or to convince members of an indigenous majority to accept a minority immigrant as equal. Where the direction restoration of one's lost sense of personal significance seems impossible, the individual may seek to do so *indirectly* through alternative means, including an identification with a collective loss (or one's group's relative deprivation) that affords a clear path to renewed significance via participation in militancy and terrorism. Thus, through a kind of *"collectivistic shift"* individual powerlessness may be overcome by an empowering collectivistic ideology in whose name terrorist acts are carried out.
>
> (26, emphasis added)

Case 2: Azad-P

Azad was born into a Kurdish-Alevi family in 1976, in a village in one of the eastern provinces of Turkey. Because of a large migration that was taking place from eastern provinces to the metropolises in western Turkey, his family moved to Istanbul when Azad was two years old. He has three siblings; two elder brothers and one elder sister. He grew up and studied in Istanbul until he joined the PKK at the age of 26. When I asked Azad to recount his childhood, the first thing he mentioned was the social structure of the village where he came from. I was little surprised by such kind of a prelude, thinking that he could not possibly remember anything from that village. I was tempted to interrupt him; but preferred to be patient as he carried on by explaining how non-violence was the most significant feature of culture in that village and how it affected his family, while emphasizing the significance of all of these in his own life within the family and outside it. To be more specific, Azad did not experience any violence at home in his childhood and afterwards, which he attributes to this culture of non-violence. I will come back later to his predisposition to non-violence and the effects of it with regard to his entry into, and exit from, the PKK. [Family] [Political socialization]

Growing up in a non-violent family does not mean, however, that Azad's childhood life was perfect and free of emotional difficulties. His father was working in Europe, which meant that Azad had no time with his father between the ages of two and eight. This lack of paternal time, in turn, led among other things to the establishment of strong bonds between him and his mother. One year after his father's return, however, Azad lost his mother at the age of nine, which was one of the most important "turning points" in his life. "I get emotional when I talk about it. I remember my mom; she was sick and they were taking her to the bathroom. After that, something developed in me ... like I wasn't very eager to take shower. For instance, a person may take a shower once or twice a day, whereas I used to take shower only once a week. I hadn't thought about it, until I realized it much later. Besides this, for example, the day when my mother died I realized a hustle and bustle on the first floor. I didn't know until then, and still didn't know. The son of our superintendent came and said, "your mother died." I said "No I don't believe it". But when I became sure that she was dead, I went near the window and cried; all by myself... I was about ten years old. I mean, it was something unforgettable for a child. In those days I became very quiet; for instance I remember my father giving money to our neighbor's son to take me out, outside the house. I mean, I had locked myself at that level." [Lack of paternal and maternal time in childhood] [Turning point]

Separation stage

As we shall see in the upcoming sections, various other factors also led to the formation of his introversive characteristic trait that has had a big impact all aspects of Azad's life. Thus, in order to make it more intelligible, I shall delve into it. The following text from the interview is quite telling in this respect: "I had a teacher whose name was Mehmet. For instance, I was good at drawing pictures, but since he was convinced that I was a lazy student; he asked 'Did you draw this picture?' Then he said that I'd cheated and failed me. In fact, I had drawn it myself. There I developed a kind of judgment ... like unjustness; it stung me for a long time. In addition, there was beating at school; when I returned home as beaten up, it really affected me. When I was beaten up, a peculiar psychology would develop in me, I would not go out, I was ashamed. Think about it; you are beaten up at school, you are lazy ... it was a psychology that developed automatically. And I would not participate in social events; because of this, I preferred to stay alone all my life. For instance, I even wanted to be alone in jail, I stayed in solitary confinement. I did not feel any disturbance; I did not feel the need to be with other people. I always wanted to be with few people. I want the same now. After all these years, it would not be right to enter a new environment so rapidly. When I enter a new social setting, I warm up very slowly anyway. I slowly fit in, but over time I can dominate. Since I know myself, I don't rush." *[Formation of his introverted personality pattern]*

As seen in the above quotes, Azad's introversion after his mother's death and the need for detachment from social environment seems to have led to the formation of his personality pattern; i.e., prudence. As hinted in the last sentences of the foregoing paragraph, Azad used this prudence consciously to produce positive results for himself throughout his life. It also had an important influence in his life in the PKK and exit from it (Chapters 5 and 6). *[Forming of his 'prudent' personality pattern]*

A couple of years after his mother's death, Azad's father got married again, making home for him a difficult place to be. Although his stepmother was trying to be nice and loving, it was not good enough for him to fill the void created by the loss of his mother. After a while, problems started to surface within the family, as one of his two brothers, who was the main financial provider of the family, started to complain about the fact that his hard work was being exploited by their father and stepmother. The tense family structure became unbearable for Azad, as he started thinking for the first time of running away from home. He summarizes those years by saying: "I was aware of the tension between my father, brother, and stepmother. I can say that it had an impact on my desire to run away from home. There was *[Tense family structure]* nothing attractive at home. I mean, I did not have a regular home environment."

At this point, a serendipitous event took place. After finishing secondary school in Esenler district, a poor neighborhood inundated by internal migrants from the east, Azad started high school in Bakirkoy, which was one of the most upscale neighborhoods in Istanbul at the time. With this change of social field, his introverted nature started to slowly wane, and he became relatively more sociable and extroverted, largely due to the influence of his peers. In addition, the high school he attended was a commercial high school, which was different from regular high schools. The students of commercial (occupational) high schools were attended school only on certain days of the week; otherwise, they were doing practical training in various factories depending on the type of the commercial high school. Azad benefited from this greatly in the sense that he was able to work and make money while studying, with which he supported his family financially. This gave him a sense of "empowerment" and "independence" given that his father was not scolding him anymore if he was not at home. Azad's high school years and afterwards until his enrolment at university was pretty stable and could be considered as "ordinary." He worked in multiple locations; his finances were in good condition given that he was able to buy his own car at such a young age and to lend money to family members and friends.

Azad became aware of his Alevi and Kurdish identity very early on, as does any other Alevi and Kurdish person; because, as explained earlier, these groups have historically been "differentially incorporated" (Smith 1998) into Turkish society. His peculiar Kurdish name was another reason for his early awareness of his identity, proven by his frequent subjection to "strange looks" of people when his name was announced in a social setting. At school, the situation was even stranger because one teacher put down a Turkish name in his "mark book" in lieu of Azad's Kurdish name. In terms of politics and ideology, he did not inherit strong political views or attitudes from his parents, notwithstanding the fact that most people in his environment observed the Republican Party (the CHP) ideology. Illustrating this, Azad said, "In terms of political identity, I can say this: there were always people from CHP (People's Republican Party – statist ideology) around me, but I didn't grasp that Marxist-Leninist (PKK's initial ideology) atmosphere." He was not totally indifferent to political issues, nevertheless. He mentioned that one of his teachers, for instance, was a leftist. This teacher spoke about various artists and singers who were considered to

Experience in school – political socialization

be icons for Turkey's left. Azad recalled his feelings towards this teacher by saying, "That teacher was talking about different things, for instance. I liked him a lot; I would see him in my dreams sometimes. He left a big impression on me."

It appears that until enrolling at university, his identity and inclination towards leftist narratives did not play an important role in his interactions with other people. He was not tied one place; rather he was in search of camaraderie no matter who provided it. For example, during his high school years, Azad was hanging out with non-Alevi and non-Kurdish friends all the time. He did not even see any problem being friends with youngsters who were members of various religious groups that follow, for instance, Nakshibendi Sufi orders, despite the fact that he and his family was not religious at all. They did not even go to *Cemevis*. When I asked about his religious views he said, "Personally, I didn't grow up in an Islamic environment. If I tell you that there is no God, I have a culture and background which would support that."

Cemevis (singular Cemevi) are Alevi gathering places for prayer, the equivalent of mosques

Yet, when he decided to go to university, like most students in Turkey he had to go to a preparatory school in order to be successful in the entrance examination; and the preparatory school he chose was run by religiously conservative people. Besides being open to such interactions with religiously conservative people, he saw no problem in working with people who were staunchly "nationalist." This, too, was almost unthinkable, considering that political exclusionism was at its peak in Turkey in 1990s, i.e., the formative years of Azad. Those who had nationalist ideology and those with Alevi-Kurdish backgrounds were the least likely people to be seen together, let alone work together. These examples from Azad's childhood and adolescent years are important in the sense that despite his cultural context (Alevi-Kurdish), the neighborhood in which he grew up was predominantly "patriotic" (*yurtsever* in Turkish), which is used to define PKK sympathizers), and the potential pressures emanating from these two, he was able to transcend these intrinsic "compulsions" and act relatively independently in weaving his web of social networks.

When Azad was around 22 years old, he fell in love with a girl in his neighborhood. Even though she was a frequent visitor of their house, Azad could not express his feelings to her for a long time. When he finally gathered his courage and confessed his love, he was rejected: "I have always seen you as my brother, and you will remain the same," she said. This affected him significantly and, once again, Azad turned into himself. He even experienced difficulty breathing when she was in his vicinity. Eventually,

Turning point

intensifying emotions started to become insurmountable, which compelled him to make a choice between joining the army[3] and attending university. His friends persuaded him to choose the latter. This was another "turning point" for Azad, for despite not being radicalized for ideological reasons, Azad's journey towards the PKK began with his decision to go to university.

Unbeknownst to him, the first step towards the PKK was taken on the first day of the university. When he went to register for classes, there were representatives of different student clubs in the quad and one girl gave extra attention to him when she heard that he had a Kurdish name. Thinking retrospectively, he said that those orientation days were very important as they function as a screening tool for the groups under the guise of student clubs. The clubs that are connected to the PKK are usually involved in social activities such as arts, music, and dance, which are very appealing to newcomers to the university. In addition to such activities, these groups are well-versed in various social sciences including philosophy, sociology, and political science, which seem promising for the new students because of the potential gain to be obtained as a result of participation in such activities. Eventually, Azad registered for one of the groups associated to the PKK, without exactly knowing this connection. He was guessing, however, that such connection was possible with one of the illegal groups, even though not necessarily with the PKK. He did not question this that much at the time, because he was open to join any group, but he did not mind joining a leftist group in particular. When I asked why he chose that particular students' club and not the others which are connected to less militant groups, i.e., affiliates of the nationalist party (the MHP), various religious groups (these groups are called Cemaat in Turkish), or the likes of them, he did not have a definitive answer, but sufficed to say that he needed some kind of affiliation and the activities of the group he chose looked very enticing to him. Because unlike others like religious and nationalist clubs, the club he joined was more welcoming, the people were more sociable, and "girls and boys were always together" in all activities. *[PKK recruitment strategy]*

Azad stayed in the student hostel during the first year, visiting his family only at weekends. He participated in many activities with his club, all of which were legal. In his second year, he moved into the apartment of his friends from the club. That was in a way his "initiation" into the group, given that that apartment was in fact a PKK cell, to which only trusted people would be accepted. This cell-like lifestyle appeared quite interesting for Azad in several aspects; first, their life was not like it was made out to be in public discourse, e.g., the gender relations were not *[Initiation into the group]* based on promiscuity. Second, these people were always reading and debating for long hours. After starting to live in that apartment, he read many books including ones written by the PKK leader Abdullah Öcalan. He confessed, however, that he did not understand anything from these books, while adding that it was his lack of knowledge that led to this difficulty. Thus, he asked his friends to make a list of ten crucial books in order to better understand Öcalan's books and other heavy political texts that all PKK members had to read. So he did, and after a while he realized the importance of this newly gained knowledge; he was more successful at school and more persuasive in informal debates with other students.

During his junior year at the university, he participated in numerous legal activities. The only one that "seemed" illegal, because they had not received permission from state authorities, was his participation in a walk for "education in native languages." However, nothing happened to him because of this participation. His most important job in the club was publishing a journal along with his friend Harun who was "the most successful, charismatic, and convincing student" in his class. Eventually, he told Azad that the journal was doing well, but they needed to do better; and for this reason, he should go to the "mountain" to get intensive training on press matters. Azad faltered for a moment, but could not say no to Harun. He decided to go, thinking that he would be back in three months anyway. He returned eight years later and surrendered himself to the police. *[margin: Role of peers]*

When I asked Azad to explain why he joined the PKK in one or two sentences, he mentioned the following concrete issues: "When Öcalan was captured in 1999, there was a retreat. He ordered guerillas to retreat to Northern Iraq. He spoke about democracy, brethren, etc. My entry into the PKK coincided with this period; I mean, with the time when peace doves were flying. Before that period, there was YCK (Yektiya Civanen Kurdistan); they were bombing everywhere, they were going to Romania to get training. But when I started university, in the first two years we were not involved in such illegal activities. We were involved in activities like publishing a journal, organizing conferences, meetings, etc.

> ...In our second year, we had gone to Newruz[4] celebrations. But we didn't face any problem, because at that time the state was also implementing mild policies. There was such an atmosphere. Because of the withdrawal, there was no news of 'martyrdom' on TV. A student to go to the 'mountain' to join the PKK! Never heard of it... Had I come to know

[margin: The effects of disposition to violence on his entry in PKK]

this organization five years ago, I would definitely not join. I mean I was influenced by that peaceful environment. Post-99 period was the reason for my entry. If they asked me to throw a Molotov in the first days, I would definitely not go. I was never arrested by the police when I was at the university; had I been arrested, I could split earlier ... or had I seen violence."

...If it were the years 2002 or 2003, meaning if I saw what happened in those years, I would most probably not join. For instance, there was a student who used to say that 'politics, culture, etc., they don't mean anything; they are empty stuff ... everything was for the war in the past.' He was right; they would demand everyone to go to the mountain; even those who have been in the organization only for two years. MKMs (Mesopotamia Cultural Centers) were the same. Take a look at the post-99 period; you won't come across a person who went to the mountain. But before that there were plenty. In those days the atmosphere was like that. Those, whose Kurdish consciousness was high, would join the PKK within one or two years, even if he went to university. And within two years, he would die. People who are familiar with the PKK know this ... this is called as the philosophy of death. *Philosophy of death will be analysed in Chapter 5 for its effects on disengagement*

What is crucial in Azad's life history is that he did not grow up in a dysfunctional family, though the relationships within the family became tense after his mother's death. Despite his Kurdish-Alevi identity, he was able to transcend the inherent compulsions that could lead to an exclusive behavior in his interpersonal relationships with religiously conservative and nationalist people. This means that he did not "demonize" other groups, which would be expected of most people who joined the PKK. According to his own accounts, his predisposition to non-violence, his charismatic friend Harun at university (idealization), and the timing of his entry (the year 1999 when "peace doves were flying" in Turkey with respect to the PKK violence) played a significant role in his entry into the PKK. As he mentioned several times during our conversations, the overarching psychological reason for his entry to the PKK had to do with his need for belonging and search for camaraderie. In this respect, it is possible to say that his case is similar to the cases of Hakan-R and Ahmet-R, whose paths to political violence, too, were marked by their quest for meaning and significance.

Case 3: Savaş-P

Savaş grew up in a village of an eastern province in a poor family whose subsistence was based on a few cattle and some crops. His parents were illiterate and he had six siblings (four sisters and one brother). On the other hand, his parents were very religious, *Family and political socialization* which demonstrates that they had no sympathy towards the PKK, which has historically distanced itself from Islam, except for several periods when it tried to instrumentalize Islam for its purposes. Having suffered serious economic difficulties, Savaş became frequently frustrated and felt deprivation. "I was having problems at the time because I was looking at other people who had many things, but we didn't ... I was often asking myself why?" These economic problems, in fact, had significant impact in his decision to join the PKK. When he was around 18 years old, he fell in love with a girl in the village but because of his inability to provide a substantial dowry; her family rejected his marriage proposal. In a few months, she got married to someone else; but Savaş could not get her out of his head. He could not accept the fact that she was married to someone else. After several months, he even sent a message to her saying that even if she was married; he wanted to "steal" her.[5] Unfortunately, although having feelings for him, she did not accept his offer, which left Savaş in a very difficult mental state. He explains the events and his feelings by saying:

The institution of 'dowries' had important ramifications with respect to social structures

> In fact she had also wanted me. But people said, 'If you steal somebody's wife, it means it's an invitation to your own death.' However, I was not afraid of this. I sent her a message with my sister in law; I said I wanted to steal her. But, she said she couldn't do this. However, I couldn't stand this; I couldn't get her out of my head. My brother in-law said, 'Forget about this, it's finished.' At that time, I said for the first time that I will go to the mountain [to the PKK]. I cannot live in this village, and had I not gone to the mountain, I would have to go to the army within one year anyway. There was no other solution; I couldn't stand seeing her face. I lived like that for a few months; my family was giving me money and other things to keep me busy. But eventually, I went to the mountain where I stayed for eight years.

Turning point – significance loss and entry into PKK

Apparently, Savaş was an unlikely *voluntary* candidate for joining the PKK for ideological reasons. But economic problems created first a relative deprivation and then a deep significance loss, stemming from his inability to provide the dowry for his love, which prompted a significance restoration. As he grew up and lived his whole life in a village, the easiest escape, and thus the most readily available means to restoration of his significance, appeared to be the PKK. Another alternative, in fact, was its complete opposite that meant joining the army, but it was one year away from this psychological conundrum. It was a valid curiosity to ask whether he would still join the army if his service time were closer. I did indeed ask, but he said he did not know what he would have done in such a case.

Concluding remarks: turning points as "triggering effect"

In this chapter, I tried to explain the Turkish Penitents' journey to political violence by focusing on a sequence of different phases in their life continuum. My findings suggest several important points with regard to their separation stage based on my ROP model. First, the Turkish Penitents' entry to both the PKK and revolutionary groups was a product of a *process* consisting of various phases, i.e., their childhood and adolescence, their experiences in education and schooling, their political socialization, radicalization, and entry. Each phase within this process was of crucial importance in terms of their effect on my informants' entry to their respective groups, but the level of the effect of each phase varied in each individual. For some, early life experiences seemed to have played the most crucial role (e.g., in the cases of Gökhan-R and Soli-R, their dysfunctional family structures), while for another the phase of political socialization during adolescence (e.g., Recep-P's exposure to political violence). Second, despite the similarities that I will summarize below, there is high level of heterogeneity with regard to the ways (pathways) that led the Turkish Penitents towards their respective groups. Even my small sample size shows that they traveled different pathways that ended in political violence, even within the same group, be it the PKK or revolutionary groups. Hence, I argue that it is quite difficult to make predictions as to whether an individual is likely to become involved in political violence or not based on the same approach. This approach, however, can still be useful in that it provides a general idea about joining violent groups and emphasizes the importance of each and every phase within the "separation" stage in understanding an individual's eventual participation in the armed struggle.

The most important finding of this chapter is that the concepts of *significance quest* and *significance loss* played an important role in all of my informants' paths to political violence, either in their radicalization or entry phases. "Significance quest" was the main motivation for two of my informants from the revolutionary groups (i.e., Hakan and Ahmet) and one of my informants from the PKK (i.e., Azad). Whereas, all of my remaining six informants who joined their respective groups voluntarily were deeply affected by a "significance loss" which prompted a "significance restoration," culminating in their joining criminal or their respective groups which seem to have manifested themselves as viable instruments for significance restoration. An important issue here, however, is that significance loss emerged for different reasons in each of my informants, e.g., for political, economic, or psychological reasons, and affected them in different phases during their processes towards political violence. For instance, Recep-P's personal exposure to state violence, coupled with the national trauma of the Kurds, created a significance loss during his political socialization phase, whereas in the cases of, for instance, Gökhan-R, Soli-R and Savaş-P, significance loss arose as a result of psychological problems during their childhood and adolescence. In any way, my informants' losses of significance were prompted by their life experiences, which I call "triggering turning points."

These turning points, in turn, had important ramifications on my informants' transition from one phase to another in their paths to political violence. In some cases, a turning point was marked by negative experiences with persons (actors), in other cases by negative life events (factors). Thus, I believe that an equally important focus must be placed on the links and transitions between the different phases in the Turkish Penitents' separation stage. To this end, I embark on the notion of "turning points" envisaged by Sampson and Laub (1993) based on life history data of 1,000 men, for turning points led to both incremental and abrupt changes in my informants' paths to political violence, and often functioned as a determining factor in their transitions from one phase to the other.

Sampson and Laub (1993) propose a sociogenic approach in which they argue that turning points, along with social capital, are important concepts in understanding changes in the adult life course (302). Their main goal indeed is to advance a framework that would challenge theories of crime that "presuppose a developmental determinism in which childhood experiences set the course of later development" (1993:302). Their first argument in such a framework is that "social bonds in adulthood – especially *attachment to the labor force* and *cohesive marriage* (or cohabitation) – explain criminal behavior regardless of prior differences in criminal propensity" (1993:304). In other words, they contend that "pathways to both crime and conformity are modified by key institutions of social control in the transition to adulthood (e.g., employment, military service, and marriage)" (1993:304). The authors emphasize, however, that the occurrence or the timing of discrete life events is not sufficient to create these transitions; instead they emphasize the quality and strength of social ties in these transitions. For example,

> employment by itself does not necessarily increase social control ... It is employment coupled with job stability, commitment to work and mutual ties binding together workers and employers that should increase social control, and all else equal, lead to a reduction in criminal behavior.
>
> (1993:304)

Another key point in their framework is its dynamic nature whereby "the interlocking nature of trajectories and transitions generates turning points or change in the life course" (1993:304). Put differently, although there is a connection between childhood events and experiences in adulthood, turning points can modify life trajectories, as the authors argue, they can "redirect paths."

As indicated above, these authors placed a greater emphasis on the importance of marital attachment and job stability as turning points in terms of understanding the decrease in adult crime.[6] Building on a similar line of thinking, I found that in my study turning points also played significant role in the Turkish Penitents' lives as "triggering events," especially on their transitions from one phase to another along the continuum of their "separation stage," i.e., their paths to political violence. To illustrate this, consider the following examples from my data.

Some authors have argued that

> in traumatized individuals the emotional and psychological overload from traumatic events becomes so intense that a psychological boundary is passed inside the individual in which he becomes extremely vulnerable to those who would encourage him to make terrorist acts – especially those who use a religious and nationalistic ideology to motivate him to martyrdom.
> (Speckhard and Akhmedova 2005:130)

Hakan-R's earlier personal exposure to violence, i.e., his own subjection to torture at the police station when he was a high school student, did indeed move him from being a politically conscious person to a leftist radical. Interestingly, however, it was his secondary trauma caused by the humiliation of his father by the police that functioned as a *triggering event*, catapulting him from radicalism to the heart of the group he joined. It appears that the beatings he endured and the humiliation of his father pushed him beyond all senses of psychological normalcy. Similarly, Recep-P's secondary exposure to violence while he was in the village coupled with his personal subjection to violence by the police in Istanbul were the most significant turning points in his journey towards political violence in the PKK.

In the case of Gökhan-R, he had several turning points until he became a member of a revolutionary group. The first turning point for him was his experience in his childhood with three children who stole the money that he earned by selling shortcakes. For Gökhan-R this was an unforgettable event as he explained it was quite a heavy weight for a child to see the fruit of his hard work being taken away from him. The second turning point was his encounter with a leftist person while he was in prison who constantly talked about leftist ideals and politics. Although it did not play a direct role in his entry to the group, it undoubtedly created a political awareness within himself. The last turning point he had was his meeting with the revolutionary groups while he was working in a teahouse in the city of Izmir. The overarching determinant factor for his official membership in his group was perhaps this last turning point given that those groups showed him the moral agents of his lifetime suffering.

For Hikmet-R the most important turning point was his brother's capture by the police, which gave him no choice but to take his brother's place in his revolutionary group. In the case of Fatih-R, his father's ultimatum pushed him towards the group; but it was the shootings when he was in a coffeehouse that triggered his radicalization, solidifying in turn his loyalty to the group. In Azad-P, the most significant turning point was the rejection by a girl he fell in love with, which compelled him to make a choice between attending university and serving in the army. With the influence of his friends, he chose to go to university at the age of 26 (very late by Turkish standards) where he finally met with people from the PKK. The crucial turning point indeed was his meeting with a charismatic student Harun whom he adopted as a role model. Thus, it is possible to say that his idealization of Harun not only facilitated his entry to the PKK because of his quest

94 Separation stage

for significance, but also solidified his loyalty to the group afterwards, leading to his extended stay in the PKK.

I will not prolong this list here as I emphasized above in the side notes to life-histories when and how turning points influenced the paths of my other informants towards political violence. The crucial point is that explaining different phases in my informants' separation stage is a necessary undertaking in deciphering their processes of adoption of political violence; but exhibiting the transitions (turning points/triggering events) between these phases is a *sine qua non* for a full understanding of their motivations in becoming a member of a terrorist organization. For, as my informants made it clear, in the absence of these turning points they would probably taken different paths instead of political violence. All in all, the Turkish Penitents' paths to political violence were characterized by a process consisting of various phases that include their experiences in childhood and adolescence, schooling, political socialization, and radicalization. The transitions from one phase to another in this process occurred as a result of cumulative experiences obtained in the aforementioned phases and individual self-reflection and they are marked by different turning points. I shall now turn to my exploration of the Turkish Penitents' lives within the groups by discussing their perceptions and internal dynamics of the groups, the causes of disillusionment and departure from their respective groups (paths from political violence) and finally, the difficulties and resources related to disengagement.

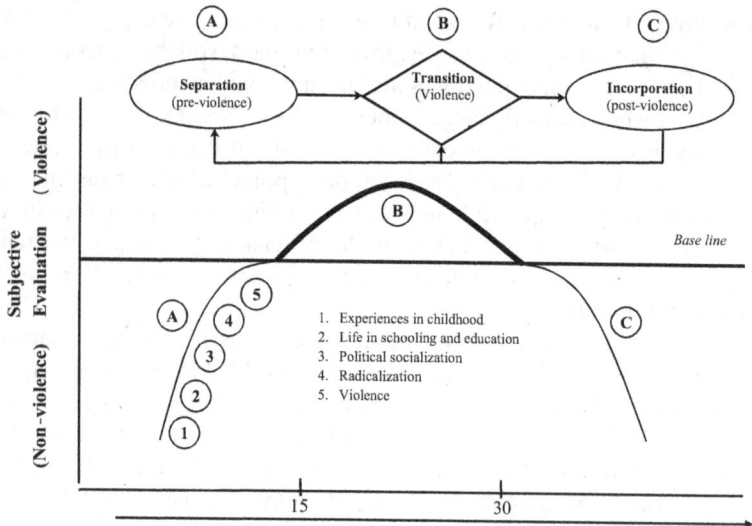

Figure 3.1 Rite of passage (ROP) model for political violence

Table 3.1 Separation stage – Turkish Penitents' paths to political violence

Name	Group	Family situation				Education		Political socialization (e.g., awareness of ethnic identity)		Turning points		Radicalization and entry into the group			
		Stable	Un-stable	Loving	Un-loving	Negative experiences (e.g., abusive teachers)	Positive experiences	In family	In school or other (e.g., prison)	Effects of individuals	Effects of events	Significance quest	Significance loss: Personal trauma	Significance loss: National or collective trauma	Involuntary or forced recruitment
Zilan	PKK	×		×		×			×	×					×
Selim	PKK	×		×		×			×						×
Nadir	PKK	×		×				×			×				×
Savaş	PKK		×	×		×			×	×			×		
Recep	PKK	×		×		×			×	×	×		×	×	
Azad	PKK			×				×	×	×					
Gürkan	PKK	×		×				×				×			×
Hikmet	Rev.	×			×					×	×		×		
Gökhan	Rev.		×			×			×	×	×		×		
Ahmet	Rev.	×		×					×	×	×	×			
Hakan	Rev.	×		×		×			×	×	×	×	×	×	
Soli	Rev.		×		×	×			×	×			×		
Fatih	Rev.	×		×					×		×		×		

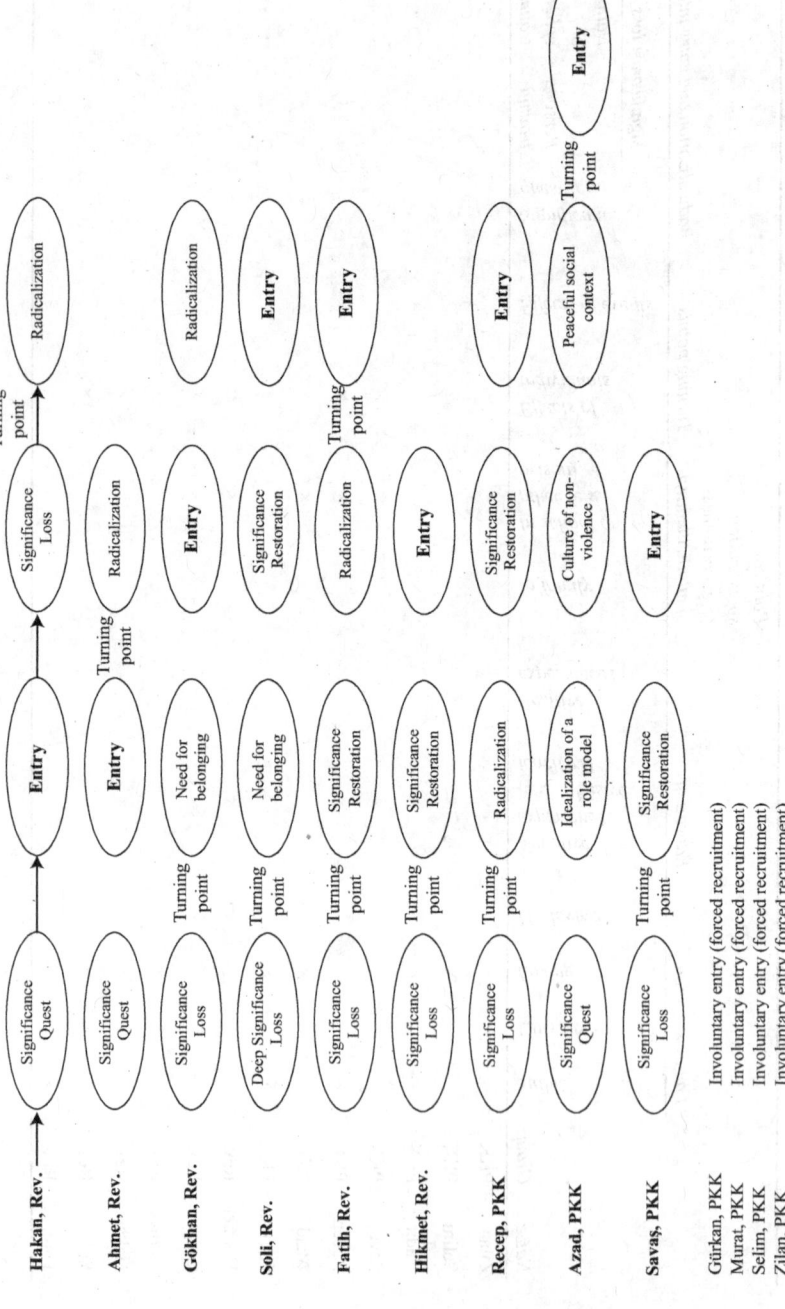

Figure 3.2 Turkish Penitents' processes towards political violence

Gürkan, PKK   Involuntary entry (forced recruitment)
Murat, PKK   Involuntary entry (forced recruitment)
Selim, PKK   Involuntary entry (forced recruitment)
Zilan, PKK   Involuntary entry (forced recruitment)

Notes

1 I do not mean his official, ritualized entry, which occurred after his radicalization. The point I make has to do with his voluntary involvement in the activities of his group which took place before his radicalization.
2 As implied in my analysis here, in the separation stage of Gökhan and Soli, I took them as "moral patients" who have the ability to *experience* things. As we shall see, however, in the next chapter in the discussion of their exit from the group, while Gökhan will be conceived as "moral agent" of his own salvation (exit from the group), thus having the ability to do things (*agency*), Soli will still be seen as a "moral patient" but in this case as the "receiver of good" by God.
3 In Turkey, military service is compulsory for every man when he reaches the age of 20. But Azad was skipping it illegally, meaning that he could be caught by the military at any moment when he was compelled to make *this* choice.
4 Newruz means the Kurdish New Year. It is also one of the letter days for the PKK, on which it is usually expected to strike with deadly attacks.
5 Bride stealing, or bride kidnapping, has been also a common practice in especially eastern parts of Turkey.
6 Turning points were also crucial in the Turkish Penitents' disengagement processes from political violence. Thus, this concept will be revisited in Chapter 6.

4 Transition stage I

Life in the PKK and revolutionary groups

This chapter and the next two chapters are about the Turkish Penitents' transition stage, i.e., how they describe their lives within groups (current chapter), their causes of disillusionment and release from them (Chapter 5), and difficulties and resources related to disengagement from political violence (Chapter 6).

The inner workings of terrorist groups have always been mysterious not only to society in general, but even to their sympathizers, generating a great curiosity in people to know what is really going on in such groups. In the case of the PKK, for example, the "mountain" as a mystical place has always been at the heart of political discourse in Turkey, but the extent of our knowledge about its internal dynamics remained limited. In the case of urban revolutionary groups, the same issue has been linked to their enigmatic cellular structures. My interviews with the Turkish Penitents were invaluable in that they enabled me to glance what is "behind" the mountain and what is happening in those clandestine "cells." They also allowed me to situate my informants within these social contexts and to understand their grievances about them, which contributed significantly to their disengagement from political violence.

As a theoretical construct to understand my informants' lives within, and their paths away from, political violence, I use the concept of *situated learning* in *communities of practice* through *legitimate peripheral participation*, envisaged by Lave and Wenger (1991) as an alternative and contribution to earlier theories about learning. The core idea of their theory is the relationship between learning and the social situations in which it occurs. As William Hanks explains in the introduction of their book, rather than defining learning as the acquisition of propositional knowledge, "Lave and Wenger situate it in certain forms of coparticipation" (1991:14). In other words, learning takes place in participation in daily life and is "situated" in a process of engagement in a community of practice. The basic argument about communities of practice, on the other hand, is that they are everywhere, at work, at home, in doctors' offices or religious congregations, public events, and so on. Interactions in all of these settings involve limited, but highly asymmetric forms of co-participation designated as legitimate peripheral participation (1991:18).

These concepts will be deconstructed shortly, but I should state at the outset that rereading of Lave and Wenger's theory after my fieldwork sparked immediate interest in terms of its applicability to Turkish Penitents. First, it was readily apparent to me that the whole lives of my informants in terrorist groups were, in fact, about learning as it is expressed by one of the informants, "A guerilla's daily life is nothing but about learning." Second, the learning process they were involved in was not only cerebral, i.e., it was not taking place in the mind of the individual, but in the activities in which they participated while in their respective groups. Put differently, their learning was about "becoming" an integral part of a community of practice. The only difference from ordinary communities of practice was the notion of violence; thus, I conceptualize my informants' lives in terrorist groups as "lives in communities of *violent* practices." Second, given that the chief focus of this book is on Turkish Penitents' disengagement, I felt that Lave and Wenger's theory was a perfect tool in order to account for their renunciation of political violence, for I realized that most of the reasons leading my informants to leave their groups appear to have sprung from the *problems* and *contradictions* that are inherent in the concepts of communities of practice and legitimate peripheral participation. These issues and contradictions emanate from unequal power relations within the groups, from their teaching curricula for identity transformation, and last but not least, the problem of access to partial or full participation.

Legitimate peripheral participation in communities of practice: an overview

The notion of situated learning contributed greatly to a body of literature in human sciences that explores "the situated character of human understanding and communication" (Lave and Wenger 1991:14). According to Lave and Wenger, the individual learner is not acquiring a discrete body of knowledge in order to transport and use it in later contexts. Based on this approach, learning does not take place in an individual mind, but in a participation framework, which means, *inter alia*, that it is mediated by the differences of approaches among the coparticipants (1991:15). The authors call this participation framework as communities of practice, some of which have formal organizational structure, while some are very fluid and informal. Within the community of practice, members are brought together by joining common activities and by their newly gained knowledge in their mutual engagement in these activities (Wenger 1998). From this perspective, a community of practice exhibits discrepancies from a community of interest or a geographical community in that it involves a shared practice.

In explaining the ways in which individuals participate in a community of practice, Lave and Wenger coined the term "legitimate peripheral participation," a process that is the central characteristic of learning as a situated activity. By legitimate peripheral participation, the authors meant to "draw attention to the point that learners inevitably participate in communities of practitioners and that the mastery of knowledge and skill requires newcomers to move toward full participation" (1991:29). Moreover, legitimate peripheral participation offers opportunities to understand the relationships "between newcomers and old-timers, and about activities, identities, artifacts, and communities of knowledge and practice" and to speak about the ways in which "newcomers become part of a community of practice" (1991:29). More importantly, learning through legitimate peripheral participation takes place regardless of the type of educational form providing a context for learning or the intentionality of individuals to learn in such contexts. This is indeed a fundamental distinction between learning and intentional instruction (1991:40).

Before moving further, I shall make the definitions of these concepts more explicit given that the authors suggest, "each of these concepts is indispensable in defining the others and cannot be considered in isolation" (1991:35). What is the meaning of legitimate *versus* illegitimate, peripheral *versus* central, and participation *versus* nonparticipation? Briefly, the legitimacy of participation is about the defining characteristic of ways of belonging. With regard to peripherality, the authors express that

> there may well be no such simple thing as 'central participation' in a community of practice ... [because] peripherality suggests that there are multiple, varied, more or less engaged and inclusive ways of being located in the fields of participation defined by a community... Peripherial participation is about being located in the social world.
>
> (1991:35–36)

In other words, insofar as the continual interaction of "new perspectives in communities of practice is sanctioned, everyone's participation is legitimately peripheral in some respect ... [and] everyone can to some degree be considered a 'newcomer' to the future of a changing community" (1991:117). Lastly, in terms of participation, the authors argue:

> Legitimate peripherality is a complex notion, implicated in social structures involving relations of power. As a place in which one moves toward more-intensive participation, peripherality is an empowering position. As a place in which one is kept from participating more fully – often legitimately, from the broader perspective of society at large – it is a disempowering position.
>
> (1991:36)

The nuances between the aforementioned terms have important ramifications for understanding the Turkish Penitents' processes of disengagement, which I will explore in the next chapter. I shall now focus on my informants' lives in communities of violent practice, by describing their lives within the mountain and groups' cells, their activities and tasks, as well as their goals and aspirations.

Turkish Penitents' lives in communities of violent practices

Before addressing the question of what it takes to move from partial to full participation in terrorist groups, it is a valid undertaking to explore how individuals become members, what type of activities they engage in, and what full participation entails in a community of violent practice. Despite the apparent analogical similarities, there are striking differences between my study and the five studies of apprenticeship[1] Lave and Wenger (1991) examine in their book in terms of membership, the technologies employed, the forms of recruitment, the relations between masters and apprentices, the organization of learning activity, what is being produced, what is learned by the members and participants to become a master, etc. The crucial question related to my informants is, "to become a master in what?" A novice Vai apprentice ceremoniously becomes a member and attends tailoring workshops to become eventually a master tailor. To this end, his journey towards full participation in craft production equips him with the necessary knowledge and skills. In Alcoholic Anonymous, a newcomer to the meetings of AA starts from a negative position to a positive one, i.e., a drinking individual to a non-drinking one. Considering the activities that individuals participate in terrorist groups and their destination in such groups, my informants, perhaps, present semblance only to meat cutters, in the sense that productive activities and mastery in both involve "killing," "cutting," and a lot of "blood." I do not mean to be facetious, but becoming a part of a group immersed in such activities is quite puzzling to an outsider, having many implications on the notion of fundamental human motivation of protecting the integrity of individual body. To make sense of *this* seeming "nonsense," the role of ideology and operating in a "group psychology" become indispensable in that they conquer individuals' inhibitions in terms of both putting the integrity of one's body (self) at risk and taking others' lives.

Life in the PKK: membership, the domain and goals

As mentioned in the previous chapter, some of the Turkish Penitents from the PKK joined the group voluntarily while some of them were thrown into the group through forced recruitment at the beginning of 1990s. Membership in the PKK occurs almost automatically around the age of 15 regardless of intentional or contractual (involuntary) entry into the group, given that individuals are thought to be bound together by a common denominator, i.e., Kurdish identity. This is not to say that legitimacy of membership is not questioned, given that members are asked constantly to prove their loyalty and attachment to the cause. I will come back to this issue later in the discussion of "access to participation" in terrorist groups.

Membership of the PKK is obtained voluntarily or through recruitment in three different domains: (1) in an urban environment within the borders of Turkey; (2) in rural areas both within Turkey and beyond, mostly in Northern Iraq; and (3) abroad including European countries, Russia and, to a lesser extent, the countries in Central Asia. In all these domains, individuals engage in different trainings and activities that have important effects on terms of the notion of disengagement. However, since almost everyone in these three groups has to go through a training on the "mountain," (that is, the PKK camps located today predominantly in the

102 Transition stage I

Qandil mountains in Northern Iraq), and given that most of my informants from the PKK spent their time on the mountain, I will focus more on the inner workings of it here as well as how it affected my informants' processes of disengagement in the next chapter.

When a novice arrives at the mountain, he is received warmly by the old-timers and the leaders because he is viewed as a "new warrior" who is ready to sacrifice himself for the Kurdish cause. During the first couple of days, he is allowed to rest, for the journey to the mountain usually takes up several days in the company of alternating couriers starting from the city centers, continuing through difficult terrain mostly on foot or riding mules, and ending on the mountain. As soon as they arrive at the mountain, newcomers start to sketch out the enterprise, as Lave and Wenger put it, to understand the "culture of practice" which include who is involved; what they do; what everyday life is like; how masters talk, walk, work, and generally conduct their lives …what other members are doing, and what members need to learn to become full participants" (1991:95). In this sense, the first impressions of the newcomers regarding mountain conditions are important, which in fact differ significantly when the time of their entry and place of origin are taken into account.

Before the year 2000, in particular, physical conditions on the mountain were said to be quite dire, but those who came from villages and who were used to village conditions seemed to have easier time than those who came from an urban environment. Newcomers in the latter group were more likely to experience a culture shock. As my informants mentioned, there was no toilet and no bathroom in the regular sense, and there was not much to eat. For breakfast, they ate lentil soup; for lunch, various types of pasta; and for dinner, lentil soup again. There was almost no fruit or dessert, and more importantly, this menu did not change for a long time. The most luxurious and readily available provision was tea. I should add that the scarcity of food affected female guerillas more than males.

After the year 2000, the conditions were said to have become relatively better because of the financial support the PKK obtained through various sources, including fees collected from Kurdish businessmen both voluntarily and by force, from various foreign governments, as well as from drug trafficking and organized crime in the city centers within Turkey and abroad. Azad, who joined the group in this period, expressed the new conditions by saying, "When I arrived, I couldn't believe my eyes ... They had even built dams, giving electrical power to the nearby villages. I said to myself 'what a powerful organization this is.'" Regardless of the time of entry and place of origin, however, one important first impression common to most newcomers is that people who stay on the mountain for some time look quite different, or as one of my informants put it, they look "wilder" than normal people. Besides this wildness, the presence of blind people, deaf people, or amputees does not escape the attention of any newcomer as they become aware that such disabilities are the probable consequences of spending some time on the mountain. These, however, appear to be the more preferable outcomes given the fact that a sizable number of the "new warriors" die within a couple of years in clashes with the Turkish military.

After several weeks, the novice is initiated more formally into the group in a two-fold process. First, he is asked to write his life history on paper and hand it in to the group leaders, and second, to stand up and tell his life story in front of the group members. These talks are quite important in terms of the transformation of identities and their impact on my informants' disengagement, but I postpone this until the next chapter. The whole structure on the mountain is organized on the military lines including a system of hierarchical ranks, types of training, or hierarchical nature of the relationships among newcomers, old-timers. and leaders. Thus, a typical day on the mountain is only slightly different from one in a military compound. The day starts at 5 am with roll call followed by a breakfast; from 5:30 am to 9 am guerillas take their positions as "ready battalions" in case there will be a raid by the Turkish military; from 9 am to 12 pm there is theoretical training; from 12 pm to 1 pm they have lunch; from 12 pm to 5 pm theoretical or military training; at 6 pm dinner; from 6 pm to 9 pm theoretical training; and at 9 pm they go to bed. Male and female guerillas have separate dormitories but they all receive training under the same roof, which they call "the school."

The inductive training usually takes about four months, which starts with a class on "cadre" and "education" in the PKK. The former focuses on the genealogy of the group in which historical figures and events are examined, whereas the second course is designed to explain the goals of education in the group. More specifically, the teaching curriculum is divided into two sections, "theory" and "practice." The theoretical section includes history of socialism, philosophy, world history, history of Kurdistan, history of the party, leadership (meaning the personality and ideas of Abdullah Öcalan), public movements, cultural history, the influence of culture on mass movements, etc., while the practice section focuses on the group's history of war, which is dubbed as "history of self-defense." Depending on the importance of the class, different time-slots are allocated for each class, which ranges from four to ten days.

Learners are tested for each class with three questions. The first question aims at testing their general knowledge, while the second focuses on group's historical periods. The most important question is the third one through which learners' analytical skills are evaluated. The main goal of this approach is to teach learners how to make a "reductive" analysis. The theoretical curriculum is designed impress some learners as they perceive it to be "enlightening" and "empowering," whereas others regard it as an escape from heavy practical training. Since there is usually a "reassignment" (*düzenleme*) after each training session, some members try to put their names on the list for those sessions in an effort to change their current locations. The group leaders see this approach as "pragmatic" and criticize it harshly.

On the other hand, there is almost no leisure time, except for watching the news on TV for a short period before going to bed.[2]

The tasks that the guerillas undertake look also similar to those carried out the military service; e.g., manning the posts, cooking, and housekeeping, etc. In terms of duties, there are different divisions, which include military, logistics, security (responsible for guarding those captured by the group), training, and so on. Horgan argues that "for some roles, the leadership of terrorist groups will often place a psychological premium on certain high profile roles, aside from the "reward" of granting membership more generally in the first instance" (2005:86). In the PKK, the most prestigious roles are in the military division for it is the most important path for promotion in the group by way of demonstrating one's bravery, dedication, and loyalty. The crucial task of the military division is to attack Turkish military posts. Carrying out such attacks in a continuous manner is not feasible, but they still have to stay vigilant all the time lest the Turkish army attack them. This means that a significant portion of their time on the mountain is allocated to waiting, i.e., "idleness" permeates life all the time on the mountain, which has significant influences on the "disillusionment" of PKK members in the sense that idleness leads to psychological burn-out of individuals and degeneration of interpersonal relationships among guerillas, old-timers, and leaders.[3]

The distribution of tasks and duties on the mountain, in fact, are important but quite puzzling. Fathoming what the notion of full participation entails and what is being produced in the PKK is an extremely difficult task. Does full participation for the learner mean learning the necessary skills to kill the "enemy," which is equally dangerous for him because of the inherent risk of his own fatality? Alternatively, does full participation mean becoming an old-timer and thereby escaping largely from the encounters with the Turkish military? Does production mean production (or construction) of an independent Kurdish nation through violence, as the PKK originally claimed but changed it over the years? More importantly, what are the "intrinsic rewards" (Lave and Wenger 1991:111) of full participation in a terrorist group? The list can be extended, but as far as I understood from my interviews, answers to these questions differ depending on individuals' ideological and psychological backgrounds.

For those ideological guerillas, full participation means engaging in practices that will eventually emancipate Kurdish men and women who are believed to be oppressed and subjugated by the Turkish state. For them, killing human beings does not seem terrifying at all and it is justified because of their "dehumanization" of the enemy; and the salience of their own mortality as a result of such activities, too, is not important given that the same activities promise immortality through martyrdom. For others who join the group for psychological reasons, e.g., individuals who see the PKK as a refuge because of their psychological problems, the foregoing analysis applies but this time for psychological ends, i.e., the meaning of full participation means being immersed in violence that guarantees one's own death.

However, considering those who join the group involuntarily, the meaning of all terms associated with communities of practice shifts significantly. Such individuals try, if they can, to remain a *legitimate member* but only a *partial participant* in violence and in all kinds of relations and activities from the beginning, because they seem to have at the outset the idea of leaving the group when opportunities arose. Since they do not believe in the ideology of the group, they try to be assigned to divisions like training, facility management, or logistics.

The last division is more desirable because of the possibility to get in touch with "ordinary" people and the chances of escape it provides.

Life in revolutioary groups: membership, the domain and goals

Membership in revolutionary groups in Turkey occurs also on a voluntary basis and recruitment starts around the age of 15; and the activities that members engage in usually take place in an urban environment. Unlike the PKK in which membership becomes legitimate through a common Kurdish identity and starts usually upon arrival at the mountain, in a revolutionary group, members generally come from all walks of life and there is a *blurred line* between a sympathizer and an actual member. Individuals who sympathize with the leftist ideology, thereby think that Turkey's social, economic, and political problems can only be solved through a revolution, find themselves engaged in various activities, most of which are legal at the beginning such as attending debates at student clubs, distributing leaflets, journals, or newspapers promoting socialist ideas, etc. Once the individual is thought to be reliable and ready to do more, he is usually initiated into the group more ceremoniously than in the PKK, by gathering around a table and taking the socialist oath in front of a *small* group of people in one of the group's cells. This last point is important as it dominates the whole lives of people in such groups, i.e., a revolutionary's life is spent usually within the society but because of the associated illegality, it must be lived invisibly. Not surprisingly though, this cellular structure of revolutionary groups is one of the most enticing features that facilitate the attraction of potential recruits towards the group.

On the other hand, compared to the members of the PKK, members of revolutionary groups in Turkey seem to be more ideologically oriented, in that they dedicate their lives to *the* revolution. In this respect, production in revolutionary groups means the reproduction of the idea of a socialist revolution in the minds of people every day through participation in political violence. Thus, for a novice revolutionary, the most important goal is to equip himself with the necessary knowledge and skills to become a full participant in such a reproduction. However, when the influence of ideology is diminished, or lifted, the secret lifestyle starts to become unbearable and this leads to the disillusionment and disengagement of group members which I will discuss in the next chapter.

I will allocate the remaining part of this chapter to my focus group interview with Fatih and Ahmet, two of my informants from the same revolutionary group. Their ideas in this interview illuminate various issues to which we are not privy, such as life in revolutionary groups, interpersonal relationships within them, their cell-structures, their *modus operandi*, and so on and so forth. Thus, I prefer to place the relevant excerpts from our conversation below "as it is" without a detailed interpretation.

Case: focus group interview with Fatih-R and Ahmet-R

Anthropologist: Can you talk about the cell-structures in revolutionary groups? How does it work? When did you use such organization in your group?

Fatih: Well ... We worked in a cell-type for several years, at the beginning of 1990s when the incidents had reached an apex. At that time, we followed a cell-type in theory and practice. I mean, every team member stayed with one or two others in an apartment. This applies to the members of the military committee, but other committees did the same as well. For example, the political committee which was responsible for political practices such as writing and publishing, as well as other *ad hoc* committees that were throwing Molotov cocktails, printing and hanging banners and placards, etc. Their cell-like activities were based merely on a specific practice; not in the sense of sharing the same apartment for 24 hours. But we ... I mean, everybody has an area of work; some in the region A, some in the region B and, some in region C. They were pursuing political and organizational activities in those regions. Each of these A, B, and C regions has a leader and there is another leader who is responsible for the A, B, C regions as a whole. However, these individuals have a maximum of one or two hour meetings every day or every other day.

Anthro: Where do they stay at other times?

Fatih: They live in the regions in which they work and, if they are not followed by the police, they live in the houses of their "contacts." I mean, they live in the houses of their parents, uncles, or other relatives. But if there is a search warrant issued for them, they live with their distant relatives or their contacts.

Anthro: Do you mean that not every member lives in the cells?

Ahmet: They may stay but if they are seriously followed by the police.

Anthro: So, in that case, are you using what's called "extreme protection measures"?

Fatih: Sure. In that case, the group first rents an apartment. Second, it finds a couple among the group sympathizers and convinces them to move to the apartment that the group has just rented. Third, it places the group member in this apartment, telling the couple that he/she will act as their child. The bottom-line is, they become a cover for that group member. But if the group member is in a more serious situation [i.e., requiring extreme cover], he takes a female group member with him, finds an apartment and lives with her as a married couple. He institutionalizes himself in this way. Alternatively, he finds a girl studying in the big cities whose parents are living in the village. He tells her that he will take care of her if she agrees to live with him. This is another way to institutionalize one's self.

Institutionalization in a terrorist cell

As I said before, we had some cells at the beginning of the 1990s when the military activity was at its peak. Let me explain how the cell structure is thought out. Let's say, there are five people in a cell. Two apartments are rented for these people; two of them stay in one apartment, while the other three stay in the other. They are together for 24 hours.

Anthro: Do these people know each other? I mean, the members living in the same cell but in different apartments...

Fatih: These five group members know each other, but they don't know where they live. Only the one who is responsible for the apartments knows the location of both apartments. This individual is the cell leader; he doesn't give the location of the apartments to other group members. To summarize, one cell consists of two apartments; two stay in one apartment and three in the other. Sometimes, a cell may be composed of three individuals, but as far as military committees are concerned, three individuals are not sufficient. Military committee cells usually comprise five group members who are cognizant of all activities they are supposed to undertake. One among these five individuals is the cell leader who can meet with the group's senior leader. The other four members cannot see this senior leader. These senior leaders, on the other hand, constitute the higher committee of the group. In addition, why do we need five individuals in a cell? Imagine that the activity is not directed at an individual but at the state, i.e., to the police or soldiers; three people will be insufficient to pull it off. That is why, five people is ideal for such actions.

Anthro: Does this senior leader see the cell leaders separately?

Fatih: Yes, but if he wants he can bring all of them together sometimes. It depends on the situation at the time...

Anthro: In this case, it means four individuals participate in the meeting. Do they all know each other and what they do?

Fatih: They know for sure. For instance, he knows that one of them is the leader of Beyazıt region; one of them, the

108 *Transition stage I*

     leader of Topkapı region; and the other as the leader of Şişli region. But they don't know the specifics of what they do on a daily basis, as well as the exact locations where they live. Only, the senior leader knows all of these. They work like this …

Anthro: So, can you explain life in the cells, for instance how is life in the apartment in which three group members live?

Fatih: It depends on the position of the individuals. There are usually newcomers and old-timers among these individuals. In the first couple of months, old-timers teach newcomers how to adapt themselves to the cell, that is, they teach them how to institutionalize themselves. To specify, they teach how to live in the cell without attracting the attention of outsiders, how to protect yourself from police surveillance and from people in the vicinity… While they do these theoretically in the apartment, they go out in groups of two in order to teach them through practice. They constantly do surveillance or practice how to escape from surveillance. In addition, the newcomer learns how to do intelligence in the company of an old-timer. *[Life in the cell]*

Anthro: What exactly do you mean by intelligence?

Fatih: Let's say there will be an action against the police. First of all, you need to know who the target is; you have no information in your hand.

Anthro: Who is giving this information?

Fatih: Sometimes, it comes from outside. They might have found a name and address from miscellaneous group channels. That information is raw information; they say, take this info and clarify it. This needs to be done, because around 40 percent of such intelligence is inaccurate, while 60 percent is accurate. But many problems arise during the implementation of this accurate intelligence. Anyhow, the group says clarify this intelligence and report back to me so that I can do my plans. Within the cell, some people do these clarification activities while others implement those military practices. There is usually list of such activities that are implemented by the cell members who are in charge of the military activities. To sum up, most of the cell members are busy with the issues of institutionalization, e.g., protection from police surveillance, working discipline and other general issues about intelligence. Others who are more advanced, on the other hand, are involved with activities that are based on more sophisticated intelligence. *[Daily activities in and out of cell]*

Cell members usually leave the apartments at 8:30 am in the morning and return at around 5 pm in the evening, as if they are working somewhere as a normal worker. They either do not go out of the apartment, or if they do, they follow the aforementioned schedule. They return in the evening. Even if they finish their work outside, they don't come back at 12 pm, for example. They wait until the evening. They must return at the same time every day; they have to give an impression that they have a normal working schedule. They can come back at a later time, but not after say, 9 pm; because of the members of the military committee, it is very dangerous to wander around in the street at night. Since the streets are quiet at night, it is easier to be detected by the police. As I said, they have to take care of their work when there is crowd on the street and retreat to their homes like a normal citizens. How terrorists cover themselves

Anthro: Can you explain more; how is life in the apartment?

Fatih: There is division of labor in the apartment. Some people deal with the cooking and housework, while others have their personalized training. There are also collective training sessions. A daily schedule is made, which must be followed by everybody. If you woke up at 8:30 am, you would have to read if you are not going out to gather intelligence. You have to take notes while you read. In brief, everything is scheduled at home; you wake up at this time, take theoretical training at this time, and military training at that time. By military training, I mean theoretical and practical training, as much as the conditions of the apartment permit. For example, there is usually training on how to assemble and disassemble weapons, how to prepare and execute actions, etc. Besides of these, you read books constantly; you cannot wait idly. Life in the cell

Anthro: As far as I understood, life usually passes with training. Is this so because it is not feasible to commit violent actions all the time?

Fatih: I mean, in principle, the main task of a group member in the military committee is to gather intelligence and prepare for action. In particular, those military committee members active in urban environments dedicate the most of their time to prepare for action. The remaining time is allocated to carrying out the action.

Anthro: Let's say you have an order for action. How long does it usually take to prepare and act?

Fatih: That's the easiest part. He [the military committee member] finishes the job within one day. Because it became a habit for him, he does the necessary preparation and, if there is to be a bombing, he goes and finishes it within one day. Or, he can do something else, such as armed robbery, murder, etc. But I am talking about old times; it used to be very simple back then, only today have they gained enormous importance. I mean, they used to say 'you are going to bomb certain institutions like banks, big enterprises or the like ... these take only a couple of days. But, there are more serious actions, say, against the army, the police, or MİT (Central Intelligence Agency). Or, actions against specific transfer points... These require special preparation. Otherwise, normal bombings do not require much time and planning, because there is constant preparation anyway. Specific places are previously designated and earmarked, which can be bombed when necessary. [Preparation for action]

Anthro: Did you stay in one of these cells?

Fatih: I stayed for a while, before escaping from prison. I stayed during the most active times of the group. I stayed with the Istanbul military committee of my group, together with ... and ... . After a while though, I left that apartment, saying that I don't understand these things. Such a lifestyle is not for me; you are going to sit down, prepare for military action, blah blah blah. I said I couldn't do these ... I said, I am impatient and what you want requires patience. For instance, we had a friend whose name was ... . He was very patient; he could kill the day by working with a needle and thread. I can put up with this for half an hour; then I get bored. I told them that I am a man of the streets and left the apartment.

Anthro: I see. So, do any problems occur between the newcomers and old-timers in the cell?

Fatih: Yes of course ... Problems arise not only between newcomers and old-timers, but among old-timers as well. If there is woman, for instance, there definitely arises a problem. This happens usually because of an emotional relationship. And before you know it, you see that they started to have sex and stuff like that. This did not happen so much in the old days. [Interpersonal relations]

Anthro: How many female group members are there usually in a cell?

Fatih: In general, there is one woman and two men. But sometimes there can be three men in an apartment. When she is engaged with one of the men, problems arise with the others. If she has an emotional relationship with one of the men, others usually do not look askance at her. But if another man has a crush on her too, there may be problems. He displays his discontent indirectly, day and night. I should add that most of such relations are emotional, not sexual. If it occurs, what does the group do? The group punishes them, demotes them to the zero-level and sometimes sends them to the mountain. I mean, it takes care of itself as soon as possible. In the old days, there were few problems like that, because most of the group members were quite mature individuals. They transcended such things; but if they occurred, the group used to deal with the problems as I explained.

Anthro: So, can you talk about the allocation of tasks and responsibilities? What kinds of tasks are given to the newcomer, for instance?

Fatih: The tasks depend on the situation. Let's say there is a novice, who has just joined student associations, legal or neighborhood organizations. Old-timers watch closely the newcomers' activity in those places. In particular they follow and test their energy, courage, knowledge of theory, etc. The leaders receive reports from the superiors of the newcomers as to what kinds of persons they are. In these reports, there is information about the foregoing issues, in addition to information about their character traits and skills. More often than not, newcomers are closely supervised and trained based on these reports. After a while, they are definitely sent to actions and tested this way.

<small>Tasks of newcomers</small>

Anthro: When a person is assigned to a certain duty, does it create any change in the person?

Ahmet: Sure. It is possible that his responsibilities increase, even if he is not a member of the cell; for example, he is sent to the "student field" from "neighborhood field." However, if he cannot be successful, he is called back … And by neighborhood field, I mean the activities to organize shopkeepers and neighborhood residents.

Anthro: How does this work? I mean, don't they go out and knock on people's doors?

Fatih: It is simple. You are living in that neighborhood anyway. You are a member of the neighborhood. So, you start with establishing relationships in public places like coffeehouses, sport centers, etc., and move on to their houses.

Anthro: But, if there is a search warrant issued for you, aren't those people afraid of this?

Ahmet: Yes you are right. But those for whom a search warrant is issued do not do such work. Neighborhood organizations are created by their legal members. How do they do it? They do not simply say "Hi" and invite them to destroy the existing regime. They find an entry point, say, for instance, the neighborhood has a problem. They try to attract the neighborhood person by using various ideological arguments and narratives, such as notions of unjustness, inequality, etc. Or to be more specific, let's say there is a sewage or telephone exchange problem. They approach them with arguments like "You are going to have cancer" or "You are going to die," if we don't do something about it. When the whole neighborhood's attention is directed to those issues, naturally some individuals come to the fore. Then, you try to convince those individuals and recruit. The same method applies to the student societies as well. Each society mobilizes people by utilizing their own problems. Turkey is full of issues anyway …

Fatih: This, in fact, is the most important issue. First of all, there are many issues of discontent that you can use in Turkey. Second, somebody gets up and rightfully expresses his concern about the telephone exchange, saying that it will cause cancer. Then, five people follow, and they start shouting on the streets. The police come and break the heads of these people. At that point, the damage is already done! You don't have to ask those people to be the enemy of the state. I mean, there are many problems like that. That is the major difference between Europe and Turkey. The state is acting differently nowadays, nevertheless. But if you really want, you can find enough problems, although they will be ineffective because we don't have an established system yet. For example, *ergenekoncus* [plural of *ergenekoncu* means those who are charged with involvement in the "alleged" Ergenekon Terrorist Organization] are in jail. But, for instance, Tayfur Havutcu [a famous soccer coach] is taken into the custody for "match fixing" and released in a couple of days. The same happened with the soccer player who is a relative of the Prime Minister's wife. I heard that when he was taken into the custody, the police chief provided him with his own bed so that he got some rest. He was released in the morning anyway; he did not even remain

> Modus operandi

in custody for 24 hours. This definitely makes people angry; even an ordinary citizen is aware of such things …

Anthro: What do you think about the improvements made in terms of democratization in the last decade?

Ahmet: I can say that the AKP government did a lot of good things in terms of democratization. Otherwise, explosions similar to those during the Arab Spring would occur in Turkey as well. Today, everything can be discussed in Turkey, which is good …

Fatih: For example … If the AKP had not started to implement its conciliatory policies several years ago, people [ordinary Kurds] would have exploded over the KCK operations. The mild rhetoric that the AKP adopted, in fact, created spaces for Kurds. What's more, the state does not attack ordinary Kurdish individuals. Unlike previous governments, it does not say "Why did you support the PKK." It deals with the higher echelons and lets people talk. It doesn't touch them; otherwise a civil war would have already begun in Turkey.

Anthro: I see. So, I am curious to know something … Let's say there is a bombing; how does the person who executes this action feel when he returns home? For instance, remember the bombing in Anafartalar Shopping Center in Ankara; the scenery is bloody and graphic. How does he feel in such a situation?

Fatih: Let me give you a personalized example. Sometime in the past, we blew up the office of " … Syndicate," which was located near the National Police Headquarters, the Ministry of Interior, and other government buildings. We went to their office, tied up approximately 20 people who were working there, placed them in a secure place so that they would not be hurt and then blew up the whole floor. The building was located in one of the main streets; so, if someone threw a stone at the window and broke it, we would have finished.

Anthro: Why?

Fatih: Because we were very close to the police headquarters. We would be caught.

Anthro: How many of you were there for this action?

Fatih: There were four of us. One of us was wearing a police uniform, because the target place was a special, protected one … He knocked on the door; they opened it and after that we entered and tied everyone up. The building had six floors; we were on the top floor. And then …

Perception of contemporary Turkish politics

Anthro: What message were you trying to give?

Fatih: The message was this: in that year, ... organization was the most effective group in Ankara. With this action, we wanted to give a message to both the leftist groups and the state, saying that we, too, are in Ankara. " ... organization is no longer in Ankara, gather around us." This was the message. Moreover, the location we selected was intentional; it was the heart of the state. We wanted to say, "We have infiltrated your veins." Of course, we did our planning accordingly, making sure that risk was minimum. We did not want to lose any group members. As I said, one of us went ahead of us in police uniform; if they asked, "Who are you?" we would have been finished. The risk was very high, which is why the organization did not want us to execute such an action. I said, "I will do it." I gathered people together and the idea of a police uniform occurred to me at the last moments of planning. We also thought thoroughly about how to place the bomb. I put a long wick on it so that we had enough time to get out of the building before the explosion. It worked; the bomb exploded one minute after we left the building. To make sure that this would work, I had sent somebody to rehearse the whole process of leaving the building without using the lift. We did not use the lift lest we would be stuck in it. All in all, the bomb exploded with a thunderous sound. That was our purpose anyway; to create a sensation ... [Purpose of actions]

Ahmet: At the same time, we bombed a similar institution in Istanbul. But we did not know about the simultaneous action, only the leaders knew about it. But anyway, the bombing in Ankara resonated greatly within the group and in the country in general.

Fatih: So, we left the scene and I took a cab home. But on the way, I got out and called the group leader. He said, "Have you done all preparations?" I said, "We finished it already." He was very surprised but excited, and he congratulated us. I mean, how can your psychology be like? I returned home, thinking that we pulled off an action in Ankara that was dominated by ... organization. We had such audacity ... We were overcome by such a spirit for a while as we started to persuade people to gather round us. The organization was also explaining how we undertook such an action in Ankara. You could carry out similar actions in Istanbul, but you couldn't get

Anthro: 　the same reaction from the masses. For, the masses are inured to such actions in Istanbul anyway.

Anthro: In that action, nobody died right? If someone died, would you be upset?

Fatih: No, nobody died. If someone died, our morale and motivation would plummet to zero in a minute. As a group, if somebody was our target, we killed them. But we were never involved in indiscriminate and haphazard killings. In recent years, this rule might have changed little bit, but it did not happen in the old days. With regard to the killings, our philosophy is this: if we denounced someone as guilty or a criminal, that person could be killed. But if others, too, were killed together with our target, that action was considered to be an "unsuccessful" one in group assessments. In our history, there is no action in which we put a bomb in a navel. If innocent civilians die, you lose anyway. Such actions are not carried out by the leftist groups in general; instead, the PKK and religiously-motivated groups used that method frequently. They legitimize the killing of innocent civilians in some way. But since leftist groups base themselves on humanistic rhetoric, you cannot explain such actions ... You have to know that if you do it, it means you shoot yourself in the foot. Post-action psychology

Anthro: Imagine that a PKK member carries out an attack in which 100 people die. What's more, there are Kurds among the casualties ... How would he feel?

Ahmet: In that case, it would be the same ... He would be happy regardless of the killing of Kurds. He sees them as collateral damage and says, "What can I do? My people died as a result of this action but my target was Turks." He does not feel any distress, because he legitimizes the action, which is carried out for protecting the rights of Kurds. But among the leftist groups, you cannot have such discussion. Let's say you planted a bomb in a police house and caused the killing of women and children. You cannot say that they deserved to die because they were also guilty... There is no such action on the left. If you want to carry out such an action, you place the bomb when there is nobody there. Of course, there may be several officers on duty who may die; it can be justified ... Post-action psychology: comparison of the PKK and revolutionary groups

Anthro: As far as I know, leftist groups carried out a lot of raids on police and military stations, during which many officers died. What goal did you try to achieve with those raids?

Ahmet: Yes we carried out such raids. But not too many... Our goal with those raids was to create awareness of the issue of torture, which was endemic especially before the 1980 military coup and at the beginning of the 1990s. We wanted to prevent those officers from torturing us when we were taken into custody.

Anthro: Let me put the question differently; which actions are carried out by the leftist groups and for what purpose?

Fatih: We divide the types of actions into several groups. For instance, at one time, a campaign was launched against torture and torturers. First, various academic papers about torture were written, which were followed by writing graffiti on the walls. Then, placards were printed and hung in various locations. Step by step... Then, illegal demonstrations were organized, police checkpoints or stations bombed. Finally, at a certain point, a police chief could be killed. [Purpose of actions]

Anthro: Since this person has a symbolic value, everybody gets your message...

Fatih: Yes indeed. This incident takes place in every venue associated with your group and you claim responsibility for the action anyway. As a second example, I can mention the IMF policies... Let's say that the IMF will impose on us numerous policies that will lead to austerity measures, i.e., downsizing in business and governmental institutions. A campaign is launched against it as well. All syndicates are against this anyway. You may follow the steps I enumerated above in order to show your discontent. In particular, you first make a list of institutions that are associated with the IMF, banks, associations, business enterprises, etc., which constitute an "economic target" as a whole. During the demonstrations, businessmen set the police at the demonstrators. Then you start attacking those businessmen. Another example pertains to the conditions of students. You may organize events to protest against the YÖK (Higher Education Council), for example. You can attack various institutions affiliated with the YÖK or the Ministry of Education. I mean, the actions you plan are directed to relevant institutions.

If the 1990s conditions still prevailed in terms of leftist groups, they would attack on the police and prosecutors in big cities because of KCK operations. You may ask what you have to do with the Kurdish issues and the PKK. I would say it doesn't matter ... Leftist groups killed General Hulusi Sayin and General Ismail Selen, too. We would kill anyone who is oppressive, because we don't see the victims simply as Kurds; we see the whole Turkey as the victim. If Kurds say they want to be separated, we reject it though. We'll tell him or her that there is no Kurd or Turk; we are all one and the state destroys us without discriminating between us. The crux of the issue has to do with the problem of the "oppressed." So, what I mean is, by utilizing such a line of thought, actions of the leftist groups today would be directed against the police and prosecutors. There cannot be any action without a purpose. There are many opportunities for action in Turkey anyway…

Anthro: But don't you think that sometimes terrorist groups order attacks without a purpose in order to revitalize their members who have been idle for a while?

Fatih: Yes it is possible, but not in Turkey … You may organize actions like that maybe in Europe, in Germany, for example. But you don't need that in Turkey. For instance, imagine the people of the Black Sea region today. They were assimilated by the Turkish state but previously they were the staunch supporters of the left. If I go to the Black Sea region today, I could easily organize them around the notion of HES (Hydro Electric Stations). I can revitalize the democratic masses as a whole around this notion, because even those who vote for the religious and nationalist parties are against the construction of those stations. They say "I won't give my house whatever it takes." So, I can get their support by organizing some action on their behalf. And those people don't care about who you are; the house owner pays attention to the fact that you saved his land. More importantly, if I carry out such actions, the state cannot delegitimize me no matter what it does. However, if I organize actions against KCK operations, it could be claimed and people could be convinced that my actions are illegitimate, unfair, and planned to obscure these operations. People could also be convinced that I am a terrorist because of the reasons I explained with regard to the relationship between the state and KCK operations. But in the final analysis, I don't think leftist groups today have the power to regain the support of the masses by utilizing the problems linked to the construction of HESs. They can participate in the democratic demonstrations in Taksim Square, but they don't have the power and effect to revitalize themselves around such notions. They are almost irrelevant today…

_{The end of the Turkish left}

118 *Transition stage I*

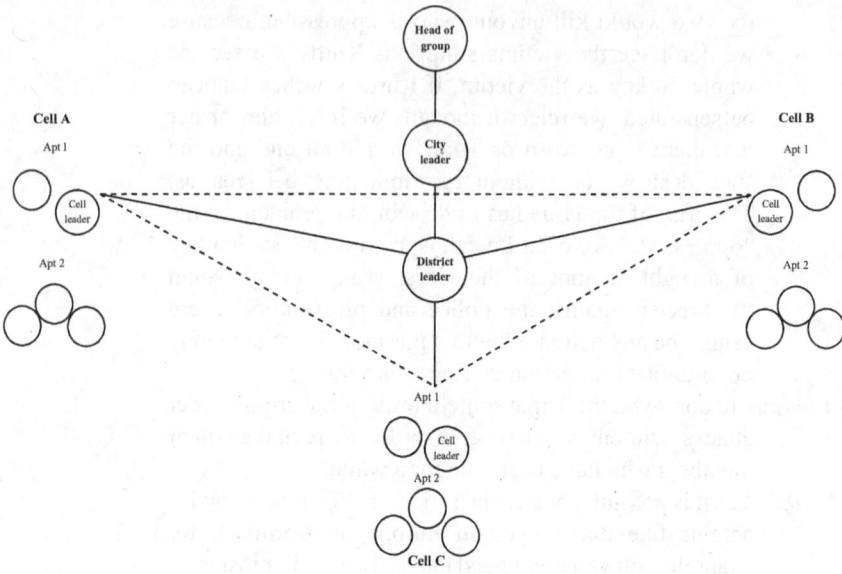

Figure 4.1 Cell structures (networks) in revolutionary groups

Notes

1 These five studies of apprenticeship entail: (1) Jordan's study of Yucatec Mayan midwives; (2) Goody's study of Vai and Gola Tailors; (3) Hutchins' study of naval quartermasters; (4) Haas' study of meat cutters; and (5) the study of Alcoholic Anonymous. See Lave and Wenger (1991), pp.59–84.
2 Most of my informants mentioned that the existence of a TV on the mountain does not mean that mountain conditions are good. As they suggested, the TV is the most luxurious thing on the mountain which came only several years ago, and its use is extremely limited and depends on the discretion of group leaders.
3 In times of ceasefires, the negative influences of idleness are felt perhaps at its extreme. For instance, the PKK had announced a ceasefire that lasted for five years, starting with Öcalan's capture in 1999 and ending in 2004.

5 Transition stage II

Causes of disillusionment and exit from the groups

> If you scrape the ideology off the surface, what you get is the human being.
> (Gökhan-R)

As I explained in the theoretical section at the beginning of the previous chapter, most factors contributing to my informants" disillusionment and exit from their respective groups seem to be related to the *problems* and *contradictions* that are inherent in their legitimate peripheral participation in communities of violent practices. In an effort to decipher these problems and contradictions, this chapter will be divided into several sections. In the first section, I will explain how conceptualization of learning as didactic teaching and indoctrination by the groups I studied backfire. I will then delve into the nature of the "goals" of the subject groups of this study, by which I will attempt to demonstrate the impact of what I call "the postponement of the utopia" on the Turkish Penitents" disengagement. Finally, I will explain how the problems of access and sequestration while being a participant in a community of violent practices led to their disillusionment and exit from their respective groups.

Didactic teaching and indoctrination: the PKK and revolutionary groups as "cults"

Some of the aforementioned problems and contradictions related to participation in communities of violent practices can be found in the following areas: (1) interpersonal relationships within the groups, particularly between leaders and members; (2) group leaders" approach to learning as didactic teaching; and (3) transformation of identities through indoctrination. As Lave and Wenger argue, when the community of learning in practice is viewed as a form of apprenticeship, the nature of relationships become triadic: "the community of practice encompasses apprentices, young masters with apprentices, and masters some of whose apprentices have themselves become masters" (1991:57). In the terrorist groups I studied, the triadic relationships include newcomers, old-timers, and the leaders. Because of the strict, vertical structure of the groups, it is almost impossible for a newcomer to be a leader, though he might have chances to become an old-timer. In particular, this difficulty is exacerbated by the number of PKK members, which has vacillated around 5,000 any given time since its inception in 1978. Leftist groups have been historically smaller, their sizes ranging from several hundreds to 1,000. This is important in terms of access in becoming a master participant in these groups, to be explored towards the end of this chapter. For now, I will focus on the perception of the leaders on learning.

Lave and Wenger distinguish between a learning curriculum and a teaching curriculum. A learning curriculum is described as "a field of learning resources in everyday practice from the perspective of learners" (1991:97) whereas a teaching curriculum is constructed for the instruction of newcomers. "When a teaching curriculum supplies and thereby limits structuring resources for learning, the meaning of what is learned (and control of access to it) is mediated through an instructor"'s participation, by an external view of what knowing is about" (1991:97). The learning curriculum in such didactic situations, then, takes the form of a prescriptive view of the target practice as a subject matter, in which educators act as "pedagogical authoritarians" viewing apprentices as novices who "should be instructed" rather than as peripheral participants in a community engaged in its own reproduction (1991:76). In so doing, they aim to achieve two things: First, they want to make sure that the learner "internalizes" knowledge given to him; and second, they attempt to transform the identities of newcomers in such as way that newcomers make the culture of the group theirs.

In light of these arguments, it is possible to argue that both in the PKK and in revolutionary groups, learning is too easily construed as an unproblematic process of absorbing the given, as a matter of transmission and assimilation. Like Alcoholics Anonymous (AA), they use various processes in an effort to reconstruct the identities of newcomers, processes that can be found in cult-like structures. To specify, as opposed to other studies of apprenticeship in which identities are reconstructed for a positive end, identities in terror groups are reconstructed through indoctrination such that non-violent identities of newcomers are transformed into violent ones. In the PKK, this transformation takes place in the form of a top-down imposition of its ideology on its members, whereas in revolutionary groups, identities are transformed largely through engagement, persuasion, and negotiation. In both cases, however, it is possible to see certain aspects of cults. It is now my task, then, to explain what the term cult refers to and to illustrate the simulacrum between cults and the groups I studied.

The term cult "refers to a group with a given belief system, to a specific way of recruiting its members, and to the way it exerts control over the lives of its adherents" (Alexander and Rollins 1984:1). In cults, the autonomy of individuals is surrendered, which may lead cult members to exhibit robot-like behavior. Alexander and Rollins suggest that a cult can be identified by two variables: (1) its ideology; and (2) its methodology, while adding, "All cults may share a methodology, but they do not share a theology [ideology]" (1984:1). Proceeding from this idea, they argue, "There is agreement in the literature that cults use some or all the techniques identified as thought reform" (1984:1). Given that most of my informants talked about various thought reform techniques that their respective groups use, I will examine eight different techniques of thought reform used by the foregoing authors, which are indeed slightly modified version of Lifton's (1961) early work on this concept. I will enumerate below the relevant ones to my study and give examples to demonstrate how the PKK and the revolutionary groups use them and how they affected my informants" processes of disengagement. In particular, my informants' experiences prove, as suggested by Salter, that indoctrination is inefficient even though it is seen as a necessary condition for producing terrorists (2008:63).

> *Milieu control*; where control is established over the person's environment. Usually this refers to the individual's" communication with both outsiders and members within the cult group. Careful control is exercised so that the individual is put into situations where the reality that he or she experiences can be defined by other cult members. The purpose of this control is to keep the content of the group's ideology as the dominant reality.
> (Alexander and Rollins 1984:2)

Milieu control influences group members in the PKK and revolutionary groups in two ways, the first of which has to do with the structure of these groups. Because of their size and clandestine natures, these groups can be called as close-knit social networks (Bott 1957) based on fictive kinship. According to Bott, a close-knit network is described as "a network in which there are many relationships among the component units" (1957:59). One of the most important characteristics of close-knit networks, on the other hand, is their power in terms of exerting social pressure on their component units to conform. Bott elaborates on this phenomenon by saying:

> The networks of the component families are so closely connected and the relationships within the local group are so clearly marked off from external relationships that the local population can properly call an organized group. Families are encapsulated within this group. Their activities are known to all and they cannot escape from the formal sanctions of gossip and public opinion. The group to which they belong governs their external affairs.
> (1957:99)

A second way in which milieu control affects group members is linked to groups" conscious efforts in that regard. That is, the groups maintain milieu control especially by way of labeling recalcitrant members as "subjective" or "objective agent." The former term is used for those who are thought to have harmed the organization by their mistakes or failures in groups' operations. Since their loyalty and good intentions are not questioned, such individuals are said to be labeled as a "loose cannon" and receive minor punishments in that they may be asked to do a "self-criticism" in front of other members and to promise that they will be more careful and not repeat the same mistakes in the future. The latter term, on the other hand, is used to define people who are thought to be "traitors" because they collaborate with the "enemy," i.e., the Turkish state. Since a majority of its members spend their time in the group on the mountain, this type of labeling in the PKK is frequently attached to members who attempt to escape from the mountain but fail to do so. I should, in fact, note that this tactic is still being used by the PKK. To give an example, in an attack on 20 September 2011, three PKK militants killed four women and wounded two, who were en route to a celebration dinner in the city of Siirt. At the crime scene, the police found 114 cases of Kalashnikov bullets and two hand grenades. On a website close to the PKK, the group announced that this incident was a "mistake" and an investigation was launched against those three guerillas. After the incident, I called one of my informants from the PKK and asked what would this investigation entail and he responded by saying,

> Nothing ... these individuals will just be labeled as "subjective agents" and be asked to do self-criticism because of the fact that this attack on civilians damaged the image of the group as a "self-defense" institution; but it does not mean that these militants will receive severe punishments as in the cases of objective agency.

In revolutionary groups who are usually active in an urban environment, individuals are called traitors if they are thought to be displaying bourgeois behavior, or especially if they are thought to be criticizing the group, its ideology, and modus operandi.

In cases of being labeled as "objective agent," the punishment is more severe and, more often than not, the person who is labeled as such ends up being executed, as one of my informants said, after a "phony" trial run by "unqualified group leaders." According to Çiçek (2009), more than 3,000 PKK members were executed in this way. In order to increase their deterrent effect, the trials and executions are implemented transparently in front of all group members, or in ways that could be heard by all members even though they are not seen. In addition, specific to the PKK, the milieu control included even the houses and families of its members. Especially in the first half of the 1990s, if one of its members managed to escape from the mountain, representatives of the group's urban wing (militias) would go to the house of that member in the town or city and force the family to give another son or daughter of in place of the one who escaped. In order to illustrate the points made hitherto, I invoke Nadir's narration. He was one of my informants from the PKK.

Case: Nadir-P

> In place of those who escaped, they would take another child from the family. I mean, it is a very difficult situation because those who escaped are married and have kids, which need to be taken care of. Albeit being reluctant, the father has to send another child. If the escaped person was a girl, they would take another girl from that home. This is quite difficult for

us culturally; if my sister was on the mountain, I would go so that she could come back home. The PKK knows this weak point and exploits it considerable. I mean this practice continued for a while; they were replacing escapers with other family members. However, after that, they changed tactics and started to kill those who attempted to escape. For example, there was a guy from our village whose name was Suat. He tried to escape from the group but the group chased him in the field and he was caught. They put him on a platform and said, 'He is a traitor. He would escape and surrender himself to the enemy. He would give information to the enemy. Instead of allowing him to harm our group, we will harm him.' He made such political statements after which he made the verdict; he said, 'He deserves to be punished by execution' and added, 'We will do the same to those who attempt to follow his path.' He wanted simply to deter us. That squad commander fired four shots; there were about 200 of us watching the incident. That guy was about my age [around 13 at the time]. He was my childhood friend. We are mute because we are terrified. We want to cry but cannot cry ... We don't have any power to oppose their decision anyway. What can we do? We are compelled to say, 'Yes, you are right. He deserved this punishment.' Anyway, they killed him, dug a hole, and 'threw' him inside. There was no funeral, no ceremony, no grave; they just covered him with dust, just like that ... and we moved on. They do this consciously; and the newcomers went into a state of panic right there..."

After two months, people started to escape again. Some of them were from the nearby regions, so they were able to escape because they knew the terrain very well. However, they caught two of them who had come from different regions. He [the commander] said, 'Are you stupid? Haven't you had enough lessons yet?' I mean their goal was to silence us, but it is difficult to talk about these. Only those who witnessed would believe these things, others don't believe. I didn't know that person, but the choice of execution ... I think that choice could not be made that simply anywhere in the world. One of them was newly married and had a child, while the other was still single. They [commanders] said a few words, but we knew what they would do.

Their hands were tied up behind and they took all of us to a rocky place. There was a deep hole, like a cave in there. First, they threw a small rock in it; we heard the sound of the rock hitting the ground only after two minutes. Its diameter

Description of an execution

was about two meters but inside was very dark. It must have been so deep that we heard that sound after two minutes. They kicked one of the guys into that hole; 'Alive!' They did not shoot and kill him before throwing him in. They closed our eyes, but we all heard his scream, which I cannot forget to this day. They shouted at us, 'Are you afraid?' We were petrified but couldn't say anything. Since they were scrutinizing us by looking into our eyes, we said we were not afraid. The other guy started to scream and beg, 'Please don't kill me, I have a child. I promise I am not going to try to escape again.' However, they did not pay attention to what he was saying. They threw him too into the dark hole. We did not hear anything from him; I guess he died in the air ... So, they executed like that. Then they made an admonishing speech, saying that you will end up being like them if you try to escape. They said, 'We, too, have lives. We are same like you; why do you think you are privileged? We, too, have fathers and mothers, but we are here for our homeland. We have a cause ... You will turn yourself over to the enemy, which exploits us for centuries.' They made such political remarks. The bottom-line was, 'You have two choices: You will be with us, or else we will kill those who try to escape ... we will do this even if you go to Şırnak or Istanbul.' They were making such terrifying propaganda.

Furthermore, the mountain conditions in the PKK were quite difficult, especially until the year 2000, and organized in such a way that members were cut off from other people. Individuals felt as if they were living in a bubble, in an abstract environment devoid of anything presenting a semblance of real life. A member's only chance of seeing another human being depended on his duties in the group, i.e., people in the logistics division could go to the nearby villages to get supplies where they would interact just a little bit with normal people. Nadir-P's case exemplifies this:

> Personally, it was my third year into the group that I saw the first civilian. I was together with them [the PKK members] all the time. This is really difficult, I mean ... You live in an abstract environment. The only sound you hear is the sound of animals and passenger planes at night ... and sound of weapons. There is nothing else. There is no TV, no radio. Newspapers are forbidden. You cannot see anything, you cannot know anything about the outside world. Now, the situation is quite different, there is even the internet ... So, we were living in such an environment, we saw no civil person. We wouldn't know what was going on in the world

or in Turkey. Their goal was to objectify us, and make us like robots. They wanted to produce wild humans who do not think and know anything. The main goal was to nihilate and exploit us according to their needs. You cannot follow the developments in the world. You have to do whatever you are told by them. You have to go through their channel. Even if we start discussing our former lives ... we would be prevented. They would say, 'Why are you talking about former lives? Hmm, it means you have a longing for your former life ha!' They had such mentality.

Another example for milieu control in the PKK can be found in Zilan's case. Given that one of the most imporant aspects of such control is to keep the content of the group's ideology as the dominant reality and make members *submissive behavior types*, anybody who challenges or criticizes its ideology is punished harshly for specific and general deterrence purposes. For instance, after witnessing the killing of Kurds in Northern Iraq by the PKK, Zilan thought, "These people say they are fighting for the rights of Kurds, but these men, women and children they just incinerated are also Kurds; so I cannot go one step further with these people." This incident, in fact, marked her disillusionment. As a result, she wrote a report to the management saying that what she saw was not acceptable and she wanted to return home.

Case: Zilan-P

I wrote a report to Murat Karayilan [the current operational leader of the PKK] and expressed my wish to go home. He said, 'Are you out of your mind? You want to go home after all these years? You better forget about it. The PKK is a sea and if you don't walk in it, you get drowned. We cannot accept your request; what's more, if it was somebody else, we would kill him/her.' The reason why they didn't kill me was my cousin, because he was killed by the Turkish military. However, they killed several other people who dared to challenge the group. For example, there was an Iraqi girl, whose name was Pervin. They killed her. I cannot forget that moment ... they took her behind the hill and we heard several shots. A close friend said, 'They took Pervin and several others behind the hill to kill them.' When I asked why, she said, 'They wrote reports like you did.'"

The reason why they killed them behind the hill was the proximity; they wanted other people to hear the fate of people who challenge the group ideology. This was a tactic; they take into account the psychologies of other people when doing these ... they were doing this concsiously. After a while, we sensed a smell of a fire and burning bodies. In fact, they had burned the bodies after killing them to prevent putrefaction. I mean, you feel that smell and watch the smoke; all was happening right behind the hill. When I felt that smell, I said, 'Dear God, what wrong I did I do to see this?' There was the smell and smoke of a dead body near me. I could not help myself going to see it. Surreptitiously, I went there. Her clothes and ashes were there. I cried there for about an hour. The way she died was unpleasant for a human being. The pieces of her body were all over the place, most of which were burned except her finger tips. I wanted to touch them, eventually I lifted one of them and touched it faintheartedly. The reflex was sensible even two days after her death. As if she shook my hand; I was frozen ... like an icebox. As if her hand was moving, or I felt like that because of the shock I was in. I cannot comprehend what happened to me. Pervin was a beautiful girl; she was innocent, impeccable ... She was from Iraq, and couldn't speak Turkish. She was very little, may be about 14 years old. Her vulnerability affected me greatly; I was really hurt. At that time, I got really sick. My back was hurting a lot because of an accident I had in the mountain. I started to think as if it was my turn to die. I said to myself, 'get ready.'

Altruism born of suffering (ABS) of others

In the revolutionary groups, milieu control is done a little bit differently, i.e., first psychologically, largely due to the conditions of the urban environment. Like the PKK, the most important means of control is also labeling members who pursue a life different from that dictated by the groups. For example, if a person gets in touch with people from outside the group, and uses the jargon other than the group's, he is severely criticized and labeled as "bourgeois", "police informant," or a person who is "lacks revolutionary personality." The punishment includes also execution, but unlike the PKK it is applied through a serious examination of the case and seen as a last resort.

Case: Gökhan-R

When I entered the group, what I needed was emotional satisfaction. In my life, material interests were secondary to my emotional needs, which is why the leftist narratives looked more appealing to me. In other groups such as MHP (Nationalist Action Party), relationships were more closed; the environment was more official. In such an environment, someone will talk and you will listen. However, in revolutionary groups it is different. I say this in quotation marks, which means, it was indeed the same in those groups too. However, since they maintain a broad spectrum, you don't realize this at the beginning. Only after delving into the group, do you start realizing ... For instance, if you smoke Marlboro cigarette; they say, 'Ooo, so you are smoking Marlboro? You still maintain your bourgeois features. You totally ignore the values of our group.' I mean they control every aspect of your life; they watch what you eat, what you drink ... In addition, they say, 'Learn the thoughts of our opposing groups.' But if you read liberal ideology books, they start to label you again ... Then you say, 'What should I do to prove myself?' The bottom-line is, there are many inconsistencies like these. Their rhetoric was on freedom, as you know ... However, when you start drawing the lines of this freedom, you face several choices: you are either accused of being a police informant, traitor, or of being a person who lacks revolutionary personality.

What is more significant is that the groups use various types of punishments for milieu control, which are perceived by group members to be extrajudicial. This feeling of unjustness creates a state of vulnerability in members of the group, which functions usually as a first "seed of doubt" in the process of their disillusionment with the group and its ideology. After experiencing the first seed of doubt, they seem to find themselves in an irreversible path towards the exit and start seeking for opportunities to realize that. In this respect, considering the fact that the average length of stay of my informants within the groups is around 12 years (outliers being four and 26), and that the time difference between their psychological disengagement and physical exit is about seven years, it is possible to say that the power of milieu control is quite strong and it is one of the most important factors explaining the extended stay of my informants.

Mystical manipulation; Lifton's second technique, involves the personal, social manipulation of the individual. Above all else, the neophyte is asked to trust the group. Members of the group explain to the initiate that they have developed a way to achieve life's "higher purpose." The group has identified and incorporated a special law, a new truth along with a special rule, which is the foundation of their ideology, and hence the basis of the new way of life. By the same token, any thought or question which challenges the goals or methods of the group is defined as coming from a lower or malignant purpose, or that the initiate is exhibiting a stubborn strain which means that he/she does not yet fully accept the group's way. To increase the possibility of achieving trust in the group, the individual is encouraged to participate actively in the conversion of itself. The conversion to the cult is complete when the individual himself sets out to proselytize others. Also included in the idea of social control, mystical manipulation introduces the use of ritual. Ritual works to reduce an individual's focus of attention, and increases the person's susceptibility to emotions. Rituals act as "an avenue to the merging of the self with the cult and the cult ethic." This can create an "orgiastic" sense of oneness of the most intense sort with fellow confessors and a dissolving into the cult or movement.

(Alexander and Rollins 1984:2, internal citations deleted)

In the groups I studied, mystical manipulation is one of the most used techniques of thought reform. In the PKK, I identified several methods of mystical manipulation: (1) the concept of "life" (*yaşam* in Turkish) is used incessantly to describe what "real life" should look like for a Kurdish person; (2) in their training sessions, "story-telling" is used in a ritual-like process of transforming identities, for which life stories of groups symbolic and historical figures are told in a class called "Cadre." More specifically, the lives of the group's "martyrs" are told and retold to the members throughout their membership of the group in order to strengthen interpersonal relationships and create a sense of "oneness" within the group. Similarly, in revolutionary groups: (1) narratives and ideas in published materials are often used to confuse group members, given that writing most of those stories is perceived to require great depth of knowledge and intelligence; (2) the concept of "freedom" is used quite often in order to increase solidarity within the group and reinforce members' illusions about the notion of emancipation of humanity and communist utopia; and (3) narratives of "torture" circulated in the journals and group discussions are aimed at keeping the enmity of members towards the state at its peak.

Mystical manipulation in the PKK

A newcomer to the PKK hears the concept of "life" even before joining the group, but once he is physically in the group, that is, when he arrives at the mountain, he starts to be inundated with the concept until he leaves the group or dies, for that matter. The group does not consider pre-PKK life as life, given that Kurdish people are thought to be stripped of their freedom, which is considered to be a "fact" that they are not aware of. Group leaders argue that a life without freedom is not a life; it is at best a state of lifelessness. In this respect, the PKK is asked to be a movement that defeats the kind of life imposed upon a people [Kurds], a life that indeed is worse than death. The life that the group promotes today instead is a *Democratic Confederation System* that will belong to Kurds, in which they will weave their own freedom. In this process, the PKK claims to be a bridge to this life system.

This idea of "life system" has many implications for the group's life. For example, until the life system is reached, sexual relationships are strictly forbidden and no one is allowed to start a family. In fact, this rhetoric resonates in most of the group's members as stated by one of my informants, Azad-P:

> He [the PKK leader Apo] says, 'You will definitely have a relationship and a family when you have established a free country, a free society and a free

world. Let us say you established a family in which you will have children. However, in Turkey, there is no education in Kurdish. So, do you have the right to give birth to that child?' It is like a person who is begging on the street with a kid. More often than not, we resent the fact that he/she bore that child, because he/she put that child's future in jeopardy. This analogy is used so often in the group, in order to make group members internalize this; I mean the life system ... In fact, most people internalize it; they find it to be believable. 'Your homeland is not free; there is no 'life' there. You don't even believe in it yourself; how can you add one more person to it?' This is the logic behind the life system spoken in the group.

Second, martyrdom is one of the most important concepts in the group, frequently used to create a sense of oneness by instilling an emotional intensity in the group's members. Because, as Kruglanski *et al.* suggest, "a martyr is not an anonymous militant who carries out a mission, and whose name remain unknown ... a martyr is a volunteer who will be remembered by his fellow countrymen through photographs, posters, murals, and plaques exhibited in public places" (2007:12). To this end, in the PKK, stories of historical martyrs are narrated in a ritual-like format. Like the concept of life system, the stories of martyrdom are aimed at keeping the group together in that the place of martyrs in the group's structure is regarded by Öcalan to be above the level of the "leadership." To specify, after his capture in 1999, the group has seen Öcalan as a "personality" rather than a person, that is, he is no longer called as the "leader" but "leadership." I invoke Azad-P once again to demonstrate how the concept of martyrdom is used in the group.

> The group [the PKK] has an ideology and a goal, which is why you are in the group. So if you die while in the group you become a martyr no matter how you die. It has a deep meaning; and martyrs are located very high in the group hierarchy. Even Öcalan says, 'I am subordinate to our martyrs.' For example, to be candid, if a friend of mine from university becomes a martyr while in the PKK, I would feel heartbroken even if I left the group. You remember that I had mentioned a friend from my village; if he became a martyr, for instance, I would probably not leave the group. Martyrs strengthen one's loyalty to the group. I am 100 per cent sure about this ... To give an example, this organization [the PKK] is called 'the school of cadre.' Despite this, there is no discrimination in the group *vis-à-vis* martyrs; Mazlum Doğan has a special place in group's genealogy. He became a martyr in 1983 in the Diyarbakır prison. He burned himself in Newruz [the Kurdish New Year]. [And he adds that he heard another story about his death from the police while in custody.] So, why do you think the organization is not celebrating Newruz like any other special day? Because, the group politicizes the Newruz and gives it a special meaning by associating it with Mazlum Doğan's personality ...
>
> On the other hand, martyrdom is very important for the recruitment of women into the group. When you look at the most notable martyrs, there

is a sizable number of women. For instance, the name of Zilan (*nom de guerre* of Zeynep Kinaci) is very important. She blew herself up in a military compound, killing eight soldiers, remember? And the story of Gülnaz Karataş (code name Beritan) is quite important. Her life, her bravery in defending her squad was even made into a movie. She had not even seen Öcalan, but when she killed herself, she was dedicating her action to him by screaming his name. There are not many men in the PKK that reached their level in terms of heroism. It is an interesting issue, because this movement has existed since 1984, it was a male-dominated organization, but it was a woman who executed such an act after a decade. More importantly, Zilan left a report before that suicide mission in which she wrote, 'If only I had a more valuable thing than my life to sacrifice for the PKK.' Can you imagine, she gives her life but makes such a statement ... it is an extremely powerful statement. I should add in this respect ... that Öcalan, for instance, reads Zilan's letter to a group of people where he says 'these are our commanders, we will follow their paths.' After these examples, the number of female guerillas increased in the group that became, in fact, a driving force in the group. Because men started to say, 'War conditions are extremely difficult, so if women can do it, I can do it too ... I should do even more.'

In order to understand the effects of the stories of martyrdom, when I asked Azad-P how effective they were, what people felt while listening to these stories, and whether they cried, he said:

I mean there is an emotional density, but I rarely saw people crying. It can best be described as an eruption of emotions, which occurs at an extreme level. Another example in this respect is the story of Kemal Pir. His story is very often used in the group. He was indeed a Turk ethnically, and the leader of a faction that had opposed Öcalan at the beginning. He died in Diyarbakır prison as a result of a death fast. He was subjected to incredible torture before dying, and his torturers said many times that they would kill him. His answer was, 'We love life (*yaşam*) to the point that we can die for it.' I mean this resonates strongly with people in the group. What he said indeed became a motto; if a PKK member is subjected to torture, he used that motto. It is very influential in the group. Kemal Pir said, 'this struggle will be won one day; if the only thing in your hand is killing me, I am taking it away from you.' And finally he dies of hunger ...

...There are many statements like this. For instance, I joined in the group in 2001 and heard these statements in 2003. Let us say someone joined the group today, in 2010, no later than several months after his entry will he hear such statements. This can be considered, in a way, a ritual. I mean martyrs are as important in the group as in other communities. When I think of a ritual-like phenomenon in the group, this comes to my mind right away. There is quite a high level of mystic ambience in the organization.

Despite the group's efforts to create such a mystic ambience, however, some of my informants from the PKK pointed to the mismatch between the narratives and the deeds of the PKK. According to Zilan-P for example, although the PKK argues that Kurdish women are oppressed by men and claims to emancipate them in its utopian "life-system," the situation is quite different in the production of that system, i.e., life in the PKK, as she said, "Even women within the group are oppressed by men; so, how can you believe that they will emancipate other Kurdish women?" She adds, however, that some women in the group believe in this rhetoric:

> One day a big fight broke out between men and women in the group. It was a tug of war; men always tried to dominate us and act as our superiors. We did not accept, nevertheless. One of the woman squad leaders said, 'You want women like slaves. You cannot take a woman who acts by her own conscience and who improves herself. You would rather prefer women who will serve you, who will satisfy you sexually. I will not, however, let this to happen. I will create an army, a Red Army, in which all women will be equal to men.'

When I asked Zilan whether female guerillas believed in this, she continued:

> In fact, most of them believed this. To be honest, I liked it too as a woman. However, there was inconsistency within the group in almost everything. Theory and practice did not match; life in practice was not lived like that ... What's more, people had different backgrounds; some of the theoretical stuff did not resonate in everyone in the same way. For example, in the training, they used to talk about materialism or idealism. However, some of the women in the group had come from feudal environments; when you spoke about materialism, they wouldn't understand a word. They were simply stuck ... When they were told that there was no God, for instance, they would say, 'Come on!' They wouldn't understand a person who doesn't believe in God.

Mystical manipulation in revolutionary groups

In revolutionary groups, mystical manipulation is usually done through their published materials, which are both legal and illegal. Because these groups operate in an urban environment, they have to maintain and protect their clandestine structures. To this end, various illegal materials are published for internal circulation, which function as their chief means of communication and manifest themselves as the media for sharing ideas and creating a sense of connectedness among group members. Newcomers and old-timers wake up every morning with an enthusiasm to see what has been written by their masters with regard to the developments in the country and all around the world. The "intelligence," "depth," and the "uniqueness" found in these narratives, ideas, and analyses written by group masters literally mystify group members. Hakan-R explains this phenomenon as follows.

> I became a member of the group, but I have no duty yet. I go to work normally. But after that time [his formal initiation to the group], I started to see more things about the group that I hadn't seen until then. Legal materials go to everyone, but the party's internal journal is not available to the general public. Only members can see and read it. It's indeed a free platform; everybody can write, but you need to be very knowledgeable to have the courage to write ... which is why I remained as a reader for a long time. There are incredible writings about revolution in that journal, which changed my view of revolution and the country. Because even local parties were analyzed and depicted differently ... there were very deep analyses. Just this fact alone was enough of a reason to keep you connected with the group. I mean there were many notes in there about how to motivate yourself, how a militant should live, what a militant should be careful about, what family is for a militant, etc. I mean it is so powerful to the point that it gradually distances you from your family; you think that you have nothing but the party. You even reach to the point where your own parents seem to you your enemy, because they try to prevent you from being with the group. When masters gather information about 1,000 people and write their stories, you tell yourself, 'Wow, look at this guy, he is talking about me, is he an oracle?' But in fact, almost everybody goes through the same processes; since you don't know about them, what they write appears to be too interesting for you. This, in turn, increases your loyalty to the group.

A second tool for mystical manipulation in revolutionary groups is the narratives of torture, for the terms "torture" and "inequality" were the most commonly used concepts by these groups both in their recruitment processes and afterwards in order to maintain the unity among group members.[1] These groups trained newcomers on what needed to be done in instances of subjection to torture. In order not to scare newcomers, they did this gradually, particularly after a newcomer proved his loyalty to the revolution. They warned newcomers against the potential dangers of being a revolutionary. Most members knew that torture was being exercised by the police or military, but until experienced personally, they did not have a full understanding of its effects on the human body and soul. That is why, if a revolutionary was subjected to torture, he was required to tell his experience to his colleagues. This was important in terms of transparency and one's promotion in the group in that it increased the person's reputation in the group in a significant way. Openness was seen in these groups as an added value. The opposite was quite dangerous for group members, that is, by hiding personal experiences the individual would put his own future in jeopardy. Anyhow, it was common practice in these groups to listen to the story of a tortured member in the aftermath of torture, which were formulated and published in book format in order to make group members aware of the effects of such experiences.

Furthermore, the main motive in these narratives was "resistance" in the face of torture. As one of my informants put it, "It is possible to say that the history of revolutionary groups in Turkey indeed is the history of resistance." Resistance, on the other hand, has historically been displayed by these groups in multifarious ways; first in the form of silence; and second, as hunger strikes, death fasts, etc. Silence and non-display of emotions during police interrogation was seen as an asset or as "power," so to speak, in all revolutionary groups. Not giving-in in the face of torture in this way and conveying one's experiences not only enrich his outlook considerably, but also his experiences were carefully transformed into narratives that were inherited by potential members and future generations.

As a third way of mystical manipulation, the concept of "freedom" is used abundantly, particularly in recruiting people and in the first stages of membership in revolutionary groups. Members are told that people's freedom is taken away from them by the oppressive state and in order to free people and one's self, each individual must work relentlessly to bring about a communist revolution. However, as newcomers climb up the steps towards being an old-timer, they start realizing that even though their groups claim to have set out to emancipate people; their deeds do not match the narratives that they promote. It is possible to say that, in the conceptualization of Varenne and McDermott, recognition of these groups' legitimacy as a freedom-loving institution is maintained by production and reproduction of "misrecognition" of the symbolic violence which they exert (1998:173). Thus, with the passage of time and because of relevant lived-experiences within the groups, group members become cognizant of this "misrecognition," become disillusioned, and finally start looking for a way out of the groups, which my informants admitted to be extremely difficult indeed. For example, Gökhan-R's experience describes this situation vividly:

> Speaking of freedom … When you join a group because of its noble aspirations towards freedom and you realize that your freedom is sanctioned by the same group, you start to feel yourself as constricted, which in turn makes you start looking for a way out. However, these organizations have a peculiar approach… You don't reach to this consciousness overnight. Your whole life in the group is about climbing, or jumping one step at a time. When you do these, you are given certain tasks and responsibilities; which mean that you are thrust into a criminal life. This is to say that you don't have a chance like a normal person to say, 'OK, enough of this group; I will kick this door and get out to a normal life.' You don't have such luxury. This is called, 'the policy of contamination' [of identities]. I mean, in order to achieve this, you need a special formula. When you return to normal life, everything is a problem … when you see a police officer, at a checkpoint, or when you are running your official errands … You have to be ready to put up with all these problems.

Lifton's third technique refers to the *demand for purity*. The world is divided into a moral dichotomy of good and evil. Good is defined as those thoughts, feelings, and actions which are consistent with the ideology of the group; and evil is defined as every other kind of thought or behavior. Since no one can achieve this level of purity, a feeling of shame and guilt is engendered.

(Alexander and Rollins 1984:2)

Demand for purity is at its highest level in both the PKK and the revolutionary groups, according to which the group's ideology is defined as the ultimate good, whereas anything other than those ideologies is thought to be the ultimate evil. To specify, members in both types of groups are asked to sacrifice everything they have for their ideals, i.e., a life system in which all Kurds will be free, and in the case of revolutionary groups, a communist revolution. As an overarching concept, being "bourgeois," or leading a bourgeois "lifestyle" are defined as the ultimate evil, which all members are expected to shy away from. In order to achieve that kind of purity, members are asked occasionally to turn to themselves, a process that can be defined as "concentration" or "purification" (*yoğunlaşma* in Turkish). What happens as a result of such episodes of purification is that it backfires, that is, it leads group members to the adoption of new approaches in which groups' ideological underpinnings are reevaluated and often discarded. It is a process in which the real power relations in the groups are unmasked, which in turn dissolves the misrecognition of their own situation as true believers.

Case: Gökhan–R

When you first join the group, your behavior is different. You try to maintain a high standard based on the group values because you want to prove to yourself that you are a good revolutionary. You always try to be on the forefront in group's actions, and you try to demonstrate the most radical of all behaviors that are asked by the group. However, after a while, you start realizing that what you do is indeed wrong; when you throw a Molotov cocktail on a bus, you don't think that you are burning a vehicle of the system. After a process of self-evaluation, you think that when I burn this bus in order to destroy the system, I am in reality harming my people. You may relieve your conscience by saying that you are doing such acts just to expose the ugliness of the system; but this thought doesn't satisfy you.

...When I talk about my own situation, it is quite easy in theory. You may sacrifice your father, your mother and the whole family for the revolution. However, these are nothing but lies that you use to ease your own dissatisfactions. Why does a person become a revolutionary? Why does he join this path? Individuals don't become revolutionaries because they believe in the revolution. I had mentioned before, that individuals become revolutionaries to create alternatives for themselves. How can I put it? For instance, people may have grievances or humiliations that may lead them to seek escape. They think that 'I need something to protect me; I have to be part of a whole.' What these groups say, in fact, is nothing but propaganda; when you carry out actions on their behalf, you are indeed trying to earn a position for yourself. If you are not strong enough to face your own conscience, you continue to follow this propaganda, which promises even higher levels for you in the system. In that case, you become free of all moral scruples that you had; you start legitimizing the war as a tool to achieve your own interests. This, in fact, is the business of people who lack conscience. If a person calls himself a revolutionary, he has to know where to stop in terms of his praxis [violence]. Otherwise, he is no one but a savaged war-machine. Most people in my environment had such kind of approach.

In the case of the PKK, members are often told about the virtues of democracy, freedom of speech in the group, balanced relationships between male and female guerillas, dedication, loyalty, and so on. If a member failed in any of these aspects, like in revolutionary groups, he is encouraged to withdraw for a while to purify himself by rethinking his own situation based on the group values. What most members see in reality after self-evaluation, however, creates a sense of confusion and dissatisfaction in them, which eventually leads to their disillusionment with the group. In the case of Azad-P, for instance, his visit to Mahmur camp[2] was a turning point in this respect:

> One day, I went to the Mahmur camp in civilian clothes. It was 2005 when we had many tumultuous events within the group. No one knew that I was a cadre [of the PKK]. They said, 'Hevals ['comrade' in Kurdish, and used among the PKK guerillas] came here, they [males and females] were on each other's laps.' I mean in Kurdish culture, sexuality starts normally with marriage. These types of relationships are not tolerated anywhere in Kurdish territory, which is why it was a perverted development... I mean when people are freed, they consider no limitations, the balance gets broken in that case. I mean, I haven't seen it, but I was convinced that such things happened in that camp. In addition, when I was in Romania, for instance, two [Kurdish] families went to Moscow to bring their girls back from one of the PKK's village camps there. They were about 18 years old at the time, but when they sent their girls, they were only 13 years old. They brought them back because of such rumors about corrupted relationships [*yozlaşma* in Turkish]. They said, 'We didn't send our girl for this.' In brief, my visit to Mahmur camp in 2005 had an enormous impact in me. I started to make sense of things slowly. When I was returning from the camp [to his own group in Europe], I said, 'I will no longer be the person I was.' Who was I? I was a very dedicated person; I was breaking myself into pieces for the group. When I went back, even my friends said, 'Azad you are different; you have changed.'

Lifton's fourth technique, *the cult of confession*, is perhaps one of the most psychologically powerful. As a concomitant to the search for purity, there is an imperative demand to make a confession of one's shortcomings. Sins are defined by the cult's ideology. The function of publicly confessing one's sins maximizes the vulnerability of the self. Three mechanisms come into play with public confession: (a) a device is created to maintain focus on personal imperfections, thus augmenting feelings of guilt; (b) a means is devised to surrender the self to the group in a dramatic fashion; and (c) a method is generated by which knowledge of one's sins demands forgiveness. "I ... practice the profession of penitent to be able to end up as a judge ... the more I accuse myself, the more I have a right to judge you."

(Alexander and Rollins 1984:2–3)

The cult of confession, too, is one of the most powerful tools used by the PKK and revolutionary groups. However, it is applied more elaborately in the PKK, manifesting itself in the forms of policies of "criticism" and "self-criticism." Some of my informants have quite a positive view about these concepts, while others have opposite feelings toward them. To specify, those who spoke positively about these concepts expressed the benefits of these concepts to teaching methodology, reducing stress by allowing people to open themselves up and creating a sense of togetherness. Those who held negative views suggested that group's encouragement to speak up is insincere and there is indeed a latent discrimination in terms of their implementation, disguised by the seeming transparency and nobility associated with these techniques. The approach of the latter group can be conceptualized such that

> when there are explicit rules saying not to do certain things, it means implicitly that one should do it; and by the same token, if there are explicit rules allowing one to do certain things, implicitly, it means that one should not do it.
>
> (Žižek 2011)

In this context, consider Azad-P's opinions as an example for the former group:

> In the PKK, the concepts of criticism and self-criticism are used very effectively. When a person is asked to criticize himself before the group members, the goal is not to judge him, which is why people speak quite freely.

I asked him, "Is it not difficult to expose one's deficiencies in front of everybody? How do people overcome this psychological conundrum?" He responded:

> Of course it was difficult especially at the beginning, for newcomers in particular. However, trust me; people disclose everything about themselves because of staying together for ten years or more. They talk about their experiences, impressions, and practices that they had in life. Even if he doesn't open up, others help him in this process. Sometimes we saw people who went through these processes after which we thought, 'How will this person continue his life normally tomorrow?' I mean the dose of criticism reaches the point where it is almost unthinkable for that person to resume his work

the next day. However, it is not like that; I mean everything is not normal of course, the person has intensified emotions, but the negative reaction remains be less than 10 percent. In general, it is seen as a positive thing.

I pushed a him little bit further to better understand the dynamic of this process and asked, "Do you think this process is eased by the fact that everybody goes through it, if needed?" He said:

> You are right. Everybody does the same thing. You remember that I had mentioned the concept of martyrdom as being one of the pillars of the PKK; the mechanism of self-criticism is another pillar of the group. For example, even Cemil Bayik [one of the top-brass of the PKK] undertook self-criticism in front of everybody. His self-criticism produced an approximately 150-page document, which is used in training in a class called 'the history of the party.' He described all of the rights and wrongs that the group did. The same thing is said for Şemdin Sakık and Osman Öcalan [they were also high-level commanders, but they are currently not in the PKK]. They are asked to go through a self-criticism process because of their [faulty] practices. Do you know what punishment they got? They were asked to write a book, in which they were told to write their life histories with all of the negative and positive aspects. Their life histories, in fact, became voluminous material for the group, which has been used in theoretical and practical training. Instead of making a theoretical and historical chronology, analyzing the history of group in the light of a prominent individual's life is seen to be a better approach. The language used in such an approach, on the other hand, becomes more effable for the people in that environment.

In contrast to Azad-P's views, Zilan-P says that these concepts are used selectively in the group; if they tried to criticize certain people, for instance, they were immediately silenced and ostracized. More importantly, the group leaders make their life after that experience quite difficult, even unbearable.

> There was an elite group on the mountain. These people were different from us in terms of the autonomy that they had. They were able to get anything they wanted from the villages. They had a lot of money on them. They had private lives. However, the same people wanted others to be like sheep; they wanted them simply to be obedient. *Criticizing them would mean your own destruction.* All information about you, e.g., your real name, your code name, the report written about you by your former commander are in the hands of these people. Even if you want to present your criticism in writing, you don't have a right to do it secretly. If you write, you know that the senior commanders will recall that person, and that he will come back with anger because he knows that it was you who wrote that report. Then, he will start to watch you more closely; the pressure will be intolerable. He will even send you to such actions [clash with the Turkish military] where he knows

that you have no chance of survival. Therefore, for many reasons, you avoid expressing your criticism.

The highlighted sentence reminds one of the concept of *acidiae* during the dark ages and during the inquisition: "depression" indicated a lack of faith in God and was therefore heretical and punishable.

> Litton's fifth variable, *the sacred science*, refers to the aura of fundamental ideological purity. If one holds the tenets of the "true" faith, then it becomes blasphemous to question that faith. One does not question God.
> (Alexander and Rollins 1984:3)

In the PKK, the sacred science refers to the group's ideology and the "infallibility" of its leader Öcalan who views himself, as do many of his followers, as a prophet, or even a demigod.[3] For instance, as Azad-P mentioned, group members are told that the Kemalist state does not want this problem to be solved politically, for it is insufficiently intelligible. They are told,

> Nobody can debate with Öcalan ... He is now in prison; thus he doesn't have access to resources he wants. But still, there is nobody in Turkish politics that can beat him in a debate. They have everything, e.g., the parliament but they cannot do politics; but Öcalan manages and dominates the politics even through one-hour meetings that he holds with his lawyers.

It is therefore safe to say that questioning his personality, his deeds, and ideas is perceived to be blasphemous in the PKK. Moreover, since criticism of the group leaders and their ideology is prevented, both manifestly and latently, individuals who are not happy with the sacred science of the group and cannot get out are left with one alternative, i.e., committing suicide. As many of my informants mentioned, although suicides are quite common in the group, the leaders do not think that there is something wrong with the group; instead, they think that such individuals blow up themselves because they cannot improve themselves. Nadir-P describes this phenomenon as follows:

> During my time in the group, I witnessed a lot of suicides. Many people took their lives, not for no reason. It means that there was something deep in them that they felt helpless; and they kept everything inside. Then they blew themselves up ... I experienced several cases like this; I mean he doesn't blow up himself in front of everyone; he usually goes behind a hill, but you hear the sound and run towards there. You hope that it was an accident, but many times it is not. The group leaders say, 'These people take their lives because they cannot improve themselves.' The group is always right; it doesn't think why these people killed themselves.

I asked him how they were affected by such incidents and whether they spoke about them among friends, and he responded:

> Of course it is difficult to speak with everyone. Unless you are close to the person, you cannot make any assessment about the incident. You have to say, 'The group is right. He couldn't improve himself; he had many faults, which is why he took his own life.' If you oppose, they say, 'You pushed him to this.' I mean you cannot make a defense on his behalf. On paper, everybody has the right to criticize, but in reality you have no such right. Some people were too naïve to believe in this that they were speaking up. As a result, he is scolded by the commander before everyone, and he writes him up. This means, there is no democratic environment in the group as it is claimed. Because, in a couple of months, he will definitely face something terrible; he will be trapped by the commander ... It is definite.

In the revolutionary groups, sacred science usually refers to pursuing a revolutionary lifestyle and avoiding a bourgeois one. The former requires full loyalty, self-sacrifice, and relentless efforts to achieve and maintain it. Moreover, like the PKK, if the group makes a mistake, it does not accept it and instead says, "The bourgeoisie is disturbed by our actions, which is why they are acting out." If a group member, for instance, attempts to criticize anything about the group such as its ideology or modus operandi, he is considered to be unfaithful and is even punished, depending on the level of criticism he has put forth. Gökhan-R's opinions exemplify this:

> The [revolutionary] groups don't think that they are doing bad things. They say, 'The people under the tutelage of the bourgeoisie are disturbed by our actions. Look, our actions are so influential that it [the State] gets tougher… They know that if a member starts questioning, and feels remorse, it marks the beginning of the end of the group. When we look at the groups historically, such examples of questioning usually brought about separations from the groups. However, the groups never accept their deficiencies, they are too proud to do this. In fact, this is a good thing for the state; because groups cannot explain their wrongdoings to their own members.'

The seventh mechanism used by Lifton refers to the *reinterpretation of an individual* so that his/her past conforms to his/her present identity. Lifton calls this "doctrine over person," by which he means that the behavior of the person's entire history is reexamined to show that he/she always was the kind of person that he/she is now revealed to be. Using the group's jargonistic language, it becomes easy to cast all previous life experience as the fulfillment of the ideology's mythic prophecies. This form of retrospective interpretation of an individual's life means that the individual is reconstituted. "The former identity, at best, receives the accent of mere appearance ... the former identity stands as accidental; the new identity is the 'basic reality'." What he is now is what, "after all," he was all along."

(Alexander and Rollins 1984:3)

This technique is also used by the groups I studied in a way in which the identities of their members are reconstructed based on the group's ideology. This meant the denial of their former identities; yet, like the other techniques employed to the same end, this too usually backfires in that after spending some time in the group, members realize the mismatch between who they were and who they are being forced to be. For example, consider the case of Nadir, who joined the PKK as a child (13 years old) via forced recruitment.[4]

He did not feel he belonged to the group from the outset, but even though he tried to escape from the mountain several times, he failed. He met with his future wife in the mountain (Zilan) who also joined the group involuntarily and for a long time wanted to find a way out. When they were chatting one day, they opened themselves up by telling each other stories, which encouraged them both to make an escape plan. Although it took almost two years to realize the plan, they succeeded:

> Even though having failed several times, I still wanted to escape from the mountain, but I was afraid. I did not have the courage. When I spoke with her, we both gave each other a feeling of trust, felt encouraged, and made a plan to escape. Because since I joined the group, I never felt part of the group. I could not associate myself with it. I was angry all the time; I never had the urge to accept this life. On the other hand, I was missing my normal life. I saw many wrongs on the mountain, all of which piled up in me. The execution of those two people, for instance, doesn't fade from my memory. Also, the people who were killed before my eyes; I still cannot forget them.
>
> I was thinking, 'What am I doing with these people? In what way am I related to their narratives?' What they say will never happen, and we will never be able to finalize this task. I don't know anything about these things; when you talk about Russia, Vietnam, or Cuba, for that matter, 'What the hell are you talking about?' That's not my business, that's not who I am. My business was to pursue a normal life. My business was our work in the village, with our cattle ... It was, 'How will we protect our families?' I mean you want something from me that is very very far from me. You want something that is very far from human psychology. This was really difficult to accept.

In addition to Lifton's delineation of six techniques of thought reform, Alexander and Rollins talk about two other techniques that cults use: (1) love-bombing, and (2) the substitution of a "good family" for the family of origin.

> Love-bombing refers to the apparent unconditional acceptance of the individual. The person is accepted, and he/she is not given any privacy or time to be alone. Never again will he/she experience loneliness, but never

again will he/she have time to reflect or engage in critical thinking. The second cult technique – substitution of a 'good family' – provides direction and meaning for the person's life. He/she is thrust into a situation where he/she does not have to question the merit of any of his/her actions; his/her behavior has meaning for his/her new family, and therefore for him/her. The new family provides acceptance and understanding for his/her behavior. The neophyte is repeatedly told, 'Only we can love you, and understand you. We are like you, and know what your life is really like. This is the only place you really belong.' The convert's family of origin is denigrated into a position of little value, or even negative value. His/her old frame of reference is steadily eroded, and the cult is substituted as the new family.

(1984:3)

In an effort to create a close-knit social network (Bott 1957) based on [fictive] kinship among group members, the groups I studied used both of these techniques in a conscious and strategic manner. Considering the fact that some of my informants joined the groups because of their dysfunctional family structures and the lack of love, it makes sense that some people are more susceptible to the influences of such techniques. Doubtless, love-bombing impresses especially the newcomers to the groups, but it is also effective during their life in them. The substitution of a good family occurs a little differently, however, in the sense that the families of origin are not denigrated by the groups; instead, members are told that they now have a larger family including their own that is oppressed by the state, and thus, that it needs to be emancipated. In the case of the PKK, the real family is the PKK and real family life is the one lived in the mountain and the real homeland is Kurdistan. In the revolutionary groups, the meaning of real family refers to a larger community, which encompasses all people who are discriminated against, oppressed, and subjugated. Hakan-R describes the importance and effects of these techniques as follows:

I mean ... You have two eyes and two ears; but the party has a thousand eyes and ears. It has a thousand brains. You tell yourself, 'What kind of an institution this party is; they know everything.' But, in fact, it is his business; nothing is strange with this. They have seen a lot of things, including betrayals of their own friends, some of whom sold them and escaped abroad. In brief, you realize that they are really experienced and wise ... At that point, you realize that your own father became your enemy; you dedicate yourself to your comrades, but nothing else ... Because when you go there, everybody understands you and you understand everybody as well. You have a common language. When you leave that place, you don't understand and be understood by anyone. You become a stranger in there; I felt like that at least ... When I am with the party people, feeling that comfort, I become united with them."

This is indeed how they recruit people and build their cadre. Some people are impervious to the effects of groups; they don't get separated from their families. I was not like that, for instance... I was touched by many things that the group spoke about; this is in my character I guess. I cry even now when I watch a sentimental movie; I get affected easily. Sometimes the same thing happens when I read a book. I mean, one side of me is like this; I am an emotional person. Most people around me wouldn't know this, because I did not display my emotions. Anyhow, because of my emotional side, I became easily detached from my family; my home was like a hotel for me ... My whole life was about 1 May neighborhood; the party offices, café-houses, and my friends in there. You couldn't find anybody else in there anyway; there was no nationalist person for instance. It was a breeding place of all revolutionaries, except for the PKK, because it did not exist at the time.

* * *

To summarize this section, like in the case of AA and in religious cults, indoctrination plays a central role in the construction of identities both in the PKK and in revolutionary groups. These groups view education as a process, in which a body of knowledge is transmitted to their members in order to fashion their identities so that the members see the identity of the group as theirs. On the other hand, the timing of indoctrination seems to differ in the two types of groups I studied, because it appears that the PKK recruits Kurdish youth to indoctrinate them, whereas revolutionary groups indoctrinate youngsters in order to recruit them. The processes of recruitment and indoctrination are not mutually exclusive, and more often than not, there is a blurred line between them; but the aforementioned argument becomes logical, should membership types of these groups be taken into consideration. To specify, given that the least common denominator for membership in the PKK is the "Kurdish identity" of its members, the process of entry into the group occurs faster than in revolutionary groups, although more effort is required later to reshape the identities of youngsters with different backgrounds to maintain their conformity to the group identity and ideology. In contrast, revolutionary groups have to embark on a longer process of indoctrination in order to cajole and allure youngsters to recruit them, while it does not require later on as much effort as in the PKK to maintain their identities aligned with the group ideology. In any case, indoctrination is a necessary condition for entering and staying in terrorist groups. Yet, although being effective for a certain period, indoctrination appears to produce unwanted outcomes in the long run, as group members start to experience or see the contradictions inherent in it. This, in turn, leads to their realization of the misrecognition of their subjection to the negative effects of indoctrination, e.g., loss of autonomy, lack of freedom, and contamination of the self, etc., resulting in group members' disillusionment with their respective groups and their eventual desire to separate from them.

"Imagined" communities of practice and the effects of "postponed imaginations"

Despite the similarities between the five studies of apprenticeship analyzed in Lave and Wenger's book and my study, there are important differences between them, for instance, in Marxist terms, with regard to the type of production, means of production and relations of production, etc., which in turn have enormous impact on the notion of disengagement of the Turkish Penitents that this book has set out to explore. To clarify, in the study of Vai tailors, for example, apprentices observe and participate in the processes of "garment" production, during which they enter in various types of relationships, either conflictual or consensual, with the objects of their work, with other apprentices, and with master tailors. Production processes involve "learning to sew by hand, to sew with treadle sewing machine, and to press clothes" (1991:71). Furthermore, apprentices can see and touch the produced material (garments), and that the developmental cycle of such communities of practice takes five years on average. The terrorist groups I studied, on the other hand, engage in multiple productive (destructive) activities simultaneously, i.e., they produce an *enemy* (the state) and *public fear* via indoctrination and violence in order to produce a product that has a phantom quality. That is, newcomers, old-timers and masters alike participate in the production of violence to reproduce a community of practice (the groups), which has an ultimate goal of producing an *imagined community*. In the case of the PKK, this imagined community is an independent Kurdish state; while in the case of revolutionary groups, it is a communist Turkish state.

I use the term "imagined," by focusing on its *spatial* and *temporal* aspects, in two ways. First, Anderson (1983) argues that a nation is a community socially constructed, that is to say, imagined by the people who perceive themselves as part of that group. In other words, a nation is imagined because "the members of even the smallest nation will never know most of their fellow-members, meet them, or even hear of them, yet in the minds of each lives the image of their communion" (1983:x). Similarly, following Lave and Wenger, I use the term community to argue that an imagined community does not necessarily imply co-presence, a well-defined, identifiable group, or socially visible boundaries (1991:98). Second, I use the term "imagined" to connote the temporality of the communities that the PKK and revolutionary groups aspire to build. Put differently, I argue that they are indeed mental projections in the minds of the members and supporters of these groups, which they wish and struggle to arrive at an *unknown time* in the *future*.

Several dynamics are at work in this analogy of imagined community. First, in such communities members might make diverse contributions to activity that may elicit different feelings and hold varied viewpoints. In light of this, I argue that the mode and the means of production in communities of violent practice is unique in the sense it involves killing human beings, destroying infrastructure, inundating the memory with countless indelible graphic images, etc., in the production of an abstract, imaginary craft (violence) which cannot be touched (like garments), but only felt by its producers in the form of not only "exhilaration, anger and fear"

(Aretxaga 2000:49), but also pain, empathy, and remorse. Second, the goal of the whole production process in terrorist groups, too, has an abstract, cerebral feature, which can potentially be objectified and actualized through various actions; but the current "productive" activities in which group members participate may not necessarily be the only activities conducive to the achievement of that goal. For instance, since its inception in 1978, except for the frequently claimed "mythical" gains for the Kurdish people through violence, the PKK organization not only failed to establish an independent Kurdish state, but also caused more than 40,000 deaths, most of whom being ethnically Kurdish citizens. Similarly, numerous revolutionary groups have existed since the 1970s and claimed thousands of lives; yet, the social, political, and economic developments in the last three decades have proven that the destination the country wanted to head towards has been far from what these revolutionary groups aspired it to be, that is, "a communist state."

Furthermore, these failures are also crucial in terms of their explanatory power for understanding the developmental cycles of the groups. As Lave and Wenger (1991) mentioned, for the quartermasters, the cycle of navigational practice is quite short, i.e., about six years. Given that the PKK keeps around 5,000 guerillas in its mountain and urban cadre, and that around 35,000 guerillas hitherto have been killed by the Turkish security forces since 1984, it is possible to say, roughly, that the group reproduced itself seven times and each cycle took about four years on average. The same logic can be applied to revolutionary groups, though their numbers are significantly smaller than the PKK, ranging perhaps from a hundred to several hundreds. The crux of the issue here is that numerous reproduction cycles did not bring tangible results in terms of the groups' goals. Thus, I claim that the postponement of these utopian and imaginary goals, propounded by the PKK and revolutionary groups over three decades, created in some members and supporters of such groups a sense of disappointment and hopelessness, making them in turn believe that these goals are no longer attainable.

In the case of revolutionary groups, it is possible to say that improvements made in social and economic reforms in the country marked the end of their ideological arguments, the most important of which being the concepts of social and economic "inequalities," and "torture" exerted by law enforcement officials. Particularly in the last ten years, the Turkish economy jumped from twenty-sixth to sixteenth in the world, which allowed the AKP to pursue the welfare-state policies that were stipulated in its party program and have been the leitmotif of its political campaigns since its rise to power in 2002. Specifically, the country has made significant improvements in terms of the principles of equitable distribution of wealth, equality of opportunity, and positive discrimination for the disadvantaged citizens. Moreover, in an effort to ameliorate the country's human rights record, the AKP started in 2002 to implement its policy of "zero-tolerance for torture." With the adoption of this policy, and with the assistance of the European Committee for the Prevention of Torture, Turkish prisons and detention centers have been open to international control. Even though there are still instances of torture, the situation is significantly better than the pre-2002 period. In fact, all six of my informants from revolutionary groups mentioned that these improvements in a way marked, *inter alia*, the end of the Turkish left, as they believe that propaganda tools that leftist-revolutionary groups capitalized on in recruiting members were taken away from them.⁵

More importantly, these developments seem to have created in my informants a feeling that the goal of bringing about a communist revolution and a communist state is no longer attainable. The following excerpts from my interviews exemplify clearly the effects of the postponement of imaginations (utopia) and this new situation:

Case 1: Gökhan -R

> For a long time, ideologies played an important role in transforming individuals. For this, you had to create a consciousness in people based on the group's values. However, today the situation is different; most things that people need became available to them. I mean, they can easily satisfy their needs and emotions, which in turn decreased the number of people that the leftist ideology could attract. As a result, their portfolio has shifted significantly, given that they are now only able to recruit substance addicts, drug addicts, and so on. They have difficulty recruiting new members today. Think about this, what are the propaganda tools that the groups use to recruit people? All of the wrongdoings of the opposite side (the state) are available to the organizations for exploitation. However, it is not possible to find potential recruits in the towns like Şişli, Mecidiyeköy, or Etiler [upscale neighborhoods]. It was easier for groups to recruit in shantytowns where people have many grievances. That is why; leftist organizations promote a utopian world. Even China is building such a world today, because socialist ideology cannot respond to the needs of people; it does not provide any alternatives. As I mentioned before, the capitalist system is quite successful in showing people so many things through colored media and colorful materials, which means that even ordinary individuals can dynamite their potentials. Socialist thought cannot provide this; everything is structured in it. They say people must have everything on an equal basis, but in reality, it does not work that way. It is very difficult to translate theory into practice. I mean, no matter how hard you try, you get stuck at a certain point because you run out of lies that you can use … There is only so much material remaining in your hand.
>
> To be honest, I never believed in the revolution. I was just interested in the group because of thinking that maybe I would die and become a hero. I can sincerely say to you that

among more than one thousand revolutionaries that I know may be ten people really believe in the revolution. If people turn to their inner selves, they will realize that they joined the group in search of something because of their material or emotional deficits, because of their need to be meaningful and their desire to verbalize their rebellion. I don't believe in and accept growing up in an ideology of the leftist narrative. Because it is against human nature; human beings have unlimited wants, but there is only a limited life that the leftist narratives can provide for you. Despite this, they talk about collective and individual freedom, you see in reality that that freedom is confined within certain borders."

Case 2: Hakan-R

I can say that the conditions for the revolution had already ceased to exist, both globally and in Turkey, when I decided to leave the group. One of the most important reasons for the end of the Turkish left was the end of police torture. It was, and still is, almost impossible to organize people around this notion of torture. Furthermore, it is possible to say that the level of poverty is not as bad as 20 years ago. I mean, you cannot organize people with this narrative too; you have to say something new, because the foundation on which you stand has slipped off your feet.

On the other hand, revolution is almost unthinkable today, unless you created a new 'human type.' Unless you could get rid of bourgeois morals, it is impossible for communism to come into life in this soil. For instance, in Turkey the revolution cannot take place in a regular format, i.e., 'I will go to the mountain, from where I will strike the state, which will create a consciousness in people and will follow me …' This could happen in Cuba, because of the dictatorship there; but in Turkey, this is almost impossible, for there is a democracy in your country, though with its deficiencies. It is not perfect but at least you have elections, parliament, etc. What is more, this perception is shared by the masses too. Even if you say, 'Let's bring about the revolution,' it is meaningless; because revolution cannot be brought about without the support of the masses. I cannot make a revolution by myself; it is a problem not only of cadre but also of the masses.

> Reference made here is similar to Fanon's desire to create a "new man"

Case 3: Azad-P

> Let me tell you something else; there was a man in the PKK, whose name is Ali Haydar Kaytan and code name Fuat. He is a friend of Öcalan from university. He separates from the group and marries someone. Öcalan talks to him and says, 'So, you want to start a family? How can you think so simply? We have a cause; we have a revolution to bring about. Just to have a child, you cannot abandon the cause.' I can say that there was a problem connected to this; everybody wants to start a family in the PKK, but on what do they fixate themselves? They are fixated on the cause and a certain timeline for it: 'You will do this before 1993, you will do that by 1999, etc.' So, what really happens is, these dreams get postponed at every crossroad that in fact has a significant impact on people's and my own separation from the group. They say, 'Of course you will have a family when we have established a free country and a free world.' On the other hand, we were told the following by the PKK: 'So, you will establish a family and have a child but there is no education in Kurdish in Turkey. Do you have the right to give birth to that child?' Many people indeed internalize this; they think that 'your homeland is not free; there is no life in it.' But overall, there are a lot of people who are affected by the postponement of the utopia."

Moreover, in addition to postponement of utopia, the shifting nature of the PKK's goals and ideology over the years also created confusion among its members and supporters. The PKK was founded originally with an aim of establishing an independent Kurdish state, for which it had adopted a Marxist-Leninist ideology. However, over the course of time, and based on the imperatives of the changed local and global conditions, the group replaced its Marxist-Leninist ideology with an over-reliance on ethnic nationalism. In terms of its goals, the group shifted from an independent Kurdish state to a Democratic Confederation System, which Öcalan formulated as a "democratic, ecological and sexist" system, in which gender roles would be reconfigured. In addition, despite the fact that most of the Kurdish population are Muslims, the concept of atheism was forced upon the group members for a long time, which was then replaced by Zarathustra. The problems emanating from these developments are twofold: (1) the language that the group use is ineffable to many of its members, e.g., terms such as ecological and sexist system, Zarathustra, etc., are quite difficult concepts for the group members who come from feudal family structures; (2) shifting ideologies and moving targets in the group create confusion among its members. The biggest disappointment for the PKK members, which had also shocked general public at the time, however, was linked to Öcalan's capture in 1999, when he uttered that his mother was Turkish and that he was ready to work with the state. Hundreds of PKK militants had left the group at the time, and as my informants suggested, the effects of his aforementioned statements continue to linger in the group.[6] About the foregoing arguments, Azad-P said:

> I should tell you the following with regard to historical dimension of the PKK. Most people think that Öcalan's main goal was to establish Kurdistan; but he told us that it was not a determining factor for him and people around him who had the same level of consciousness. He used to say, 'If there is a utopia, you can use it within the circumstances and geography in which you live.' As you were mentioning instrumentalization, it is possible to say that they might have instrumentalized the term 'dream of Kurdistan.'

When I asked him what the goal of the group was then, if not to establish the Kurdistan, he continued:

> The term Kurdistan was a utopian term. For instance, when the Turkish government started its Democratic Opening in 2010 and invited militants to lay down their arms in exchange for amnesty, in Romania people [Kurds] asked us, 'So, if there will be peace, does that mean that everything is finished?' Or let me give you another example; they are talking about disarmament; but Duran Kalkan, one of the PKK leaders, said, 'we cannot lay down our arms; they are our *raison d'être*.'[7] So, my point is that even if the PKK achieved its military and political goals, the current utopia of the group will not cease to exist; it will find another contradiction in society and continue its struggle. Whatever contradiction that epoch has to offer ... it will use it."

On the other hand, you remember Harun, my role model at the university. I saw him in 2005, when the group had come to the brink of disintegration because of those 'heated debates.' He had said the following phrase that I cannot forget, '*Yes to struggle, but no to the PKK*. If struggle means working at a level of utopia for the improvement of humanity, today the means to that end is the PKK, but tomorrow it can be something else. Alternatively, it was something else a

Those heated debates were about the so-called social project defended by Osman Öcalan, brother of the PKK leader. The gist of the project was to allow more relaxed relationships between male and female guerrillas

hundred years ago; think about it. Che Guevara brings about the revolution in Cuba and goes to Bolivia to bring about the revolution in that country. So, you became a finance minister, what else would you want?' It is a similar issue here; I mean I am talking about the people who live for this utopia.

With regard to utopian thinking, the group leaders used to tell us, 'Don't be too realistic, or else you will drown yourself.' The people would tell us, 'You are only a handful of people, but look at your enemy; they are so powerful, what can you do against them?' You see, this is exactly what being realistic means. Mostly, people who had reached middle age talked like this; but if you have this type of thinking, you have to leave the group from the beginning. You have to be utopian instead and say, 'What is Turkey; we can do this, do that ... and defeat them.' The point is that the group follows the developments in the world closely; if there is a change in the real situation, the utopia is modified based on that; the group can use any contradiction that exists anywhere around the world.

Furthermore, whereas postponement of utopia creates in group members a sense of hopelessness, exhaustion, and disenchantment, the notion of "idleness" exacerbates these psychological problems. As I mentioned earlier, life in communities of violent practice differs significantly from other conventional forms of apprenticeship in terms of the production process. The production process in terrorist groups involves violence, but for obvious reasons, it is not feasible for such groups to produce violence in a continuous manner. It is possible to say, for example, that if an individual spent ten years in a terrorist group, the time he was engaged in the production of violence and training for this would not exceed, perhaps, one year. The remaining nine years are dominated by a state of idleness, or at best "active idleness," for an indefinite time and an amorphous target, which potentially lead to the *burning out* of individuals, as well as the *degeneration* of interpersonal relationships within such groups. In addition, the concept of "missing normal life" complements this process and facilitates members' exit from their respective groups. For instance, Hikmet-R said the following about the merging of his disillusionment and longing for a normal life:

> One day, they relocated me as a punishment from X town to Y because of ... However, even though the other guy had failed big time, he got nothing. So, where are the democracy, equality, and justice that you talk and brag about in the

group? What are you talking about! I mean, the internal dynamics within the group were different; the reality was totally different ... You may say that agents who infiltrated the group might have an influence; but do you think: 'Are all of these people working for the deep state? Aren't there a few revolutionaries or communists like us? Is the situation messed up this much? and so on.' I mean you smolder over these things; do you know why? Because you see your friends from high school and think, 'He has a house, a car, and a job. He has a family.' And you look at yourself, at the same age, but you see that you didn't get anything for yourself but gave all that you had. You are not even at a point zero. Your situation is below zero, because you lost even your own and your family's savings... When you are in prison, it is your family that supports you, not the organization. I mean they pay a visit to you several times a week; they spend money for this. They are your parents, you need to support them, but instead they are the ones who support you financially. I mean I was really resentful.

People who join terrorist groups and participate in violence are usually thought to be individuals who have nothing to lose. However, this example demonstrates that this argument does not hold at least for some individuals in terrorist groups, especially for those who joined the groups voluntarily for significance quest, and not for restoring their significance loss stemming from negative prediction definers such as having "dysfunctional, unloving, or tense" households, being exposed to political violence in the process of socialization, and so on.

The problem of access in participation

Lave and Wenger argue that learners must be legitimate peripheral participants in ongoing practice in order for learning identities to be engaged and developed into full participation (1991:64). For full participation, on the other hand, they suggest that "problems of access, of its embedding in the conflictual forms of everyday practice, of motivation, and of the development of membership and identity into object of analysis must be realized" (1991:87). To be more specific, they argue that several factors distort, partially or completely, the prospects for learning in practice: (1) conditions that place newcomers deeply in adversarial relations with superiors; (2) exhaustion through over involvement in work; (3) involuntary servitude rather than participation (1991:64). Lastly, their point of view suggests, "communities of practice may well develop interstitially and informally in coercive workplaces" (1991:64).

Proceeding from the foregoing arguments, I assert that another important reason behind my informants' disengagement stems from the problems and contradictions inherent in the process of "gaining legitimacy" in their respective groups that display the features of both voluntary and coercive organizations. In an effort to explain how legitimate access is gained in violent communities of practice and to outline the kinds of problems and contradictions intrinsic to it, I will focus on the following issues: (1) master-novice and peer-to-peer relations and the issues of transparency; (2) the problems of access and sequestration.

Master-novice and peer-to-peer relations and the issue of transparency

Lave and Wenger argue that "in shaping the relation of masters to apprentices, the issue of conferring legitimacy is more important than the issue of providing teaching" (1991:92). For example, among the five studies analyzed in their book, neither Yucatec midwives nor quartermasters learn in specific master-apprentice relations. "Newcomers to AA do have special relations with old-timers who act as their sponsors but these relations are not what define them as newcomers," while in the case of Vai and Gola tailors, "Master tailors must sponsor apprentices before the latter can have legitimate access to participation in the community's productive activities" (1991:92). On the other hand, the authors argue, "Apprentices learn mostly in relation to other apprentices" and added, "The effectiveness of the circulation of information among peers suggests that engagement in practice, rather than being its object, may well be a condition for the effectiveness of learning" (1991:93).

Within this framework, at first glance, it looks as if there is no problem in terms of the legitimacy of membership in the PKK. For, all members belong to a common identity before coming to the group and they all work, both voluntarily and involuntarily, for the production of the same imagined community. Coming from the same background and working for the same future, in a way, provides an automatic, "ascribed" legitimacy to the newcomers and quickly establishes solidarity between them and the old-timers, facilitating in turn their process of learning. However, in reality, this sanguinity remains ephemeral for two reasons. First, despite being accepted into the group quickly, the nature of relationships within the group (especially on the mountain) compels "supposedly" legitimately-peripheral group members to try hard to gain an "achieved" legitimacy and to become a full member because of their bravery, dedication, and loyalty to the group, as well as their obedience to masters, are tested in a continuous manner throughout their membership of the group. Failing in one of the enumerated attributes expected of group members brings their ascribed legitimacy into question; hence, they cannot rely on their automatic membership based on sharing a common identity. Second, the problem of "nepotism" based on members place of origin (called *hemşericilik* in Turkish; *hemşeri* means "fellow townsman") appears to be quite salient in terms of interpersonal relationships and access to participation within the group.

152 Transition stage II

To clarify, given that there are 150 members and less than ten commanders (masters) on average in each PKK camp, a novice's legitimacy and learning through participation is deeply affected by two factors: (1) number of guerillas coming from their own place of origin or its vicinity, and more importantly; (2) the place of origin of the masters. Most of my informants emphasized the importance of these issues; as one of them said, "There are many cliques based on *hemşericilik* and if you don't have any *hemşeri* in the group, you are treated as if you are a stranger ... if one of the commanders is your *hemşeri*, then, you don't have to worry about anything." Thus, the notion of *hemşericilik* has the potential to impact both positively and negatively on the process of learning in relations with peers and deeply influences the legitimacy of membership in that being hemşeri with a master increases the legitimacy of a member, whereas not having one brings his/her legitimacy into question.

In terms of the interpersonal relationships within the PKK, there is perhaps more than catches the eye. That is, there are issues related to transparency, which have important consequences for the legitimacy and increased access to participation. Besides the natural opaqueness of relations within the groups I studied, as necessitated by their violent and secretive structures, I realized that despite the potential positive effects of *hemşericilik,* all relations within the group, be it peer-to-peer or master-novice relations, or even relations among the voluntary and involuntary members for that matter, are characterized by the notion of "prudence." Put differently, as my informants reported, there is a high level of distrust among group members and masters. As I mentioned earlier in the discussion of milieu control, the relationships between peers is controlled and constricted anyway, i.e., the group prohibits relations between males and females, and closely watches who is "teaming-up" with whom. Thus, I assume that one of the most important reasons for the prudent nature of interpersonal relations is that members are prospectively securing their lives within the group, as well as within society in case they will be able to return to it. They all know that there may be state agents within the group, and that some members who leave the groups become a "confessor" and work for the state. They also know that in both cases, such individuals are asked by the police to identify and incriminate group members who participated in the killings of Turkish soldiers. Therefore, it is possible to say that prudence translates itself as a "resource" for disengagement from the groups. Accordingly, some of my informants did not disclose their real identities even to people that are close to them, i.e., *hemşeris*, and tried to maintain a low profile within the group in an effort to avoid the potential wrath of security forces in the future. For example, I had mentioned in the third chapter that Azad-P's most conspicuous personality pattern was prudence (because of his introvertedness), which he would use as a resource in his departure from the group. As an illustration of this, consider the excerpt below from my interview with him:

> For example, my separation from the group shocked many people within the group. They couldn't make sense of it as they said, 'How come this person

...' They would occasionally ask why I was quiet and I used to respond to them by saying that everything was normal. Some people would be really disturbed by my taciturnity and introverted nature. People who saw me for first time would find me a cold person; I had difficulty finding something to share with them. Other group members perceived me as being a man of duty, a self-confident man who doesn't refuse given tasks, etc. I had such a profile within the group. I can say that I used this knowingly; I hid myself by doing this. Because I always knew that I would leave the group someday...

In the revolutionary groups I studied, there were similar problems with respect to the nature of interpersonal relationships. All of my informants from the revolutionary groups made emphasized the negative feelings elicited during the interpersonal relationships within their respective groups such as betrayal, dissatisfaction, and, more importantly, a sense of worthlessness, which can be considered as a loss of significance that prompts significance restoration. What is seen here is the reversal of the process of significance quest. That is, in their paths to political violence, I had argued that most of my informants joined the groups for significance quest, either initiated personally or triggered by a loss of significance. However, spending some time in the groups, the aforementioned problems seem to have created a feeling of the loss of significance in them, which could be restored only by leaving the groups, regardless of the costs attached to it. As an example, consider the experiences of Gökhan-R:

> Anyway ... I came to Istanbul and started to live in my sister's apartment. At one time, I had rented my own apartment in Istanbul, but this time I had to live with my sister. I was a person who dedicated his 24 hours for the revolution. However, in that time, I was still with the group but I had many doubts ... I was thinking, and asking myself, 'Is it possible that the group does not give sufficient care to human relations within the group?' I felt betrayed; weren't we comrades to each other? Weren't we supposed to support each other in hard times? When I saw people [other group members] eating out in restaurants when I was wandering around with an empty stomach, I wasn't saying anything to them. But, I was indeed reproachful of them. I mean, couldn't they think on their own? Is it necessary for you to say your situation? If you look carefully and truthfully, you see the condition of the person in front of you. His lifestyle is quite obvious [that he is in need]. Thus, as a comrade, you have to look out for him. You have to understand the emotions of the person on whom you rely [at other times].

Problem of access and sequestration

According to Lave and Wenger (1991), access to practice as a resource for learning rather than for instruction is an important issue. For instance, in the study of butchers, it has been described that some meat cutters received instruction but the practice, that is, some apprentices worked on the wrapping machine and did not watch journeyman cut and saw the meat. On the other hand, the authors argue that when masters prevent learning by acting as pedagogical authoritarians, "viewing apprentices as novices who should be instructed rather than as peripheral participants in a community engaged in its own reproduction" (1991:72), gaining legitimacy and access to participation becomes an extremely difficult task for the newcomers.

In the groups I studied, the nature of access to participation appears to be paradoxical when it is compared with the notion of access in conventional forms of apprenticeship, in which the issues of continuity and replacement function as a barrier for novices increased participation. Depending on the different developmental cycles, it appears that there was no shortage of access to participation for novice Turkish Penitents, given that they were encouraged from the beginning to participate in the production process, i.e., violence. To specify, in the PKK and in some of the revolutionary groups I studied, newcomers are thrown into violent clashes with the security forces even without receiving sufficient theoretical instruction and proper practical training and equipment. This appears, in turn, to create a sense of confusion and worthlessness in group members, which they define as "philosophy of blood and death" in the PKK, and "revolutionism through marketing the blood of martyrs" in some of the revolutionary groups. The process of recognition of these phenomena takes place faster among those members who joined the groups involuntarily and tried to remain "legitimately-peripheral but not participant" than those who joined the group "voluntarily." These groups seem to implement practices based on such philosophies for several reasons.

First, by sending inexperienced members to violent actions, the groups think that there is a high possibility for them to be killed by security forces. These people are then called "martyrs," whom the groups use in their processes of mystical manipulation to reinforce the groups' existence. In addition, these martyrs provide some political parties operating in the shadow of terrorist groups with an opportunity to "do" politics in the parliament. As Recep-P put it:

> For instance, I asked myself so often, why did they die? They died for nothing. Because they [the PKK] have ten guerrillas killed so that they can make propaganda with them. They have them killed so that they can do politics with the arrival of dead bodies in Diyarbakır [the capital of 'imagined' Kurdistan]. In order for them to influence the people [Kurds], the children of the people must die ... because in such cases, Diyarbakır turns into a battlefield for a month. And since the police respond in kind, it means that a chaotic environment has been created. As a result; the cycle of violence continues. More importantly, all these are being done so that Karayilan [one of the PKK leaders] could make a speech on Roj TV. I mean, everything is being done in an organized way; nothing is happening by chance. In this case, who bears the brunt? The people who died, the businessmen whose shops are vandalized, and the police who scamper around the streets to no avail ... In addition, people receive punishments and they die in prisons. I mean, the

lives of at least 300 people darkened by one incident for one-hour speech, over which ...

On the other hand, although accepting the existence of such policies, Azad-P paid attention to the distinction between the pre- and post-1999 periods with respect to the PKK. He said that these philosophies governed the group's practices especially before the capture of Öcalan in 1999, and hardly ever did they occur after that; because actions based on such philosophies were criticized by the group as "peasantization" (*gundileşme* in Kurdish) and they were convinced that a *stalemate* had been reached, which could not be broken by killing more soldiers:

> I will tell you about a concept ... Öcalan says, 'I don't call that a victory, if it is won over blood.' I mean we [the PKK] don't breathe a sigh of satisfaction over the death of a soldier. It had existed before 1994, but that approach has changed. For instance, there was a term in the group, 'the status of pata-pat' [stalemate]; I mean the PKK understood that it could not kill all the Turkish soldiers, but argued also that the Turkish army could not kill all the guerrillas. Before the 1999 period, there was peasantization (*gundileşme*) in the group; some group leaders said, 'We take more action' to revitalize the group members, even though it was not needed. In that case, they embarked on actions, which led to big casualties let alone bringing any results. Just to give an oral report to the leaders [to show that they are working], some commanders recklessly sent their groups to actions without any preparation. Most of these commanders had village backgrounds; which is why that era was called 'peasantization' by the group.

As mentioned above, my informants criticized some of the revolutionary groups for their conception of *revolutionarism through marketing the blood of martyrs*. In this case, full participation in practice means one's own elimination. The main difference from the PKK is that not only did these groups send inexperienced novices to fatal actions, but also experienced old-timers might be asked to engage in actions that would result in their deaths. Gökhan-R said, for instance,

> Dev-Sol (Revolutionary Left) had a mentality of war, according to which it practiced politics based on blood. It tried for many years to organize itself around the notion of martyrdom, which in turn created a vicious cycle that led to its members' disenchantment.

To give a vivid example to illustrate this, consider Hikmet-R's experience in one of those revolutionary groups that exploited the blood of its members:

> One day, Mustafa [one of the group leaders] came to me and said, 'Rent an apartment for three of you [military committee members], and I will bring you Kalashnikov rifles. The organization is entering into a new phase of attacks, because it has reached a very powerful status in Turkey.' He continued, 'Our

ability to resist torture is good, but we don't have experience in fighting with the police in our cells. Other groups are better than us.' I said, 'OK, why don't you do it?' He responded: 'No, the apartment which I told you to rent will be uncovered and you will have skirmishes with the police... and you will die.' He said exactly this... I told him, 'What are you talking about?' That was the first time I started to feel that I am losing my belief in the group.

On the other hand, Hakan-R said that although many revolutionary groups exploited the blood of their members, there were exceptions. The MLKP (Marxist-Leninist Communist Party), for example, did not resort to such practices.

> Because the MLKP is not fed by such policies; the first goal of the MLKP is to protect its members and not have them killed, for they are needed for the revolution. If in any case one of its members dies, starting from his/her family, it gives its utmost to support them; because he/she has a golden value for it, for he/she died for it [the group]. However, if you send your members to death every day, it means that they have no meaning for you ... It happens in those groups. But in the MLKP, each individual is valuable; I spend 10–15 years training him, how can I send him to death just like that? I need him/her; because he/she is a cadre; and the revolution is a problem of cadre, without which the revolution is impossible.

A second reason for these groups' policies of blood and death has to do with the question of "who is benefiting from the protracted violence?" A commonly held belief among my informants, which corresponds also with general public opinion, is that two parties benefit from the perpetuating nature of spilling the blood, namely, *terrorist groups* and the *deep state*. A crucial aspect of this protracted violence providing members with increased participation in the "production" process has to do with the nature of relations between terrorist groups and the deep state, which can be subsumed under three categories: (1) some of my informants argue that there is a symbiotic relationship between terrorist groups and the deep state, which explains their convergence of interests, i.e., perpetuation of violence; (2) some believe that the deep state cashes in on already existing terrorist groups and their actions through infiltration into these groups; (3) a more radical argument is that at least some terrorist organizations were founded by the deep state to create an ambience of chaos in the country, when "necessary," in order to maintain its stranglehold on power. For instance, Azad-P seemed to have subscribed to the symbiotic relationship argument:

> Yes, what is certain about the PKK is that some people in the group want to see more blood. In 2004, the group took a decision to wage an all-out war against the Turkish army. The logic was, 'A military power [the PKK] is doomed to failure and dissolution, if it does not engage in wars. If you are a real war organization, you have to fight as much as possible; otherwise your raison d'être will be questioned.' Some people in the group staunchly defended, and

still defend this and want that the Turkish army keeps attacking. They want blood and deaths. And the same rule applies to the Turkish military; they also want to see more blood and deaths ... because they know that if there is a death, others will unite with the feeling of taking revenge. I think this psychology of war is used by both sides.

Similarly, and interestingly enough, Fatih, one of my informants from a revolutionary group, had a firsthand experience of such a kind of relationship between his group and the deep state. As implied earlier in the second chapter, the concept of the deep state has an amorphous nature. So it is not easy to define it. But a popular belief is that the Turkish military, or better to say some factions within the military (i.e., Özel Harp Dairesi- The Special Warfare Department), is the major component of the deep state, a behemoth that has been disguised until recently by various "epistemic murks" (Taussig 1984) around it. The group in which Fatih-R participated in violence was famous for its targeted attacks on state infrastructure and certain individuals who are thought to be serving to the interests of imperialist powers and institutions. When I asked him who was providing intelligence for those attacks, he said the following:

At that time [in the beginning of 1990s], we had a real self-esteem boost; we were attacking everywhere like crazy, which indeed generated huge support from the masses. When we decided to attack a target, we knew every minute detail about that person or place; because our relations were quite solid at the time. For instance, even though a search warrant was issued for me, I was entering to General Command of the Gendarmerie, filling my bag with weapons, and exiting freely. They knew that I was a member of X group. [I asked how come? and he continued]: I mean these men [gendarmes] were our contacts, but I didn't know the nature of this. I was just receiving the weapons from them. However, as far as I know, three groups had been established at that time, composed of officers who received training in America. They were on duty in the east [duty refers to extrajudicial killings of Kurds] on a rotating basis. I knew about this, but never questioned it at the time.

This generated a curiosity in me about the nature of those relations, and therefore I took things a little further by asking, "How come you trusted those people? Security forces were behind you, and these soldiers were also state officials, were you not afraid of being arrested?" He replied by saying, "Yes, but the process does not work that way. We had experience of such relationships before; we have always been in close contact with the state. Remember the era of Pol-Der/Pol-Bir; this is no different from those days." Here, he refers to the era before the 1980 coup when society was divided into two groups; on one side the rightist nationalists and the leftist revolutionaries on the other. Security forces were not exempt from this. For instance, police forces were divided into two groups: nationalists gathered around the Pol-Bir (Police-Union) while revolutionaries were organized under the umbrella of Pol-Der (Police-Foundation).[8] The crucial point here is that the formation of such groups undermined the objectivity of police forces in that illegal groups on both sides benefited a great deal from such a division in the police. Thus, it is possible to say that Fatih-R did not question the peculiarity of his relations with the officers in the Gendarmerie because of drawing similarities between pre-1980 era and the time of his experiences in the 1990s. Anyhow, regardless of the nature of such relationships, his experiences demonstrate the existence of *a kind* of the aforementioned relationships between terrorist groups and the deep state.

Furthermore, Fatih-R also believed that his group indulged in too much violence, which he thought was not necessary at the time. Accepting that such excessive violence which his group exerted in the beginning of 1990s increased considerably mass support for the group, he argued that it was not sustainable and pragmatically beneficial for the group in the long run. Long discussions with other group leaders (he was one of the group leaders) did not yield any fruitful results in that sense, which marked his and many other group members' first disillusionment with the group.

> So, we had long debates about these. I said, 'We are constantly escalating our attacks; but until where?' How many soldiers or generals can you kill? Even Mahir Cayan [a symbolic leftist leader] did not kill an army general every day; they paused every once in a while. You cannot hold that much weight anyway; you lack that capacity! If you want to pursue such tactics [attacks], you need to have such capacity. What we did indeed is that we tried to take on more than we could bear. This, in turn, led to heated discussions within the group, because the police struck a significant blow to our group at the time. Then, we started to find excuses; we said, 'We couldn't get organized well enough; we gave this to the police, etc. If we behaved in a principled way, we wouldn't have gotten these blows.' However, that was a wrong interpretation of reality; because if you always approach problems technically, you make a mistake. For, technically, this is all you got anyway; this is your human capital, you have to work with them. The problems lay in our strategy; if you ratchet up your armed attacks and get struck by the police all the time, public support naturally starts to wane. But we tried to overreach our capacity, tried to punch above our weight, if I may, and the man [state] slapped us on our necks.

In some group members, the possibility of murky relations between their groups and the deep state created a sense of suspicion about their respective groups' encouragement of their members in increased participation in the production of violence. To give an example, remember that Hikmet-R was asked openly by his group to be killed in a police raid on his cell. I invoke his experience once again to indicate that his disillusionment occurred because of his suspicion about the link between his group and the deep state.

...He said, 'No, the apartment which I told you to rent will be uncovered and you will skirmish with the police ... and you will die.' He said exactly this ... I told him, 'What are you talking about?' That was the first time I started to feel that I was losing my belief in the group. Because I know what happens to you if you engage in terrorist activities normally. I don't need to be told that I will be killed, because if you are living in a terrorist cell and you encounter the police, you know that you will have to use your weapon. However, what you [the group leader] say is different; there is something else in that logic. It has nothing to do with being an organized revolutionary. It is an insult for you to say that 'You will be killed.' If you say to one of your fellow group member that there will be an armed struggle in the cell, and you will use your weapon; it is worse than cursing him, especially if this person is on the military committee. He is not stupid, he knows that he will fight ... But the point here is, I became suspicious that day. That action was cancelled somehow, but I was right. Because I came to know several months later that that person [Hayri] was working for the deep state and it was him who betrayed me when I was caught by the police.

Overall, the link between the deep state and terrorist groups in understanding my informants' exit from the groups appears to function in two ways. First, in terms of the provision of *full participation* in violence, which elicits a sense of "exploitation," "worthlessness", and "disenchantment" in group members who are asked in a way to volunteer in actions that will bring their own deaths; and second, in terms of prevention of access to full participation in *mature practice*, to which I now turn.

Lave and Wenger argue that the crucial point about legitimate peripherality "is access by newcomers to the community of practice and all that membership entails" (1991:100). Among the benefits that should come with the membership of a community of practice, on the other hand, is "access to a wide range of ongoing activity, old-timers, and other members of the community; and to information, resources, and opportunities for participation (1991:101). In addition, the authors argue that although access is essential for the reproduction of community, it has a problematic nature at the same time. One of the most conspicuous problems about access is the notions of *control* and *selection*.

I mentioned earlier that in the PKK, there was no shortage of participation in practices for the newcomers. Access to participation and information was a major problem for the Turkish Penitents from revolutionary groups, which played out differently in the experiences of each of them. For instance, Gökhan-R thought that it was not that his access to participation was prevented, but his group itself as a whole was not participating *enough* in reproductive activities, i.e., violence. He expressed his disappointment by saying that the group did not want to attract too much attention; and accordingly it always tried to maintain a low profile by keeping the group small and its aspirations as narrow as possible. For a person who was after "heroism," it did not make sense that a group refrained from engagement in mature practices, which was established in the first place to bring about a revolution that intrinsically requires *praxes*, and more often than not, the violent types.

> You start by distributing leaflets about revolution; but after a while, it does not satisfy you. At least it was the case for me. Anyway, in our group, they always tried to keep the group narrow. They didn't want to expand, but ironically they had set out to bring about a revolution with 10 or 15 people. At the beginning, it made sense, because theoretically a revolution would be made possible with a small number of people, who would mobilize millions. At this juncture, psychologically, you choose yourself a lot; you ask yourself, 'What is my duty in this process.' Then you say, 'OK, as a militant, I will do this, do that, etc.' Over the course of time in the group, and through your interpersonal relationships, you start realizing what is best for you. They say, 'You are more suitable for progression in theory, and you in militancy, etc.' Personally, I always thought of myself as having the abilities required for militant structures. I think, because of the issue of 'heroism,' because I wanted to be a hero all the time, I thought that heroism was always at the barrel of a gun. That is why; I compelled the organization in this respect, to engage in more actions. The group always gave us great missions; but the activities we were involved in were so trivial that at one point you start to have a feeling of dissatisfaction. Then, you start questioning, 'Do they really want a revolution?' If you want that, then, you have to persuade the masses, and your organization must be made based on this. But, our group did not do this; it always kept its narrow structure, which is why I had a lot of heated debates with group leaders.

This example and similar others led Gökhan-R to question his group, demonstrating the fact that his psychological disengagement from the group occurred before his capture by the police that marked his physical exit, which I had mentioned in Chapter 4.

On the other hand, the problem of access manifests itself differently in the cases of my other informants from revolutionary groups. Some of my informants expressed their feelings that they were being sequestered by their respective groups in the participation of practices, although in a subtle way given that their sequestration was done under the guise of protecting them from police detection. Some of my informants from revolutionary groups were members of their respective groups' Central Military Committees (MAK in Turkish) that operate, to adopt the jargon of such groups, under "heavily illegal conditions." That is, given that MAK is the most important branch of the revolutionary groups after their Central Committees (MK in Turkish), and that the whole military propaganda is based on the work (bombings, robberies, murders, etc.) of these MAK members, such groups claimed that it is required for them to take extreme care and caution to protect the MAK members. Another reason for this has to do with the size of MAKs, which are comprised of three individuals who then supervise several Red Battalions of nine soldiers. Hakan-R, for instance, was a MAK member for more than ten years before being captured by the police and as he described, this period was the most important reason for his psychological disengagement from political violence and departure from his group.

A strong believer in leftist ideals and communist utopias, Hakan-R believed that in order to bring about the revolution some of his fellow group leaders wanted to move from illegality to politics by establishing a legal party. Nevertheless, the crucial point for him was that it was not that these individuals had a "mentality shift" and lost their belief in violence; it was rather their *conformism* and desires to become bourgeois that gravitated them towards legality. Yet, they did not disclose this idea to the other group members and instead expressed some excuses for the lack of "action" in the group, i.e., the sequestration of MAK members, by saying that they would maintain a low profile until the heavy scrutiny of the state security apparatuses was loosened. Hakan-R described his subjective feelings of his and his like-minded friends' sequestration through a philosophical explanation. According to him, the organization or the party must be a means to an end (the communist revolution); but some of his group's leaders started to take the party as an end in itself.

> I mean, what is a party? It is not an end in itself; it is just a means to an end. However, if means become an end, you lose. This was the problem of Turkey's revolution, as it was my own problem. For instance, we started as a movement, then became a path, and eventually established the party. However, after becoming a party, what happened? The party became an end for us, which meant that from that moment onwards; we had to protect the party. However, the issue is, why should I protect the party? Let it be destroyed if it is its fate; let it be dissolved by the police, I can reestablish it. In fact, we forgot about the revolution, and instead started to trouble ourselves only about protecting the party. I was entering the houses of our supporters at night; I was participating in the syndical meetings; I was taking notes and writing. But after we started taking the party as an end, we started to bureaucratize. Especially after becoming a MAK member, we were told not to participate in 1 May events for instance. They said, 'don't participate in 1 May events, because what will we do without you if you get caught by the police?' This was nonsense; what will happen to the party? Nothing! Others will come after us and the party will continue walking. But if you think, 'If I go, the party will no longer exist,' it just means that you became a bureaucrat, though under the guise of heavily illegal conditions. After that, we started to live in upscale neighborhoods side by side with the bourgeoisie. In 1999, I was paying 500 TL (Turkish liras) for rent. Can you imagine this? I mean, I was staying in a castle. Why? Because, I could get caught by the police who were cruising the streets of shantytowns ... What happens if I get caught brother! I don't care; but all revolutionary groups were like this. They all did this in the name of protecting the parties. However, I believe that 'a person thinks as he lives.' Losing all my hope from revolution ... I mean, you start struggling against this, but some people already made this a lifestyle.

Ooh, what a beautiful life! Especially after all you suffered ... This was not expressed however; this lifestyle was undergirded ideologically.

The real issue, in fact, was conformism. You talk about revolution, but what do you do now? It is not your concern indeed; what you are trying to do is to legalize. You want to legalize the party [illegal party] with hopes that the state will open up opportunities for you. You are just trying to prepare yourself for that kind of life [legal life]. However, this is not right ... I have to die for the revolution; I don't have to survive. I am a revolutionary; how can you impose such a lifestyle on me? If you are imposing this, then, you are a revisionist. Our group was not the only one however; most revolutionary groups were the same. My group used to mobilize more than 30,000 people, but it arrived a place where it couldn't manage even a handful of people. Because the masses recognize the change in you, the fact that you gave up on revolution can be seen in your writings on the walls, in your narratives and inclinations. When the theory and practice don't match, it is quickly detected by the people.

What is significant about Hakan-R's case is that he did not leave his group because of losing his belief in revolution; rather, he became disillusioned with his group for its sequestration of him and several of his friends from participation in group's activities. As they had experienced the first seed of doubt about their position in their group, and in fact reached their psychological disengagement, Hakan-R and his friends (about 50 of them) started to think about splitting from the group and establishing themselves under the umbrella of another group. He claimed that since the group or some people within the group who had ties with the deep state detected their intention, it sold them out to the state by cooperating with it for their capture.

One year before our capture, we, about 50 of us, had started to pull the weapons from the group in order to separate from it. Unfortunately, we got caught; but I am one 100 percent sure that the deep X [his group] was behind our capture. They blatantly sold us to the state authorities, because they were aware of our thoughts, because we were disclosing the wrongs and writing about them ... They were not, however, being published in our newspaper [illegal], as we were being censured by the group. Additionally, Mahmut [one of the group leaders] said to me, 'Comrade Hakan, look; this organization is a khan [public house], it has two doors. You enter from here, and exit from there. You do whatever you can to stay in the khan.' But he didn't say, 'Be the owner of the khan.' Pay attention to this ... After a while, in fact, I intuitively started to think that there were the owners of this khan and I would not be able to be one of the owners no matter what I do.

Furthermore, their sequestration under the guise of heavy illegality conditions generated some psychological problems among them, e.g., feelings of *worthlessness* and boredom out of *idleness*, *alienation* from the cause and the people, and so on. Being disconnected from practices and the masses made my informants feel like a "fish out of water," and in an effort to protect their anonymity and to avoid exposing their identities to the residents in their buildings and neighborhoods, they had to be extremely careful in their daily lives. This lack of practice led to psychological idleness, notwithstanding the fact that they were physically active and mobile, camouflaging themselves through blending into society as ordinary citizens. Given that this period of idleness lasted so long, it seems to have created strong feelings of dissatisfaction and loss of significance in my informants, which in turn contributed to their disillusionment and departure from their respective groups. Hakan-R described the foregoing issues as follows:

> Anyway, I mean, since we were in the MAK, we became disconnected from the organization. Everything was forbidden to us, even actions in the legal sphere. All battalions had to obey this. To be concise, we were a group of people who were living under heavily illegal conditions, in a glass lantern so to speak. We were checking our cells often and in a serious way. All eight of us had apartments and everybody was watching each other; they would inform the group if you did something against group strategy. Why? Because when you rented an apartment, you said you are working in a factory; so you have to prove that you are working every day. I mean, if a worker left his house at 9 am or 10 am, it would attract a lot of attention. Everybody went through training on these issues; I mean, they were pumping these ideas on us constantly; 'Pay attention to this and that, etc.' There was constant indoctrination. As a result, our mentality started to change; we were like 'fish out of water.' Why? Because you are a revolutionary; if you are cut off from the masses, you will start ganging up after a while. Because all day … I mean, we leave the apartment; what will we do all day? Time does not pass in the corners of coffeehouses. I mean, you cannot go anywhere; even passing through central locations was prohibited. So, what will I do the whole day?

I asked him, 'How did you get motivated then?' and he responded:

> Forget about being motivated; I became a maniac. I mean, you sit in the apartment, but you cannot even use the toilet. When you flush the toilet, will people not think that there is somebody in the apartment? I mean, you are on tenterhooks even in the apartment.

Summary of the theoretical explanations related to individual disengagement

The purpose of this section was to examine Turkish Penitents' causes of disillusionment and departure from their respective groups. Following Lave and Wenger (1991), I conceptualized the groups in which Turkish Penitents lived as *communities of violent practices*. My findings suggest that the crucial reasons behind my informants' disengagement and exit are located in the problems and contradictions inherent in legitimate peripheral participation in communities of practice, which were sought in four different areas: (1) gaining legitimate membership and the nature of interpersonal relations; (2) the didactic nature of teaching and indoctrination as well as the effects of the groups' cult-like structures, i.e., thought reform; (3) the nature of the means, modes, and relations of production in communities of violent practice; that is, the effects of imagined communities of practice and postponed imaginations; (4) the issue of access and sequestration in participation. I will elaborate on these issues in the concluding section of the next chapter (for the purpose of coherence since they are connected chapters), but it is safe for now to say that the experiences of the Turkish Penitents in these four areas caused their disillusionment with the groups and eventually facilitated their disengagement from them. However, since there is a time difference between having the first seed of doubt, psychological disengagement, and physical exit from the groups, it is necessary to account for the extended stay of the Turkish Penitents in their respective groups. To this end, in the next chapter, I will talk about the individual reasons (willingness to stay) and difficulties emanating from external factors to explain their delaying departure from those groups. I will then explore the personal and other resources that the Turkish Penitents used in order to overcome those difficulties and realize their physical exit from their respective groups.

Notes

1. I use past tense here, because of the fact that torture by law enforcement officials is almost extinct due to recent governments' policies of "zero-tolerance" for torture. This, in fact, has important role in my informants' decisions to exit from their groups, which I will explore in the next section.
2. The United Nations established Mahmur camp as a refugee camp in 1998 in Mosul, Iraq, for Kurdish people living on Turkey's Iraqi border that were evacuated for security reasons and took refuge in that region. There are currently 12,000 people living in the camp, which is managed by 60 people. Turkey demands the closure of this camp by arguing that the PKK uses the camp inmates and that the camp harbors PKK guerillas and their weapons.
3. Öcalan declared himself as Demigod in his book *Dialogues with the Free Life* (*Ozgur Yasamla Diyaloglar*), which was published in 2002.
4. Since its establishment, the PKK has claimed to have fought a war of "self-defense" based on the Geneva Conventions. However, it appears that the group has used international laws selectively, evidenced by its forcible and voluntary recruitment of young children, before they make their normative transition from childhood to adulthood. The Geneva Convention's Additional Protocol I provides that children should be protected from participating in hostilities and that a person who has not reached the age of fifteen is considered to be a child. In addition, according to the United Nations' Convention of the Rights of the Child (1989), the definition of child was changed such that a person is considered a child if he has not attained the age of eighteen. See Honwana (2008) for details.
5. As mentioned in Chapter, the events of Taksim Gezi Park may have changed this situation, i.e., police use of excessive force and the government's discriminatory and authoritarian tendencies may have radicalized some individuals. Also, they may have been exploited by leftist-revolutionary groups, in particular.

6 A commonly held view in Turkey among people, and even among most terrorist organization including the PKK, is that Öcalan was indeed working for the state (deep state) from the beginning, which I will explain in more detail in the next section when discussing the problems of access in participation.
7 In a TV interview in January 2012, Kemal Burkay, a renowned Kurdish poet and politician, said that Duran Kalkan, too, has been working for the deep-state since the late 1970s. More specifically, he argued, the deep-state/counter-guerrilla movement commissioned Öcalan and Kalkan to establish the PKK before the 1980 military coup, and have supported them ever since and, more importantly, used them when it was deemed "necessary."
8 In 1979, the total number of the Turkish National Police (TNP) was 47,662; and the number of officers who were members of Pol-Der was around 17,000, while 2,000 officers were registered to Pol-Bir (Evren 1990:402).

6 Transition stage III

Difficulties and resources for disengagement

Extended stay in groups: willingness to stay and difficulties related to disengagement

Just like in any other collective group and in conventional forms of apprenticeship, hundreds of individuals leave every year from communities of violent practice as a result of the disillusionment similar to what was described in the previous chapter. However, because of the nature of their violent, bounded, and secretive structures, as well as the close-knit interpersonal relationships within them, exits from such groups differ significantly from departures from conventional groups. Therefore, for a full understanding of the notion of disengagement from political violence, the following factors that seem to influence the extended stay of individuals before exiting violent groups must be taken into account: (1) strong ideological beliefs and loyalty to the group; idealization and identification with the group; a sense of empowerment and satisfaction; and routinization of practices; (2) the state of liminality when disengaging, i.e., being betwixt and between the fear of failure to exit on the one hand and anxiety over being accepted by, and integrated to, society on the other; and lastly, (3) the fear of punishment upon return.

My informants from revolutionary groups appear to have had stronger ideological beliefs and loyalties to their groups than my informants from the PKK. Except for Gökhan, all of my informants from the revolutionary groups saw themselves as professional revolutionaries until they left the groups; while some of them have retained their revolutionary ideas even after their disengagement. Ahmet-R, for instance, expressed his dedication to his group and the revolution by saying that his group had gone through several transformations since the beginning of 1970s and that he has been a part of every move in this evolutionary process until he had his first seed of doubt about his group. Moreover, "acquisition of certain skills is important to understand prolonged engagement in terrorist activities" (Horgan 2005: 85). Since Ahmet-R developed strong leadership skills and assumed a leadership role in his group from the beginning, his process of disengagement took longer than of an ordinary group member's. Hakan-R, on the other hand, felt a great sense of satisfaction and empowerment by being a member of his group; as he said, "being a Sunni member in a predominantly Alevi group was a big honor; I always saw an extra respect for this and never been subject to contempt," and added, "when you are a member of such a group, you are always at the forefront of everything; people come and ask your advice."

Pyschologist Jerald Post argues that "when we join a group, and our views become evident from discussion, we may seek approval by sharing those views in an attempt to display a greater level of commitment to the group's ideal and thereby demonstrate our loyalty over time" (1987:312). On the other hand, becoming part of collective entities is an important aspect of extended stay in groups; as Castano and Dechesne asserted, it "allows individuals to extend their selves in space and time [and hence] to overcome the inherent limitations of their individual identity inextricably linked to a perishable body" (2005:233). When this collectivist shift occurs, "a group can take on a sense of 'fictive kin' and group loyalties can become as strong as blood ties (Speckhard and Akhmedova 2005:135). Furthermore, dehumanization of the enemy ("the Other") is also a potent feature of justifying continued membership and attacks, and "commitment to a special, focused community to which the terrorist belongs" (Horgan 2005:112). Lastly, the process of the routinization of practices is also important for making sense of extended stay in groups, which functions in two ways for the individual:

> (1) there is a reduction in the effort required for conscious, deliberate decision-making, minimizing the likelihood of situations occurring where the individual has to engage in moral evaluations; (2) the individual finds it easier to avoid the implications of their behavior by focusing on the details of his job rather than on its meaning.
>
> (Kelman 1973:46)

In light of these arguments, it is possible to suggest that strong ideological beliefs, loyalty to and identification with the group, adopting the group-think approach and dehumanization of the Other all contribute to the extended stay of individuals in communities of violent practice. Nevertheless, as mentioned earlier, the lifting of the ideological influence results in the dissolution of the misrecognition of "the real conditions," in which members of such groups live and function. To be more specific, various factors leading to disillusionment facilitate the lifting of the ideological influence such as perceived injustices, unattainable nature of the group's goals, adoption of new approaches through introspection and concentration, and so on. In particular, these latter two factors provide them with an opportunity to focus on the meaning of their practices, leading in turn to a reevaluation of their continued membership of the groups and eventually resulting in their disengagement from them.

On the other hand, while all of the factors enumerated above played a role in the continued membership of my informants to revolutionary groups, the extended stay of my informants from the PKK appears to be linked largely to their *liminal state* (liminality) in the group and *fear of punishment* upon return. Both liminal and liminality are derived from Latin *limen*, which means "threshold" – that is, the bottom part of a doorway that must be crossed when entering a building (La Shure 2005:1), or, as I view it, a "vestibule" between two train carriages. Thus, the concept of liminality refers to a state of being *betwixt and between*, which gained popularity with the work of Victor Turner who focused on the second (liminal/transitional) phase in Van Gennep's schema of the rites of passage. In formulating his thoughts on liminality, Turner developed a conceptual framework around "social dramas," which is based on his personal experience of Ndembu life in Zambia. He argues, "our quotidian life, social dramas, whether in small groups or large, is offspring of both culture and nature, although the cultural ways of becoming aware of them – rituals, stage plays, carnivals, films, etc. – vary with culture, climate, technology, group history, etc." (1987:100). Proceeding from the abovementioned distinction between the cultural and natural worlds, Turner argued that "one of the most arresting properties of Ndembu social life in villages is propensity toward conflict ... which arises in the form of public episodes of tensional irruption" (100). He called these irruptions "social dramas," on the basis that the conflict-ridden nature of Ndembu social life provides nothing but "loyalty and obligation" as available choices for people; in other words, in Ndembu society, choice is overwhelmed by duty (Turner 1974:35).

Likewise, the analogy of social dramas is helpful in understanding my informants' lives in the PKK as it also provides nothing but "loyalty and obligation" for its members, and in it, "choice is overwhelmed by duty," especially because of the group's expectations from all Kurds to fulfill the "necessities" of their Kurdish identity. Most of my informants from the PKK wanted to leave the group at the outset but could not realize this goal, for they were always betwixt and between the fear of failed attempts of exit on the one hand, which would mean the member's execution, and anxiety over being accepted and reintegrated into society on the other. Since I mentioned in earlier sections in the discussion of groups' strategies of milieu control, I will not reiterate here the examples related to my informants' fear of attempting to exit from the groups. It suffices to say that exit from the PKK was, and still is, harder than exit from the revolutionary groups because most of my informants from the PKK spent their time in political violence in *the* mountains, a bounded environment with high levels of group control and pressure; whereas, my informants from the revolutionary groups spent their time in urban environments where they would have higher chances of survival if they left, as it would be easier to escape and live relatively incognito in such environments.

Furthermore, for a better understanding of the extended stay in groups, it is important to address the effects of anxiety over the likelihood of being accepted into communities of origin. This latter issue played out in several ways for the Turkish Penitents who wanted to exit from their groups: (1) when considering exit from the groups, my informants, especially those from the PKK, felt compelled to return to their communities of origin because, prior to their entry into the group, most of them used to live in small villages and towns and they could not imagine living in places other than their previous communities; (2) this obligation made them hesitate to leave the groups because they knew that they would most likely be treated as a "traitor" and "wolf in sheep's clothing" by people in those societies, if not being subjected to harsher physical harassment or even more severe punishment by group members living in those communities (these people are called *milis* (militia) in the PKK); (3) since they are unsure whether a search warrant had been issued for them, they were afraid of being subjected to severe and lengthy punishments by the state authorities. This third point is crucial also in the sense that terrorist groups have a strategy to send every member to at least several serious attacks on Turkish state infrastructure and people (incursions into military posts, bombings, assassinations, robberies, etc.) in an effort to make sure that members think twice before attempting to leave the group for the fear of punishment by the Turkish state because, as my informants put it, of their "contaminated identities."

Resources for disengagement

Despite the risks and difficulties associated with disengagement from terrorist groups, individuals use various resources in overcoming those difficulties and that facilitate their physical exit, which is preceded by a process of disillusionment with their respective groups. These resources can be divided into four categories; (1) the change of mentality in individuals and their adoption of new approaches and philosophies of life; (2) their personality orientations and styles of coping; (3) turning points and serendipities; and (4) the prospects of repentance laws. Following Moss (2001), the last category will be explored in the next chapter in the discussion of "the politics of repentance" where I will conceptualize the relationships between my informants' confessions and collaboration and the Turkish state's promises of rewards as "gift exchanges," from a Maussian perspective. I will now examine the effects of the first three categories on the processes of Turkish Penitents' disengagement.

Change of mentality and adoption of new approaches and philosophies of life

My findings suggest that most of my informants had an incremental change of mentality as a result of various factors that caused their disillusionment such as perceived injustices in interpersonal relationships within the groups, indoctrination through thought reform, postponement of the utopia and unattainability of goals, problems of access and sequestration *vis-à-vis* participation in practices, etc. This change of mentality manifested itself as renunciation of violence and adoption of non-violent behaviors and pacific approaches.

Among my seven informants from the PKK, four of them joined the group involuntarily. Azad-P, one of the other three, had a penchant to non-violence from childhood to adult life; Gurkan-P joined the group not for his ideological beliefs but because of his psychological problems, while Recep-P joined the group voluntarily and believed, before joining the group, in the role of violence in achieving political aspirations. Thus, it is sensible to argue that six of my informants from the PKK did not believe in violence from the beginning while Recep-P's approach to violence altered as a result of a change in his mentality while living in the group. On the other hand, all of my six informants from the revolutionary groups that previously held strong ideologies and belief in revolutionary violence had a mentality change, which manifested itself differently in each of them. Some of the Turkish Penitents from the revolutionary groups kept their ideology and maintained their belief in the justifiability of "revolutionary violence," while thinking that their political goals were no longer attainable through violence. In the words of one of my informants, they said "Yes" to struggle, but "No" to violence. Others, however, had a mentality shift, which led them to renounce ideology and violence altogether. I call the ones in the first group as "detached" individuals and others in the second group as "repentants."

Such typology is much akin to McAdam's perspective on change in social movements, who distinguish between a radical transformation of one's life – "conversion" – and the more common form of personal change – "alternation" (1989:745). The latter is not as drastic as conversion; "the crucial difference between conversion and alternation centers on the degree to which the change is continuous with the individual's previous life and conception of self" (Sampson and Laub 1993:312). In light of McAdam's perspective, it is possible to argue that repentants have been through an incremental process of conversion, whereas detacheds' incremental transformation took the form of a process of alternation. For, although renouncing violence and leaving terrorist groups, the detacheds do not impugn socialist ideals and lead a politicized life, mostly with a small group of like-minded individuals. Repentants, on the other hand, not only left terrorism behind, but also felt remorse and have tried since to compensate for the wrongs that they have done. According to these definitions, all of my informants from the PKK showed tendencies to fall into the second category, i.e. they are all "repentants"; whereas four of my informants from the revolutionary groups appeared to be "detached" while Soli-R and Gökhan-R seem to be more like "repentants."

Being contrite about the damage they have inflicted, repentants embark on constructive works with the state authorities in preventing other individuals to resort to violence, i.e., they share information about their groups, about the psychology of individuals in terrorist groups, about the notion of political violence in the country, the links between the deep state and terrorist groups and so on. These activities, in fact, help them in terms of *reengagement* in *something* after disengagement; but since they are only in touch with state officials, such activities do not help them reintegrate into society fully. The stage of reincorporation into society is indeed an important aspect of disengagement from political violence, which I shall explore in the next chapter. For an understanding of the effects of mentality change and new philosophies of life on disengagement, consider the following examples, both from the PKK and the revolutionary groups.

Case: Gökhan-R

In my group, there was even a philosophy of exit from the group. They said, 'He who doesn't become a revolutionary at the age of 20 is heartless; but he who doesn't quit at the age of 30 is brainless.' In a more limpid life, you start seeing that revolutionary process is not an instantaneous thing; achieving this utopia takes a process that is beyond the lifespan of an individual. When you look at people who motivated you in the first place, you realize that they have operated for several years in the group; they spend some time in prison; they come out and retreat from violence, and finally establish a normal life for themselves. Then, you also want to distance yourself from this (violent) life and live in tranquility. On the other hand, most groups argue that they are defending the rights of people. However, as I have familiarized myself with numerous groups, I can say that I haven't seen such thing in any of those groups. I mean, in reality, I haven't seen them doing something for the service of people. It is quite wrong to portray shantytown-resistance as service to people, because you are looting people's property. Trying to maintain this (shantytown settlements) is not a service to people; but they say this in order to justify their actions. In this respect, mafia and terrorist organizations are not different from each other. They exploit the property of individuals that are products of their personal labor. In fact, if you compare fascism and socialism, you will see that they are the two sides of the same coin; they both prioritize their own interests. If you narrow down these people, the numbers of these people (elite) will come down to several thousands. With them, you can deal with different formulas instead of violence. But as long as you are in a void, you cannot see this...

In addition, the distribution of wealth in Turkey today is better, but I don't think that the left had anything to do with it. When you look historically, the Turkish left tried to save the whole population of 70 million all at once, which indeed put it in a vicious cycle. Instead, it had to try to change people by starting from individual households, to the streets, and finally to the whole country. If you want to do something, you start respecting others; but if you try to put yourself on an exaggerated mission, idolize yourself and say, 'I am the protector of your rights,' you just satisfy your feelings at that moment ...

Here, Gökhan refers to another reason for the change of mentality among my informants which came about as a result of a macro level development in Turkey, i.e., the end of the Turkish Left.

I asked him if he meant to say that change should come about through a bottom-up approach instead of top-down, he continued:

> Yes ... I experienced it in my life personally. I mean, if you become friends with bad people, there is no positive outcome. You have to have dialogues with good people; but this doesn't mean that you go to a community (*cemaat* in Turkish), to the state, or the like. You can distinguish a good person from a bad person. You should be friends with people who protect their dignity, who respect others and work in an ethical way; such people will not harm you. But if you befriend people who hold guns in their hands, both from terrorist groups and the deep state, these people are not doing you any good. Why? Because, they will ask you to use that gun one day; no doubt about it ... Using guns with good intentions and for the purpose of the 'goodness' of people, too, does not help; as Lenin said, 'The road to hell is paved, gilded and furnished with stones of good intentions.' I mean, this doesn't take us anywhere; but if we act with our minds and hearts and choose to serve people, this takes us to good places. You hold somebody's hand; he holds others', and so on ... Then, we can develop each other; but this cannot be found in the left.

For the effects of the end of the Turkish left for the change of mentality, consider also the following case:

Case: Hakan-R

> When you look today, you see that there is no armed group from the left. The state did not do anything; the left destructed itself. In fact, it was supposed to be this way: We should have gone to people and told them our problems, dreams, and goals, and asked for their help ... and if they said no, we should have stopped there. It was supposed to be this way, because this business [revolution] must be based on voluntariness. Because, if you [the left] were a true power, they would bring everything to you voluntarily ... If you are powerful enough, the masses are on your side anyway. If the state is stronger, they are on the side of the state; if mafia is stronger ... this is normal. We were not aware of the fact that people were with us not because of their socialist views and revolutionary identities. They were with us because we were instilling fear in them, with our power and watchmen at nights in the neighborhoods. They were feeling that they

would say, 'the state is not here, they are here ...' In addition, the biggest reason for the end of the Turkish left is that their materials are taken away from them. Tell me, how can you mobilize people around the notion of torture today?

In addition, in explaining the role of the adoption of new approaches and philosophies of life, Hakan-R emphasized the importance of his mentality shift that led him to abandon his Cartesian dualisms of good and bad, black and white, etc., which he previously used to demonize the Other during his time in the group. As a result of this mentality shift, he started instead to identify and sympathize with, and learn about, the Other.

Now, I don't believe in the division between black and white: 'you are bad, I am good, etc.' I don't believe this. There is no absolute goodness or badness; this is now my philosophy of life. Humans are born as equal, they do have both of these aspects in their genes, but one of them comes upfront through experiences in life ... In other words, good and bad are in constant conflict with each other; in this way, we understand that people are good at certain times and bad at other times.

In his book, "On Suicide Bombing", Asad (2007) takes issue with the notion of "just war," in which it is assumed that there is a legal definition of war, but also that there is a moral distinction between warfare (a state function) and terrorism (the disruptive activity of ruthless individuals). He suggests that because of this mentality the very phrase "just terrorism" appears to us as an impossible contradiction. He argues, however, that if terrorism is not only about physical violence but also about intrusion of fear into the everyday lives of people, the same applies to war as well. The brutality of state army and a terrorist group have much in common. Even though in a formal sense the state armies are subject to international humanitarian law this does not constitute as much of an obstacle to deliberate cruelty as might appear at first sight. It has been argued that sometimes wars may be necessary to justify the violence by state armies. By the same token, Asad argues, terrorists may see that the violence they inflict may be sometimes necessary. He further states that some people justify the killing of the civilians by soldiers by saying that "they would not kill if they didn't have to." Similarly, he poses the following question. Could not the same be said of the terrorist whose killing of civilians is at once deliberate and coerced? He opines that terrorists believe that they have reached their limit and had no other choice but violence; if they kill enough civilians perhaps the politically responsible would respond in the desired way.

In light of Asad's foregoing arguments, I have found that most of the Turkish Penitents from the revolutionary groups did not have a problem in terms of the "justifiability" of violence for the purposes of revolution. They thought that violence perpetrated by the state was no different from violence inflicted upon the state apparatus and people by their groups. The crucial point was that, because of going through a mentality change, they lost their belief in violence as a viable and fruitful means to achieve their ends. Moreover, they believed that the environment for violence, which they call "revolutionary state," did not emerge naturally, but was instead constructed by the deep state. Exemplifying these arguments, consider the following case:

Case: Hakan-R

We defined ourselves as revolutionary. We never saw ourselves as terrorists. I never inflicted terror on anyone; even today, I don't see what I did as terrorism. Because when you look carefully, it becomes clear who is the real terrorist [implying the state as terrorist]. If the goal is to protect the indivisibility of the state ... it was the same for us. So if it is the right of the state, why do I not have the same right? [I reminded him the Weberian definition of the state as having the monopoly of legitimate use of violence based on law and he continued.] Yes, but the law is written by people; they sit down and make laws based on their needs. I mean, the law is a subjective phenomenon. Everyone can create his/her own law. You may be illegal, but if you manage to gain power, you may create your own law. For example, if the Sultanate was not destroyed, we would be reading that Atatürk was a traitor today ...

On the other hand, the notion of state is a new, modern phenomenon. So, do I have to accept its definition? If I don't feel like that and if I can undergird this argument, why should I accept your definition of the state? I accept that the state does something on the grounds of law. But I may struggle against that law in an effort to establish a new type of state. Now, is this not my right? People may not think this way, but this is how I think; this is what the right of the minority means.

When I was captured, Mr. Fatih [a senior chief in the terrorism division in Istanbul Police Department] said, 'Hakan, look; what we did here to you is unforgivable [torture] ... but I apologize to you, please forgive me.' This was one of the best things I could hear in this country at this age. I said to myself, 'I think this country will be better from now on. Our lives have gone, but at least things will improve for the future generations [his eyes are watering]. Because we suffered a lot in this country; but we didn't do anything. We did, but in the final analysis, the state forced us; it took us and threw into that pool. It was the state who did all these things to us; neither America nor Russia ... Or, politicians who were the puppets of those powers did it to us. They destroyed the youth of this country; they killed the future of this country. Three generations have been destroyed for nothing. Why? Because, they did not want this country to develop ... what does this country lack? Do you think its farmers are lazy, not hardworking, or not creative? Or, its workers, for that matter ... Leave them alone and watch; they will build airplanes. I worked for many years in factories; I know how smart they are. But, they were not left alone lest they make both ends meet [direct translation]. People ask about the deep state; here is the deep state. Here is the Ergenekon; here is the Gladyo ...

Hakan-R's opinions, in fact, are shared by most of my informants who think that even though violence can be justified for various reasons, the conditions for violence in Turkey have been historically fabricated by the deep state, which has been able to maintain its stronghold on power by capitalizing on the chaotic environment created by such violence.

All in all, change of mentality and adoption of new philosophies of life influenced the Turkish Penitents' processes of disengagement in a significant way in that, through introspection and reevaluation, they started to focus on the *meaning* of their actions rather than their technical features, which contributed to their humanization of the Other and disillusionment with their groups' ideology, tactics, and goals.

Personality orientations and styles of coping related to disengagement

In their Pathmakers study, Harrington and Boardman (1997) explored the lives of 100 Americans who achieved success in their careers by "beating the odds" which are stacked against them. Calling these individuals "Pathmakers" and presuming that social support and redundancy of opportunity of Pathmakers might be far less common than of demographically advantaged people, the authors expected that personal resources would be more crucial to Pathmakers' career success. Building on various authors, they looked at some of these resources that they subsumed into two categories, i.e., motivations and personality orientations. My informants present strong similarities to Pathmakers in the sense that despite extreme risks and difficulties associated with physical exit from terrorist groups, and given that there are hundreds of people who succumb to these risks and difficulties, my informants managed to exit from the groups physically, if not mentally, as is the case for some of my informants. Thus, borrowing from these authors, I also explored the Turkish Penitents' personal resources in my fieldwork in order to understand whether they had any effect on overcoming those risks and difficulties that influenced their exit from the groups.

Comparing Turkish Penitents with those who are still in terrorist groups would yield much better results, but since I did not have the opportunity to talk to individuals who are presently active in terrorist groups, I wanted to see if there are any similarities and differences between Turkish Penitents who left two different types of groups, i.e., the separatist PKK and revolutionary groups. Specifically, I searched for answers to questions such as, "Are Turkish Penitents from the PKK and revolutionary groups psychologically similar or different?" "Is there a common psychological orientation concerning exit from the groups?" In addition, since I could not find any significant correlation between their motivations (such as achievement, affiliation and power motivation), I focused merely on their personality orientations and styles of coping. The judgment about these orientations and styles is made by me if the behaviors associated with these orientations – which will be explained below – were encountered two or more times within the interview transcriptions.

Reward- and cost-orientation

Thibaut and Kelley speculate that "some people are particularly oriented to the rewards they might obtain, and relatively insensitive to the costs they might incur in the course of striving for rewards" (in Harrington and Boardman 1997:17). They describe such "reward-oriented" people as tending to feel *confident*, *powerful*, and *oriented to success*. In contrast, "cost-oriented" people, as they are particularly sensitive to the costs they might suffer, are described as generally "constricted, powerless, and oriented towards the avoidance of failure" (1997:17). On the other hand, it has been argued that "reward-oriented people have relatively optimistic perceptions of their past and future performances, are willing to undertake relatively difficult tasks, tend to learn more than cost-oriented people about those tasks, and therefore tend to perform somewhat better and reap greater rewards" (1997:18). It seemed plausible to me, then, to think that my informants, among other things, had to be willing to see opportunities and to take action despite the possibility that costs may be incurred in the process, that is, they would be more reward-oriented than cost-oriented.

My findings suggest some differences between my informants from the PKK and those from revolutionary groups with regard to their reward-cost orientation. All my informants from the latter groups ($n=6$) showed tendencies toward reward-orientation. From the PKK, three of my informants were reward-oriented, while four of them were cost-oriented. Interestingly, all of these three from the PKK joined the group involuntarily through forced recruitment, but they were still seeking rewards while they were in groups. To give several examples, Selim-P said "Our squad commander liked several people; I was amongst them. I was quite frail, but I made a lot of sacrifices. I was fulfilling all duties without any objection.

So he rewarded me with a badge." In another case, he said "Our squad was a perfect squad; all members were true warriors which is why regional commander congratulated us." One of the most conspicuous features of cost-orientation is "avoidance of failure," which is exemplified best in Zilan-P's case. On the mountain, intimacy between men and women guerillas was strictly prohibited and Zilan was extremely meticulous about this, for she did not even talk to her husband (remember that she was taken to the mountain by him) in order to avoid the stigma of being labeled as a "promiscuous" girl. She said:

> If I had spoken with him, they would definitely know that I had a relationship with him. Had this taken place, I would kill myself. I couldn't accept this, because I never failed on this while I was on the mountain. Maybe this emotion was springing from my feudal background. Because during my time in the organization no one said you have this or that deficiency... which is why I could not accept such accusations.

In light of the abovementioned results, it seems logical to argue that both reward and cost-orientation facilitated my informants' disengagement from their respective groups. Considering that most of my informants ($n=9$) were reward-oriented, it made their disengagement easier in the sense that life after "exit" from the group appeared to be the best reward for them. On the other hand, it is sensible to opine that my informants' cost-orientation ($n=3$) also helped them in their decision-making to exit from the groups because of the cost of staying in the group, which my informants admitted to be worse than death, seemed greater than the cost of attempting to exit, i.e., a probable death as a result of failure in exiting.

Internal and external locus of control

Building on the work of various authors, Harrington and Boardman suggested that it is useful to differentiate "two major attitudes people entertain about the causes of things that happen to them and others" (1997:18). Based on such a division, they argued that those who take the view that they are the causes of things that happen to them seem to have "internal" locus of control; while others who believe that forces external to themselves are more likely to exert the most important influence in terms of what happens to them. There is indeed a great deal of literature showing the important differences between people whose locus of control is internal and those for whom it is external. For Harrington and Boardman, most of the ideas developed in this body of literature are related to the notions about reward-cost orientations discussed above. They assumed that most of the Pathmakers who believed that their rewards are contingent upon their behavior also had a strong internal locus of control. As opposed to people who argue that each life situation requires a new assessment of the locus of control, they suggested that the locus of control as a personality variable was fairly stable overtime. Finally, their findings suggested that the key psychological difference between Pathmakers and Controls was their locus of control.

When my informants were judged according to whether they saw the locus of control over their lives in internal factors or saw external factors predominating, I realized that their orientation shifted in each life situation. In general, six of my informants seemed to have had stronger belief in their ability to control what goes on in their lives, while seven of them saw external factors to determine what happened to them, e.g., fate, God or the *state*. From the PKK, three of my informants had external locus of control while four of them had internal. Among my informants from the revolutionary groups, two had internal locus of control while four of them invoked external factors to be more influential in their lives.

However, when their orientations were judged with respect to their participation in violence and their processes of disengagement, all 13 of them alluded that external factors were more influential. My informants from revolutionary groups stated that they joined the groups voluntarily but they were compelled to resort to violence by the state. Laying the blame on an external factor in this sense seems to have helped them in their decision-making process to disengage (this corresponds with one of their styles of coping, i.e., "rationalization" which I will talk about shortly). Most of my informants from the PKK (six of them), on the other hand, said that since they had they not joined the PKK involuntarily, they would not resort to violence, while one of them (Recep) said that he joined voluntarily but it was the wrong state policies that pushed him to the group. Similar to the Turkish Penitents from the revolutionary groups, seeing the causes of their participation in violence in external factors appeared to have helped them "rationalize" their exit from the group.

On the other hand, in terms of how they were able to physically leave the groups, only three of my informants (Zilan-P, Soli-R, and Hakan-R) invoked external factors. Thus, Zilan-P said that it was her fate that she was not killed while in the PKK, and that she was able to return. Soli-R said it was God and religion which gave him power to disavow violence, while Hakan-R mentioned that it was as if he received "revelations" (epiphanies) when he finally gave in at the end of police custody. The remaining ten of my informants mentioned their decisiveness, effort and, strategy to be more influential factors with regard to their psychical exit.

Inner- and other-directedness

In a well-known book about Americans after World War II, it has been argued that "a plausible and probably important distinction can be made among people based on the sources of their standards of behavior and performance" (Harrington and Boardman 1997:19, internal citations deleted). Based on this approach: "inner-directed people are seen as creating and using their own standards of performance and conduct in judging their own and others' actions and work, while other-directed people are seen as seeking out and adopting the standards of others in judging the adequacy of their own and others' performances and outcomes" (1997:20). Thus, while inner-directed people are likely to be autonomous, independent, and initiating, other-directed people are thought to be more "dependent on the standards of others, and presumably more strongly oriented to pleasing others and meeting their standards" (1997:20).

In my study, I would expect that most of my informants would be inner-directed, given that exit from terrorist groups is an extremely difficult task that requires a certain level of courage and initiative. My findings suggest that they were all primarily inner-directed, that is, to use their own standards of performance to evaluate their own and others' actions. If it they had used the standards of others for their physical exit, they could perhaps not succeed given the inherent risks and difficulties, as well as pressures from both the groups and the communities to which they would return.

Styles of coping with stress and conflict

Proceeding mainly from the psychoanalytic literature in which "ego mechanisms of defense" are viewed as a characteristic of neurotic functioning (e.g., Anna Freud 1937), Harrington and Boardman (1997) suggested, like Hartmann (1958), that it is more useful to view "ego mechanisms of defense" not as protecting against unacceptable endogenous wishes, but as coping strategies in which the self deals with conflict in the external world. Thus, instead of thinking ego and external coping styles separately, they opined that it is sensible to assume that "defense mechanisms that a person uses in dealing with intrapsychic conflicts are related to how one copes with the problems and obstacles encountered in the external world" and that

> intrapsychic conflicts are, after all, often stimulated by real-world events, and the real-world consequences of defense mechanisms (such as projection in the case of authoritarian attitudes and behaviors) have often been documented ... the distinctions that have been made, then, can seem indistinct and arbitrary.
> (1997:21)

As opposed to the body of research that emphasized coping styles as characteristics of pathological functioning such as being maladaptive, rigid, or distorting, Harrington and Boardman benefited from studies (e.g., Haan 1963 and Kroeber 1963) that focused on coping mechanism preference among men and women as being strongly associated with behavioral indicators of mental health and maturity (1997:21). For example, in Haan's longitudinal data on adolescents, she suggested that coping mechanism preference in adulthood is associated with shifts in social class. Harrington and Boardman assumed that "persons in her study whose styles of adaptation can be seen as productive or mature were more likely than others to move upward in social class" (1997:21). For their Pathmakers study, however, the authors benefited most from George Vaillant's work on preferred coping styles largely due to the similarity between their Pathmakers study and his longitudinal study with Harvard undergraduates in that Vaillant distinguished between those "whose life outcomes were particularly good and those whose career, interpersonal, and health outcomes were relatively poor" (1997:22). More importantly, in his descriptions of the lives of people, it is implied that many of those who are thought to have mature coping styles started life in relatively modest conditions, and "a number of the men who were socioeconomically advantaged during childhood did not develop productive styles of adaptation" (1997:22).

In my study, I only have data on what they say today. But I thought it would be useful to assess their coping strategies in this way. I expected that Turkish Penitents from the PKK would have less mature coping styles because of growing up in socioeconomically disadvantaged circumstances (all seven but Azad-P were born and spent their childhood in a village with poor economic resources), and that they would develop more mature coping styles as they grew up, for they not only failed to succumb to undesirable conditions within the groups but succeeded in exiting from them. On the other hand, given that the Turkish Penitents from revolutionary groups except Soli and Gökhan were born and lived in relatively better socio-economic conditions, they would not be expected to develop mature coping styles based on Vaillant's model. Moreover, since Soli-R and Gökhan-R grew up in dysfunctional families (Gökhan also grew up without parental time since he was reunited with his mother at the age of 17 and father was absent most of the time because of work), they would have immature coping styles in childhood. But since all six of them were also able to transcend their own "disillusionment" within the groups and left, I expected that regardless of their childhood, they would also develop mature coping styles (level III and IV in Vaillant's model), or more productive strategies, like the Turkish Penitents from the PKK.

Altruism (n=13)

Altruism, a "mature" coping style in Vaillant's scheme, is defined "as vicarious but gratifying service to others" (Harrington and Boardman 1997:158). As indicated in the previous chapter, altruism played an important role for most of my informants' entry into the group despite the fact that they would not be expected to have mature styles of coping in childhood. But it is sensible to argue that their significance loss prompted a significance restoration, which led to their acceptance of ideologies that promise such restoration by promoting altruistic sacrifices for one's individual, national, or universalistic aspirations. Being more interested in how my informants' coping styles would influence their disengagement, I was more vigilant to find their coping styles during my interviews *vis-à-vis* their processes of exit from the groups. My findings suggest that all of my 13 informants, regardless of the type of group, used altruism in their processes of disengagement, this time not necessarily in the sense of "gratifying service to others," but more as "feeling for" the suffering of others. This may sound paradoxical since altruism and pro-social behavior are usually thought to originate in positive experiences and processes, "whereas violence and antisocial behavior is often rooted in negative life experiences" (Berger and Zimbardo 2012:3). However, as Staub (2005) has suggested, adversity and suffering may contribute to increased violence and antisocial behavior, but it may also enhance the motivation to help others. He called this phenomenon "altruism born of suffering" (ABS) and suggested that some individuals transform the meaning of past suffering and promote psychological change in the direction of caring for others rather than turning against them.

Similarly, I conclude that Turkish Penitents' witnessing of other people's suffering stemming from their subjection to various injustices, torture, and mistreatment within and by the groups functioned sometimes as a *first seed of doubt* and sometimes as a *defining turning point* in their processes of disillusionment and exit. As an example, consider the following incidents experienced by Selim from the PKK:

Incident 1

> I was responsible for logistics in the PKK. One day, we went to a village in an Eastern province to get victuals for the group. The villagers cannot do anything; they have to provide it, because it's the organization (the PKK) that is asking. We entered the storage room in a house and I saw that there were many sacks full of flour. We loaded them on the donkeys. When I returned to the house, I saw that there was a newly-wed couple. They cried, and said, 'Please don't take our flour ... we will starve without it.' I was really touched by this; I gave them US$200. They said, 'No! Please give us our flour back, we don't want money.' I am offering an amount of money way above the value of the flour. But at that time, flour was more valuable than money. Because there was an embargo by the Turkish state [to minimize the logistical support to the PKK]; it was a big mistake.

Incident 2

> One day we had a skirmish with the [Turkish] army. Seventeen of us died in that operation. Our leader, Murat Karayilan [current operational leader of the PKK], was shot in the chest, but he survived. In our group, there was a man from my village. He made a lot of sacrifices for the group and during that operation he truly demonstrated his dedication to the group. He tried so hard to save Karayilan, but he was wounded himself that day and we had to leave him there. When we returned from the operation after two weeks, they said, 'Hozat [code] was a traitor because he surrendered to the enemy.' I said to myself, 'How come? This man should be declared as a hero.' And at that time, I understood that everything is nugatory in the PKK. I mean, you fight as a hero but they say you are a traitor. Why? Because you didn't die ... I said to myself, 'This is how we all will end up; we will be killed for nothing, no matter what; either by the state or the PKK. I was not loyal anyway because I had entered by force, but over time you start to internalize it and identify yourself with the group. I was even promoted to squad commander. But on that day, I made up my mind; my connection to the group ended completely.

On the other hand, the main reasons that caused Zilan-P's disillusionment were her witnessing of the extrajudicial killing of two guerillas that were thought to be "agents," and her participation in a raid into a village populated by the supporters of Mesud Barzani, the leader of Kurdistan Democratic Party (KDP) in Iraq. She described her feelings in that raid as follows:

> We went to that village to get supplies but they [the PKK leaders] said kill all of them, because they were supporters of the KDP. I was in the health division, so I was not directly involved in the killings. We were situated on top of a hill from where we could see everything. I was listening to their communication on the radio, which made me very upset. Because they were saying, 'Kill everybody ...' But I was thinking: you say that we are doing everything [as the PKK] for humanity, but these people whom you kill are also Kurds. There were many children among them. They were firing like crazy; we could see the clouds of fire. They [the villagers] were screaming. The commander was saying: 'Bump off all of them, don't leave anybody alive.' I mean at that time my emotions became very intense, I was really hurt by these. There, I became psychologically detached from the group. I said to myself, 'I cannot walk one more step with these people.' I had indeed become inured to the group because of the training, but after this incident, I became completely alienated from the group; it really affected my feelings. These people say they are working for a cause, but their deeds don't match their narratives. What's more, they were doing such things even jubilantly; it was unacceptable.

Anticipation (n=13)

Anticipation is described as a "mature" coping style in Vaillant's scheme that involves "the realistic anticipation of, and preparing for, future inner discomfort" (Harrington and Boardman 1997:160). I was not surprised that all of my informants used this style, because all of them expressed that they knew about the difficulties and risks of disengagement from groups. On the one hand, as they personally observed during their time in the groups, that a failed attempt to exit by a group member would definitely mean death for him or her on the basis of being labeled as an "agent." On the other hand, they knew that it was quite difficult to reintegrate with the society, this time for being labeled as a "traitor" by the supporters of groups, or a "wolf in sheep's clothing" by the larger community. Despite these difficulties, once they made up their minds about leaving, they did whatever it took to execute their decision. This coping style is, in fact, linked to another mature coping style, i.e., "rationalization," which I found in all of my informants, although there were some differences between them.

Rationalization (n=13)

Rationalization occurs where a person convinces him or herself that no wrong was done and that all is or was all right through faulty and false reasoning. An indicator of this coping mechanism can be seen socially as the formulation of convenient excuses – making excuses (Vaillant 1971). In this respect, all of my informants seem to have used this coping style in their disengagement processes. But there was an apparent difference between the Turkish Penitents from the PKK and those from revolutionary groups. In order to disengage, my informants from the latter groups had to come up with "excuses" not only to convince themselves but also the people whom they would encounter within the society upon return, especially the people who knew about their past. They did not try to convince fellow group members because from the perspective of terrorist groups, there could be "no excuse" for leaving; a commonly held view was that it was at best the "weakness" of the individual. But convincing themselves was the hardest part because all of the Turkish Penitents from revolutionary groups joined the groups voluntarily, and most of them were staunch defenders of the leftist ideals until their belief in those ideals was diminished by their disillusionment. To this end, they usually put forth the injustices against them and others within the groups, while some of them said that they had some "epiphanies" which facilitated their decision to exit.

In order to satisfy other people upon "return" to society, they propounded the idea that it was not their fault; because they were not given any alternatives and they were "made" by the state to resort to violence. Another significant point for their use of rationalization had to do with the fact that all of my six informants from the revolutionary groups expressed their desire to exit from the groups when they were captured by the police. Highlighting this, they reported that even though their decision was made while in custody, their psychological disengagement had occurred long before their arrests. For instance, Soli-R said that even though he was informed about the police raid into his cell, he did not leave the apartment but waited for hours for the police to come.

On the other hand, my informants from the PKK only had others to convince, for all except Azad and Recep joined the group involuntarily, and they knew that they had to leave the group sooner or later. As they expressed themselves, they had no doubt about that. The main problem for them was the reactions of people upon return if they left the group. Their return, in fact, was more complicated than that of the Turkish Penitents from revolutionary groups because five of my informants from the PKK were on the "mountain" when they made their decision and they would go back to their villages or small towns in the southeastern provinces of Turkey, where the pressure of being labeled as "traitor" is greatest. Only Azad-P was living abroad when he made his decision and he would go back to Istanbul where he could possibly live relatively "incognito." In fact, most of his neighbors and relatives did not even know that he had joined the PKK; they thought that he was abroad simply for business purposes. When considering his disengagement, Azad-P was cognizant indeed about this fact, which in turn helped his "rationalization" of cutting his ties with the group.

Moreover, Recep-P had joined the group voluntarily because, as explained earlier, of his feeling of exacting revenge emanating from his exposure to violence by the state. But over time, he became disillusioned with the internal dynamics of the group on the mountain, e.g., mistreatment, injustices by the leaders, and their hedonistic lifestyles while other guerillas were literally suffering in mountain conditions. His own decision was rationalized by these reasons but he had no hope of being accepted especially by his father who was a staunch supporter of the PKK and he would never accept Recep's "betrayal" to the Kurdish "cause." Fortunately, a turning point eliminated this problem as his father visited him on Qandil Mountain (presently main PKK camp) and witnessed with his own eyes those negativities that caused his son's disillusionment from the group. All in all, although having slight differences, all of my informants used rationalization in disengaging from their respective groups.

Other coping styles/idealization (n=1)

Idealization is described as an "immature" coping style (level II) in Vaillant's (1971) scheme which refers to unconsciously choosing to perceive another individual as having more positive qualities than he or she may actually have. As mentioned in the previous chapter, most of my informants had "idealization" in their processes of entry into the groups. Idealization of charismatic schoolmates, friends, or historically legendary figures for the groups seems to have facilitated their decision to join the groups. But, although "idealization" is an immature coping mechanism and could not yield productive results for the individuals, one of my informants used idealization as a coping style which played a crucial role in his disengagement. Remember that Azad-P had taken his friend Harun as a role model. When he had his first seed of doubt and later became disillusioned, he talked to Harun about his doubts and realized that he too had similar doubts and questions which he "could not" resolve in his mind. "If Harun could not resolve these issues, I definitely cannot," he said. Although Harun did not eventually leave the group, that conversation provided Azad-P with the necessary justification and courage to leave the group.

To conclude, when the emphasis is placed on their psychological and physical disengagement from political violence, it seems that there is a common psychology among the Turkish Penitents. That is, they seem to be predominantly inner-directed and reward-oriented and they seem to have internal locus of control. In terms of coping styles, despite differences in their socio-economic backgrounds which would mean that at least some of them had immature coping mechanisms, considering the processes of their exit it appears that they developed and used "anticipation" and "rationalization" which are described as mature styles of coping in Vaillant's model. It can be argued that spending time in terrorist groups might have had an equalizer effect in terms of individual coping styles.

The role of turning points and serendipities related to disengagement

In the previous chapter, following Sampson and Laub (1993), I had argued that turning points played an important role in the transition of Turkish Penitents from separation stage (pre-violence) to the stage of transition (violence). Similarly, in addition to personal and other resources, the importance of turning points and serendipities cannot be overlooked for a full understanding of Turkish Penitents' disengagement. Following Sampson and Laub, I do not deny the reality of selection or the fact that "persons may sometimes 'create' their environment" (1993:320). However, as the authors suggested, "once in place, those environments take on a history of their own in a way that invalidates a pure spuriousness or self-selection argument" (1993:320). In addition, self-selection argument, according to these authors, is much too deterministic and it overlooks the importance of the role of "state sanctions, chance, luck, structural location, historical context, and opportunity structure in shaping the life course" (1993:320).

Overall, the turning points and serendipities *vis-à-vis* Turkish Penitents' disengagement appeared to be related to my informants' encounters with certain persons and/or experiences in a variety of events. For example, Recep joined the PKK at the age of 15 on a voluntary basis because of his personal exposure to violence and his subjective view of the collective trauma of the Kurdish people. After being disillusioned, however, he made up his mind about leaving the group, but because of his cultural background that prioritizes the "authority of elders," he was concerned with the reaction of his father who, as a staunch supporter of the PKK, would never forgive his "betrayal" of the Kurdish cause. He grappled with this psychological dilemma for a long time, yet he could not gather up his courage to face his father upon return, despite the fact that he was ready to pay the price of a failed attempt to escape from the mountain. Eventually, a serendipitous event occurred three years after Recep-P's final decision to leave the group.[1]

His father came to visit him in the Qandil Mountains, which lasted for two weeks. As Recep stated, his friends and he tried to hide the negativities in the camp and strove hard to show the best of the camp in terms of the physical conditions and interpersonal relationships that had caused his disillusionment in the first place. One day, his father and several of his friends were chatting, when one of the guerillas let slip from his mouth that a guerilla was killed a day before and he was buried to a place several feet away from where they were chatting. On the other side were a couple of commanders who were drinking tea, listening to loud music and burst into laughter. This did not escape the attention of Recep's father as he later said to him that he was shocked by that fact: "if these commanders treat our martyrs like this, they will do the same thing if my son died." Because of his strong belief in the PKK, however, he did not express his disappointment to his son immediately. Nonetheless, when one of his friends told about this event and the signs of confusion he saw in his father's eyes, Recep had a sudden realization as he felt that he had jettisoned the most important weight springing from his fear associated with escaping from the mountain. With this boost of courage, he escaped from the mountain and returned to Istanbul, but it took almost two years to face his father. During this time, he lived with his brother illegally until he turned himself into the police with hope of benefiting from the repentance laws. In fact, he did not receive any punishment based on the "Effective Repentance Law," which was enacted in 2005. When he went to see his father, he did not say that he had turned himself in to the police; but stated instead that he was caught by them.

This is indeed an important aspect of disengagement, for all of my informants stated that being caught by the police or being known as such eases out the tension emanating from potential reactions as a result of exit from terrorist groups.

In the case of Zilan-P, several turning points and serendipities contributed to her disengagement without which she could perhaps not manage to escape from the PKK. As I mentioned earlier, Zilan-P did not join the group voluntarily; she had joined at the age of 13 because of her fiancé. Thus, she had no doubt from the beginning that after spending a short time on the mountain, she would go back to normal life. However, it was quite hard for her to rescue herself from the clutches of the group because of its ironclad control and scrutiny of individuals on the mountain. During her time on the mountain, she saw many incidents that not only disgusted her but also made life unbearable for her. The most important of such incidents have been mentioned before; but to recap, the first incident was the killing of a 15-year-old Iraqi girl, Pervin, for being labeled as "traitor," whom Zilan thought to be innocent and the second was related to her experience of a PKK raid in a village of Iraqi Kurds, where she saw indiscriminate and nonsensical killings of Kurdish men, women and children. The accumulation of such incidents (turning points) brought her to a point of no return; she had to escape from the mountain, but she was powerless. Moreover, escaping from the mountain would require a deep knowledge of the geography of the region, but she had only a vague idea of the position of her camp.

At this juncture, another serendipitous event occurred: she met Nadir-P, a fellow *hemşeri* who would also become her future husband. Like Zilan, Nadir was also a long-term disillusioned PKK member and he had tried to escape from the mountain several times. Being *hemşeri* provided them with an instant trust in each other and increased their communications in the camp, which resulted in an establishment of an intimate relationship, which was in fact strictly forbidden in the PKK. At some point during their conversations, they started to talk about their disillusionment with the group and desire to escape, and started to sketch out plans to escape from the camp. Nadir was more experienced than Zilan, and his brother was living in a little town in Northern Iraq, controlled by the KDP of Mesud Barzani. Thus, the first idea was to escape and go to that town, which would be followed by finding out ways to return to Turkey. After a carefully made plan, they were able to escape from the mountain, but as Zilan indicated it was their "fate" that they did not get caught because at one point during their escape, they were trapped by three PKK squads. In brief, they made their way to that town in Northern Iraq, but it took more than eight years for them to go back to Turkey since when they arrived in that town they were tried by Barzani forces who gave them two choices: be a *peshmerghe* (soldier in Barzani's army) and receive numerous benefits including a house and a stable job, or else, they would be returned to the PKK, the upshot of which would mean their execution. Of course, they accepted to be a *pesmerghe*. It is important to note here that the conditions that Barzani forces offered played, and still play, an important incentivizing role in terms of escape for those disillusioned PKK members in the camps located in Northern Iraq, who are in the throes of leaving the group.

On the other hand, among my informants from the revolutionary groups for instance, Soli-R's introduction to religion was a turning point in his process of disengagement, which came about because of a serendipitous encounter with a religious friend who was a member of a religious derwish lodge (*dergah* in Turkish) in the city of Adiyaman in southeastern Turkey. About his feelings towards religion and its role that influenced his philosophy of life, Soli-R said:

> When I made up my mind about leaving the group, I started to live outside in the parks. I worked occasionally, but most of the time, I was suffering from hunger. Living for two years in such conditions, I met with a friend who was a tenant of my family's apartment. He was a religious person; he said, 'Why are you wandering around? Why don't you go to the Dergah? They need someone to look after the facilities, make tea, etc., anyway. Why don't you go there?' After that, I went to the Dergah and stayed there for four and a half years. While I was there, I didn't even want to go out to the street; I was preparing food and tea for the visitors, and cleaning up the facilities. While I was living there, I learned a lot about religion."
>
> "After leaving the group, religion was the only subject that I didn't know anything about. While in the group, I had an opinion about everything except religion. My new philosophy became leading a life without harming anyone. The crucial thing is that I didn't make my final decision to cut my ties completely from the group because of the unattainability of their ideals. I left that thought [leftist ideology] because I *chose* religion. I understood that you shouldn't harm anyone in this life; there can be no justification for the wrongdoings. Maybe leftist and Islamic narratives are close to each other, but Allah and what He said about afterlife is more accurate. I mean, the other side of the line of death was dark for me; but now, I see it as bright as the inside of this room.

In addition to his newly gained knowledge about Islam that made him a more relaxed, tranquil, and considerate person, he had also an epiphany, which solidified his belief in his new philosophy of life.

> One day I saw something; it was like a dream. I was standing by the river where I felt as if the water level was rising to the level of my eyes. There were three fishes jumping in the water before my eyes while uttering at the same time, 'Salamun Aleykum' [religious greeting]. The color of the water also changed; it turned into a beautiful scene. The voices of those fishes and that water have always come pleasant to me.

Sampson and Laub (1993) argue that marriages and finding stable jobs are two important turning points in individuals' life-courses in terms of decrease in criminality. Similarly, marriage played an important role in the chain of events that led to Gökhan-R's incremental process of conversion from violence and belief in violence to non-violence and abandonment of leftist ideology. Regarding this chain of events, Gökhan -R said:

> As I said, the organization is a kind of structure, in which you realize over time that there is nepotism. You also start understanding, solely by looking into their eyes, that there is also distrust against you. It is hard to express these with words; you can only understand through personal experience. For instance, in the organization some policies [e.g., of secrecy] are imposed on you under the guise of heavily illegal conditions; but you know that there is no illegality in it, it is just that some things [information] are being kept from you. But you have to kowtow to that in such a structure, or in other words, you remain silent for your own benefit. When there is coldness against you, you feel it right away as well. When I started having such feelings, I started a feeling of coldness towards the group. My emotional satisfaction had started to dwindle anyway.
>
> When my wife entered into my life, my intention to cut ties with the group was solidified, because I felt that I had a more meaningful direction in my life, i.e., a normal family life. In other words, I had put a more valuable person in my life in lieu of the organization, it was my wife. I started to build my dreams on her, and wanted to lead a life away from violence.

Another important turning point related to disengagement in the groups I studied occurred on a macro level, i.e., the commotions and turmoil within the groups provided disillusioned members with an opportunity to exit with relative ease. To give examples, two important incidents led hundreds of PKK members to leave the group, the first of which took place in 1999 when the group leader Abdullah Öcalan was captured in Kenya and brought to Turkey for trial. It was sensible to expect that such an incident would unify the group members. However, Öcalan's words on the plane were shocking to not only his followers but also to everyone in Turkey and beyond. Below is the conversation that took place on the plane between state officials and Öcalan:

State official: Welcome to the homeland. How are you?
Öcalan: [Surprised and demoralized] Thanks, I am fine.
State official: ... [He asks some questions about his health and he replies that he is fine.]
State official: Now, you are our guest, relax. I mean don't trouble yourself with anything; tell us if you need anything.
Öcalan: I love my country. Also, my mother was a Turk.
State official: Can you speak louder?
Öcalan: If there is a chance for me to serve, I can do it. Other than this, don't tell me anything. If I am required to serve, I am ready.
State official: If you answer our questions, it means you have served. Let us wipe your face if you are bothered [by the blindfold].

Öcalan: When I return to Turkey, I will serve. If you give me the chance, I can serve. I talk about these before the public. I won't say anything else. If there is a chance for me to serve, I believe there is, if you inform the top brass, I will serve with pleasure. I will serve, in a perfect way.
State official: Look, we are recording what you are saying ...
Öcalan: Publish or broadcast them. You didn't torture me; they are coming from my heart. But, really, I love Turkey and Turkish people. I believe I will serve them perfectly. If the opportunity is given, I will do it.
State official: You will be given the opportunity, but what do you really want?
Öcalan: [He doesn't say much; just reiterates that he is ready to serve.]
(Stratejikboyut 2009, my translation)

The second tumultuous incident in the PKK occurred in 2004, when Osman Öcalan, Abdullah Öcalan's brother, and two other PKK leaders were thought to have made an agreement with the United States to dismantle the PKK in exchange for being given an opportunity to live in exile somewhere in Europe. What preceded these disturbances within the group was Osman Öcalan's so-called "social project" which was designed to loosen up the relationships between male and female guerillas in an effort to prevent, as my informants suggested, further "barbarization" of the male guerillas. As I alluded to earlier, this project was seen as a corruption of ethical values within the group and among its supporters (patriots/*yurtsevers*), which gave hundreds of disgruntled and disillusioned group members the chance and extra justification to separate from the group.

A similar example of macro-level turning point related to revolutionary groups can be given with respect to the so-called coup within the Dev-Sol (Revolutionary Left) that occurred in 1991. Two factions within the group started to clash at the time; Dursun Karataş and his friends on the one side, and Bedri Yağan and his supporters on the other. As a result, Yağan and his friends were killed in a police raid of the cell where they were staying.[2] What is significant about this and similar commotions and elimination of top-level leaders within terrorist groups, as one of my informants from the revolutionary groups argued, is that they give disillusioned group members a chance to leave the group without being bemused by the reactions they are to receive after their separation, for the fact that there is simply nobody that can hold them accountable.

Lastly, in the case of some of my informants, the time they spent in prison played a serendipitous turning point in their processes of disengagement. This sounds quite ironic, should one consider the common conviction that prisons are the breeding place for terrorist organizations. As some of my informants, both from the PKK and revolutionary groups, had their first seeds of doubt about their respective groups and found themselves in prison (in the case of my informants from the PKK, it meant the "security" section within the mountain), it provided them with an opportunity to make an introspective journey towards the inner-self, which resulted in their reevaluation of the meaning of their actions within the group and the way they were treated by group leaders, as well as the injustices they encountered throughout their time in the groups. In this respect, most of my informants believe that solitary confinement in prison translates itself as a resource for disengagement from terrorist groups in that it provides them with a shield against the authority of the groups in prisons. That is, it prevents other group members from reaching out out to disillusioned members, change their ideas about leaving the group, or threaten them.

Conclusion (related to the "transition stage" as a whole)

The transition stage of the Turkish Penitents, i.e., their lives in groups and paths *from* political violence, is a process that is as complex as their paths *to* political violence. Although it is difficult to point to a single issue to understand the cause(s) of political violence, in the previous chapter I presented a taxonomy of processes and factors to account for the Turkish Penitents' entry into terrorist groups by examining their lives in different phases of the "separation stage" based on my ROP model, which includes their experiences in childhood and adolescence, schooling, political socialization, radicalization and entry into the terrorist groups, and argued that transitions from one phase to another were marked by various turning points. Similarly, although it is equally hard to make a final judgment about the Turkish Penitents' disengagement from political violence, I argued in the last three chapters that their disengagement had to do with various problems and contradictions that are inherent in *legitimate peripheral participation* in *communities of violence practices*. Miscellenaous factors played a role in the creation of these problems and contradictions, which can be subsumed under two groups; namely, internal (individual) factors and external (structural) factors. It appears also that the former are secondary to the latter.

The first internal factor of disengagement from political violence emanates from the nature of interpersonal relationships within the terrorist groups. Lave and Wenger argue that "there is a fundamental contradiction in the meaning to newcomers and old-timers of increasing participation by the former; for the centripetal development of full participants, and with it the successful production of a community of practice, also implies the replacement of old-timers" (1991:57). My findings suggested that the replacement of old-timers was not a serious problem in terrorist groups, given that group members are allowed, or even expected, to stay in groups as much as possible and become full participants in the production of violence. The contradictory nature of interpersonal relationships in the terrorist groups I studied plays out differently from conventional forms of apprenticeship in the sense that there is a high level of *distrust* among group members and leaders, which appears to be more crucial than the issue of displacement of old-timers. From the perspective of the group members, there is also a significant sense of *unjustness* in master-novice relations. A combination of these perceived feelings of distrust and unjustness, in turn, seems to have contributed to *psychological degeneration* in my informants.

A second internal factor is linked to the Turkish Penitents' subjective views with regard to access to participation in their respective groups, which manifests itself in multifarous ways. In the PKK, it appears that there is no shortage of access to participation in the production of violence. That is, excessive violence is encouraged and especially newcomers are sent to violent clashes with the Turkish military without proper military training and equipment.[3] This phenomenon is called by group members as "the policy of death," which leads to the generation of the feelings of *disappointment, worthlessness*, and *disillusionment* in them. A similar policy is seen in most of the revolutionary groups, dubbed as "revolutionism based on the blood of martyrs," which elicits similar psychological grievances in group members who reportedly sacrifice their whole lives for their groups.

On the other hand, in some revolutionary groups my informants felt that their access to participation is prevented, rather latently, in that those who are on the military committee of their respective groups, and who thereby operate under the "heavy illegality conditions," are kept away from the production process (violence) under the guise of being protected. My informants' perceptions about this seem to differ as they thought that their sequestration from participation was not done for their protection; on the contrary, they were being sidelined by the groups which would mean their eventual *discharge* from them. Furthermore, since they spent a long time in this state of mind, lack of access to participation created in them a sense of "active idleness," engendering in turn some psychological problems such as *burning out, dissatisfaction*, and more importantly, a sense of *significance loss*.

Furthermore, both in the PKK and the revolutionary groups I studied, excessive access and lack of access to participation appeared to have sparked off a suspicion in my informants in terms of the existence of a potential (symbiotic) relationship between their respective groups and the deep state. They felt that, since the deep state and terrorist groups benefit from the protracted violence, their individual existence does not matter much for both parties, and that they were being "exploited" by one or both of these parties by being encouraged to participate in excessive violence. In terms of the lack of access to participation, they believed that the deep state use terrorist groups when necessary and eliminate individuals who are thought to be creating hindrances to a smooth operation of the workings of the deep state and terrorist groups, and thus, who also appear to be existential threats to the very existence of such types of symbiotic relationships.

External factors of individual disengegement from political violence appear to reside in two areas related to legitimate peripheral participation in communities of violent practices. The first of these areas covers the notions of production and mode of production. I argued that in both the PKK and revolutionary groups, what is being produced has a phantom quality, i.e., the groups I studied have all tried to produce for almost three decades an *imagined community* (Anderson 1983) through the reproduction of communities of violent practices by using violence as their main mode of production. In the PKK, this imagined community was claimed to be an independent Kurdish state, whereas in the revolutionary groups, it was a communist state that would emancipate all citizens who were allegedly subjugated thenceforth by the "oppressive" Turkish state. Nearly three decades of armed struggle did not bring any fruitful results in terms of arriving at such communities, which my informants interpreted as the *postponement of utopia* that led them to believe that their goals were no longer attainable. In this respect, the main difference between the Turkish Penitents from the revolutinary groups and the PKK is that unattainability of the goals of the revolutionary groups came about largely due to a reflection of the changed global conditions on Turkey. To clarify, the people's infatuation in the 1970s with a communist revolution, and thereby their romance with revolutionary violence, was diminished worldwide in the 1990s and Turkey was not an exception. In addition, increased economic development and the democratization of the country marked the end of the ideological underpinnings of Turkey's revolutionary groups in that their main arguments (economic inequalities and torture) for recruitment and mobilization were largely taken away from them.

Moreover, specific to my informants from the PKK, the aforementioned feeling of the postponement of utopia was coupled with a sense of confusion created by the shifting nature of the group's goals; that is, the PKK was initially created to establish an independent Kurdish state, which was then downgraded to a "democratic confederation" and lately to an "autonomous" Kurdish region within the borders of Turkey. Most of my informants from the PKK claimed that they did not believe that the PKK would cease to exist even if the most extreme of its goals, i.e., "independence," was achieved by the group, and that the group would perpetuate its existence by finding a new contradiction within the system at any given time. More importantly, some of my informants even argued that violence, which was supposed to be the means to an end, or the "mode of production," has become an end in itself. To clarify, the PKK appears to have forgotten about the creation of a Kurdish state, or even an autonomous region for that matter, and instead became immersed in unfathomable violence for the sake of perpetuating its *raison d'être*.[4]

The second area related to external factors of individual disengagement of the Turkish Penitents has to do with the nature of didactic teaching in groups that have cult-like structures, in which learning is understood not only in the context of pedagogical instruction but also as the transformation and construction of identities through the utilization of numerous thought reform techniques. At first glance, it seems logical for the leaders of both the PKK and revolutionary groups that they ought to reconstruct the identities of the newcomers who come from diverse social, economic, and political backgrounds. To this end, they embark on a process of indoctrination, in which learning is thought out as a didactic activity of absorbing the given, and behaviors of individuals attempt to be modified through various techniques of thought reform. More importantly, even though the carrots and stick approach is a perennial behavior modification system in social collectivities, the cult-like structures of the groups I studied are dominated mostly by the sticks approach. For a short period, individuals do not realize their own situation under the effect of ideology that masks the real power relations within groups. Over the course of time, however, the accumulation of experiences that elicit negative feelings lead to the lifting of ideological influence, which in turn results in the disillusionment of them with their respective groups that marks their *psychological disengagement*. This analysis does not apply to my informants who joined the PKK involuntarily, given that their psychological disengagement started as soon as they were thrown into the group's camps on the mountain.

Moreover, considering the time differences between my informants' entry, first seeds of doubt, disillusionment (psychological exit), and physical exit from the groups, it was necessary to account for the notion of "extended stay" in their respective groups.[5] My findings suggested that the extended stay of the Turkish Penitents was linked to the following issues: (1) strong ideological beliefs and loyalty to the group; idealization and identification with the group; a sense of empowerment and satisfaction; and routinization of practices; (2) the state of liminality when disengaging, i.e., being betwixt and between the fear of failure to exit on the one hand and anxiety over being accepted by, and integrated to, society on the other; and lastly, (3) the fear of punishment upon return to society. While the issues in the latter two items had an important effect in the disengagement processes of all of my 13 informants, the issues listed in the first item were related mostly to my informants from the revolutionary groups. Another significant difference between my informants from the PKK and revolutionary groups was their ideological orientations. That is, all of my informants from the revolutionary groups, except for Gökhan, had strong ideological beliefs; whereas among my informants from the PKK, only Recep and Azad had weak ideological beliefs while others did not commit themselves fully to the PKK ideology as a whole from the outset.

Another important difference between the Turkish Penitents from the PKK and the revolutionary groups related to their disengagement was that the effects of "liminality" were stronger among my informants from the PKK. This had to do with the structure of the mountain, a bounded environment in which individuals are scrutinized closely, and the fear of return to communities of origin in little towns of Turkey's southeast where the reaction of public towards the "detacheds" or "repentants" is extremely harsh. The effects of liminality were less for my informants from the revolutionary groups, for all of them participated in revolutionary violence in an urban environment, which allowed them to lead a relatively invisible life after their exit from the groups. The foregoing arguments point to another difference between Turkish Penitents from the PKK and those from the revolutionary groups, i.e., disengagement from the PKK is usually coterminous with guerillas' physical exit (escape) from the mountain, whereas in the revolutionary groups it generally means a severance of ties with accomplices, groups' cells, and also their offices that function in the legal sphere.

Despite the risks and difficulties associated with disengagement from terrorist groups, my informants were able to overcome those difficulties for which they used several personal resources, namely; (1) change of mentality and adoption of new philosophies of life; (2) their personality orientations and styles of coping. With respect to the first, another significant difference emerges between Turkish Penitents from the PKK and those from the revolutionary groups when *cognitive* and *behavioral* aspects of disengagement are taken into account. I found that all of my 13 informants had a behavioral change that led to their conversion from violence to non-violence. However, in addition to renouncing violence, my informants from the PKK also discarded their ideologies, felt remorse for their wrongdoings, and decided to repair the damage that they had inflicted on society; whereas all of my informants from the revolutionary groups, except for Gökhan and Soli, did not think that they had done anything wrong and maintained their leftist-revolutionary ideologies, believing that the conditions for *the* revolution no longer exist in Turkey notwithstanding.

When the emphasis is placed on their physical disengagement from terrorist groups, it seems that there is a common psychology among the Turkish Penitents. That is, they seem to be predominantly inner-directed and reward-oriented and they seem to have internal locus of control. In terms of coping styles, despite differences in their socio-economic backgrounds which would mean that at least some of them had immature coping styles, considering the processes of their exit, it appears that they developed and used "anticipation" and "rationalization." It can be argued that spending time in terrorist groups might have had an equalizer effect in terms of individuals' coping styles. These findings also suggest that coping styles are not stable throughout the life-course and they should be assessed separately for each new life situation. Lastly, besides the personal resources that explain Turkish Penitents' *agency* in terms of disengagement, various turning points and serendipitous encounters, too, played an important role in their processes of disengagement, particularly in terms of their transitions from *suspicion* to *disillusionment* and finally to their *physical exit* from their respective groups.

Overall, the Turkish Penitents are unique individuals because not only did they present resilience in the face of diabolical conditions within terrorist groups, but they also managed to overcome extreme difficulties associated with physical exit from such groups. Their experiences, or success in exiting so to speak, prove in a sense that at least some people in terrorist groups make *rational choices* in order to extricate themselves from an unwanted situation or state of being. This, in fact, runs counter to the conventional thinking that terrorists are irrational, abnormal or crazy individuals who are ready to kill others and sacrifice themselves unconditionally for a noble or trivial cause. Even though terrorist groups try to reconstruct their identities to germinate in them robot-like behaviors, that is, to downgrade them to a level of *a thing*, experiences of the Turkish Penitents demonstrate that they resist such endeavors of "objectification" by the terrorist groups and that, like any other human being, they too have emotions, desires, fears, dreams, and so on and so forth. Following Heidegger (1962), it is possible to argue that the aforementioned problems and contradictions associated with participation in communities of violent practices led to the creation of Turkish Penitents' "inauthentic-selves" and prompted in them a quest for their "authentic-selves," which could come about only by exit from their respective groups. Since the feelings enumerated above helped them in their processes of disengagement, it is now time to explore whether their lives after violence conform to their dreams and what types of difficulties they have to put up with. Exploring their lives after violence, however, requires understanding the role of "repentance laws" for their disengagement. This is so partly because in the absence of such laws most of them would possibly not exit from the groups. Besides, the process of disengagement starts in the mind of the individual, which is significantly influenced by the confessions to be made and rewards to be received in an exchange relationship with the state through the repentance laws. Hence is the discussion of the "politics of repentance" as a prelude to the next chapter.

Table 6.1 Information about the Turkish Penitents' entry and exit

Name	Name of Group	Sex	Age	Year of entry	Age at entry	First attempt to exit	Second attempt to exit	Year of exit	Length of stay	Mode of exit
Zilan	PKK	F	32	1993	14	Upon entry	—	2002: she went to Northern Iraq 2010: came to Turkey Considers 2010 as her return	17	Surrendered
Selim	PKK	M	32	1993	14	Upon entry	1995–1997	1998	5	Surrendered
Nadir	PKK	M	36	1986	11	Upon entry	1997 – caught	2002: he went to Northern Iraq 2010: came to Turkey Considers 2010 as his return	24	Surrendered
Savaş	PKK	M	41	1989	19	1990– after seeing an execution of a guerrilla	Caught two times	1996	7	Surrendered
Recep	PKK	M	34	1990	13	—	— (but he was thinking of exit all the time)	2008	18	Surrendered
Azad	PKK	M	34	2002	26	Upon entry	2006: failed 2009: failed	2010	8	Surrendered
Gürkan	PKK	M	40	1992	21	Upon entry	—	1994	2	Surrendered
Hikmet	Rev.*	M	37	1993	19	1996: failed	—	1997	4	Captured
Gökhan	Rev.	M	41	1989	19	—	—	1992	3	Captured
Ahmet	Rev.	M	50	1975	14	—	—	2003	28	Captured
Hakan	Rev.	M	55	1974	18	—	—	1999	25	Captured
Soli	Rev.	M	42	1998	29	—	—	2002	4	Captured
Fatih	Rev.	M	51	1976	16	—	—	1996	20	Captured

* Revolutionary group

Table 6.2 Factors contributing to the Turkish Penitents' disengagement from political violence

				Postponement of utopia		Problem of access and sequestration in the production process (i.e. violence)		
Name	Name of group	Problems in interpersonal relations (e.g., feelings of distrust and injustice) (Yes/No)	Negative effects of indoctrination (i.e., brainwashing) (Yes/No)	Objective perception (i.e., about group in general) (Yes/No)	Subjective perception (i.e., personal effect) (Yes/Indifferent)	Lack of access (Yes/No)	Excessive access (Yes/No)	Turning points and serendipities (Yes/No)
Zilan	PKK	Yes	Yes	Yes	Indifferent	No	Yes	Yes
Selim	PKK	Yes	Yes	Yes	Indifferent	No	Yes	Yes
Nadir	PKK	Yes	Yes	Yes	Indifferent	No	Yes	Yes
Savaş	PKK	Yes	Yes	—	Indifferent	No	Yes	Yes
Recep	PKK	Yes	Yes	Yes	Yes	No	Yes	Yes
Azad	PKK	Yes	Yes	Yes	Indifferent	No	Yes	Yes
Gürkan	PKK	Yes	Yes	—	Indifferent	No	Yes	Yes
Hikmet	Rev.*	Yes	Yes	Yes	Indifferent	Yes	Yes	Yes
Gökhan	Rev.	Yes	Yes	—	Indifferent	Yes	Yes	Yes
Ahmet	Rev.	Yes	Yes	Yes	Yes	No	No	Yes
Hakan	Rev.	Yes	Yes	Yes	Yes	Yes	No	Yes
Soli	Rev.	Yes	Yes	Yes	Indifferent	Yes	Yes	Yes
Fatih	Rev.	Yes	Yes	Yes	Yes	No	Yes	Yes

*Revolutionary group

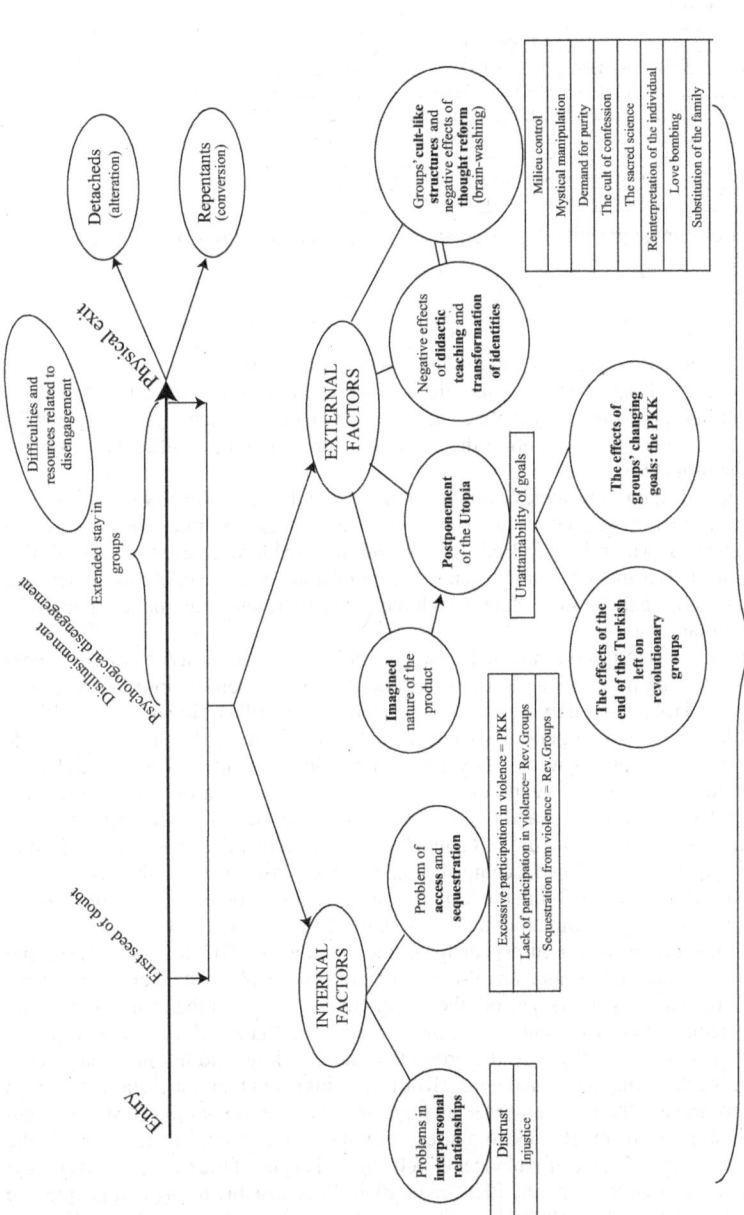

Figure 6.1 Processes of individual disengagement from (imagined) communities of violent practices

Transition stage III

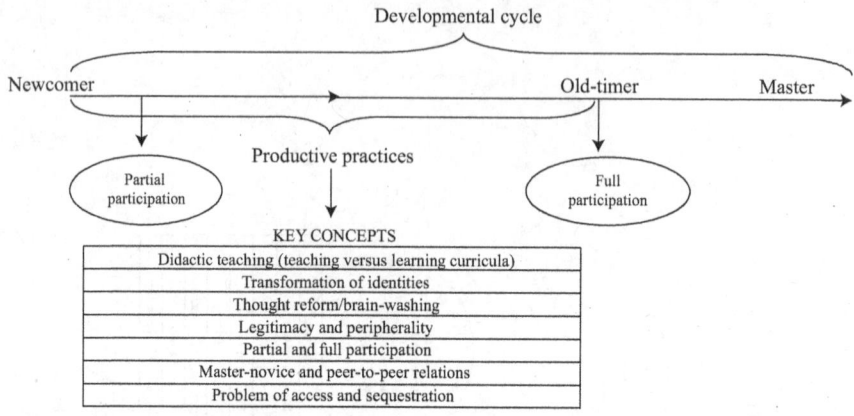

Figure 6.2 Legitimate peripheral participation (LPP) in communities of practice

Notes

1 It was, in fact, Recep's tenth year in the group when his father came to visit him on the mountain. Thus, if we combine the periods of his disillusionment and his final decision, it is possible to say that he had to stay in an environment against his will for at least *five* years, demonstrating the level of control in and the difficulty of escape from the mountain.
2 Many people, including some of my informants from the revolutionary groups believe that that incident was a deep-state operation because Dursun Karataş was working for the deep state, which is why Bedri Yağan and his friends were eliminated with that operation. This is indeed an important case for understanding the relationship between terrorist groups and the deep state, which requires a thorough examination along with other similar cases.
3 This policy seems to continue and create turmoil within the group as of November 2011. Following the months of August through October when the PKK increased its attacks on Turkish military and civilians (including Kurdish citizens), the military responded with intense operations which resulted in the killing of more than 100 PKK militants in a couple of weeks. Given that more than a quarter of these dead were female guerillas, Zozan Cewlik, the head of the PKK's woman division, warned the male leaders Duran Kalkan and Fehman Huseyin by saying, "You are responsible for the death of comrades who did not enough practice." When Duran Kalkan wanted to give a speech in the women's camp, she said, "In the last three months, we suffered more casualties than we did in the last 30 years. You are responsible. Comrades don't want you," and turned him around (*Sabah Daily*, 12 December, 2011).
4 Such arguments were raised especially in the summer of 2011 by many Turks and Kurds, when the PKK waged an all-out war against the Turkish state and its citizens. In numerous attacks in that period, the group not only targeted the state officials and infrastructures, but also went on a killing spree of civilians, which was interpreted even by people sympathetic to the group that those killings did not make any sense in terms of the group's claimed goals (Kurdish rights), and that the group was indeed trying to prevent the government's attempts at the peaceful solution of the problem by provoking it to revert back to aggressive policies that would then guarantee the perpetuation of the cycle of violence; thereby the existence of the PKK. In this context of non-sensical violence by the PKK on civilians, it is possible to say that people, the members of the PKK included, are likely to start distinguishing the larger Kurdish

problem as a problem of cultural rights and the PKK as a problem of terror. It is also sensible to argue that this distinction has a potential to create more confusion among the PKK members on the "mountain," leading in turn to the disengagement of large numbers in the years to come.
5 For all of my informants, the time difference between "psychological disengagement" and "physical exit" from the groups was seven years on average, demonstrating that physical exit from terrorist groups is quite a difficult task to achieve.

7 Reincorporation

Politics of repentance and life after violence

> Men say that gift-exchange brings abundance of wealth.
>
> Mauss (1967:9)

Do states' promise of rewards and confessions of repentants bring abundance of peace?

On 9 November 2005, a bookstore was bombed in Semdinli, southeastern Turkey, killing one man and injuring others. The bomber was caught by local people with two other suspects in a car along with Kalashnikov rifles, bombs, maps and documents that contained a "death list." Shortly after, the police and military officers came to the scene, saved the three suspects from the anger of the locals, and whisked them away (Biner 2006:347). The incident attracted huge media attention and created public uproar.

The three suspects were working for the operation team of Turkish Gendarme Intelligence and Counter Terrorism (JİTEM), which had been founded as a paramilitary force for state counter-terrorism. The bomber, Veysi Ateş was an erstwhile member of the PKK who was recruited by JİTEM after benefiting from the "Repentance Law," while the other two, Ali Kaya and Özcan İldeniz, were non-commissioned military officers (2006:347). All suspects denied their involvement in the bombing, arguing instead that their visit to town was related to gathering intelligence from local members of the intelligence service and discussing with the local procesutor the activities of the book shop owner, Seferi Yılmaz, "who was suspected of harbouring PKK guerrillas and of providing logistics for the organization's activities" (2006:348). The public prosecutor of Van province was sacked because he accused General Yaşar Büyükanıt, then the Commander of the Land Forces, of organizing an illegal group to create unrest in the country's southeastern region (Chislett 2006:8). When he was asked about the incident and the involvement of the soldiers, Büyükanıt responded, "I know them, they are good boys." The three suspects were initially tried in a military court and released; but they were later tried by a civilian court and sentenced to around 40 years in prison.[1]

The Semdinli incident brought into the limelight Abdülkadir Aygan, whose confessions about the dirty workings of the state had largely been overlooked thus far by the mainstream media. Almost two years before the incident, two pro-Kurdish newspapers, *Özgür Politika* and *Ülkede Özgür Gündem*, had published a series of accounts based on the public confessions of Aygan that exposed the atrocities committed by the state during the turbulent years of political violence in the persona of "repentant" terrorists (Biner 2006:345). Aygan himself was a former PKK member, who once worked as a security detail of the PKK leader Öcalan, but later left the group, benefited from the "Repentance Law" and joined the shadowy organization JİTEM with a new identity and a name, "Aziz Turan," where he *served* for ten years.

Two years after this incident, in June 2007, the police found 27 hand grenades in the attic an Istanbul slum. The investigators claimed that they were stored there by an ultranationalist retired army officer, who was linked to an illegal group called Ergenekon, named after a legend and a mythical place in Central Asia that has significance for Turks. The group is thought to be the latest embodiment of the "deep state" in Turkey, and documents found by the police in a key intelligent agent's house showed that it had a well-organized structure, having links to earlier unresolved incidents that include *inter alia* thousands of disappeared persons. Among the members of the group were retired army officers and generals, police chiefs, politicians, journalists, university professors, and businessmen. Alleged members of the group have been indicted for various crimes such as plotting to foment unrest; assassinating intellectuals, politicians, religious leaders, military staff, etc.; and among other things, toppling the incumbent government. Since 2007, and with the unfolding of other incidents and plots, the Ergenekon case was prosecuted with other cases such as "Sledgehammer," "Poyrazkoy," "Assassination of Generals," "Attack on the Council of State," and others. In addition, in his official assessment submitted to the court, the public prosecutor argued that Ergenekon's Trabzon[2] branch was behind the assassination in 2007 of Hrant Dink, a Turkish journalist of Armenian origin. By January 2012, 415 people have been tried for their alleged involvement in 13 different cases (Zaman 2012). Similar to Aygan's confessions, statements made by numerous former members of terrorist organizations who became *anonymous state witnesses* played an important role in the development of the aforementioned cases. These individuals were known to the public by their pseudonyms "Dilovasi," "Gurbet," "Ismet," "Efe," "Aydin-1" and others, some of whom could have been among my informants.

Many researchers, journalists, and academics have analyzed such confessions made by individuals that benefited from Turkish repentance laws, enacted eight times since 1985 under different names. In her article, for example, Biner (2006) aptly demonstrated the dialectical relationship between the state discourses and the PKK counter-discourses of terrorism by analyzing the discourses and imagination surrounding the subject of "repentant." Proceeding from the ideas of Foucault, she argues that discourses created out of confessions made by repentant subjects have the power of truth making, i.e., they have "truth-effects," which constitute the social body by creating specific subjectivities (2006:341). She further asserts, "power could be contaminated by its mode of operation, that is, that discourses and practices could be transformed by the subjectivities they produced" (2006:341).

Following Taussig, she describes this transformation as the "space of death," which is quintessential for creating meaning and consciousness in societies where torture is endemic and "where culture of terror florishes" (2006:341). For Taussig, the space of death is qualified as a threshold zone "where victims and victimizers are modified and blended into each other and where narratives with the capacity to create an *uncertain reality out of fiction*, an *epistemic murk* are produced" [emphasis added] (2006:341). Citing from Taussig's formulations, Biner opines that "it is these narratives ... that 'mediate the culture of terror' and that lead to political practices and discourses dominating victims as well as victimizers" (2006:341). To sum up, in light of these concepts, she examines the "Reinstatement into the Society Law" as a complex text and event that produces discourses and practices, which give rise to narratives and imaginations of "the repentant." In so doing, she engages in an analysis of victimhood through an examination of the epistemic murkiness created by such narratives and imaginations and challenged the "official manifactured categories of victim and of perpetrator" (2006:341).

Like Biner, most researchers examined the effects of the laws of repentance in terms of their *functional* value for the state and/or terrorist groups. In this chapter, besides their functional value, I will focus on these laws from the perspective of the state and the Turkish Penitents *vis-à-vis* the notion of disengagement from political violence. That is, by using the Maussian concept of gift-exchange, I will attempt to explicate the politics of repentance in Turkey, in which I will explore the exchange value of both the state's promised rewards and the Turkish Penitents' confessions and collaboration. Such undertaking was inspired by a similar approach used by David Moss who looked at the issue of *pentimento* in Italy. There are many reasons for my embarkation on the same concept.

First, based on my ROP model, the purpose of this chapter is to explore the Turkish Penitents' reincorporation stage, i.e., their lives after violence. However, their lives after violence indeed started in their minds long before their physical disengagement. In other words, their period of rumination over physical exit from the groups was deeply influenced by the prospect of the repentance laws. As I mentioned in the previous chapter, these laws manifested themselves as a crucial *resource* for disengagement; thus they are worthy of examination. Second, between the first repentance law enacted in 1985 and now, more than 3,000 individuals reciprocated the rewards (prestations) of the state with their confessions and collaboration (counter-prestations). The *contents* of the confessions have been indispensable for understanding and writing the history of political violence in Turkey, but it is equally important to comprehend the *practical* value of these laws from the perspective of both the state and the individuals. Thus, following Moss, I will explore the *practice* of the confession itself – "the rules and relationships through which those contents have been elicited, shaped and given the imprimatur of reliable historical evidence" (2001:298).

Several opportunities arise from this approach: (1) it enables us to explore the application of Mauss's ideas to the very area which "he regarded as the principal justification of his own interest in gifts: the deliberate creation of exchanges to prevent violence and maintain peace"; (2) examining the notion of the disengagement of the Turkish Penitents as a type of gift-exchange "encourages us to continue broadening the study of gifts beyond the economic and commodity contexts ..."; (3) the actuality of repentance laws in Turkey provides a "rather rare opportunity to track in detail the creation and evolution of a particular exchange relationship and identify the pressures responsible for its modifications" (2001:298–299); and lastly (4) by analyzing the relationship between the Turkish Penitents and the Turkish state as gift-exchange, I am hoping to provide a comparison, where appropriate, between the politics of repentance in Turkey and *pentimento* in Italy. The fact that Moss started analyzing the chain of relationships in the exchange with confessions offered by *pentiti* and that I start my analysis by putting the state-initiated rewards (through repentance laws) first in the exchange is likely to yield interesting results from such comparison.

Mauss's concept of gift-exchange: a brief introduction

Mauss' reputation as a founder of the modern discipline of ethnology is attributed to his short essay on *The Gift*, the greatness of which lies in "Mauss' aspiration to embrace human condition in its entirety by exploring the moral relationship between concrete persons and society as a whole" (Hart 2007:7). *The Gift* was indeed a direct line of descent from Durkheim's *The Division of Labor in Society*, in which he had focused on "the non-contractual element of the contract in his critique of Spencer's utilitarianism" (2007:8). Mauss' guiding questions in the essay were: "In primitive or archaic types of society what is the principle whereby the gift received has to be repaid? What force is there in the thing given which compels the recipient to make a return?" (Mauss: 1967:2).

His chief argument in *The Gift* therefore was the notion of obligation as he argued, "in many civilizations contracts are fulfilled and exchanges are made by means of gifts [which] are in theory voluntary but in fact they are given and repaid under *obligation*" [emphasis added] (Mauss 1967:1). This obligation emanates from the spirit and power of the gift, from its *hau* so to speak, which establishes a *bond* between the giver and the receiver. For this reason, even when abandoned by the giver, the gift still forms a part of him, and "through it he has a hold over the recipient, just as he had, while its owner, a hold over anyone who stole it" (1967:7). Because of this bond between giver and gift, failing to reciprocate means to lose honor and status, but the spiritual implications can be even worse: in Polynesia, for example, failure to reciprocate means to lose *mana*, one's spiritual source of authority and wealth (1967:5). Furthermore, Mauss distinguished between three obligations: giving – the required initial step for the creation and maintenance of social relationships; receiving, for refusing to receive is to reject the social bond, and reciprocating in order to demonstrate one's own liberality, honor, and wealth (1967:8).

A second focus in the essay was on "the system of economic prestations between component sections or sub-groups of 'archaic' societies [in which] social phenomena are not discrete; each phenomenon contains all the threads of which the social fabric is composed" (1967:2). Mauss called these social phenomena "total social phenomena" because in them "all kinds of institutions find simultaneous expression: religious, legal, moral and economic" (1967:2). On the other hand, he isolated one important set of social phenomena, "prestations," which are in theory "voluntary, disinterested and spontaneous, but in are in fact obligatory and interested" (1967:2). In other words, the gift seems to be generously offered, but the accompanying behavior is usually "formal pretence and social deception, while the transaction is based on obligation and economic self-interest" (1967:2). Lastly, his key idea about these transactions was their collective forms, i.e., according to Mauss, "the earliest forms of exchange took place between entire social groups and involved the whole range of things people can do for each other" (Hart 2007:8). He argued that these groups do not just exchange "goods and wealth, real and personal property, and things of economic value," but also "courtesies, entertainments, ritual, military assistance, women, children, dances, and feasts; and fairs in which the market is but one element and the circulation of wealth but one part of a wide and enduring contract" (Mauss 1967:3). Proceeding from these arguments, he called these prestations and counter-prestations as the system of *total prestations* (1967:3).

The evolution and politics of "repentance laws" in Turkey

Since 1985, eight different laws of repentance have been enacted by the Turkish state which can be divided into three major types: (1) although having different official names, the first six laws (of 1985, 1988, 1990, 1992, 1995 and 1999) came to be known as the "Repentance Laws;" (2) the seventh law was called the "Reinstatement into Society Law" or "Returning Home" (*Eve Dönüş*) law, as it was called by the general public, enacted in 2003 and the *offer* was good for six months; and (3) the "Effective Repentance Law" was enacted in 2005 and is still in effect as of February 2012. Despite sharing some similar features, these three different types of laws have had different meanings and significance both for the state and individuals who benefited from them.

The *Repentance Laws* and the *Reinstatement into Society Law* were similar to the juridicial mechanism of plea bargaining" in that

> members of terrorist organizations would receive amnesty or a reduction in sentence in exchange for becoming state witnesses ... [and] sentences for those who submitted to the law were to be reduced to half or three quarters, and upon their release they were to be protected with a new identity, including a change of name and appearance, and assurance of employment after their testimony had been verified.
>
> (Biner 2006:339)

Moreover, these laws were similar to Italian *pentimento* (625/1979), in which "obtaining reduction required a full confession, unequivocal rupture of all contact with terrorist organizations, and active collaboration in identifying former accomplices and averting further violence" (Moss 2001:300). Put differently, "the benefits of collaboration were directly conditional on *practical* results – preventing the illegal activities for which the group had been formed or repairing the damage already caused" (emphasis added) (2001:301). Furthermore, law 15/1980 in Italy brought an innovation: "it demanded collaboration not just to avert a crime or reduce its effects but to identify and capture accomplices" (2001:301). By so doing, the Italian government aimed, as did the Turkish one, at a radical transformation of the exchanger's identity and social relations.

In the *Repentance Laws* and the *Reinstatement into Society Law*, the exchange relationship between the state and individuals in terrorist groups was initiated by the former's prestations (promise of rewards) and continued with the counter-prestations (confessions and collaboration) by the repentants, a process mediated by police and the courts. These rewards were announced through the booklets prepared by the Turkish National Police and delivered to the families and the militants, which were also published in the newspapers. For instance, an article published on 9 August 2003 by one of the mainstream newspapers, *Hürriyet*, reads:

> To the parents, we are sure that you do not want to see our dearest, valued children involved in the terrorist organizations. We also do not want that because he/she is also our child. This is the right time to protect our children from unpleasant and unwanted conditions in order to reduce the suffering of the past and make sure it never happens again. We do not want our young people to suffer at the hands of the terror organizations. With your support, let's prepare our children for a new life. Let's save our children.
>
> (*Hürriyet* 2003)

From the Maussian perspective, this system of total prestation can be interpreted in several ways. First, the exchanges were collective in nature because even though they were personalized, they "bring participants together as representatives of wider collectivities" and as the laws clearly indicate, the value of being repentant depends on his/her membership and knowledge of a terrorist organization and the benefits are not available to lone gunmen (Moss 2001:309).³ Making a confession initiated a type of event characterized by Mauss as a total prestation, in which the repentant's "own past, present, and future selves were donated to the state by repudiating violence and breaking off relations with accomplices, removing the mask of a 'battle-name' and resuming a former identity" (2001:309). Second, although these laws were "imputed to symbolize the *paternalistic* state calling its *deviant citizens* back *home*" (Biner 2006:343), such prestations cannot be seen as a free gift; for in a type of exchange involving political violence, a free gift would be a general amnesty issued by the state without any conditions. Third, it can be argued that although the content of prestations created a "legal obligation" (Testart 1998) for the state, offering these prestations (enactment of these laws) in the first place was not obligatory; thus, that they were made with altruistic intentions that showed the state's magnanimity. I argue, however, that beneath this apparent altruism lies self-interest because even though the state was not legally obliged to make such prestations, it was in its best interest to do so given that potential reciprocation of repentants in the form of confessions and collaboration were quintessential tools for the state in maintaining the *social order* and claiming *legitimacy* to its authority.

It is sensible therefore to argue that the force of the confessions came from repentants' insider knowledge of terrorist organizations which, to the outsiders, have been the objects of fear, mystery, and even fascination. In this respect, like a Maori gift, confessions had "magical" powers that compelled the state to initiate the exchange. Moreover, considering the cost of terrorism to the country (estimated to be around 300 billion dollars since 1984) and potential reduction of this cost by information obtained from the confessions and collaboration, it is equally sensible to argue that there was also economic self-interest associated with the state's enactment of the repentance laws. Fourth, repentants, too, were obliged to reciprocate, an obligation that emanated partly from the *hau* of prestations, in this case the lure of benefits promised by the state (*pull factors*), and partly because of their own condition in terrorist groups as disillusioned individuals, which made life unbearable for them in such groups (*push factors*).

Despite the obligatory nature of exchanges, social, political, and economic constraints attached to repentance laws as a *legal system of total prestation* were quite strong for both sides. Whatever the potential benefits in reducing political violence, the institution of repentance laws, like the Italian *pentimento*, "aroused a moral ambivalence that Mauss ascribed to the nature of the gift-exchange itself" (Moss 2001:311). In Turkey, the governments who proposed and enacted these laws were criticized by the political opposition and by citizens with nationalist tendencies for the "futility" of such laws; or, in other words, because of forgiving the "terrorists" without any assurances about their potential recidivism. It was argued that rather than reducing political violence, the hope of the enactment of repentance laws in the future instead encourages people to join terrorist groups. With respect to the *Reinstatement into Society Law* in particular, enacted in 2003 and coincided with United States' invasion of Iraq, the criticisms by the opposition parties centered around the notion that the government's desire to pass the law was in fact demanded by the US that was in line with its strategy to get rid of terrorists based in Northern Iraq by "sending" them to Turkey. Thus, as the criticisms went, since the law was "ordered" by a foreign government, it was undoubtedly against Turkey's national interests. Within society, the criticisms of the government were based on nationalistic narratives such as "How can you forgive those who committed crimes against humanity?," "How can you maintain peace in society by forgiving those 'villains' who kill babies and women alive in cold blood?" and so on.

The governments usually defended themselves on the basis that they were cognizant of the multiplicity of factors that cause terrorism (political, cultural, economic, etc.), but repentance laws were one of the solutions to a complex problem in the legal sphere. The main reason for such an argument, in turn, depended on their conviction that "not all individuals join the terrorist groups voluntarily, or even if they join the groups consciously, they should be given an opportunity to come back on certain *conditions*;" and because of the existence of these conditions, these laws cannot be regarded as "amnesty" as generally claimed by their opponents. In addition, it was asserted that the possibility of recidivism was prevented by increases in penalties for committing crimes after benefiting from the laws. Lastly, as opposed to Italian *pentimento*, in which the expense of protecting *pentiti* was a significant element in decisions for expansion or restriction of eligibility for exchange, in Turkey financial issues of repentance laws have been secondary to social and political considerations.

From the perspective of potential repentants, the social and psychological constraints were equally strong. To participate in the exchange would be construed as acquiescence with the state's political and legal authority. In fact, when these laws came into force, contrary to mainstream and official media, the pro-Kurdish and pro-leftist newspapers and journals criticized the laws in terms of submission to the state's authority and disavowal of the suffering and atrocities caused by the state (Biner 2006: 344). In addition, media outlets such as "*Özgür Politika* provided a forum in which the positions ascribed to both the state as 'forgiver' and to the people as 'repentant' were denounced, by highlighting the 'hidden' and 'real' objectives of the state behind its veneer of transparency" (2006:344). The terms attached to those who had already benefited from the laws such as "undignified," "traitor," and "lesser" made it very difficult for those disillusioned members of terrorist organizations to participate in the exchange. They were indeed in a paradoxical state in that their willingness to reciprocate the gifts of the state by their confessions and collaboration would allow them to preserve their "individual" dignity, while being interpreted as destroying the "collective" dignity of their respective groups.

Furthermore, potential reciprocators of the state's promised rewards had a concern with regard to the implementation of the exchange. Since the prestations made by the state were non-material in nature, that is, state's promises, the fulfillment of which was stringent upon the counter-prestations of the individuals in terrorist organizations, and the fact that the average time difference between the first installment of confessions in police and court decisions for the completion of the exchange (receiving the rewards) was more than five years, individuals who were considering participation in the exchange found themselves in a dilemma, pondering that this technical issue increased the risk of their participation. This risk emanated to a great extent from the uncertainty about obtaining a positive decision at the end of the process.

What prolonged this process was the investigation of the accuracy and reliability of information given by repentants, a process which was administered by the Ministry of Interior. After receiving confessions, courts sent a written request to the Ministry of Interior in order to check the reliability of the content of those confessions. Similar to the standard rules of judicial confidentiality (*segreto istruttorio*) in Italy, the contents of the confessions were protected by the standards determined by the said ministry, based on which the violators could recieve up to three years of punishment in prison. During this period, i.e., from the first installment of confessions until the court decision, repentants were kept in jail but they could be taken out with a court's permission if their collaboration was deemed necessary for the investigation procedures. This, in fact, created a significant problem given that repentants were put in a separate place in jail called the "repentants' ward," but it did not prevent their subjection to harrassment by their former "comrades" in the jail's communal areas. At times, pressure manifested itself physically in beating, torturing, or even killing if the circumstances permitted.

Despite these difficulties, however, around 1,800 individuals benefited from the laws by their confessions and collaboration by being "repentants" between 1985 and 2005 (see Table 7.1 below). The statistics show, however, that nearly 3,000 applications had been rejected in the same period. One of the *leitmotivs* of the Maori custom was the obligation to reciprocate, which stemmed from the *hau* of the gift that was not itself inert. Mauss argued that "the *taonga* or its *hau* constrains a series of users to return some kind of a *taonga* of their own, some property or merchandise or labour, by means of feasts, entertainments or gifts of *equivalent* or *superior* value" and continued, "such a donor will give its donor authority and power over the original donor, who now becomes the latest recipient" (1967:7–8, emphasis added). While turning down the applications, the Turkish courts made an assessment of whether the applications conformed to the provisions of the laws. In Italian *pentimento*, given the secretive structures of the terrorist groups, information was already a scarce and highly valued resource and "its circulation [was] subject to various safeguards against the risk of police infiltration and its distribution roughly correlated with the organizational hierarchy" (Moss 2001:303). This, in turn, put the more-deeply involved individuals who were in possession of a store of valuables in an advantageous position in the exchange with the "enemies" (2001:303). In the Turkish *Repentance Laws* and *the Reinstatement into Society Law*, however, the aforementioned issue played out differently. First, founders and senior commanders of the groups were excluded from benefiting from the laws, which is why their confessions and collaboration were not accepted. Second, the exchange value of information in some individuals' confessions and their collaboration was not deemed to be *equal* or *superior* to the offer made by the state. In that case, the rejection made was directly related to the quality and reliability of information given by the members of terrorist organizations.

Furthermore, another reason for exclusion from the exchange had to do with the above-mentioned "collectivity" issue regarding prestations, as well as the "sensitivity" of the cases that the applicants were formerly involved with. For instance, on 2 July 1993, Madımak Hotel was burned down in Sivas, which had resulted in the killing of 37 Alevi citizens. After a long judicial process, 33 individuals were sentenced to death, which was then downgraded to "aggravated life imprisonment." These individuals applied to the court in 2006 in order to benefit from the "Reinstatement into Society Law," but the court decided that since no ties had been found between these individuals and any terrorist organization, they could not benefit from the law. This example demonstrates the importance of the collective nature of prestations for eligibility in the exchange with the state.[4] However, considering the identity of individuals who were killed in the incident, i.e., they all belonged to the country's

Table 7.1 Statistical data about the repentance laws in Turkey

"The Law of Provisions to be Applied to the Offenders of Some Crimes," known as "Repentance Law" by the general public, first enacted first in 1985. (Law Number: 3216)

This law was revised and the deadlines extended as follows:
Law 3419 dated 25.3.1988, (Official Gazette: 30.3.1988)
Law 3618 dated 21.3.1990, (Official Gazette: 27.3.1990)
Law 3853 dated 26.11.1992, (Official Gazette: 29.11.1992)
Law 4085 dated 28.2.1995, (Official Gazette: 8.3.1995)

The law was revised on 26.8.1999 once again, and remained effective for six months.
The breakdown of numbers related to applications to benefit from these laws (1985 to August 1999):

Date	Accepted	Rejected	Assessed	Total
11.6.1985–11.6.1987	202	197	–	399
30.12.1988–30.3.1991	160	370	–	530
26.11.1992–28.2.1995	213	843	–	1056
28.2.1995–13.8.1999	200	1311	13	1524
Total	775	2721	13	3509
Last enactment				
29.8.1999–1.2.2000	359	100	614	1073

Based on confessions between 1985–1999;

# of members of terrorist organizations identified:	2,320
# of members of terrorist organizations arrested:	755
# of incidents (crimes) revealed:	591
# of bunkers and weapons cache found and destroyed:	233

In the same period, the following witness protection measures were applied to the beneficiaries of the law:

# of people who were helped to establish a business:	54
# of people who were placed into a job:	78
# of people whose identity cards have been changed:	43
# of people to whom a gun licence was given:	54
# of people whose physical appearance was changed:	1
# of people who received financial support:	99
Total:	329

# of people benefited from the "Reinstatement into Society Law" (2003–2005) 731
(applications: over 1,000)
# of people benefited from the "Effective Repentance Law", Article 221 (2005– present): over 1,200

Source: www.belgenet.com/belge/pismanlik_03.html (4.2.2000) and various newspaper articles

Alevi minority, it is also possible to suggest that, while sending the applications to the courts, the public prosecutors took into account the sensitivity of the cases in terms of potential political and social reverberations.

The Effective Repentance Law (Turkish Penal Code – Article 221), which has been effective since its enactment in 2005, introduced several innovations that have important ramifications in terms of disengagement from political violence. First, contrary to earlier repentance laws that excluded founders and leaders of terrorist organizations from benefiting from the stipulations of the law, Article 221 included them in a way that no punishment will be imposed on them if they dissolved their groups or helped state authorities in their dissolution. Second, whereas earlier laws had set in motion a potlatch of comrades and weapons by compelling repentants to identify and incriminate others, or even participate in their capture, Article 221 removed also these obligations in the exchange that facilitated potential exchangers' (members and leaders) participation. Third, like the other laws discussed above, the requirement for "sincere repentance" remained in the "original" text of the law; but the wording of the law has been changed later such that the need for the utterance of "repentance" from terrorism has been removed from the text, jettisoning an important portion of the psychological weight of potential participants. Beneficiaries of such type of an exchange based on Article 221 prefer to be called "state witnesses" instead of "repentants." The nuance between these terms is quite important, which I shall discuss later.

Fourth, according to the conditions of the initial form of Article 221, participation in the exchange was a process that started with volunteers' oral confessions to the police, followed by a written document sent to the Interior Ministry for verification of the content of confessions and completed with a court appearance where the decision was read directly to the applicant. The change made in the law in 2009, however, loosened this complex process dramatically in that prosecutors have been given the necessary authority to complete the exchange with state witnesses, provided they have no criminal record. Lastly, some authors wrote about the partibility of the gift-giver in Melanesian exchange (Strathern 1988), but in Turkish law it is the gift that is partible in the exchange between the state and members of terrorist organizations. Like in the Italian *pentimento*, "the courts have carefully discriminated between relative value of different parts of a confession" (Moss 2001:328). It means that confessions do not have to be admissible in their entirety; the related parts are used as proof, while irrelevant parts can be discarded without invalidating the value and the usability of accepted parts. Moreover, if supported by supplementary evidence, the value of the parts of a confession which is based on secondhand information is deemed to be tantamount to the value of information obtained through firsthand experience or observation (2001:328).

In brief, with the enactment and innovations of Article 221, individuals have been able to benefit from the state's offer *just* by applying to the state authorities and expressing their willingness to disengage from political violence without being compelled to collaborate with the state in terms of identifying or incriminating others, showing the weapons cache of the terrorist organization, or partaking in operations to capture or decapitate active members. This evolution, in a way, followed closely Mauss' sketch of the historical shift from total prestation via exchange-by-gift to individual contract (Moss 2001:313) that allowed individuals who could not supply more (total prestation) to reciprocate with the lesser gift of self-incrimination (2001:214). Hence it follows that the evolution of repentance laws in Turkey was a reversal of the evolution of Italian *pentimento* given that Italian law of 1980 had made the conditions more difficult for benefiting from the law *vis-à-vis* its predecessor, law 625/1979.

In terms of the incentives and risks of participating in the exchange with the state, there emerges a big difference between Article 221 and its predecessors, i.e., the Repentance Laws and Reinstatement into Society Law, which were in effect from 1985 to 2003. As mentioned above, the number of people who benefited from the repentance laws during this period was around 1,800, whereas more than 1,200 individuals benefited from Article 221 in just seven years between 2005 and 2012. More importantly, these two types of laws produced two different kinds of repentants, i.e., "confessors" (*itirafçılar*) like Abdülkadir Aygan – whose confessions were analyzed earlier (Biner 2006) – who participated in the production of violence in the 1990s, this time exerted on Kurds on behalf of the state; and others, some of whom became "anonymous state witnesses" (*gizli taniklar*) and offered their confessions to the *existing* state in its attempts to dissolve the epistemic murkinesss around the deep state, e.g., Ergenekon. Mauss stated that gifts, in the sense of presents, are a source of both pleasure and of "poison" (1967:24). It can therefore be said that confessors took the dose of poison they were given, whereas state witnesses took the poison but did not swallow it ; they savored it, mixed it with their own saliva to dilute its toxicity and spat it out for others to see (Williams 2006:105). One of the most important reasons for this difference was a paradigm shift that took place in Turkey about a decade ago with regard to the state's and society's understanding of the notions of governance, democracy, and security. To understand this paradigm shift, it is necessary to account for the state's mentality before and after the year 2000, during which the gift-exchange with the state led to the production of two different types of repentants.

Gift-exchange with the state and deep state: production of two types of repentants

Mauss (1967) argues that "every exchange embodies some coefficient of sociability, and it is a means to create peace and bonds of trust." The gift-exchange relationships between the state and repentants in the 1990s, however, were far from producing these positive outcomes. In justifying the usefulness of the repentance laws, the state was keen to reassure public that repentants' confessions and collaboration would protect it from renewed violence by the terrorist groups, but in reality their confessions and collaboration as turning into a state's hitman functioned only to guarantee the perpetuation of the cycle of violence. In that period, the state not only fashioned an epistemic murk out of the narratives of repentants in creating the space of death especially in the country's southeast, but also repentants themselves were exploited in that creation along with other symbolic figures such as Mahmut Yıldırım (knows as Yeşil) and Abdullah Çatlı, as well as other military institutions that operated as a paramilitary organization such as Gendarme Intelligence and Counter Terrorism Division (JİTEM) and Special Warfare Department (Özel Harp Dairesi). It has been said that more than 17,000 individuals (mostly Kurds) disappeared in the 1990s, who have yet to be accounted for. A common conviction among political and civil society today is that most of these individuals were killed by the aforementioned people and institutions, in which the institution of confessors (*itirafçılar*) played a significant role. It is sensible to argue that the characteristic of the state's prestations before the year 2000 seemed to have taken the form of what Mauss called "polite fiction ... and social deceit," because political violence produced in that period not only blurred the line between victim and perpetrator, but it also led to a dubious but indecipherable link between the state and what is called "deep state."

This brings up the questions of "why would the state/deep state do *this* (social deceit)? Some answers to this question were explored in the second chapter, but to reiterate briefly, Smith's (1960) categories of *politics/administration* and *power/authority* in his "Government in Zazzau" become practical concepts as they resonate in Turkish politics as the distinction between government and power[ful] (*iktidar* and *muktedir*). Despite being elected as legitimate governments (authority), many political parties have historically failed to rule the country because of their lack of *power*, which was in reality in the hands of a small number of people that has come to be described as the bureaucratic-military elite. In other words, even though these governments had the "office," they did not necessarily have the "power" to rule the country. The power that this elite held, nevertheless, had an insecure character, which is why they have resisted any attempt aspiring to alter the status-quo that benefited them. This status-quo, on the other hand, is called the "system of tutelage," through which the Pan-Turkic/secularist ideology of the aforementioned elite has been protected and its power has been exercised through the bureaucratic, judiciary, and military institutions since the establishment of the Republic in 1923. Doubtless, this tutelary system was not based on popular consent; it was based on domination disguised by the notions of the "sanctity of the state" and "state secret," which were inherently open to resistance and attack by the masses that the elite tried to engineer as a flock.

The tension stemming from the foregoing domination and possibility of resistance led this elite to resort to exploiting various non-democratic tools because of their cognizance of the fact that pursuance of democratic ways and policies would mean their extinction. To this end, they capitalized on the fundamental human need for security through the fabrication of a chaotic environment and its reiteration when necessary, which seemed to them a viable tool promising the maintanence of their stranglehold on power. Ergil (1980) explained state violence by saying,

> state violence is a control strategy that rulers choose consciously to maintain their sovereignty in the absence of other strategies or when the current policies become obsolete ... what makes this strategy possible, on the other

hand, is the disorganization of the ruled and their lack of resistance due to insufficient institutionalization.

The chaos created in the wake of three military coups (1960, 1971, and 1980) and the post-modern coup of the 1997 are commonly cited examples for such strategy, which transformed the country into a "state of exception" (Agamben 2005) whereby the sovereign would be able to transcend the rule of law in the name of public good. The actors that were utilized in the creation of these states of exception, as well as those who exploited them, constitute the deep state which worked as a parallel institution to what is known as the conventional state. I had enumerated earlier some of these actors, but as a reminder, they were: Army's Özel Harp Dairesi, Gendarme's JİTEM, *itirafçılar* (confessors), and some symbolic figures whose names were identified with the deep state such as Yeşil and Abdullah Çatlı. It is possible to view the Özel Harp Dairesi[5] as the umbrella institution under which other actors worked together for the same goal, i.e., the maintenance of the status-quo by the production of chaos through violence.

The elusiveness of the link between the state and deep state was the main factor that precluded society from pinning down the responsible people and institutions behind the cycle of violence. It has been a common conviction that there was an entity called the deep state; but it was hard to define it because many of its actors were inextricably intertwined with state institutions; i.e., they were individuals from *within* and *without* the state who were working *for* the state/deep state nevertheless. From this angle, it is possible to suggest that the deep state was one of the faces of *the* Janus-faced state. This opaqueness associated with the deep state, or its imbricated/parallel existence *vis-à-vis* the state, in fact, was an important issue for understanding the cycle of violence in Turkey and making sense of the actions and motives of multiple actors that worked together to perpetuate the cycle of violence, which benefited the aforementioned power-elite in maintaining their advantaged position in society.

To specify, terrorism has been an important problem in Turkey since the beginning of the 1970s. In terms of its causes, there have been countless explanations, which none the less boil down to two: the first suggested that terror emerged in the country as a *natural phenomenon* due to various groups' social, political, and economic grievances that created discontent, which then led them to resort to violence to eliminate those grievances. According to the second, terror did not emerge naturally; it is a *constructed phenomenon*, constructed by the power-elite for the reasons explained above. I argue that these two explanations are not mutually exclusive; they delineate the existence of a symbiotic relationship between terrorist groups and the deep state. Given that terrorist groups' *raison d'être* is to produce violence and the power-elite's maintenance of the status-quo depended on the creation of a chaotic environment through violence, the aforementioned symbiotic relationship is almost automatically created, which describes the protracted nature of violence in the country.

On the other hand, the deep state cannot be seen as a homogeneous entity, in which all actors were "conscious" of its "real" intentions. There have been two types of people in it: the designers of policies and their bona fide implementers. As I mentioned above, the link between the state the deep state was not clear; bona fide state officials who were responsible for implementing the state's counter-terrorism policies were not privy to the fact that their actions were designed by the malevolent actors of the deep state.[6] The reason for their inability to detect this was that most of the deep-state actors occupied leadership positions in state's counter-terrorism institutions like the army, the National Police and the National Intelligence Organization (MİT). Their double functions and overlapping positions in the legal and illegal spheres in a way provided them with a shield, with which they could pursue their "dirty" policies and praxes with considerable freedom. Since the policies were fashioned by these higher echelons, the rest had to implement them without questioning, and their good intentions did not make any difference in terms of the resulting atrocities.[7]

As part of the counter-terrorism policies in the 1990s, the state/deep state seems to have convinced the majority of state officials and even society in terms of the prospects of two strategies. One of these strategies was to infiltrate the terrorist organizations through undercover state officials. This strategy resulted in the production of more violence, let alone preventing it. Because when these officers infiltrated terrorist groups, they felt compelled to exert the most extreme violence to the level of barbaric savagery to prove their dedication in order to get promoted in the group, which would supposedly give them access to more qualified information about it. For example, a senior police officer mentioned during my fieldwork that most of the "terrorist violence" they saw in certain districts of Istanbul's (e.g., Kanarya, Küçükçekmece, Esenler) in the 1990s was organized by such state/deep-state officers. The second strategy was to use repentant terrorists (*confessors*), which seemed to be quite effective for eliminating terrorism because of their in-depth knowledge of the groups, their ideologies, and modus operandi. It is easy to understand the motives of those "patriotic" state/deep-state officials; but what were the motivations of the confessors who not only disclosed highly-valuable insider information about their groups but also participated in the internecine acts against their former comrades and people for whom they had previously fought?

In the Maussian gift-exchange system, what is given becomes the manifestation of its giver. Because of this connection between person and property, an interpersonal link is generated between those who participate in the act of giving and taking. As mentioned earlier, Mauss explains the creation of a bond by the transfer of a possession (1967:8), using Maori custom as an example: the "bond created by things is in fact a bond between persons, since the thing itself is a person or pertains to a person. For this reason, to give something is to give a part of oneself" (1967:8). From this angle, it appears that confessors gave a part of themselves figuratively by their confessions, while offering their *whole selves* by collaborating with the state/deep state in its atrocities against their own people. Acquiescence to the state's terms and conditions in the repentance laws postulated the vow: in "giving you, I give myself" (Mauss 1967:57), it promised a commitment of the self to the other by the "act of transfer," and it put in place a "more generous but dangerous form of social contact as a social contract" (Williams 2006:37). As Mauss noted:

> The gift is thus something that must be given, that must be received and that is, at the same time, dangerous to accept. The gift itself constitutes an irrevocable link especially when it is a gift of food [nourishment or sustenance]. The recipient depends upon the temper of the donor, in fact each depends upon the other. Thus a man does not eat with his enemy.
> (1967:58)

In light of the foregoing, considering the gift as bad, dangerous, and poisonous was particularly relevant to confessors' willingness to collaborate with the state/ deep state in the production of violence under the guise of counter-terrorism. Agreeing to be described as a murderer in the eyes of public would make the giver vulnerable. Under normal circumstances of gift-exchange, giving brings respect and virtuous reward, but in this context, "giving hazards exposure, the possibility of ridicule and humiliation" (1967:58).

Despite shedding light on the potential consequences of a poisonous gift-exchange, the above arguments are insufficient to account for the individual motivations of confessors in participating in acts of violence on behalf of the state/deep state against their former comrades and supporters. The answer lies in Mauss' focus on the morality of the gift-exchange, i.e., "the ambivalence of the gift, of freedom and obligation, of altruism and self-interest in giving, that makes such a system of exchange ripe for the manipulation of sentiment, for emotional, moral, financial and discursive improvisation" (Williams 2006:42). Although not denying the possibility of altruism, Mauss suggested that "giving, as a social transaction between individuals, is impossible without an engagement of self, without a concern for self-interest" (1967:1). As I mentioned earlier, the state/deep state had a self-interest in offering rewards through repentance laws as the *quid pro quo* for information given by confessors and more importantly their collaboration in "counter-terrorism." My informants were not among the confessors but my in-depth interviews with them, and related archival data about *confessors,* revealed the following in terms of the confessors' self-interested motives, as well as the conditions that were conducive to such motives, to participate in the system of total prestation with the state/deep state.

First, they offered their confessions and willingness for participation after being captured or while they were in prison. Their vulnerability was skillfully exploited by the representatives of the state/deep state in turning them to a confessor through torture. One of the most notorious officers was Esat Oktay, who worked in the infamous Diyarbakır prison that I had mentioned earlier in terms of exemplifying the Kurdish people's collective trauma. A former confessor recounts those days:

> Those who were put into Diyarbakır prison know better. Lieutenant Esat Oktay turned some people into confessors. Then, these individuals tried

hard to make others confessor. Those who became confessors knew that what they were doing was wrong. They knew that they were in conflict with themselves, with their pasts and their conscience ... To escape from this situation, they had two options; to reject being a confessor or to work hard to turn others into a confessor. To choose the first choice required volition, but they lacked it because in order to make them confessors, their volition was already broken. They were left with one choice; to become a poodle of those who broke their volition, and to break volitions. Because, they knew that they would be empowered as much as the increase in the number of flaccids.

(JİTEMciler.blogspot.com 2011)

Second, their vulnerability was increased due to the notion of reciprocity as a "between relation" (Sahlins 1972:170). Since they were in prison, in participating in the exchange with the state/deep state, they spoke from an indeterminate position with regard to the duration of their actual prison sentences and the nature and validity of reduction in sentence that they would supposedly receive as a result of their counter-prestations. Furthermore, Mauss argued that the return must be bigger than the gift and more costly. Or, the return should at least appear to be so, for the gift-exchange is about appearances (1967:7–8). In such a position of vestibular temporality (Williams 2006:66), or a state in-between, they were more vulnerable because their confessions were in the hands of mediators (law enforcement officials and courts) who might have had malevolent intentions and could manipulate them. Moreover, since the benefits stipulated in the repentance laws depended on the reports of these mediators, there was a risk of "exaggerated generosity" on the part of the confessors, which might have led them to go to extremes in their violent performances on behalf of the state.

Third, apart from the significant financial rewards, they were reassured by the state that there would be no legal consequences and public hostility for their activities on behalf of the state, because they would be performed behind the shield of counter-terrorism and they would remain as a "state secret." This, in turn, led them to perform those acts with an incredible impunity, evidenced by the confessions of some confessors that they made in their memoirs or in the media, e.g., Abdülkadir Aygan.[8]

The second type of repentant appeared especially after the introduction of the above-mentioned innovations with the Effective Repentance Law of 2005 (Article 221). For the reasons given earlier, i.e., the negative connotations associated with the term "confessor," this second type of repentant rejected being called confessors and instead preferred to be called as an "anonymous state witness" (*gizli tanık*). As the innovations took away a big portion of the pressure associated with being a repentant, compared to their predecessors, anonymous witnesses disengaged from political violence with significant ease. Enactment of the new law, in fact, coincided with the emergence of the concept of a "new Turkey" that came into being with a paradigm shift in Turkish politics and society especially after the year 2000. It behooves me then to account for this paradigm shift.

The crux of the issue had to do with the fact that *change* became the way to peace, order, and stability, whereas it was seen theretofore as antithetical to those concepts. This new understanding was generally attributed to the emergence and rise of the Justice and Development Party (AKP in Turkish), which was indeed a product of the change of mentality in society in terms of its conception of the balance between democracy and security, individual rights and freedoms and their limitations, citizens' rights and state responsibilities, and so on. In other words, it was a demand-driven change for democratization that brought the AKP to power. It is sensible to argue, however, that the AKP also shaped the demands of society with its policies and achievements in the economic, social, legal, and political realms. In this vein, it should be noted that the increased pace of accession process to the European Union was the main catalyst for the *mentality change* of both the AKP and society. After the AKP's rise to power, Turkey jumped from twenty-sixth to sixteenth among the largest economies in the world. Even during the recent global economic downturn, the country's economic growth has made many countries envious. This economic advancement has translated itself also as an increase in the GDP per capita that crossed over the threshold of $10,000 in 2011 whereas it was around $2,000 before 2002.

In terms of political changes, the AKP has emphasized the importance of the complementary nature of its domestic and foreign policies. Its charismatic foreign minister Ahmet Davutoğlu, for example, formulated a new foreign policy based on his own theory of "strategic depth." The first of the five pillars of the new foreign policy was an emphasis on the balance between the democracy and security in the country's domestic politics. Turkey's former administrations had mainly focused on the country's military might (hard power), a focus that stemmed from their perceptions of threat, that is, the idea that Turkey was located in a peculiar geographical location, surrounded by enemies. In this respect, the AKP's emphasis on democracy as Turkey's soft power was unprecedented that contributed to the increase in Turkey's clout in regional and global affairs.

The most important changes made by the AKP that have had important ramifications on individual disengagement from political violence, however, were the innovations made in the legal sphere. In general, most of these innovations were interpreted within Turkey and abroad as important strides towards a mature and advanced democracy.[9]

Smith (1960) had argued that structural changes made by a political *authority* that does not have *power* are doomed to failure. Hence it follows that taken together, all of the structural changes mentioned above became possible as a result of the transfer of power from the country's former elite, i.e., the bureaucratic-military elite, to the new conservative elite that constitute the main constituency of the AKP. On the other hand, it can be argued that the processes of gaining power and making structural changes can be coterminous. The AKP's victory in the past three consecutive general elections was the manifestation of its achievement of power, but it is also sensible to assert that that achievement came about abreast with the structural changes made in socio-economic, political and legal fields. Anyhow, the AKP's boost of self-esteem that came with its globally acclaimed achievements and power, coupled with popular public demand, allowed it to give political support to the judicial process of the Ergenekon trials that started in 2007 and other cases related to coup plots that followed them. All of these cases have been interpreted as country's desire to face up to its dark history, and as an opportunity that "sheds light on alleged crimes on Turkish democracy, increases the public trust of the rule of law and the operation of democratic institutions" (European Commission 2011). In this process of *aletheia*, of the "disclosure of the truth" as such (Heidegger 1972), "anonymous witnesses" played an important role in that their in-depth knowledge of the terrorist organizations, as well as their dubious relationships with the deep state, contributed greatly to police's investigation.

To sum up, Turkey's repentance laws as a system of total prestation between the state and former members of terrorist organizations had important social, political, and psychological ramifications on society that had long been suffering from protracted violence. This system of total prestation also had practical significance for both the state and its beneficiaries. The first two types of repentance laws examined here produced less than dreadful consequences in the sense that they not only led to the conversion of (some) former terrorists from violence *against* the state and citizens to violence *on behalf of* the state/deep state, but also to the perpetuation of the cycle of violence in the country, during the 1990s in particular. The main reasons for these negative outcomes had to do with the nature and conditions of this exchange relationship, as well as the characteristics of the parties that participated the exchange. To specify, the prestations (promise of rewards) made by the state in the 1990s, in fact, appeared to be made by the actors of the deep state who were embedded in the state apparatus with motivations of self-interest of the power-elite. In other words, the main purpose of the promise of rewards through the repentance laws at that time was not to create harmony and bring peace in society as Marcel Mauss had expected from traditional gift-exchanges, but to generate a chaotic environment by stoking the already existing terrorist violence, which would serve the maintenance of the status-quo that benefited the country's power-elite for decades. In such a process, some members of the terrorist organizations reciprocated those prestations by their confessions and collaboration. The problematic part in these counter-prestations was the latter part, that is, their collaboration by way of acting on behalf of the state/deep state and killing their former comrades and own people. While some of the confessors chose this path for psychological and material gains, most of them participated in such an exchange from a vulnerable position, which I explained above. Upon realization of the negativities of such participation, i.e., their "instrumentalization" by the deep state, most confessors eventually experienced a loss of meaning and expressed enormous regret. To give an example, Abdülkadir Aygan said:

> I know that I was used by the state. When I think about it, I realize that I was used against my own people. When I came back home, I asked myself, 'What am I doing?' There was no way of going back. I became the enemy of the party [i.e., the PKK]; neither my tribe nor my family could protect me

in this situation. We all knew that whatever we did, we would never be the favorites of the state. We knew that the state would dispose of us after it got what it wanted. This is not a life worth living. I get ashamed of myself around other people. I am continuously troubled, anxious. I know that I am being followed. My phone calls are tapped. I am interrogated about whom I see and visit. There is the risk of being killed if I want to get out of it and leave everything behind.

(*Özgür Politika* 16 March 2004, quoted in Biner 2006:346)

The last type of the repentance laws, i.e., the Effective Repentance Law of 2005 (Article 221), removed from its text the obligation of *uttering* the word "repentance" and collaboration in the form of divulging the organization or former accomplices. An individual who participated in political violence became able to reciprocate the state's offer *merely* by contacting the state authorities and saying that he/she wants to cut his ties with the organization. In the case that he/she did not commit any crimes, no punishment is imposed upon him/her; otherwise, a reduced is granted. Hence, these two innovations took away an important portion of the psychological weight and difficulty associated with disengagement from political violence. Moreover, as opposed to the long duration of the completion of exchanges in earlier repentance laws, Article 221 expedited the process by authorizing public prosecutors, instead of judges in courts, for the completion of exchanges. Because of these practical simplifications, more than 1,200 individuals left terrorism behind in just seven years after the enactment of Article 221, whereas about 1,800 individuals had participated in the exchange through the former repentance laws in more than 20 years (1985–2003). As a penultimate note, these innovations came about as a result of a paradigm shift in political and civil society especially after the year 2000 with respect to the ways in which counter-terrorism ought to be pursued. Briefly, this new paradigm appears to be marked by a more altruistic, conciliatory, and democratic understanding.

To conclude, in this section, I tried to make a general analysis of the effects of repentance laws. To personalize the exchange in relation to my informants' individual disengagement from political violence, I should add the following. Of my 13 informants, six of them participated in the exchange with the state based on Article 221, that is, they were state witnesses; whereas although benefiting from the earlier repentance laws, the remaining seven reciprocated the state/deep state's prestations with *only* their confessions and refused to collaborate by exerting violence on its behalf. In addition, I had made earlier a distinction between the behavioral and cognitive aspects of disengagement from political violence, according to which I had characterized my informants from the PKK as "repentants" (should not be confused with confessors) and four of them from the revolutionary groups as "detacheds." With regard to the gift-exchanges with the state through the repentance laws, it is possible to suggest that repentants' participation in the exchange was expiatory in nature, whereas the detacheds' initial participation can be attributed to individual self-interest so as to escape from an unwanted situation. Their continued collaboration with the state by way of helping the police investigate and dismantle the deep state, nonetheless, can also be considered as efforts of atonement, or, at the very least, of *spiritualized self-interest*.

Life after violence: Protracted conflict and absence of healing mechanisms in Turkey

Many researchers have historically examined the postwar or post-conflict situations by exploring their social, political, and economic ramifications, while placing the larger emphasis on understanding the effects of those wars and conflicts on victims and victimhood. Very few people examined these phenomena in terms of their influences on perpetrators and how they are received by society after violence. Given that the attacks of terrorist groups are directed towards disruption of the social fabric or undermining the incumbent governments, it has been quite difficult for both civil and political society to accept those individuals that disengaged from such groups. Despite this difficulty, however, there have been numerous examples of peaceful settlements of conflicts and reconciliation efforts between parties of conflicts and wars.

One of the most notable and informative examples was Honwana's (1998) analysis of the Mozambican peace settlement of 1992, which brought to a close a 15-year war between the government and the Mozambique National Resistance (Renamo). This peace settlement remained fragile, however, as local tensions persisted for a long time between Frelimo and Renamo largely due to "social divisions spilling over from the long war and the desperate survival tactics of many Mozambicans attempting to rebuild their lives in the face of overwhelming poverty" (1998:1). In this context, consolidating peace was dependent on extending its benefits to all sections of society, especially in rural areas where the majority of the population lived. One aspect of the broader challenge was the healing of psycho-social traumas associated with war and upheaval. *Trauma* includes a wide range of afflictions affecting society in multifarious ways. "*Healing* goes beyond the alleviation of individual traumas and includes the mending of the social divisions which exist both within and between communities" (1998:1). War-affected communities in Mozambique drew on a variety of traditional rituals to deal with the traumas of war and to open the way to reconciliation, which include "Mpfhukwa spirits," "cleansing and purification," and "venerating spirits" (Honwana 1998).

Instead of assuming that the government or other outsiders would meet their needs, Mozambicans used the means available to them to heal the social wounds of war and to restore their meaning and significance, as well as stability in their communities. Within the context of Turkey, even though such local processes of healing were at people's disposal culturally, several factors have precluded the utilization of those processes, complicating the reincorporation of the Turkish Penitents in society in a significant way. First of all, despite the fact that the Turkish Penitents disengaged from political violence individually, the conflict with the terrorist groups and the state is still ongoing. Correspondingly, in such a context, the effects of coming clean has been often "humiliating" because of the negative reception of the Turkish Penitents' return to communities by their naming and shaming of "repentants" with the terms of "traitor," "sold-out," or "wolf in sheep's clothing," etc. In addition to the psychological pressures, my informants expressed their concerns for more severe reactions in their communities, given that most of them and their family members have been subjected to beatings or their houses became targets of Molotov cocktails by the representatives (*militias*) of their former groups. In this vein, the effects of these psychological and physical traps have been heavier for the Turkish Penitents from the PKK compared to those from the revolutionary groups, because most of the former had to return to small villages or towns where social pressure was higher, whereas the latter have remained within an urban environment where they practiced political violence, having relatively lighter social pressure.

Second, because of the foregoing reasons, the enactment of collective healing processes was almost impossible, though it could be possible to utilize such mechanisms on an individual level. However, because of the risks likely to be incurred as a result of contacting multiple persons and institutions and exposing their former identities as a former member of terrorist group, the Turkish Penitents had to establish and maintain a very narrow, loose-knit social network (Bott 1957) in which they interacted with only a handful of people, most of whom were also penitents. Thus, healing processes with these individuals does not go beyond *talking* about past experiences, traumas, and future aspirations. More often than not, however, they find themselves talking about the country's current socio-political issues –issues related to terrorism in particular – because spending a significant amount of time in a terrorist organization equipped them with deep theoretical knowledge and technical skills for the practice of violence. Since they left violence behind, what they have been left with was their theoretical knowledge, which seems to have led them to seek solace in their intellectual debates. Lastly, since only a fraction of individuals who leave terrorist groups are offered jobs and other benefits by the state, most of the penitents are in dire straits economically, which complicates their processes of incorporation even further.

The excerpts below from my interviews with my informants demonstrate some of the foregoing difficulties. Zilan-P's case is particularly important as it shows the difficulties of life in Northern Iraq where she took refuge after escaping from the mountain with her husband Nadir-P and lived there for eight years before her final return to Turkey.

Case 1: Zilan-P

> As I mentioned before, I escaped from the mountain with my husband and we initially took refuge in Barzani's government in Northern Iraq. We stayed there for eight years but I was suffering the whole time. What's more, my husband and I were always fighting. I don't remember a single night when my pillow was dry, for I was crying under it all the time ... Of course, my family didn't know any of these. They didn't know that I escaped and got

married. One day I called my mom and told her everything; she sounded cool with all of what I had been through. But when I spoke with my father and told him that I was married, he got angry. He didn't accept it. I heard afterwards that he even had a fight with my aunt, because she was angry that I had gone to the mountain with her son [her fiancé] who was killed on the mountain and that I got married to someone else ... One day, my mom came to visit me in Northern Iraq. When she left, my longing for home increased even more. I was in anguish all the time. I told my wish to my friends, saying 'If I cannot go back to my homeland and die here, don't bury me here. Take me home.' I was always telling to myself that I will go back to Turkey one day. In fact, I made it through with that hope. I never wanted my children to grow and go to school there. Because, instead of living somewhere as a refugee, I would prefer languishing in my homeland. In fact, economically, we didn't have any problem while we were in Iraq, but this longing for my homeland was tearing me apart ...

Anyway, I made my decision and came to the Turkish-Iraqi border, from where I called security forces to surrender. I crossed the river [i.e., the border] and they picked me up on the other side of the border. When I passed the border, I kissed and smelled my land ... I hadn't even told my family about this. Because, when I called them from Iraq, they were saying, 'Don't come. But if you want to have us killed, come. If you come, we will face social exclusion; they will turn our lives into a dungeon.' But after giving my statement to the police, I called them ... I benefited from the repentance laws, but still spent some time in prison, during which my mother looked after my kids. After being released from prison, I came to my family. I hadn't seen them for 17 years, except for seeing my mom once in Iraq a year before. I heard that my husband's relatives were murmuring about my return from the PKK. But I did not even have an iota of regret for my return. If only I returned before getting married; I would be OK with staying in prison. It was too late anyway. My husband's tribe was threatening my family, saying, 'Send our children [grandchildren] or tell her to go back to her husband in Iraq.' Returning to Iraq was worse than death for me, because I never liked it there. But had I not returned, I was sure that there would be blood between the tribes.

Eventually, I went back to Iraq after our families had an agreement. But, this time the KDP government didn't accept me, arguing that I had escaped from them. They even said, 'Why did you come back? Were you sent by the Turkish state as a spy' etc. ... They took my passport and even though I wanted it back a month later, they didn't give it to me. When there was a religious festival in Turkey, I wanted to go back but they did not allow it. After that, I gave up until I was sent by them. Finally, they deported me. But my husband stayed in Iraq. After several months, however, he said to KDP forces, 'You deported my wife and children; so, you have to send me too.' Then, he came to Turkey and surrendered to the police. When he came, all hell broke loose in his tribe. Because they couldn't accept the fact that one of them betrayed the Kurdish cause. It has been more than a year and we still suffer from these reactions. When my children come back from the street, they say, 'Mom, what have you done that people call you traitors.' I try not to send them to the street lest they are confused. Even though I try to tell them the truth and make them conscious, we are having problems in society. We are hiding from people. We are, in a way, invisible ..."

Case 2: Hikmet-R

Almost five years after leaving the group, I was finally offered a job by the state in a government office. I don't earn a lot, but it is enough for me to make a living with my wife and daughter. But because I had to cut my ties with almost everybody in my life, the biggest problem I have is with the people in my workplace and neighborhood. They are asking, 'Don't you have anyone in your life; don't you have any relatives; why don't you have any visitors? etc.' I have been telling them that my parents died and I have only one sister who is living in Istanbul. To show them that I am not lying, every other week or so, I go to Istanbul. But in reality, I have no sister there. When I come, I spend most of my time chatting with ... [an officer in the Istanbul police department who helped Hikmet during his disengagement from the group] and stay for two days in his office. I sleep on his couch ...

Case 3: Selim-P

People don't like us here. They call us traitors. The threats we receive from the organization are too heavy.[10] None of us is safe here; our lives are in danger. To ease the tension, I can contact the group, but I know that they will tell me to go to the BDP (Peace and Democracy Party) offices and work for them. But I benefited from the repentance laws; I cannot do it. If I do it, I will be put in prison for 36 years for being a member of the PKK. I mean, we are in the middle of many fires. If only we were not burned by one side at least. Our state has proven lately that it is strong, but nobody asks what happens to people who left their organizations. They don't ask whether we are hungry; they don't ask about the conditions of our families ... We heard that some of the repentants' families were killed by the group on the basis that they were harboring 'traitors.' Thank God, my family is taking care of us. For this reason, I contracted a consanguineous marriage; since I came back from the mountain, nobody gave their daughter to me ... On the other hand, the group used to tell us, 'If you surrender, the state will use and dump you.' We are not dead now, but our situation is worse than death. I mean, I have many economic problems. Nobody knows how many people like me fell into the hands of the mafia all around the country. If it were not my family, maybe I would join the mafia as well ...

Case 4: Gürkan-P

When I returned from the mountain, I saw that nobody wanted to talk to me. Nobody loves me. My family received me differently though; my father told me to find a job and lead a life without intervening anybody's business. I mean, he didn't want me to work with the security forces and incriminate people around us. I followed his advice. One day, somebody gave his truck to me, with which I went to Iraq [for work]. When I returned a week later, he said, 'Give me the keys.' I found another job, but the same thing happened after several days. I came to a point where I couldn't find money for bread and butter. You knock on the state's doors; to no avail ... This is a reality. Had I been given a simple job by the state, I would be able to take care of my children. Now, I have eight children. The one who is 17 years old got married and the eldest at home is now in fourth class. They all will go to school and get married. Our apartment is a rented one and I have a lot of debt for credit I took from the bank. I cannot lie to you; this is my situation, and what's more important is that there are at least 10,000 people like me. Some of them have houses, cars; but most of them are living in poverty and danger. This is a reality. Last week, for instance, they threw a Molotov cocktail at my house. The group's members or sympathizers are doing these. They are not doing these by chance; we are their targets. Some people were even killed by the group. This is a reality too.

Concluding remarks – lives in the cracks of social structures

In addition to Turkish Penitents' personal resources explained in the previous chapter, repentance laws in Turkey played an important role *vis-à-vis* their processes of disengagement from political violence. Given the fact that there was a significant time difference between their psychological disengagement and physical exit from groups, repentance laws facilitated remarkably their processes of deciding to exit, largely due to the enticing benefits to be gained from an exchange with the state in the form of reduction in sentence, no sentence, change of identity, and so on. Participating in an exchange relationship – through confessions and collaboration in exchange for the above-mentioned rewards promised by the state/ deep state – with two types of states produced two types of repentants; namely, the "confessors" (*itirafçılar*) and "anonymous state witnesses" (*gizli tanıklar*). *Confessors* participated in the exchange with the deep state in the 1990s which, for various reasons given above, compelled them not only to confess and provide information but also participate in violence against their former comrades on behalf of the state. *Anonymous witnesses*, on the other hand, participated in an exchange with a more democratically-minded state especially after the year 2000 and they were required to offer nothing but their self-incrimination even without uttering the phrase "I confess," let alone being forced to incriminate others or to collaborate with the state in its exertion of violence under the rubric of "counter-insurgency." Despite this paradigm shift in the realm of governance offering favorable conditions to members of terrorist groups who are considering disengagement from political violence, even the beneficiaries of the Effective Repentance Law (Article 221) suffer dearly in their processes of reincorporation in society, as exemplified by the problems that my informants have been facing in their "lives after violence." The most important of those problems appears to be their obligation to lead an "invisible life" which explains perhaps why society does not recognize and remedy those problems.

To clarify, consider the following analogy that was inspired by Victor Turner. In his study of Northern Zambia, Turner (1974) examined the constancy and change in Ndembu society through an analysis of its social structure. For him, there were three manifestations of social structure, namely: liminality, marginality, and inferiority. The relationship between these manifestations of social structure was expressed, in spatial terms, as being in-between (liminality), on the edges (marginality), and beneath (inferiority). He later adjusted his conception of marginality and introduced the idea of "outsiderhood." Examples of outsiders were "shamans, diviners, mediums, priests, those in monastic seclusion, hippies, hoboes, and gypsies" (1974:233). He argued, for example, that shamans and priests have opted out of the social structure and chosen to manifest social structure (communitas) through outsiderhood, while gypsies did so through inferiority.

In light of Turner's typology, then, I have found my informants not *outside* the social structure, not *on the edges* or *beneath* it, but in the *cracks* of social structure. Because of the aforementioned difficulties associated with reintegration to society, they were pushed into the cracks in the social structure where they have existed physically after leaving terrorist organizations but have remained structurally invisible in society. When they meet new people, they cannot reveal their identities and they have to be constantly cautious, which seems to create noticeable psychological problems such as boredom, melancholy, anxiety, and more importantly, loneliness.

The questions to be answered then are. How can we extricate the Turkish Penitents and thousands of similar individuals from the cracks in social structure? What policies can be designed to alleviate their current conditions and help them reintegrate into society? What benefit can be achieved from such efforts in terms of countering extremism and political violence? How can this research be improved further? In addition to a general conclusion of this book, it is therefore the objective of the next chapter to lay out this book's implications for policy and future research.

Notes

1 The trials were renewed after the changes made to the Turkish Constitution's Article 145, which regulates the military courts' area of jurisdiction, allowing civilian courts to try military officers for their crimes outside the confines of their duties. The changes came into force with a referendum, held on 12 September 2010.
2 Trabzon is a city on the Black Sea coast.
3 In Turkey, all organized/armed criminal groups were included in the law, but since my focus is on terrorist organizations, I will simply discuss these laws with respect to disengagement from them.

4 I should note that the notion of collectivity pertains to individuals' membership or knowledge of organized criminal groups. It does not mean making applications in a collective manner, as the perpetrators of the Madımak incident did. In addition, after the Ergenekon trials started in 2007, some people argued about possible links between the perpetrators of the Madımak incident and the Ergenekon Terrorist Organization; but these allegations have yet to be proven.
5 Özel Harp Dairesi was originally established in 1965 as a type of Western European "stay-behind" or "Gladio" network. The purpose of such groups was "to organize resistance in the case of a communist occupation." However, despite the collapse of Soviet Union, and thereby the communist threat, the Turkish Gladio (deep state, which is dubbed today as Ergenekon) remained in existence and has directed its violent operations against Turkish citizens who have been considered to be a threat to its Pan-Turkic ideology and its very existence. For details, see for example, Ganser (2005:224–45).
6 Those who became suspicious about the state of affairs in terms of counter-terrorism were eliminated by the deep state. One of the most remarkable examples is the case of Ahmet Cem Ersever, who was indeed a military captain and one of the founders of the JİTEM that was behind most of the said atrocities in the 1990s. Eventually, he retired after realizing that the strategies they followed under the umbrella of counter-terrorism were not right. Not long after voicing his suspicion, however, he was killed in 1993, but his murder remained unresolved hitherto. A voice-recording which came out in October 2011 revealed some of his suspicions, which also shed light on who might be the perpetrators of his killing. In that recording, he said: [With regard to the strategies] there is a genealogy that extends to the Generals... And these people brought me into a completely illegal line; they want to silence me, but I am not going to be silent." For more information, see Postmedya (2011).
7 In an internet blog, an *itirafci* wrote: "I don't know any *itirafci* who was not involved in murder, burglary, distortion, kidnapping and torture ... most of the *itirafçılar* testified that all of the claimed 17,000 disappeared persons were killed and most of the burned-villages were burned down, directly or indirectly, by them" (jitemciler. blogspot.com 2011).
8 For details of confessors' motivations, interests, atrocities, and more, see, Çiçek (2009), *Itirafci: Karanlik Donemin Tetikcileri* (*The Repentant: Hit Men of the Dark Period*), Istanbul: Timas Yayinlari.
9 The most crucial changes made in the legal structure were the following: (1) amendments to the Turkish constitution in 2010, which were hailed by the European Union as a sign of the maturation of democracy; (2) the changes with regard to undemocratic structure of High Council of Judges and Prosecutors. Since the council is authorized to appoint the prosecutors and judges, the changes in the second item were particularly important in terms of the ongoing Ergenekon trials that came to be seen as Turkey's desire to face up to the dark side of its history.
10 After leaving the group, Selim has been living in a small city in the southeast where social pressure and the PKK's threats are considerably high.

8 Conclusion

This book has set out to explore the notion of individual disengagement from political violence in Turkey by reconstructing the lives of 13 "formers" whom I call the "Turkish Penitents." The general theoretical literature on this subject and specifically in the context of Turkey is inconclusive largely due to the difficulty of access to private accounts of individuals who were once a member of a terrorist group. Having the privilege of access to such private data, I aimed to explore common processes concerning individual disengagement from political violence, rather than seeking some "truth" in those private accounts. By collecting and analyzing the life histories of the Turkish Penitents, I sought to answer the following questions:

- What motivational (individual/internal) and structural (environmental/external) factors did influence Turkish Penitents' processes of disengagement from political violence?
- What were the obstacles and inhibiting factors for leaving the group? How did they overcome such factors?
- What were the differences and similarities between Turkish Penitents who left a leftist-revolutionary group and those who exited from a separatist organization, the PKK?
- What are the Turkish Penitents' current positions in society and the states of mind?
- What can we learn from their experiences that may contribute to the facilitation of disengagement processes for others who are still involved in political violence?

In an effort to answer these questions, a theoretically-informed methodology, that is, a process-based Rite of Passage (ROP) Model for political violence was proposed. The significance of this conceptual/methodological model is that it allows the researcher to explore individuals' whole lives by focusing – before, during, and after research – on three phases in their life continuum; namely, *separation* (pre-violence), *transition* (violence), and *incorporation* (post-violence). The need for such a holistic view emanates from the fact that it is quite difficult to understand why/how an individual left a terrorist organization and who he/she has become after leaving violence unless factors that led him/her to resort to political violence in the first place are carefully examined. To give an example, before joining his group, Gökhan-R had almost no ideological inclination towards revolutionary groups and their ideologies. As explained in the third chapter, his significance loss largely due to his dysfunctional family structure culminated in his entry into the group that appeared to him as a viable means for significance restoration. Once various factors led to a loss of significance while he was in the group, this time exit from the group seemed to be the only way to restore his significance. Since he lacked a strong ideological background, his decision-making process with regard to exit occurred significantly easier, for instance, than those of Hakan-R and Ahmet-R who had very strong ideological beliefs and loyalty toward their groups. It would therefore be incomplete to embark on an effort to understand the notion of individual disengagement without examining why individuals resort to violence in the first place.

The remainder of this chapter then will be divided into four sections; the first three sections will outline the major findings of this study based on the proposed ROP model. The final section will focus on the implications of this study for policy and future research.

Findings related to the "separation" stage

My findings about the Turkish Penitents' separation stage suggest that in order to account for individual paths to political violence, researchers should shy away from deterministic, one-dimensional and/or mono-causal explanations (e.g., in the sense that "poverty leads to crime"). Instead, a process-based socio-psychological approach seems to provide better opportunities for making sense of one's killing of others or making the ultimate sacrifice. In order to better understand individual paths to political violence, we need to take into consideration individuals' experiences in various phases of their separation stage which include, as outlined in the ROP model, their lives in family and school, their political socialization, radicalization, and entry into groups. Even my small sample shows that although all of my informants have gone through the foregoing stages, the nature and the importance of each phase differed in each of them with regard to their radicalization or entry into terrorist groups. That is why; it is practically difficult to point to a particular factor or phase to make generalizations with regard to one's eventual resort to political violence or entry into terrorist groups. On a theoretical level, however, this study found considerable similarities among my informants.

First, the concepts of *significance quest* and *significance loss* played an important role in all of my informants' separation stage, either in their radicalization or entry phases. Specifically, my informants with more disadvantaged socio-economic backgrounds first felt a significance loss, which prompted a significance restoration and culminated in their joining terrorist groups. My informants who came from better socio-economic backgrounds joined their groups as a result of their quest for meaning and significance, but they too had a significance loss in their processes of radicalization, which took place after their voluntary entry to their respective groups. *Overall, therefore, "loss of significance" seems to be the common factor affecting the separation stages of all of the Turkish Penitents.*

Second, while significance loss of some of my informants was created by problems related to Turkey's *social and political structures* (e.g., the de facto differential incorporation of various ethnic, religious, and economic groups into society; relative deprivation/frustration-aggression because of personal or collective trauma, etc.), the notion of significance loss manifested itself in some of my informants in the form of *psychological problems* springing from their tense, unloving, or dysfunctional family structures and/or from their negative experiences during their political socialization in the family and/or school.

Lastly, turning points had important influences, i.e., "triggering effects," in terms of the Turkish Penitents' transition from one phase to another in their paths to political violence. In some cases, a turning point was marked by negative experiences with persons (actors), in other cases by negative life events (factors).

Findings related to the "transition" stage

This study found that individual disengagement from political violence is a gradual process which is as complex as the process of joining political violence in the first place. First of all, numerous factors influence this process which include, but are not limited to, having the first seed of doubt, disillusionment, rumination about leaving the group, the group's threats against disengagement, reasoning, planning, and exit. Second, my informants are unique in the sense that they were able to exit from their respective groups despite being aware of the heavy implications of leaving, which range from heightened scrutiny by the group and potential reactions of society upon return to execution in the case of failed attempts to escape. Some of my informants (detacheds) left their groups and violence while retaining their "revolutionary ideology" but others (repentants) not only left their groups, violence, and their ideologies but also felt remorse and went great lengths to alleviate the associated stress of past wrongdoings. To this end, among other things, they offered state officials their insider knowledge not only about their own groups but also other terrorist groups and their relationships with the actors of the deep state. This latter issue is important in the sense that such information provided by those repentants (who like to be called as "anonymous state witnesses" to differentiate themselves from "confessors"), most of whom were former members of terrorist organizations, became crucial in the processes of unmasking the Turkish deep state, and thereby opened a new page in the country's efforts towards the establishment of an advanced democracy.

Third, this study suggested that factors affecting individual disengagement from terrorist groups can be found in numerous problems and contradictions that are inherent in *legitimate peripheral participation* in *communities of violent practices* (i.e., terrorist groups). These problems and contradictions entail:

1   Problems pertaining to the *interpersonal relationships* within terrorist groups. I found that all of my informants in the PKK and revolutionary

groups perceived and experienced a high level "distrust" and "unjustness" in terms of peer-to-peer and master-novice relationships within their respective groups. Those who joined the PKK involuntarily realized such feelings from the beginning, but all others who joined their groups for ideological reasons started to realize the effects of such feelings more strongly when the influence of their ideologies was lifted. In the case of some of my informants, it was such feelings that caused the abandonment of ideology notwithstanding.

2 Problems related to *access and sequestration* with regard to participation in the production process in a community of violent practices. It appears that in the PKK, even novices do not have any problem in gaining access to participation in the production, i.e., violence. Novices are sent to violent clashes with the Turkish military without proper training and equipment which creates a feeling of "worthlessness" not only in those novices but also some of the old-timers who realize that the group has taken the political out of "political violence" and started to view violence as an end in itself. These practices of the PKK are called by the group members as the "policies of blood and death." In revolutionary groups, the problem of access and sequestration manifests itself differently. While some of my informants said that some groups encourage excessive participation in the production process (also "violence"), which creates similar feelings to those in the PKK, others claimed that their access to participation was limited or prevented by their groups. These informants also said that even though their sequestration was done by groups under the guise of protecting them against the dangers of living under "heavy illegality conditions," they felt that some murky figures in their groups were in fact cooperating with the deep state, thereby trying to sideline or discharge them. Such subjective feelings, in turn, seem to have created in them serious discontent, feelings of unjustness, and other similar feelings that led to their *psychological degeneration*.

3 Life in *"imagined" communities of violent practices* and the effects of *postponed imaginations*. With regard to their ultimate goals, this study suggested that the goals of both the PKK and revolutionary groups have an imaginary quality. Since its inception in 1978, the PKK has been through several stages vis-à-vis its objectives. To specify, the group started out with an aim to establish an "independent Kurdish state," which was then downgraded to "a democratic confederation" and most recently to establishing an "autonomous region" within the borders of Turkey. Not only has the target of the group shifted at each juncture, but also none of its goals were achieved as a result of more than three decades of struggle and in spite of almost 40,000 lives, most of whom are Kurdish citizens. (Some people say that although the PKK did not solve the problems of Kurds, it rendered them visible and made them an integral part of Turkey's political discourse. It is a reasonable argument but I argue that although the PKK made the Kurdish issue more visible, it has created serious setbacks to Kurdish people's achievement of their well-deserved democratic rights. Given that the paradigm shift in Turkish politics, which has been taking place for more than two decades towards a better democracy, led

to the inclusion of other previously subjugated groups into the system such as religiously more conservative people or Alevis, in the absence of the PKK, Kurdish people, too, would have been incorporated into the system more swiftly). Postponement of the group's utopian goals and their shifting nature as a "moving target" surely had an impact on some of its members, making them feel that the group's goals are no longer attainable and leading to their "burning out," "disillusionment," and eventual desire to "disengage" from the group. Moreover, in recent months, the suspected connection between the PKK and the Turkish deep state started to be articulated more frequently in society and especially by influential Kurdish intellectuals such as Kemal Burkay and İbrahim Güçlü.[1] Should this connection be proven, it is likely to increase the number of disillusioned members in the PKK, which may even lead to their disengagement from it in the months or years to come.

4 Similarly, revolutionary groups tried since 1970s to bring about a socialist revolution through their violent practices, which would then lead to the creation of a "communist Turkish state." Almost three decades of struggle, however, did not bring any result in this respect, largely because the global and domestic developments during this period marked the end of the Turkish Left. Specifically, global romance about a communist revolution became almost irrelevant especially in the last decade and the recent domestic policies of "zero tolerance for torture" by law enforcement and "economic advancement" have taken away from revolutionary groups their main ideological tools of exploitation and tools for mobilization.

5 The contradictory nature of groups' approach to learning as *didactic teaching* and *indoctrination*. I suggested that the life of a member of a terrorist group is defined by learning *in situ* and *in practice* in a community of violent practice. The groups explored in this study, however, see learning as a unidirectional process of "absorbing the given," or simply as "indoctrination," largely due to their cult-like structures. At first glance, it looks logical for terrorist groups to indoctrinate their recruits based on their ideology in order to reconstruct or homogenize the identities of new members who come from different backgrounds. To this end, all terrorist groups I studied in this book used various "thought reform" techniques (Lifton 1961; Alexander and Rollins 1984), but I found that these techniques backfired in that they led over time to the disillusionment of many group members including my informants and contributed to their desire to disengage from their respective groups.

Fourth, I categorized the first two of the foregoing factors as "internal" factors and the latter two as "external." My findings suggest that all of my 13 informants were influenced by one or more of these factors in their processes of disengagement. Specifically, both in the PKK and revolutionary groups, there is a high level of distrust and subjective feeling of unjustness among members in terms of their interpersonal relationships. Likewise, all of my informants reported that they have been through a process of "thought reform" in their respective groups and that they were adversely affected by these techniques which led to their discontent, disillusionment, and physical exit from their respective groups. The remaining factors, i.e., postponement of the utopia and the problem of access and sequestration, seemed to have an impact on the disengagement processes of *some* of my informants from both the PKK and revolutionary groups.

Fifth, disengagement from political violence does not seem to be role specific. This study has found that undertaking certain roles does not have a strong influence in terms of one's desire to disengage from terrorist groups. To clarify, there seems to be negligible differences between participating in violence in the group's military committee and assuming a position in the group's health division, which does not require participation in violence personally but causes, nonetheless, significant exposure to violence during terrorist actions. For instance, the cases of Zilan-P and Selim-P show that disengagement does not merely rest on an individual's own discontent, trauma, or suffering but also on the suffering of others, which I called "altruism born of suffering of others."

Sixth, my informants' personality orientations and styles of coping played a significant role in terms of the "resources for disengagement." This study has found that when their personality orientations were judged in respect to their disengagement from political violence, all Turkish Penitents are predominantly "reward-oriented" and "inner-directed" and they seem to have "internal locus of control." In this respect, in contrast to conventional thinking suggesting that personality orientations are stable over the life-course, this study found that their personality orientations changed when there was an important change in the social situation (e.g., transition from being ordinary citizen to being a member of a terrorist movement). When their styles of coping were examined, this study found that all 13 subjects of this study used "altruism," "anticipation," and "rationalization," while "idealization" made a crucial impact on the disengagement of one subject, i.e., Azad-P. Furthermore, the decisiveness of my informants was a key to their disengagement, but the importance of "repentance laws" cannot be neglected in terms of understanding their disengagement more fully. Although many of my informants mentioned that they would disengage regardless of the repentance laws, I received a strong impression during my interviews that repentance laws played a very significant "facilitating" role, if not a determining role, on their disengagement.

Lastly, similar to my findings related to the "separation stage" of the Turkish Penitents, "turning points" and "serendipities" were considerably influential in terms of their disengagement from communities of violent practices.

Findings related to the "incorporation" stage

The literature on terrorism documents that in some countries various terrorist groups, such as the IRA in Northern Ireland (Horgan 2005), Al-Gamaa al-Islamiya and Al-Jihad al-Islami in Egypt (Gunaratna and Bin Ali 2009), laid down their arms, revised their ideologies and/or established themselves as a legal political force. In addition, considering the labyrinthine peace process choreographed in secrecy in Northern Ireland, Horgan rightfully asks, "What happens to individual members of a terrorist movement when terrorism ends?"

(2005:123). In Turkey, however, no terrorist group has hitherto abandoned arms and reorganized itself in the legal political sphere. Thus, this study attempted to demonstrate what happens to individual members of various terrorist groups who are in the throes of disengagement or disengaged, when those groups are bent on perpetuating their existence by all means necessary which include, more often than not, the intimidation or killing of individuals who decide to exit from such groups voluntarily. My findings suggest that the reincorporation of the Turkish Penitents into society is extremely difficult, as was in fact expected by them while contemplating their individual disengagement. The major difficulty they have has to do with conditions compelling them to lead an "invisible" life in society. (Hence is the phrase "Lives in the cracks of social structure" in the title). These conditions comprise the threats they receive from the groups they left on the one hand; and unwillingness and/or unreadiness of society to accept them on the other. The latter problem manifests itself in two ways: the Turkish Penitents are accused of being "traitors" by their own people, i.e., those who sympathize with their former groups, while being labeled by society in general as "wolves-in-sheep's clothing" and still being suspected, albeit their disavowal of political violence. Second, society's unwillingness to give them a "second chance" complicates the Turkish Penitents' incorporation into society even further in that such unwillingness leads to their dire economic situations having renounced political violence.

In this respect, they are grateful to the state for its offering them a second chance through "repentance laws;" but they believe that the state seems to be interested only in their insider knowledge of terrorist organizations and that it does not pay any attention to facilitating their reincorporation into society, for instance, by helping them to find a stable job or providing them with various social and financial benefits. In a nutshell, a feeling of "abandonment" appears to be dominating the lives of the Turkish Penitents after their disengagement from political violence; and associated with such state of mind are the feelings of "boredom," "melancholy," "hopelessness," "deprivation," and last but not least, "loneliness."

Implications for policy and future research

The paradigm shift from undemocratic governance in the 1990s to more democratic governance in Turkey especially during the last decade presents important ramifications in terms of the country's counter-terrorism policies. To give an example, the move from the tense and murky exchange relationship between the state/deep state and potential beneficiaries of repentance laws to a more lax and transparent exchange relationship between them since the enactment of the Effective Repentance Law (Article 221) not only created favorable conditions for the latter, i.e., "potential beneficiaries of the law," but it also increased the government's credibility in terms of its counter-terrorism strategy. This general optimism about the government's efforts in incentivizing individual disengagement is noteworthy. However, like individual members of terrorist groups who are contemplating disengaging, the current government is also reminded at times of its liminal position as being "betwixt and between" in that while being cognizant of the fact that democratic policies are conducive to garnering support in domestic politics, implementation of such policies is checked by the likelihood of a nationalist backlash and more bloodshed by terrorist groups, the PKK in particular, which hangs over the government like the sword of Damocles. The current "democratic resolution process" should also be viewed in this light. This state of the government's being betwixt and between *inter alia* creates significant challenges concerning repentants' reincorporation in society. For an illustration of some of these challenges, consider the following excerpt from my interview with Fatih-R and Ahmet-R, whose ideas about state policies with regard to "reincorporation" are also shared by most of my informants.

Anthropologist: What should be done to facilitate the reintegration of individuals who come out of terrorist groups?

Fatih-R: First of all, you have to understand the psychology of those individuals. This is the most important thing, as far as I am concerned. Nobody understands this, except for those few who work in the terrorism division of the police. You have to understand that this man, who disengaged from his group and surrendered, is not an ordinary man.

Anthro: How will the police know that this man truthfully disengaged from violence?

Fatih-R: I mean I am talking about those who "say" that he/she left terrorism behind. But still, the police may determine if he is sincere after following him for two months. It can be understood with 70 or 80 per cent success that he is sincere, during this two-month period. The problem has to do with the approach to those who disengaged:

The state says, "I enacted Article 221; so come, surrender, and leave violence behind." That is it. The state assumes that everything stops there. This is the worst of problems because, in fact, everything starts there. If he has a social network, relationships, and resources, this man can adapt himself to society, but 90 per cent of those individuals lack what I listed here. That's a big problem, because the state just thinks that if this man leaves and stops pointing his weapon towards the state, it is enough. It doesn't care what he does afterwards; whether he became a member of mafia, a drug dealer, or else is not much of a concern for the state. This is the problem with the state's mentality.

So, what I am saying is that everything starts when individuals left their groups and benefited from the repentance laws. These laws are abstractions; they don't have souls but the human beings do. They are living creatures. It is good that you took a step with Article 221, for example. It is an important step. Now the state should think like this. *Will I just rescue this person from the terrorist organization or make him a constructive/contributing person in society?* I mean, it should think how to use these laws. "*What will this man do after he returns society; will he join other criminal groups?*" etc. These are the questions that the state has to ask itself.

Anthro: Is it not included in the law that the state should find a job for these people?

Ahmet-R: It is included indeed, but although it exists on paper, it doesn't work in practice. According to the law, the state has to provide him with a fixed-term or contracted government job. But for this, there are certain limitations; for instance, it says you have to be 25 years old. But I am 40 years old; then what will I do? There are also other problems in terms of where he will be sent.

Fatih-R: What's more important is that they don't give detailed information about the kinds of benefits these laws offer. It just says that "this or that type of work is found" for these individuals, but conditions for employment are no different from normal conditions stipulated in the Labor Law. There is no special agreement in terms of "our" employment conditions. Another problem is that all procedures are carried out by the Cosmic Bureau within the Interior Ministry. So what happens there? For instance, let's say the officer is a nationalist and sympathizes with either the MHP (Nationalist Action Party) or the CHP (Republican People's Party). When writing his opinion about these individuals' application to benefit from the law, this person first says, "I cannot even find a job for my own child; why should I find a job for this pimp?" Second, hmm ... but the philosophy has changed today. Now they say, "We should reintegrate these people into society." This is a new thing; it did not exist before. The approach of the judges is another impediment to this process. For instance, we stayed in Kirklareli prison with Ahmet. There were about 40 people in our ward, who sought advice from the police just because they trusted Ahmet-R. I mean, he was mediating the negotiations between the police and these individuals to convince them to leave their groups by benefiting from the repentance laws. Almost all of these individuals benefited from the law, but Ahmet, who was the main actor in this process, could not. Why? Because there was a guy at the Cosmic Bureau who somehow disliked Ahmet. We heard that he said, "As long as I am in this bureau, this guy will not benefit from this law. He won't benefit, even if the President came here for him."

Anthro: Did you benefit from the "Witness Protection Law?"

Ahmet-R: Yes, in fact, we benefited from that law because we became an intervening party to X case against the group ....

Fatih-R: Our chance here was Zekeriya Öz [Public Prosecutor of the Ergenekon case]. He trusted us because of our daring efforts from the beginning, i.e., 2007, to unmask the deep state.

Anthro: Who initiated this relationship? Did you go to him yourself, or did he call you?

Ahmet-R: We were talking about the activities of the deep state anyway, even before the case exploded in 2007. At one point, they said, "The state is preparing itself to unveil the deep state." And at that time we were

	talking about Veli Küçük [retired general who is now in prison for being one of the leaders of the Ergenekon], the individuals in the Special Warfare Department, etc. In fact, the first operations against the deep state were initiated as a result of these talks.
Fatih-R:	Yes we were talking about these. For instance, I told them that when I was a member of X group, I used to go to the Command of the Turkish Gendarmerie to receive weapons from the head of the A-team. I also told them that the same guy provided the intelligence for the assassination of General Ismail Selen. So, we were talking about these ...Why did we do this? Because of ... [naming a police chief]. We have full trust in him. For instance, a couple of days ago an officer brought a paper to me to sign. I asked him whether ... read this; he said yes. And I signed even without reading it. The officer was surprised because of this. The document was about ..., but the point is that we trust him [the police chief] unconditionally.
Ahmet-R:	Another issue is that they found an apartment for me. They are paying the rent, but even they couldn't find a job for me.
Fatih-R:	This was the issue we discussed the most in the police department. You know, we are not knowledgeable about business stuff, because our whole lives were about our groups and the revolution. We were asking them to find a job just to make a living; not to be rich ... In fact, this was done before with the "confessors" from the PKK. A big amount of money was transferred to them. But of course they were used for this. For instance, Colonel ... in Kirklareli allowed them to smuggle fuel-oil, but he took the 70 per cent of the profit.
Anthro:	I see; what else can you say?
Fatih-R:	They don't understand our emotions. Do you know what the biggest problem of those who disengage is? Those who leave their groups start to see themselves overtime as "the state." Since they left violence, they think it is normal for them to demand some rights, because they are taking risks ... But, how does the state see them? "Yes, he left violence, but he is still a suspected person." *So, the bottom-line is that the state should understand their psychologies.* There are a couple of people who understand this, such as .... They understood this and gained significant trust from us today. I always say, "If it was not ..., I would never do these [e.g., cooperate with the state during the Ergenekon case]. If he leaves this office and somebody replaces him; I will not say anything to the new officer. Because, if he [the chief that they trust] is not there, no one will listen to and understand us.
Anthro:	So, you mean only a few people can establish such relationship...
Fatih-R:	In Europe, these issues are not taken to be personal; they are institutionalized.
Anthro:	I see. You mean these personal efforts help repentants psychologically during their reintegration processes, but they need to be institutionalized.

Fatih: Yes. Whatever has been done hitherto; they are all personal. There is nothing that is institutionalized. For instance, why do you think the army tore itself apart so that Zekeriya Öz was taken off the Ergenekon case? Because he dedicated himself to the Ergenekon case and to protect those who helped during this process.

The above excerpt reveals some of the policy problems concerning individual disengagement from political violence, which can be subsumed under two main categories: theoretical and technical problems. Most of the theoretical problems are related to the concept of "liminality" which has dominated the political discourse on terrorism and political violence in Turkey for almost three decades. What should be done first is to change the narratives that govern the aforementioned discourse, a scorching discourse vented by the hatred of the Kurds toward the Turks, the Turks toward the Kurds, state officials toward "terrorists," sympathizers of terrorist groups toward the state, and so on. Many people would argue that rebranding the discourse with more peaceful narratives is not an easy task as long as terrorism keeps wrecking havoc in the country. But it is important to remember that, despite the difficulty of absorbing "potential" violence as a result of providing terrorist groups with opportunities unwittingly via expansion of democratic rights and freedoms, altering the "memorized" narratives of terrorism with the language of peace, tolerance, and reconciliation is perhaps the most effective antidote to terrorism and political violence in the long run. To this end, it is crucial to design policies that will increase public awareness in terms of understanding of and feeling for the pain of the Other.

The launching of "The Commission on Investigating the Violations to Right to Life Caused by Terrorism" in 2011 under the "Human Rights Investigation Commission" of the Turkish Grand National Assembly (TBMM) can be considered as a good example of the new approach I mentioned above. The purpose of this commission, as explained by its chairman Naci Bostancı, a renowned parliamentarian and an academic, is to understand "how victims of terrorism look at life and the world, how they view terrorism and its consequences, and what kind of messages these anguished people can give to society." Emphasizing that the work of the commission will be civilian, political, and social in nature, Bostancı (2011) further stated the following:

> As a sub-commission, we would like to show the public in Turkey and the international community that when we talk about the social costs of terrorism they do not accrue to one party; that anguish cannot have a party; that the experienced anguish belongs to all; that trying to tackle problems [related to terrorism] at the expense of these pains creates deep social trauma; that the whole issue cannot be downgraded to numbers of the dead, martyrs or their momentary images on TV; that behind all of these lie long-standing, deep and, more often than not, covered pains.
>
> (my translation)

This new approach clearly marks a successful break with the old counter-terrorism policies that were largely based on denial, detachment with the social and political reality, and often suppression. The work of the aforementioned commission was taken further by the initiation in March 2013 of the "democratic resolution process" between the state and the PKK to end violence in the country. Accordingly, the government formed a diverse group of intellectuals, called "wise people," who have contributed to the promotion of the process by organizing panels, visiting people throughout Turkey and participating in TV discussions. This and other similar policies should therefore continue and be buttressed by various *public-private partnerships* to promote this new approach, which has enormous potential to increase the admissibility and legitimacy of the implementation of such policies.

Second, *in-field* and *in-service trainings* can be planned and conducted for government officials, especially for the security and education personnel, to emphasize the importance of the consequences of their behavior during their interactions with citizens in general and youngsters in particular. As this study has shown, a seemingly simple utterance of a "bad-word" or "mistreatment" of individuals during their childhood and adolescent years can lead to results that are beyond the imagination of such personnel, e.g., they can create indelible wounds ("significance loss") in the minds of those individuals which can culminate in their entry into terrorist groups for the purposes of restoring their significance.

Third, there are multiple problems with regard to the implementation of the repentance laws. The most important problem has to do with the "intention" of individuals who are in the position of decision-making for the potential beneficiaries of these laws. In this respect, various *training programs* can be designed to explain to these decision-makers that they should focus on positive aspects of the repentance laws. A mechanism should also be designed to audit the whole process to avoid the negative effects of such self-calculated, ideologically-motivated accounts.

Another problem with the implementation of the repentance laws is connected to the foregoing problem. As my informants made it clear above, there is a lack of *institutionalization* in terms of repentants' reintegration of society. All efforts in this respect seem to be personal. It is therefore crucial to institutionalize these efforts by developing clear-cut policies and programs to facilitate repentants' reintegration into society. These programs, under the rubric of "Reconciliation, Rehabilitation, and Reintegration Program" or "Welcome Home Program," etc., for example, should be promoted and advertised to make sure that potential beneficiaries of repentance laws will have a clear idea about what they should expect in their lives after disengagement. In this way, the state will be also able to invalidate the disinformation campaigns of terrorist groups (e.g., "the state will torture you, kill you, or put into prison for life"), through which they try to dissuade their disillusioned members from disengagement. This is perhaps one of the most important policy implications of this study, because as almost all of my informants pointed out, implementation of repentance laws with clarity and sincerity and institutionalization of reintegration efforts under clearly defined and advertised programs are extremely important in terms of the state's counter-terrorism policies. Because such policies will not only facilitate the reintegration of repentants into society but their ameliorated post-violence conditions will also function as a good example and incentivize already disillusioned members of terrorist organizations to disengage.

Finally, to generate achievable policy strategies and targets with regard to individual disengagement from political violence, there is need for more case studies to allow further assessment of the subject from both the local and international dimensions. The following should be explored as future research strategies can facilitate the attainment of this goal:

- One of the purposes of this study was to compare Marxist-Leninist and separatist groups with religion-abusing groups in terms of the notion of individual disengagement from political violence. I could not have access to informants from the latter; but if such access is achieved, it will still be useful to conduct a comparative study by using the proposed ROP model to understand the similarities and differences between individuals who left the foregoing two types of groups.
- A similar study should be conducted at the international level. To specify, the ROP model that I propose in this book can also be applied to exploring the *separation* (pre-violence), *transition* (violence), and *reincorporation* (post-violence) stages of individuals who came out of various terrorist groups in two or more countries; say, for instance, in Turkey, Israel, and Iraq. Such a study will allow us to understand the country-level differences and similarities pertaining to individual disengagement from political violence.
- More case studies, both qualitative and quantitative, are justified to assess the effects of repentance laws on individual disengagement from political violence at local and international levels.

All in all, in my view, comparative studies that try to understand the notion of disengagement from terrorism are *sine qua non* of counter-terrorism strategies all around the world. This is so because I believe that it is one of the best ways to understand a host of issues related to terrorism, e.g., why individuals join terrorist groups, what happens within these enigmatic structures, what country-level and culture-specific factors should be taken into account, and last but not least, what factors lead active terrorists to become disillusioned and finally leave terrorism behind. Another reason for embarking on such an endeavor has to do with the cost of terrorism to individual governments. It has been said, for instance, that the cost of terrorism to Turkey in the last three decades has amounted to nearly 400 billion dollars. An important portion of this amount has been spent on "hard tools" of counter-terrorism, i.e., the needs of military and various law enforcement agencies. I argue therefore that even if a fraction of that amount were allocated to research, social work, and reconciliation activities, we would have achieved better social and economic returns in terms of countering terrorism.

240 Conclusion

In conclusion, it is extremely important for states to allocate more resources to reintegrate former terrorists into society. This will contribute greatly to the stability of any given society by enticing active members of terrorist organizations to disengage from terrorism. More importantly, clear-cut reintegration programs will give all kinds of former terrorists a "second chance" in life.

Does not everyone deserve a second chance?

Note

1 These articulations were made by Güçlü and Burkay on various political debate programs on TV.

Bibliography

Agamben, G. (2005) *State of Exception*, Chicago: University of Chicago Press.
Akay, H. (2011) *Türkiye'de Asker-Sivil İlişkileri: 2000–2011 Dönemine İlişkin Bir Değerlendirme*. Online. Available HTTP: http:www.hyd.org.tr/staticfiles/files/asker_sivil__hale_akay.pdf: Helsinki Yurttaslar Dernegi: Istanbul (accessed 9 January 2012).
Akçura, Y., Kemal, A., and Ferit, A., (1976) *Üç tarz-i siyaset*, Ankara: Türk Tarih Kurumu Basimevi.
Alexander, F. and Rollins, M., (1984) "Alcoholic Anonymous: The Unseen Cult," *California Sociologist*, 7(1): 33–48.
Alkan, N., (2006) *Turkiye'de Teror Orgutleri Tarafindan Gerceklestirilen Intihar Saldirilarinin Sosyolojik ve Psikolojik Acidan Incelenmesi*, Ankara: Kara Harp Okulu.
Anderson, B., (1983) *Imagined Communities: Reflections on the Origin and Spread of nationalism*, London: Verso.
Aretxaga, B., (2000) "Playing Terrorist: Ghastly Plots and the Ghostly State," *Journal of Spanish Cultural Studies*, 1(1): 43–58.
Arjmand, R., (2008) *Inscription on Stone: Islam, State and Education in Iran and Turkey*, Stockholm: Pedagogiska institutionen.
Arslan, D.A., (2005) "The Evaluation of Parliamentary Democracy in Turkey and Turkish Political Elites," *Historia Actual Online*, (6): 131–41.
Asad, T., (2007) *On Suicide Bombing*, New York: Columbia University Press.
Ashour, O., (2009) *The De-radicalization of Jihadists: Transforming Armed Islamist Movements*, London, New York: Routledge.
Aybar, M.A., (1968) *Bagimsizlik, Demokrasi, Sosyalism*, Istanbul: Gercek Yayinlari.
Aydin, K., (2006) "Social Stratification and Consumption Patterns in Turkey," *Social Indicators Research*, 75: 463–501.
Aydınoğlu, E., (1992) *Turk Solu (1960–1971), Elestirel Bir Tarih Denemesi*, Istanbul: Belge Yayinlari.
Ballı, R., (1991) *Kurt Dosyasi*, Istanbul: Cem Yayinevi.
Bandura, A., (1998) "Mechanism of Moral Disengagement," in *Origins of Terrorism*, W. Reich (ed.), Baltimore: Johns Hopkins University Press.
Barber, B., (1957) *Social Stratification: A Comparative Analysis of Structure and Process*, New York: Harcourt Brace.
Barrett, R. and Bokhari, L., (2008) "Deradicalization and Rehabilitation Grogrammes Targeting Religious Terrorists and Extremists in the Muslim Morld. An Overview," in *Root Causes of Terrorism: Myths, Reality and the Way Forward*, T. Bjorgo and J. Horgan (eds.), London: Routledge.

Bibliography

Belge, M., (2003) "Sol," in *Gecis Surecinde Turkiye*, I.C. Schick and A. Ertugrul (eds.), Istanbul: Belge Yayinlari.

Berger, R., and Zimbardo, P., (2012) *Creating a Partner: A Qualitative Study of Political Extremists and Ex-Gang Members Who Have Chosen the Antiviolence Path*, Paper commissioned by Google Ideas. Online. Available HTTP. http://peaceandconflict. voices.wooster.edu/files/2010/08/berger-zimbardo.pdf

Berkowitz, L., (1965) "Some Aspects of Observed Agression," *Journal of Personality and Social Psychology*, 12: 359–69.

Beşikçi, I., (1990) *Tunceli Kanunu (1935) ve Dersim Jenosidi*, Istanbul: Belge Yayinlari.

Biner, Z.O., (2006) "From Terrorist to Repentant: Who is the Victim?" *History and Anthropology*, 17(4): 339–53.

Birand, M.A., (1992) *Apo ve PKK*, Istanbul: Milliyet.

Birand, M.A., Bila, H., and Akar, R., (1999) *12 Eylul-Turkiye'nin Miladi*, Istanbul: Dogan Yayinlari.

Bjorgo, T. and Horgan, J., (2009) *Leaving Terrorism Behind: Individual and Collective Disengagement from Political Violence*, New York: Routledge.

Bond, G.C., (2000) "Historical Fragments and Social Constructions in Northern Zambia: a Personal Journey," *Journal of African Cultural Studies*, 13(1): 76–93.

Bostanci, N., (2011) *Terörün Safi Yoktur.* Online. Available HTTP: www.nacibostanci.com/ component/k2/item/397-terörün-safi-yoktur.html (accessed 6 February 2012).

Bott, E., (1957) *Family and Social Network: Roles, Norms and External Relationships in Ordinary Urban Families*, London: Tavistock Publications.

Bourdieu, P., (1990) *The Logic of Practice*, Stanford, CA: Stanford University Press.

Boyer, P., (2001) *Religion Explained: The Evolutionary Origins of Religious Thought*, New York: Basic Books.

Çelebi, E., (1971) *Evliya Celebi Seyahatnamesi*, Istanbul: Zuhuri Danisman.

Chislett, W., (2006) "Turkey's EU Negotiations: On the Rocks." Working Paper 19. Real Instituto Elcano.

CIA World Factbook (2008) *Turkey*. Online. Available HTTP: https://www.cia.gov/library/ publications/the-world-factbook/geos/tu.html (accessed 9 July 2011).

Çiçek, N., (2009) *Itirafci: Karanlik Donemin Tetikcileri*, Istanbul: Timas.

Çiloğlu, F., (1998) *PKK'nin 20 yili*, Istanbul: Aktuel Dergisi, Aktuel Yillik.

Cohler, B.J., (1987) "Adversity, Resilience, and the Study of Lives," in *The Invulnerable Child*, E.J. Anthony and B.J. Cohler (eds), pp. 363–424, New York: Guilford Press.

Colvin, C.J., (2007) "Political Violence," in *A Companion to Psychological Anthropology*, C. Conerly and R. Edgerton (eds), pp. 453–69, Oxford: Wiley-Blackwell.

Cumming, E. and Henry, W., (1961) *Growing Old*, New York: Basic Books.

Davison, R., (1963) *Reform in the Ottoman Empire, 1856–1876*, Princeton, NJ: Princeton University Press.

Demirel, E., (1996) *PKK*, Ankara: GHMD Yayinlari.

Demirel, T., (2001) "12 Eylul'e Dogru Ordu ve Demokrasi," *Ankara Universitesi Siyasal Bilgiler Fakultesi Dergisi*, 56(4): 65–88.

Demiroz, F., and Kapucu, N. (2012) "Anatomy of a Dark Network: The Case of the Turkish Ergenekon Terrorist Organization", *Trends in Organized Crime*, 15: 271–295

Dersimi, M.N., (1988) *Dersim Tarihi*, Köln: Komkar yayinlari.

Dechesne, M. and Castano, M., (2005) "On Defeating Death: Group Reification and Social Identification as Strategies for Transcendence," *European Review of Social Psychology*, 16(7): 221–55.

Dollard, J. and Yale University Institute of Human Relations (1935) *Criteria for the Life History, with Analyses of Six Notable Documents*, New Haven, CT: Published for the Institute of Human Relations by Yale University Press.

Dugan, L. and Huang, J.Y., (2008) "Sudden Desistence from Terrorism: The Armenian Secret Army for the Liberation of Armenia and the Justice Commandos of the Armenian Genocide," *Dynamics of Asymmetric Conflict*, 1(3, November): 231–49.

EGM (Emniyet Genel Mudurlugu) (2000) *PKK (1973–1979)*, Ankara: EGM Yayinlari.

Ergil, D., (1980) *Turkiye'de Teror ve Siddet'in Yapisal ve Kulturel Kaynaklari*, Ankara: Turhan Kitapevi.

European Commission, (2011) *Turkey 2011 Progress Report*, Brussels. Online. Available HTTP: http://ec.europa.eu/enlargement/pdf/key_documents/2011/package/tr_rapport_2011_en.pdf (accessed 10 November 2012).

Evren, K., (1990) *Kenan Evren'in Anilari, Cilt 1*, Istanbul: Milliyet Yayinlari.

Feldman, A., (1991) *Formations of Violence: The Narrative of the Body and Political Terror in Northern Ireland*, Chicago: University of Chicago Press.

Ferracuti, F., (1982) "A Sociopsyhiatric Interpretation of Terrorism," *The Annals of the American Academy (AAPSS)*, 463: 129–40.

Ferracuti, F., (1998) "Ideology and Repentance: Terrorism in Italy," in *Origins of Terrorism: Pyschologies, Theologies, States of Mind*, W. Reich (ed.), pp. 59–64, New York: Cambridge University Press.

Fortes, M. and South African Institute of Race Relations (1970) *The Plural Society in Africa*, Johannesburg: South African Institute of Race Relations.

Freud, A., (1937) *The Ego and the Mechanisms of Defense*, London: Published by L. and Virginia Woolf at the Hogarth Press, and the Institute of Psychoanalysis.

Frey, F.A., (1975) "Patterns of Elite Politics in Turkey," in *Political Elites in the Middle East*, G. Lenczowski (ed.), Washington, DC: American Enterprise Institute for Public Policy Research.

Friedland, N., (1992) 'Becoming a Terrorist: Social and Individual Antecedents', in L.Howard (ed.), *Terrorism: Roots, Impacts, Responses*, New York: Praeger.

Fulbright, W., (1967) *The Arrogance of Power*, Volume 284: London: Random House.

Ganser, D., (2005) *NATO's Secret Armies: Operation GLADIO and Terrorism in Western Europe*, New York: Routledge.

Gavan, S., (1958) *Kurdistan: Divided Nation of the Middle East*, London: Lawrence and Wishart.

Giddens, A., (1973) *The Class Structure of the Advanced Societies*, London: Hutchinson.

Göle, N., (2002) "Islam in Public: New Visibilities and New Imaginaries," *Public Culture*, 14(1): 173–90.

Gray, K. and Wegner, D.M., (2010) "Blaming God for Our Pain: Human Suffering and the Divine Mind," *Personality and Social Psychology Review*, 14(7): 7–16.

Gunaratna, R., and Bin Ali, M. (2009) "De-radicalization Initiatives in Egypt: A Preliminary Insight", *Studies in Conflict & Terrorism*, 32:277–291

Gurr, T.R., (1970) *Why Men Rebel*, Princeton, NJ: Published for the Center of International Studies, Princeton University by Princeton University Press.

Gürsoy, I., (2012) "Kizilay'da Bombalari Asker Patlatiyordu," *Aksiyon*, 9–15, Ocak. Online. Available HTTP: www.aksiyon.com.tr/aksiyon/haber-31522-33-kizilayda-bombalari-asker-patlatiyordu.html (accessed 20 January 2012).

Haan, N., (1963) "Proposed Model of Ego Functioning: Coping and Defense Mechanisms in Relationship to IQ Change," *Psychological Monographs*, 77(8): 1–23.

Haraway, D., (1988) "Primatology is Politics by Other Means," in *Feminist Approaches to Science*, R. Bleier (ed.), pp. 77–118, New York: Pergamon Press.
Harrington, Charles C. (1976) 'Schools and peers in the political socialization of the urban poor,' *Equal Opportunity Review*, August, 1–8.
Harrington, C. and Boardman, S., (1997) *Paths to Success: Beating the Odds in American Society*, Cambridge, MA: Harvard University Press.
Hart, K., (2007) "Marcel Mauss: in Pursuit of the Whole. A Review Essay," *Comparative Studies in Society and History*, 49(2): 1–13.
Hartmann, H., (1958) *Ego Psychology and the Problem of Adaptation*, New York: International University Press.
Hasretyan, M.A., (1995) *Turkiye'de Kurt Sorunu (1918–1940)*, Berlin: Wesanen, Enstituya Kurdi
Heidegger, M., (1962) *Being and Time*, New York: Harper & Row.
Heidegger, M., (1972) *On time and being*, New York: Harper & Row.
Heper, M., (1976) "The Recalcitrance of the Turkish Public Bureaucracy to 'Bourgeois Politics': A Multi-Factor Political Stratification Analysis," *Middle East Journal*, 30(4): 485–500.
Heper, M., (1980) "Center and Periphery in the Ottoman Empire with Special Reference to the Nineteenth Century," *International Political Science Review*, 1(1): 81–104.
Heskin, K., (1985) "Political Violence in Northern Ireland," *Journal of Psychology*, 119 (5): 481–94.
Hochschild, A.R., (1975) "Disengagement Theory: A Critique and Proposal," *American Sociological Review*, 40(October): 553–69.
Hoffman, B., (1998) *Inside Terrorism*, New York: Columbia University Press.
Honwana, A., (1998) "Sealing the Past, Facing the Future: Trauma Healing in Rural Mozambique: Conciliation Resources." Online. Available HTTP: www.c-r.org/our-work/accord/mozambique/past-future.php (accessed 8 Oct. 2011).
Honwana, A., (2008) "Children's Involvement in War: Historical and Social Contexts," *Journal of the History of Childhood and Youth*, 1(1): 139–59.
Horgan, J., (2005) *The Psychology of Terrorism*, London, New York: Routledge.
Hürriyet Daily (2003) Istanbul, 9 August 2003.
Inalcik, H., (1970) "The rise of the Ottoman Empire," in *The Central Islamic Lands from Pre-Islamic Times to the First World War*, P. M. Holt, A. K. S. Lambton and B. Lewis (eds); Cambridge: Cambridge University Press.
İnalcık, H., (1976) "The Rise of the Ottoman Empire," reprinted in *A History of the Ottoman Empire to 1730*, M.A. Cook (ed.), pp. 10–53, Cambridge: Cambridge University Press.
Janoff-Bulman, R., (1992) *Shattered Assumptions: Towards a New Psychology of Trauma*, New York: The Free Press.
Jenkins, G. (2009) *Between Fact and Fantasy: Turkey's Ergenekon Investigation*, Silk Road Paper
Jennings, M.K. and Niemi, R., (1974) *Families, Schools and Political Learning*, Princeton, NJ: Princeton University Press.
JİTEMciler.blogspot.com (2011) "Itirafcilar," Online posting. Available HTTP: http://jitemciler.blogspot.com/2011/02/itirafcilar.html (accessed 1 Oct. 2012).
Karademir, K., (2000) *Intihar Saldirilari*, Ankara: TEMUH Yayinlari.
Karpat, K., (1966) "Left Wing Intellectuals between the Wars," *Journal of Contemporary History*, 1(2): 169–96.
Karpat, K., (1972) "The Transformation of the Ottoman State, 1789–1909," *International Journal of Middle East Studies*, 3(July): 243–81.

Karpat, K., (1977) "Some Historical and Methodological Considerations Concerning Social Stratification in the Middle East," in *Commoners, Climbers and Notables: A Sampler of Studies of Social Ranking in the Middle East*, Van Niewenhuijze, J.A.O. (ed.), pp. 83–90, Leiden: E.J. Brill.

Kassimeris, G., (2011) "Why Greek Terrorists Give Up: Analyzing Individual Exit from the Revolutionary Organization 17 November," *Studies in Conflict and Terrorism*, 34(7): 556–71.

Kelman, H.C., (1973) "Violence without Moral Restraint: Reflection on the Dehumanization of Victims and Victimizers," *Journal of Social Issues*, 29(4): 25–61.

Keyder, C., (1990) *Turkiye'de Devlet ve Siniflar*, Istanbul: Iletisim Yayinlari.

Khan, M.M. and Azam, A., (2008) "Root Causes of Terrorism: An Empirical Analysis," *Journal of Interdisciplinary Studies*, 20(1/2): 65–87.

Kılıç, A. and Güner, A., (1996) "Teror Sivas'ta Cikis Ariyor," *Aksiyon*, 14–20 Ekim.

Kimball, S.T., (1960) "Introduction," in *The Rites of Passage*, A. Van Gennep, M. Vizedom, and S.T. Kimball (eds.), pp. v–xxi, Chicago, IL: University of Chicago Press.

Kırçak, Ç., (1993) *Türkiye'de Gericilik 1950–1990*, Ankara: İmge

Kirisci, K., (2004) "The Kurdish Question in Turkish Foreign Policy," in *The Future of Turkish Foreign Policy*, L.G. Martin and D. Keridis (eds.), pp. 277–314, Cambridge, MA: MIT Press.

Kirisci, K. and Winrow. G.M., (1997) *The Kurdish Question and Turkey: An Example of a Trans-state Ethnic Conflict*, New York: Routledge.

Koç, Y., (2008) "15–16 Haziran Olaylarinda Dev-Genc'in Rolu," *AYDINLIK,* (29 Haziran).

Kongar, E., (2002) *Social Structure of Turkey in the New Millennium*, Istanbul: Remzi Kitabevi.

Kroeber, T., (1963) "The coping functions of ego mechanisms," in *The Study of Lives,* R. White (ed.), Vol. 178–198, New York: Atherton Press.

Kruglanski, A.W., Chen, X., Dechesne, M., Fishman, S. and Orehek, E. (2009) "Fully Committed: Suicide Bombers' Motivation and the Quest for Personal Significance," *Political Psychology,* 30 (3, June): 331–57.

Kruglanski, A., Gelf, W.M., and Gunaratna, R., (2010) "Detainee Deradicalization: A Challenge for Psychological Science," *Observer* (Association for Psychological Science), 23(1). Online. Available HTTP. www.psychologicalscience.org.index.php/publications/observer/2010/january-10

Kürkçü, E., (1988) "Kapitalizm ile Komunizm Arasinda 'Geleneksel Aydinlar': Yon Hareketi," (ed.), STMA, C6, Istanbul: Iletisim Yayinlari.

La Palombara, J., (1969) "Values and Ideologies in the Administrative Evolution of Western Constitutional Systems," in *Political and Administrative Development*, Braibanti, R., (ed.), Durham, NC: Duke University Press.

La Shure, C., (2005) *What is liminality?* Online. Available HTTP: www.liminality.org/about/what is liminality/. (accessed September 2011)

Laqueur, W., (1999) *The New Terrorism: Fanaticism and the Arms of Mass Destruction*, New York: Oxford University Press.

Lave, J. and Wenger, E., (1991) *Situated Learning: Legitimate Peripheral Participation*, Cambridge, New York: Cambridge University Press.

Lee, R.M., (1994) *Dangerous Fieldwork* (Qualitative Research Methods Series 34), Thousand Oaks, CA: SAGE Publications.

Leon, M.B., and Leons, W., (1977)"The Utility of Pluralism: M.G. Smith and Plural Theory," *American Ethnologist*, 4(3): 559–75.

Lewis, B., (2002) *The Emergence of Modern Turkey*, New York: Oxford University Press.

Lewis, G., (1995) "The Articulation of Circumstance and Causal Understanding," in *Causal Cognition: A Multidisciplinary Debate*, D. Sperber, D. Premack, and A.J. Premack (eds.), New York: Oxford University Press.

Lifton, R.J., (1961) *Thought Reform and the Psychology of Totalism*, New York: W.W. Norton and Co.

Magnarella, P.J., (1998) *Anatolia's Loom: Studies in Turkish Culture, Society, Politics and Law*, Istanbul: Isis Press.

Mahmood, C.K., (1996) *Fighting for Faith and Nation: Dialogues with Sikh Militants*, Philadelphia, PA: University of Pennsylvania Press.

Mamdani, M., (2009) *Saviors and Survivors: Darfur, Politics, and the War on Terror*, New York: Pantheon Books.

Marcus, A., (2007) *Blood and belief: the PKK and the Kurdish fight for independence*, New York: New York University Press.

Mardin, S., (1967) "Historical Determinants of Stratification: Social Class and Class Consciousness in Turkey," *Ankara Universitesi Siyasal Bilgiler Fakultesi Dergisi*, 22 (December): 111–42.

Mardin, S., (1980) "Turkey: The Transformation of an Economic Code," in *The Political Economy of Income Distribution in Turkey*, E. Ozbudun and A. Ulusan (eds.), New York: Holmes and Meier Publishers.

Mardin, S., Türköne, M., and Önder, T., (1990) *Türkiye'de Toplum ve Siyaset*, Istanbul: Iletisim Yayinlari.

Marett, R.H.K., (2007) [1912] *Anthropology*, Boston, MA: Adamant Media.

Matur, B., (2011) *Dagin Ardina Bakmak*, Istanbul: Timas Yayinlari.

Mauss, M., (1967) *The Gift: Forms and Functions of Exchange in Archaic Societies*, New York: Norton.

McAdam, D., (1989) "The Biographical Consequences of Activism," *American Sociological Review*, 54: 744–60.

Moss, D., (2001) "The Gift of Repentance: A Maussian Perspective on Twenty Years of Pentimento in Italy," *European Journal of Sociology*, 42(2): 298–311.

Mumcu, U., (1987) *12 Eylul Adaleti*, Ankara: Tekin Yayinlari.

Nawaz, M., (2011) "Before and After the Norway Massacre – Symbiosis between Anti-Muslim Extremists and Islamist Extremists," Online. Available HTTP: www.quilliamfoundation.org/press-releases/before-a-after-the-norway-massacre-symbiosis-between-anti-muslim-extremists-and-islamist-extremists/ (accessed 10 Aug. 2011).

Nordstrom, C., (1997) *A Different Kind of War Story*, Philadelphia, PA: University of Pennsylvania Press.

Olson, R., (1989) *The Emergence of Kurdish Nationalism and the Sheikh Said Rebellion*, Austin, TX: University of Texas Press.

Organski, A.F.K., (1965) *The Stages of Political Development*, New York: Alfred A. Knopf.

Ozankaya, O., (1971) *Koyde Toplumsal Yapi ve Siyasal Kultur*, Ankara: AU Siyasal Bilgiler Fakultesi Yayinevi.

Perlmutter, A., (1969) "The Praetorian State and the Praetorian Army: Toward a Taxonomy of Civil-Military Relations in Developing Polities," *Comparative Politics*, 1(3): 382–404.

Peteet, J.M., (1994) *Landscape of Hope and Despair: Palestinian Refugee Camps*, Philadelphia, PA: University of Pennsylvania Press.

Post, J.M., (1987) "Group and Organizational Dynamics of Political Terrorism: Implications for Counterterrorist Policy," in *Contemporary Research on Terrorism*, P. Wilkinson and A.M. Stewart (eds.), pp. 307–17, Aberdeen: Aberdeen University Press.

Post, J.M., (2003) *The Psychological Assessment of Political Leaders: With Profiles of Saddam Hussein and Bill Clinton*, Ann Arbor, MA: University of Michigan Press.

Post, J.M., (2005) "When Hatred is Bred in the Bone: Psycho-cultural Foundations of Contemporary Terrorism," *Political Psychology*, 26(4): 615–36.

Postmedya.com (2011) "Cem Ersever'in Sok Ses Kaydi." Online posting. Available HTTP: www.postmedya.com/news_detail.php?id=45824 (accessed 1 Oct. 2011).

Powell, L. and Cowart, J., (2003) *Political Campaign Communication: Inside and Out*, Allyn and Bacon.

Rahman, F., (1984) "Muhammad Iqbal and Atatürk's Reforms," *Journal of Near Eastern Studies*, 43(2): 157–62.

Rapoport, D., (1960) *Praetorianism: Government without Consensus*, Berkeley, CA: University of California Press.

Reich, W., (1998) *Origins of Terrorism: Psychologies, Ideologies, Theologies, States of Mind*, Washington, DC: Woodrow Wilson Center Press; Baltimore, MD and London: distributed by the Johns Hopkins University Press.

Reinares, F., (2011) "Exit from Terrorism: A Qualitative Empirical Study on Disengagement and Deradicalization among Members of ETA", *Terrorism and Political Violence*, (23): 780–803

Ricoeur, P., (1981) "Science and Ideology," in *Hermeneutics and the Human Sciences*, J.B. Thompson (ed.), pp. 222–46, Cambridge: Cambridge University Press.

Sabah Daily (2011) "PKK'da Kadin Kavgasi." Online posting. Available HTTP: www.sabah.com.tr/Gundem/2011/12/01/pkkda-kadin-kavgasi-basladi-352922818266 (accessed 12 Dec. 2011).

Sahlins, M.D., (1972) *Stone Age Economics*, New York: Aldine.

Salter, F. (2008) "Ethnicity and Indoctrination for Violence: The Efficiency of Producing Terrorists," in *Values and Violence: Intangible Aspects of Terrorism*, L. Karawan, W. McCormack, and S.E. Reynolds (eds.), pp. 63–81, New York: Springer.

Sampson, R. and Laub, J., (1993) "Turning Points in the Life Course: Why Change Matters to the Study of Crime," *Criminology*, 31(3): 301–26.

Sapiro, V., (2004) "Not Your Parents' Political Socialization: Introduction for a New Generation," *Annual Review of Political Science*, 7: 1–23, Annual Reviews Inc.

Sayarı, S. and Bilgin, H.D., (2011) "Paths to Power: The Making of Cabinet Ministers in Turkey," *Parliamentary Affairs*, 64(4): 737–62.

Scheper-Hughes, N., (2007) "The Politics of Remorse," in *A Companion to Psychological Anthropology*, C. Casey and R. Edgerton (eds), pp. 469–95, Oxford: Wiley-Blackwell.

Schmid, A.P., Jongman, A.J., and Horowitz, I.L., (1988) *Political Terrorism: A New Guide to Actors, Authors, Concepts, Data Bases, Theories and Literature*, Amsterdam: New York, New Brunswick, NJ: North-Holland, Distributors for the Western Hemisphere, Transaction Books.

Şen, E., (2011) "Basbakan, 73 Yil Onceki Katliamin Belgelerini Aciklady: Dersim Ozru," Online. Available HTTP: www.zaman.com.tr/politika_basbakan-73-yil-onceki-katliamin-belgelerini-acikladi-dersim-ozru_1205730.html (accessed 25 November 2011).

Shaw, S.J., (1976) *History of the Ottoman Empire and Modern Turkey, Volume I: Empire of the Gazis: The Rise and Decline of the Ottoman Empire, 1280–1808*, Cambridge: Cambridge University Press.

Sluka, J.A., (2000) *Death Squad: The Anthropology of State Terror*, Philadelphia, PA: University of Pennsylvania Press.

Smith, M.G., (1974) *Corporations and Society: The Social Anthropology of Collective Action*, London: George Duckworth.

Bibliography

Smith, M.G., (1998) *The Study of Social Structure*, New York: Research Institute for the Study of Man.
Smith, M.G. and International African Institute (1960) *Government in Zazzau, 1800–1950*, London, New York: Published for the International African Institute by Oxford University Press.
Söylemez, H., (2011) "Duz Ovada Teror: KCK," *Aksiyon Magazine*, 878, October 3–9, Feza Gazetecilik: Istanbul.
Speckhard, A. and Akhmedova, K., (2005) "Talking to Terrorists," *Journal of Psychohistory*, 33(Fall): 125–56.
Staub, E., (2005) "The Roots of Goodness: The Fulfillment of Basic Human Needs and the Development of Caring, Helping and Nonaggression, Inclusive Caring, Moral Courage, Active Bystandership, and Altruism Born of Suffering," in *Moral Motivation Through the Life Span*, G. Carlo and C. Edwards (eds.), Vols. 33–72, Lincoln, NE: University of Nebraska Press.
StratejikBoyut.com (2009) "Ocalan Ucakta Ilk Ne Dedi?" Online posting. Available HTTP: www.stratejikboyut.com/haber/ocalan-ucakta-ilk-ne-dedi--16750.html (accessed 10 Oct. 2011).
Strathern, M., (1988) *The Gender of the Gift. Problems with Women and Problems with Society in Melanesia*, Berkeley, CA: University of California Press.
Szyliowicz, J.C., (1977) "The Ottoman Empire," in *Commoners, Climbers and Notables: A Sampler of Social Ranking in the Middle East*, C.A.O. Van Niewenhuizje (ed.), Leiden: E.J. Brill
Taussig, M., (1984) "Culture of Terror-Space of Death: Robert Casement's Putumayo Report and the Explanation of Torture," *Comparative Studies in Society and History*, 26(33): 467–497.
Tayyar, S., (2011) *Kurt Ergenekonu: Derin PKK'nin Gizli Kodlari*, Istanbul: Timas Yayinlari.
Testart, A., (1998) "Uncertainties of the 'Obligation to Reciprocate': A Critique of Mauss," in *Marcel Mauss: a Centenary Tribute*, W. James and N.J. Allen (eds.), pp. xii, New York: Berghahn Books.
Thibaut, J.W. and Kelley, H.H., (1959) *The Social Psychology of Groups*, New York: John Wiley.
Today's Zaman (2012) "Sept. 12 Victims Content as Court Accepts Coup Indictment," Online. Available HTTP: www.todayszaman.com/news-268333-.html (accessed 12 January 2012).
Tucker, W.F., (1989) "Introduction," in *The Emergence of Kurdish Nationalism and the Sheikh Said Rebellion*, R. Olson (ed.), Austin, TX: University of Texas Press.
Turan, I., (1984) "Ataturk's Reforms as a Nation and State Building Process," *Southeastern Europe*, 11(1): 169–89.
Turkish General Staff (1983) *Turkiye'de Anarsi ve Terorun Gelismesi, Sonuclari ve Guvenlik Kuvvetleri ile Onlenmes*, Ankara: Genel Kurmay Baskanligi Yayinlari.
Turner, V.W., (1974) *Dramas, Fields, and Metaphors: Symbolic Action in Human Society*, Ithaca, NY: Cornell University Press.
Turner, V.W., (1987)*The Anthropology of Performance*, New York: PAJ Publications.
Uslu, E., (2010) *Derin Devletin Tehdit Haritasi: Dun Kurtler Bugun Cemaat*, Istanbul: Karakutu Yayinlari.
Uslu, E., (2011) "KCK Mimics ANC." Online. Available HTTP: www.todayszaman.com/columnist-265387-kck-mimics-anc.html (accessed 11 Dec. 2011).

Vaillant, G.E., (1971) "Theoretical Hierarchy of Adaptive Ego Mechanisms," *Archives of General Psychiatry*, 24: 107–18.
Van Bruinessen, M., (1978) *Agha, Sheikh, and State. On the Social and Political Organization of Kurdistan*, Rijswick: Enroprint.
—— (1996) "Kurds, Turks and Alevi Revival in Turkey," *Middle East Reports* 200 (Summer): 7–10.
Van Gennep, A., (1960) *The Rites of Passage*, Chicago, IL: The University of Chicago Press.
Van Nieuwenhuijze, C.A.O., (1965) *Social Stratification and the Middle East: An Interpretation*, Leiden: Brill.
Varenne, H. and McDermott, R., (1998) *Succesful Failure: The School America Builds*, Boulder, CO: Westview.
Victoroff, J., (2005) "The Mind of the Terrorist: A Review and Critique of Psychological Approaches," *The Journal of Conflict Resolution*, 49(1): 3–42.
Vincent, J., (1988) "Local Knowledge and Global Process in Two Border Villages: Political Violence in County Fermanagh," in *Ireland from Below*, C. Curtin and T. Wilson (eds.), pp. 92–108, Galway: University of Galway Press.
Volkan, V., (1997) *Bloodlines: From Ethnic Pride to Ethnic Terrorism*. New York: Farrar, Straus, and Giroux.
Weber, M., (1968) *Economy and Society*, New York: University of California Press.
Wenger, E., (1998) *Communities of Practice: Learning, Meaning, and Identity*, Cambridge: Cambridge University Press.
White, P., (2011) "Ethnic Differentiation among the Kurds: Kurmanci, Kizilbash and Zaza." Online. Available HTTP: members.tripod.com/~zaza_kirmanc/research/paul.htm (accessed 28 July 2011).
Williams, M., (2006) *Danger in Gift Giving and Taking*, Sydney: University of Sydney.
Yalçıner, M. (1988) 'Turkiye Halk Kurtuluş Ordusu-THKO,' in *Sosyalizm ve Toplumsal Mücadeleler Ansiklopedisi* STMA (ed.). İstanbul: İletişim Yayınları.
Yavuz, M.H., (2001) "Five Stages of the Construction of Kurdish Nationalism in Turkey," *Nationalism and Ethnic Politics*, 7(3): 1–24.
Yeğen, M., (2006) "The Turkish State Discourse and the Exclusion of Kurdish Identity," *Middle Eastern Studies*, 32(2): 216–29.
Yıldırım, N., (2004) *Turk Dis Politikasinda Teror Boyutuyla Guneydogu Sorunu*, Ankara: Gazi Universitesi Sosyal Bilimler Enstitusu.
Yılmaz, K., (2009) "The emergence and rise of conservative elite in Turkey," *Insight Turkey*, 11(2): 113–36.
Zaman Daily (2012) "Ergenekon Davalarinda 415 Kisiden Sadece 94'u Tutuklu Yargilaniyor." Online. HTTP: www.zaman.com.tr/haber.do?haberno=1230055&title =ergenekon-davalarinda-415-saniktan-sadece-94u-tutuklu-yargilaniyor (accessed 16 January 2012).
Žižek, S., (2011) "Great Minds: Slavoj Žižek." Online. Available HTTP: www.youtube.com/watch?v=LKBOL6xu1Sk (accessed 20 Aug. 2011).

Index

access: problem of access 99, 150, 153, 159
Agamben, G. *see* states of exception
Alevism 26, 46
Alexander, F. and Rollins, M. 120–40
altruism born of suffering (ABS) 126, 180–1
Anderson, B. 143, 191
anonymous state witnesses 201, 211, 216
anthropological 50, 75
Aretxaga, B., 144
Asad, T. 173
Aybar, M.A. 29

Biner, Z. Ö. 200–19
Bjorgo, T. and Horgan, J. 4, 18, 19
Bourdieu, P. 7
brain-washing *see* thought reform
bureaucratic-military elite 41, 212
Burkay, K., 33, 165
burning out 149, 191, 197

cell structures 106, 118
center–periphery analysis 13, 14, 39
communities of practice 10, 98, 99, 100, 104, 143
contaminated identities 169
coups: 12 September 1980 coup 31, 33, 34, 41; 27 May 1960 coup 27–8, 39–41; 1997 post-modern coup 27, 213
cracks of social structure 224–5
cult of confession, the 135, 136
cults 119–20, 140, 142
culture of practice 102

Deep State 38–46, 156–162, 211–220
demand for purity 133–4

Democrat Party (DP) 27–8, 34
Dersim 26, 47
Devrimci Doğu Kültür Ocakları (DDKO) 32
differential incorporation 12, 13, 18, 21–2, 53, 229
difficulties for disengagement 166–9
disillusionment: process of 2, 169; causes of 10, 94, 98, 119
Dollard, J. 50

epistemic murks 157, 202, 211
Ergenekon 43, 46, 175, 201; as *ergenekoncu* (supporter of) 112;
Eruh and Şemdinli 35
escape: as failed attempts to escape 123–4, 229; from a heavy practical training 103; from the mountain 122, 140, 221–2; from surveillance 108; from an unwanted situation 216, 219
exclusionary structures 23
execution: 63, 140, 168, 186; and description of an execution 122–3
exit: difficulties of exit *see* difficulties for disengagement; from the groups 119, 159, 164; physical exit 127, 160; from political violence 23

family: 50, 132–4; and dysfunctional family structure 32, 65–6, 71, 73–4, 84, 141; importance of family ties 76, 78, 80, 86, 150, 188, 221; significance loss in family 79, 90
Fikir Kulupleri Federasyonu (FKF) 30
Fis Village *see* Marcus, A.
frustration-aggression 51–5, 76, 82

Gezi Park incidents 36–7
Giddens, A. 18

gift exchange 200–206, 211–9
gizli tanik see anonymous state witnesses
Göle, N. 18, 22–3
Gray, K. and Wegner, D.M. 74–5
Gurr, T.R. 52

Hakan 1–3
Harrington, C. and Boardman, S. 6, 56, 63, 175–182
hemşericilik (fellow townsman) 151–2
Heper, M. 13, 15, 17, 18, 20, 21, 27
Horgan, J. 4, 5, 6, 8, 9, 52, 104, 166

ideology 40, 41, 53, 54
idleness 104, 149, 162, 163; and as active idleness 149, 191; debilitating idleness 1
imagined communities 143, 164
Inalcık, H. 13, 16, 17
individual disengagement: processes of 3, 4, 197; serendipities related to 184
indoctrination 55, 119–21, 142–3, 163, 169, 192,
induced change model 20, 21, 27
inductive training 103
initiation rite 61; and as initiation 2, 87, 132
institutionalization in a terrorist cell 107, 108

Karpat, K. 15, 16, 18–21, 27–9
KCK 37, 38, 113, 116–17
Kruglanski, A.W. *et al.* 54–5, 82, 129
Kurdish nationalism 23, 24, 32, 34–5

latent control 41
Lave, J. and Wenger, E. 98–104, 119–20, 131, 143–4, 150–1, 159
Legitimate Peripheral Participation (LPP) *see* Lave, J. and Wenger, E.
life after violence 2, 8, 220
Lifton, R. J. 121–40

Magranella, P. 52–3
Mamdani, M. 23, 38
Marcus, A., 25, 32, 33, 35
Mardin, Ş. *et al.* 13–18, 23
martyrdom: marketing the blood of martyrs 155; martyrs 74, 128, 130, 154, 185; the psychology of 62, 88, 93, 104, 129, 130, 137
Mauss, M. 169, 200–218
McAdam, D. 170

Military-civilian intellectuals 27, 29
Milli Demokratik Devrim 29
modernization: as authoritarian modernism 22; voluntary modernization 18; Western-style modernization 19
moral agents *see* Gray, K. and Wegner, D.M.
moral patients *see* Gray, K. and Wegner, D.M.
Moss, D. 202–11
mystical manipulation 127–8, 131–3, 154

objective agent 121–2
Öcalan's capture: the effects of 148, 188–9
Olson, R., 24–5
organic change model 20

participation: full participation 99, 100, 101, 104, 150, 155, 159
pathmakers *see* Harrington, C. and Boardman, S.
Pentimento *see* Moss, D.
perceived subjugation 22
Perlmutter, A. 39, 40, 41
personality orientations 175–9
philosophy of death 89
PKK: the emergence of 28, 32–43; recruitment strategy of 80, 87
politics of repentance 202, 226
post-action psychology 115
postponed imaginations *see* imagined communities
practice theory 6, 7
Praetorian state *see* Perlmutter, A.
prestations 203–7, 212, 216, 218–19
protracted conflict: as protracted cycle of violence 81, 156, 191, 213, 218, 220
psychological disengagement 127, 160–4, 183, 192, 224
public sphere 22, 23

radicalization 10, 51, 56, 59–62, 69, 79–81; incremental radicalization 64
raison d'être of the PKK 148, 156, 192, 213
reincorporation *see* life after violence
relative deprivation 51–3, 56, 82, 90
repentance laws 204–211,
resources for disengagement 169
revolutionism 154, 191

252 Index

Rite of Passage (ROP) 7, 94
role of ideology 41, 51, 54, 101
role of peers 88

Scheper-Hughes, N. 3
seeds of doubt 10, 189, 193
sequestration 153, 160–9, 191
shattered assumptions approach 81
Sheikh Said 23–6
significance: as significance loss 55, 60, 67, 71, 74, 79, 82, 90, 91, 191; as significance quest 55, 56, 63, 65, 68, 70, 91, 150–3; as significance restoration 55, 69, 71, 74, 80, 82, 90–1
Smith, M.G. 21, 22, 28, 39–41, 212
social network 86, 121, 141, 221, 234
social present 12
Sosyalist Devrim 29
Special Forces Command 43
Speckhard, A. and Akhmedova, K. 71, 81, 93, 167
states of exception 213
stratification 16–18
styles of coping 179–84
subjective agent 122

Taussig, M. *see* Biner, Z.Ö.
THKO 30, 31
THKP-C 30, 31
thought reform 120, 128, 140, 164, 169, 197–8
trauma: the effects of trauma 55, 60, 72, 76, 81, 91, 185, 215; chosen trauma 53
triggering effect 91
Turkish Left: and the end of the Turkish Left 36, 117, 145–6, 171–3
Turkish nationalism 15, 18, 19, 35
Turkish Penitents: the definition of xi
Turner, V. 168, 225
turning points 1, 6, 59, 63, 91–4, 184–7
tutelage: of bourgeoisie 139; military tutelage 39, 40, 41; system of 212

Van Bruinessen, M., 25, 26
Van Gennep, P. 7, 8, 168
Van Nieuwenhuijze, C.A.O. 21
Volkan, V. *see* chosen trauma

Yavuz, H., 23, 25, 32, 33, 35–6
Yeğen, M., 24, 25

Zilan 1, 2, 125, 130, 131, 137, 140